Creative Urban Milieus

T0291409

Martina Heßler is professor of Cultural History and History of Technology at the Hochschule für Gestaltung Offenbach am Main. *Clemens Zimmermann* is professor of Cultural and Media History at the Universität des Saarlandes.

Martina Heßler, Clemens Zimmermann (eds.)

Creative Urban Milieus

Historical Perspectives on Culture, Economy, and the City

Campus Verlag
Frankfurt/New York

This publication is supported by the Fritz Thyssen Stiftung.

Bibliographic Information published by the Deutsche Nationalbibliothek.
The Deutsche Nationalbibliothek lists this publication in the Deutsche Nationalbibliografie;
detailed bibliographic data are available in the Internet at http://dnb.d-nb.de.
ISBN 978-3-593-38547-1

Cover illustration: Emanuel Opitz: »Messeszene – Die Kupferstiche«, c. 1825
Cover design: Campus Verlag GmbH
Printed on acid free paper.
Printed in the United States of America

For further information:
www.campus.de
www.press.uchicago.edu

Contents

3   The Role of Cultural Policy: City Images, Media,
and the Cultural Economy in the Nineteenth
and Twentieth Century

4   Scientific Creative Milieus in the Twentieth Century

Acknowledgements

As Urban Historians we are of course also concerned with current developments. Thus, we curiously followed the heated discussion about the new importance of creative industries, creative milieus as well as the cultural economy, which are said to revitalize cities. However, as historians we are in some way sceptical about the idea that these phenomena are basically new. Looking back helps to determine whether these phenomena are new or whether there are a number of older elements to them. Furthermore, looking back helps us assess whether or not we are actually confronted with tremendous changes in both urban and economic developments. And regardless of what the outcomes are to these questions, looking back never fails to contribute to a better understanding of current situations. Thus, this volume seeks to embed the subject deeply in its historical context by incorporating articles dealing with the sixteenth century up until the present day.

We would like to thank our colleagues for their willingness to discuss this topic with us in Saarbrücken, where we met for the conference »Culture, Economy, and the City« from February 22 to 24, 2007, as well as for their contributions to this volume.

For their organizational and editing assistance we would like to thank Jochen Leinberger (Offenbach), Aline Maldener, Martin Schreiber and Sina Schröder (all Saarbrücken). Furthermore, we would like to extend our gratitude to Rett Rossi (Berlin), for helping to refine the English in several of the articles.

Finally, we would like to express our sincere appreciation to several institutions, which through their generous funding made both the conference and this volume possible. We are particularly indebted to the *Fritz Thyssen Stiftung* for supporting our symposium as well as their assistance with the publication subvention; without their contributions, we would never have been able to realize this project. Further financial assistance for the translation was made available by the *Saarland Ministry for Education, Culture and Research* as well as the *Saarland Sporttoto GmbH*. In addition, the *Freunde der Universität des Saarlandes* provided considerable support for our symposium.

Introduction: Creative Urban Milieus – Historical Perspectives on Culture, Economy, and the City

Martina Heßler / Clemens Zimmermann

Paris, London, Berlin, New York, Venice or Milan stand for certain cultural milieus, be it the fashion of London, be it Venice as the city of the Biennale, the Paris or even Berlin of the nineteenth century as cities of spectacle, of fairs and ›events‹, or Göttingen as the place of a specific scientific milieu in the mathematics of the early twentieth century. The list goes on.

The artistic and scientific milieus in cities in particular, have often been a preferred topic for research. In a recently published book, for example, Jed Perl described the ›Invention of Contemporary Art‹ in Manhattan (Perl 2006)[1] and outlined how the city's cultural milieu, the people gathered there, along with their topography in the city and their network, not only made New York the centre of the contemporary American art of the 1950s, but also contributed considerably to the genesis of American Expressionism, and later, finally – in altered constellations – to the genesis of pop art. Jed Perl's work provides an impressive reconstruction of the genesis of specific artistic milieus in New York, portraying even the city's lighting, its architectonic character or its streets. One step in blazing the trail for this kind of research was Allan Janik's and Stephen Toulmin's book on Wittgenstein's Vienna, published already in 1972 (Janik and Toulmin 1972). In it, the authors retraced the birth of a specific style of thought in Vienna at the turn of the century, rooting it and its topics, problems and distinguishing characteristics in Vienna's local circumstances at that time.

Today, cities are once again being increasingly seen as the most suitable place for culture and creativity. There is, of course, plenty of evidence

---

1   Perl's work obviously distances itself from Serge Guilbaut's (Guilbaut 1983).

showing that innovations and new industries have originated in cities or at least have to do with the modes of communication in cities. It has often been successfully maintained that the city and culture and the city and innovation are historically closely connected. While in recent decades there has been much prophesying of the ›death of the city‹ (Mitchell 1995) or its irrelevance in view of new technologies that abolish distance, the city is experiencing something of a renaissance in the context of current debates about the significance of a cultural economy. The urban is equated with creativity; the city appears to provide the conditions necessary for the promotion of creative work, inventiveness and innovation. As a consequence – and this is of special interest here – a new connection is being postulated, namely that of the city, culture *and* the economy. It is obvious that policy makers and creatives themselves believe that creative industries, the creative class and culture will be the engine of the economy, and that cities will be both the condition of this development and its beneficiary.

While authors such as Perl or Janik and Toulmin had still left out the economic dimension, it is now at the centre of the debate. It is conspicuous, then, that the debate on ›creative milieus‹, ›creative cities‹ and a ›cultural economy‹ has recently generated a multitude of essays, lectures and anthologies that not only place their economic effects and the improvement of the cities' images at the centre of interest, however all but purport to be able to promise and predict economic prosperity. The debate about cultural economy is accompanied by the diagnosis, and above all the prognosis, of a (further) structural shift of the economy towards culture and knowledge based industries. Hopes are pinned on ›creative clusters‹ of new technologies and on the culture sector. Creative branches – whether designers, artists, architects, authors, scientists and engineers – are expected to contribute increasingly towards economic prosperity. In the debate about ›creative cities‹ or ›creative industries‹ or ›innovative milieus‹ we are thus essentially concerned with *economic questions*, whether we are talking about macroeconomic developments, urban economies, or about indirect effects like the image of a ›creative city‹ competing against other cities to attract new businesses. The ›creative milieus‹, who carouse about the districts of the inner city, in the lofts and in the ›cool‹ old factory buildings, or on the outskirts of their cities today, though, are also a symptom of a new form of self-exploitation and actually precarious living conditions, as is sometimes ignored or forgotten, while these are often praised – not least of all by the creative element itself – as the genesis of a new ›creative class‹.

Simultaneously, publications by Richard Florida (Florida 2002) or Charles Landry (Landry 2000) on ›creative cities‹ land in the bestseller lists, and serve as instruction booklets, as ›toolkits‹ for city planners who are bent on letting such creative milieus bloom in their cities and thus make cultural economy a central part of urban economy. Whereas economic aspects have been completely neglected in cultural studies and cultural history in recent decades, they are staging a comeback now in the context of the debate about cultural economy.

However, one factor still remains somewhat neglected: *a historical perspective*. As a rule, what is offered are rather current diagnoses that often affirmatively celebrate the ›creative milieus‹. Already the examples cited briefly at the beginning show that the close connection of cultural milieus, city and economy is not merely a development of the past twenty or thirty years. Even if causes for the ›discovery‹ and the immense amount of attention that ›urban cultural economies‹ receive today can be named, the conclusion still does not follow that this is a completely new development, although certain shifts and discontinuities of present development vis-à-vis earlier ones can definitely be traced. The historical dimension is missing from the political discussion in any case, but even the research on the topic is void of any systematic historicising of the topic whatsoever. This is the main theme of this volume. This volume seeks to embed the subject deeply in its historical context by incorporating papers dealing with the eighteenth century up to the present day. It will not only integrate a historical perspective, but will be interdisciplinary in its approach. It seeks to bring together the long separated sub-disciplines of cultural history, urban history and economic history, as well as economics and cultural studies, so that the relation of culture, economy and the city can be viewed from a variety of perspectives and so that what is genuinely new and successful about the urban cultural economy can be discussed.

However, before discussing our objective of historicising current debates, it is first necessary to discuss the term ›cultural economy‹. Second we then will present some considerations on the project of historicising the story of cultural economy and thereby summarize some of the main results of this volume. Third we will ask, whether the many historical case studies, presented in this volume, make it possible to draw some conclusion about necessary conditions for the ›emergence and establishment‹ of cultural economies in different periods since the early modern times. Fourth we will particulary focus on the twentieth century, where we believe to observe an intensification of efforts to generate ›creative milieus‹. Fifth it is also an important aim of this volume to challenge the promises of economic prosperity and success. We thus raise the question of failure.

On the Concept of ›Cultural Economy‹

The concept of ›cultural economy‹ is presently in use primarily in economic, cultural, scientific and city planning discourses. Currently, there is an extraordinarily vague and imprecise use of terms, which sometimes even attributes ›creativity‹ to any ›cultural milieu‹ whatsoever. Consequently, it is also not clear what is meant by ›cultural economy‹: a concrete site, a general branch such as architects or advertising managers, or, dense networks of creative people? If we look at the debate about creative industries and urban cultural economies, it is obvious that quite different phenomena are being discussed under these broad umbrella terms. Moreover, we can observe a wide variety of terms such as creative milieus, innovative milieus, creative industries, the creative class, creative city, urban cultural industries as well as the symbolic economy and the creative economy or cultural economy. Almost all of these terms entered scientific discourse – as well as the agendas of policy makers and urban planners – in the 1980s. While it is true that all these terms share the conviction that the city is closely linked with both culture and creativity, if we look more closely we see that they do indeed refer to rather different phenomena and attest to different intellectual traditions. Thus, the term ›innovative milieu‹ refers mainly to science and technology, while the term ›creative class‹, posed by Richard Florida, collectively includes scientists, engineers, artists, musicians, designers and knowledge-based professionals (Florida 2002: xiii). Members of the ›creative class‹ are defined by their potential to develop solutions to complex problems. In his terminology and methodology, however, Florida remains half-way between the designation of quantifiable members of a certain branch and the designation of professional groups characterized by their distinct intellectual disposition. The terms ›cultural industries‹ or ›cultural economies‹ have long since lost the critical tone acquired from the tradition of the Frankfurt School, and now simply denote the production of ›cultural products‹, i.e., products that have a symbolic value, products that function as signs. This research, by Alan Scott (Scott 1988, 2000) and

Lash and Urry (1999) among others, is in the tradition of Baudrillard and Bourdieu. Nowadays, the terms ›cultural industries‹ or ›cultural economies‹ refer to culture that is consumed. They make no distinction between high and low culture and instead emphasize the commercialisation of cultural practice. In particular, the term ›cultural economy‹ denotes an extremely broad range of goods, above all commodities, and all products of the media like films, television and music. Creativity is not automatically central in this discussion.[2]

Most of these terms are constantly being used overlappingly or synonymously in the debate. By taking a historical perspective, we would like to contribute to a more precise terminology. Using these terms in historical studies is, however, a particular challenge. One thing seems to be clear, namely that it stands for a close interwovenness of both spheres, culture and economy, and names (apparently exclusively) current phenomena that stand in close connection to the development of cities. Thereby, we suggest distinguishing at least two dimensions of the term ›cultural economy‹. We can principally differentiate two closely interwoven and empirically observable developments, which are combined under the term: on the one hand, the economical function of culture, which we shall here call ›economizing of culture‹ (i.e. the privatizing of cultural events, processes of de-publicizing and economizing of cultural policy), and on the other hand, a ›culturalizing of the economy‹. The latter means the increasing significance of ›creative industry‹, a symbolic economy, as well as a new, informal, small-scale, often network-based organisation of business.

---

2   Hartley criticizes the term cultural industries for failing »to combine art and culture, culture and creativity«. Instead »creative arts remained one thing, cultural industries like media and movies remained another« (Hartley 2005: 14). According to Hartley, the term ›creative industries‹ has emerged recently as a combination of ›creative arts‹ and ›cultural industries‹. He contends that it exploits the fuzziness of the boundaries between the two terms. Its fuzziness can currently be observed in Unesco's definition of the term creative economy, which implies, for example, design, literature, film, music, media, folk arts and gastronomy.
(http://www.unescobkk.org/fileadmin/user_upload/culture/Cultural_Industries/HK_Open_Forum/Backgrounder-FINAL.pdf)

The Culturalization of the Economy

For a definition of the term ›cultural economy‹, Allen J. Scott's approach (Scott 2000) is definitive, although too broadly defined. Scott takes on primarily the culturalizing of the economy, leaving the economizing of culture, which is closely connected with this process, largely unattended in his work. He includes in his inquiries both cultural industries and branches in which there is rather a lesser share of work on cultural development, but in which products are generated whose aesthetic value, whose lifestyle content, is more important than their practical function and use. Scott also makes it clear in many passages that clustering within a sector and within a city always has to do with the building of other organized networks as well. It is also important that the competitive advantage of clustering is primarily visible in the possibility of drawing upon locally present, suitable employees whose reliability and competence can be well estimated from all sides, i.e., knowledge, local employment market, mode of communication and milieu stand in close connection to one another (Matthiesen 2004). ›Cultural‹ or ›creative milieus‹ count both as central resources for urban developments and as promising, even necessary forms of organisation for innovations and creativity, be they of artistic, technical or scientific nature.

The concept of creative or innovative milieus, which is to further the genesis of innovation and creativity through network-like organisation, informal contacts and learning, is central to artistic and scientific industries, as well as to ›creative careers‹, like that of designers, architects, or advertisers. In any case, the concept of cultural economy includes also science, especially in the twentieth century, when evermore branches draw on science as an economic resource, and scientific milieus have become as important a part of city advertising and image strategies as artistic milieus. While ›creative careers‹ and artists' scenes are increasingly present in cities (Helbrecht 2004; Läpple 2003), this is not necessarily the case for scientifically innovative milieus, which are also to be found in suburban areas (Heßler 2002). This raises the question of whether or not we can talk of the renaissance of cities in the context of creative milieus.

Thus, the concept of cultural economy comprises developments that can be summed up in a first step as ›culturalization of the economy‹, and which indicate a process of economic transformation, to be understood as ›symbolic economy‹, in which the production of signs and symbols became at least as important as that of utility-based values. So-called ›creative industries‹ produce cultural goods, like fashion, design, film, advertisement, etc. Their economic significance continues to grow enormously. But what is meant in each context by the word ›creative‹? The generation of entirely new products, institutions and social practices, or only the adaptation of inventions connected to a certain radiation in a surrounding area, which originated elsewhere? How can the creative share in career activities be measured, and to what resources, even statistical resources, can one resort, especially when one moves back into a pre-statistical age? How strongly was the creativity of network connections connected to the ability of non-conformism? In John Hartley's volume ›Creative Industries‹ it becomes apparent that ›creativity‹, the ability to think of new solutions to problems, to recognise structures in the supposed chaos of new influences, to transfer competencies from one field of knowledge to another, even in that producers are simultaneously active in different careers, belonging to different subcultures; this is the main characteristic of the complex to be examined. Creativity becomes »the decisive source of competitive advantage« (Hartley 2005). In specific sectors and branches the significance of creativity is more evident than in others. Thus, the producers of lifestyle-oriented products and services (employment of the design, special forms of tourism, fashion articles) are to be included in the sector, insofar as the product's use consists in the support of individual lifestyle development and the creation of identity. It is typical of modern cultural economy and its marketing that with products a ›sense of place‹ is also conveyed, i.e., the image of a city often figures into the use of a product as a significant factor (Paris fashion, Berlin theatre). The thematizing of creativity, though, is by no means exhausted in this economic function. The term ›creative milieus‹ refers to certain urban spaces in which various actors interact and meet, formally and informally. Competition and cooperation as well as shared values and common problems are further features of creative milieus. Face-to-face communication is essential. In a more economical sense and in the words of Roberto Camagni: »Creativity and continuous innovation are seen as the result of a collective learning process, fed by such social phenomena as intergenerational transfer of know-how, imitation of successful managerial practices and technological innovations, interpersonal face-to-face contacts, formal and informal cooperation between firms, tacit circulation of commercial, financial or technological information« (Camagni 1991: 1).

The Economisation of Culture

The second process to be included in the term ›cultural economy‹ is currently, closely intertwined with the developments portrayed. It points to the ›economisation of urban culture‹. The cultural and scientific life of cities is an essential part of their identity and image building, and thus a central aspect of increasing competition of cities for the settling of industries, but also for the streams of tourists. ›Classical‹ areas of urban culture, such as theatre, museums, or opera, are placed under considerable economic pressure, while mass cultural events and productions dominate the cultural life of a city. The economizing of culture comprises institutions like theatre, museums, science, film or organized events (Sheehan 2002; Hochreiter 1994; Rooch 2001), subcultures and artistic milieus. Nor is the ›culture industry‹ to be ignored, which produces mass cultural merchandise, festivals or spectacles, and with which today's hopes for new employment potentials are connected. A city's creative industries and artistic and scientific milieus play an especially important role here. The question poses itself, however, whether culture industrial production does not displace classical forms of urban culture, and what it is about them that is really ›creative‹.

In this volume both processes, commercialisation of culture as well as culturalization of economy shall be examined and their interdependence and connection with urban development demonstrated. The individual articles deal with different fields such as books and paintings (Zimmermann), art and film (May), fashion (Breward and Gilbert), hotels (Knoch), with high as well as popular culture (Gunn), with popular music (Bottà), with tourism and media (Steward) and with port cities (Weinhold) – to name but a few. Moreover, this volume will not reduce itself to cultural milieus such as arts, design, fashion etc. Too often science and technology are left out when urban creative milieus are discussed. Thus, Heßler and Hospers deal with ›science cities‹ and ›scientific creative milieus‹, which have become the rays of hope for scientific and technical innovations and economical prosperity several decades ago, especially in the context of the ›knowledge society‹ (see e.g. Bell 1973; Kreibich 1986; Stehr 1994; Szöllösi-Janze 2004; Weingart 2001).

As already mentioned, the main objective thereby is to analyse theses cultural economies and creative milieus from a historical perspective. First we want to know why there has been so much talk of this since the 1980s.

Second we want to consider the current manifestations of the urban culture industry and creative milieus in comparison with their predecessors. The volume aims at historicising the current development systematically by comparing such different fields in different times. Although this volume is just a beginning of historicising cultural economy, we think that we can offer some general insights.

The Necessity of Historicising

The necessity of historicising the object grows primarily out of the obsession of the debate up until now with the present. The economical, geographical and sociological contributions claim as a rule that all the phenomena described today are completely new, having appeared first in the 1980s. Those who set the terms of reference in the current discussion such as Richard Florida, Charles Landry, John Hartley and Allen Scott remain focused on the present time; at most they go back to the 1980s which is when they see the development as having originated. John Hartley speaks of a significantly new development in ›post-industrial society‹ (Hartley, 2005: 18), while Allen Scott claims »that the culture is embedded in the economic; and never has this been more the case than in contemporary capitalism« (Scott 2000: ix). He does not elaborate on the claim or give any proof for it. Thus, many geographical and sociological contributions claim in accordance with these authors that all the phenomena described today are completely new, having appeared first in the 1980s. This, however, is decidedly short-sighted. There are admittedly many indications to support the claim of a discontinuity, or substantial shifts, but many developments can also be observed at a much earlier date. Where these discontinuities exactly lie, and when they are encountered, therefore, has to first be investigated. Florida's approach hardly lends itself to historicisation since it is strongly related to a particular historical situation – as for instance with the gay index as an indicator of cultural liberty. Roberto Camagni's approach on the other hand is better suited to historicisation. His research approach considers principal agents, the uncertainties of the market, transaction costs, formal and informal institutions, and relationships between cooperation/competition. It is possible to apply it to earlier forms of capitalism and early-modern states and cities, although this is not Camagni's concern.

The lack of historicisation results from the fact that many authors are policy orientated, or are trying to enlist the political support of creative industries. A historicising has two central tasks. Firstly, the current interest in cultural economy must be explained and historicized. The debate is partially one of conspicuous euphoria, hysteria and affirmation, while critical reflection is often left by the wayside, although not only the creative persons themselves often find themselves in precarious living circumstances, nor can the focus on creative industries be without its ›casualties‹. Furthermore, urban restructuring processes that coincide with cultural commercialisation are often unpredictable with respect to their long-term ramifications, such as in the context of gentrification of the city.

A historicising of the ›discovery‹ of cultural industries, creative milieus and the myth of the creative city, as it is to be found starting in the 1980s, though, would remind us that this discourse is an answer to a quite specific historical constellation, and that it is necessary to understand it in order to be able to assess yet more critically and reliably the grave historical shifts and discontinuities, supposed or factual, and the economic potential.

The historical constellation in which cities' cultural economies have been addressed can be sketched heuristically according to the following points: First, a change in macro-economic structure rooted in a loss of significance of classical industrial branches (iron, steel, mechanics, coal, etc.) in favour of knowledge-based industries, so-called high tech industries, since the 1980s. Second, such authors as Burkart Lutz (1984) or Michael J. Piore and Charles F. Sabel (1984) diagnosed a parallel end of standardized mass production, a post-Fordist age, in which the organisational forms of businesses turned to smaller scale, less formal and network oriented forms. Third, finally, Scott Lash and John Urry (1999) spoke of a »symbolic economy« meaning a shift from utility goods, whose functionality was central, toward symbolic merchandise, to lifestyle products. This was connected to the ascent of the ›creative industries‹. The significance of the latter for the economy as a whole, as they point out, has increased massively since the 1980s. Fourth, at the same time, a policy of increasing deregulation and privatisation was observable in western societies. Public-private partnerships and sponsoring became new instruments of cultural politics in the 1980s. This redoubled a waxing economisation of urban culture to accompany falling incomes and growing city expenditures.

In the context of these developments, not only did a restructuring of spaces make itself noticeable within the cities, but the entire economic geography of the cities shifted (Zimmermann 2006). The orientation toward a cultural economy that not only promised to improve the cities' image, but with which also hopes for new economic impulses for prosperity were connected, thus became a topos of political policy, as well as a new, often observable chapter of urban research, of economy and of geography, which often slipped into the role of the solution giver, yet neglected the view to the past.

In this volume Martina Heßler scrutinizes this question of why the topic of the ›creative city‹ was re-invented in the 1970s/1980s in more detail by focusing on a single science city, namely Garching near Munich. She shows how structural changes in economy, such as the growing importance of knowledge for economy as well as changes in technology/science policy forced a commercialisation of science and constituted the historical background for the re-discovery of the concept of the creative city, which is now regarded as the appropriate mode for pursuing scientific-technological research.

The second task of a historicisation consists in the search for cultural economies in different times as well as in the reconstruction of lines of continuity and breaks. If one enters into the historical dimension with the long-term goal of recognising the phases of urban cultural economic development, one will be in a better position to recognise the true potentials, but also the losses inherent in it – qualitatively and quantitatively speaking. Here, the question poses itself of whether the delineable phases can be distinguished from one another. However, it is completely unclear when the ›symbolic‹ economy began. Only with Disneyland and opera events, or already with the world exhibitions of the nineteenth century, or with the Berlin Trade Exhibition in 1896, a display of aesthetic productivity (Simmel 1992 [1896]: 71-75; Großbölting 2004), – or even with the display of art and wealth in the leading classes of London in the seventeenth century, or in the Italian city patrons of the late Middle Ages (Peck 2005; Goldthwaite 1993)?

Already at a place like early modern Venice, a close connection between favourable local peripheral circumstances such as a trade-friendly climate, the existence of a quite dense group of local specialists and publishers can be clearly seen as a creative milieu, and a most efficacious, multi-faceted and far-reaching book production, that at the same time left its seal deeply on a legacy of urban self-presentation and cartography (Wilson 2006; Burke 2000). In the eighteenth century baths, the significance of an urban economy of taste that bore a distinct city image becomes visible; from then, and from the circumstances of what urban experiences a *Kurort* has to offer, considerable economic effects are to be had. One further example is the high local concentration and continuity of the Parisian fashion business, its milieu being interconnected with other milieus and industries. In historical cities ›creative‹ milieus can also be seen, be it the London artisans, as in the case of the highly specialized manufacturers of instruments, be it the furniture workshop in the German Neuwied, or be it the history of the diamond trade in Antwerp, which reaches to the present. Moreover, the ›spectacular‹ element of a visually loaded city landscape and its economy of signs ought to be taken into account, which is characteristically a fully developed element in the metropoles of the late nineteenth century (Gellately 1993; Borsay et al. 2000; Oettermann 1980; Wischermann and Shore 2000; Schwartz 1998; Ethington and Schwartz 2006), such that, just as tellingly, at the turn of the century a first analysis with Thorstein Veblen's observations on mass demonstrative consumption appeared (Veblen 1899). Historical studies, as well, that attribute a supportive role in city marketing to cultural institutions point to the connection, but not yet to the concept of a »cultural economy of cities« (Schott 1999; Mai 2004). Hence, the history of urban events, which combine knowledge and commerciality, connected with the obvious retention of various habitual city profiles (Lindner 2003) ought also to be investigated historically (Geppert, Jensen, Weinhold 2005). Such various examples as Virchow's Museum of the History of Medicine in Berlin or ethnological shows of the nineteenth century (Matyssek 2002), as well as the amusement- and theme parks of the world exhibitions of the nineteenth and twentieth centuries display this early combination of event, spectacle, knowledge and economy. However, in the classical works of Werner Sombart on the production of luxury (Sombart 1916: 717–749) not only a multitude of further examples are to be found, but he also explains the productive effects, and that ›private‹ cultural industries can be separated neither from the patron-funded artists' milieu, nor even from the courtly and urban contexts of the production of luxury. The example also shows that in pre-modern (early modern) historical constellations other agent constellations are to be encountered than in the modern cultural industry. In this context, a historicising might be expected to clarify especially the relations between courts, or courtly societies[3] and cities, and between universities and cities.

Finally, Peter Hall described how certain metropolitan milieus gave rise to paradigmatic and new types of production systems, e.g., in Manchester, Detroit and Hollywood, in a provocative and opulent, though unsystematic work that cited all too many variables, and only introduced the theoretical premises associatively. Hall distinguishes between cultural, technical and organisational innovations, which have special chances for development in certain city types, and are ever more strongly interconnected in the historical process. Hall's book almost takes the entire history of humanity into account, from Athens under the rule of Pericles all the way to Silicon Valley, and even the most recent developments, such as ›creative milieus‹ in the media, or science as a motor for economic developments, so-called high-tech clusters. His historically comparative inquiry aims less at the description of historical change than a thorough questioning of the principal, diachronically efficacious conditions of innovations, for creativity in cities. Creativity and innovation in the urban milieu, then, are to be seen as interdependent processes that affect all aspects of urban life (Hall 1998).

It is generally clear that the relation of city and innovation does not first begin with a ›high tech‹ sector. One example is that of the technological innovations of the eighteenth and nineteenth centuries, that were often born in new types of industrial cities like Manchester, but not in classical cities (Garfield 2002). In any case, in the context of the current debate, which is characterized by attempts to establish, to increase, even to plan creative milieus, it must not be forgotten that in history centuries-old tradition of founding the ideal city exists. Especially for the twentieth century, the number of newly founded scientific cities is by no means small. The attempt to increase the generation of scientific and technical innovations in such cities, thereby guaranteeing economic prosperity, can demonstrated in such various case examples as the Soviet ›Akademgorodok‹ of the late 1950s and 1960s, the Japanese ›Tsukubu‹ of the 1980s, or the ›science cities‹ presently being built everywhere.

As this short overview based on recent literature already shows, urban cultural economy is not a completely recent phenomenon. Finally, summarizing the results of the case studies, presented in this volume, makes very

---

3   Vaubel (2005) juxtaposes high artistic productivity in Italy and Germany during the Baroque era with the existence of numerous small but competing courts (and ecclesiastical institutions), also thus with a specific local constellation.

clear that the matter is much more complicated. While the many single case studies embrace many more important aspects of a historical research of cultural economy – such as the role of media (Steward and Höpel), the extraordinary importance of city images for or within a cultural economy as well as the not yet explored questions regarding the use of material sources (Breward and Gilbert) – the following considerations do not aim at giving a summary of each article, but try to discuss their results referring to our main question as mentioned above.

Thus, concerning historicisation it is of special interest to pose the question of whether or not we can talk of an urban cultural economy in the early modern period, as Clemens Zimmermann and Peter Borsay do in their contribution to this volume. They focus on (noble and bourgeois) agents, the concepts of creativity, the significance for the economy as well as the role of networks of regulating norms. Zimmermann's study focuses on Venice and London, two leading political, cultural and economic centres of the early modern era in Europe. The branches of the economy that he analyses – art creation and the art trade on the one hand, printing and the book trade on the other – were highly significant to the export orientated economy of the two cities and were also substantial branches in terms of quantity, even though this is no longer the case in the cultural economy sectors of cities today. Both cities were decisively influenced by the presence of wealthy clients and the growing importance of an extensive market for culture, also in terms of the production of luxury articles. It appears that cooperative structures played a key role in production. There are notable parallels with the knowledge-based economies of today. The marketability of cultural products – limited in Venice, constantly expanding in London – generally was a relevant circumstance, as was the differentiation of the urban environment. The further expansion of these branches could not occur until the knowledge based economy came to have a higher status generally; the number of potential readers of books and purchasers of paintings was still limited in spite of the evident dynamism of the early modern era. Moreover, the cultural economy of the two cities differed from that of the present day in its distinct political and corporative structures. The ›economy‹ and producers were subject to sundry regulations imposed by authorities, censors, guilds and the Church. Nonetheless, London in particular, displayed characteristics of a culture economy anticipating that which we know today.

A very similar thesis is advanced by Peter Borsay, who focuses on the matter of product innovations. For Borsay, eighteenth-century Britain is a »peculiar creative economic milieu« which was brought into being by the simultaneity of accelerated cultural, economic and urban change. Borsay, like Zimmermann, dismisses the notion that cultural economy is a phenomenon of the globalisation phase of the economy in the twentieth century – although the relevant markets were numerically limited – and substantiates this by reference to a very wide spectrum of specific urban innovations. Borsay describes a tendency towards accelerated cultural and technological innovation which may be observed in towns of all sizes, although it is present to a far greater degree in the super-metropolis London than in the many very small market towns. Both authors come to the view that it is possible to talk of the existence of a cultural economy in the eighteenth century.

Simon Gunn, Jill Steward and Habbo Knoch discover specific characteristics of a cultural economy in the nineteenth century in their case studies. Focusing on the late nineteenth century Simon Gunn shows how in Manchester, England's second biggest city, a cultural quarter came into being between 1860 and 1900 which offered a wide range of ›high culture‹ well as popular culture events; this cultural quarter corresponds in many respects to today's clusters. Not only were there antecedents of the cultural quarters of today in Manchester during this period, but the contemporary culture-led regeneration of urban quarters »replicated certain features of an earlier historical phase of urban culture«. After 1900, this milieu and this type of quarter with its theatres and clubs located near to the business centre and main shopping area began to lose much of its former importance and creative potential; increasingly the sites where culture was consumed were to be found in the outskirts. On the basis of these observations it may be presumed that the rise of a cultural economy in a specific locality is a cyclical matter, in which manifestations and factors occur in parallel in different historical periods and may be compared. If cultural economy is defined as a »coherent, public commercialized sphere of art and entertainment run predominantly on capitalist lines«, then these criteria are readily observable also in Manchester in the late nineteenth century. This milieu moreover displayed certain structural features which are no longer in evidence today, for example, the substantial input into the commercial musical life of the quarter came from voluntary associations. Manchester's music scene was supported in those days by a sense of civic responsibility and public commitment – the result of a climate in which it was felt that such civic commitment was important and useful.

In her article on urban tourism Jill Steward points out in respect to the historical evolution of the cultural economy in Western Europe that a significant phase began in 1850 and lasted probably until about 1960. Looking at the phenomenon of an accelerating urban tourism in certain European cities, Jill Steward considers exactly what this urban tourism was structurally based on, and contends that it represents a significant portion of the cultural economy. She makes clear which social groups consumed here, how cities took an increasingly active role in promoting themselves and concrete local qualities and marketing their image. Cities also are becoming ever more closely interlinked, an aspect that should be taken into account in the historicisation of the cultural economy debate.

Habbo Knoch takes as his theme a significant social and cultural innovation of the late nineteenth century: the municipal luxury hotel. He does not cite concrete examples but treats it as a global phenomenon. The luxury hotel represented an innovative and specific sphere – a town within a town, sharing many points of contact with the existing town, but still striving to be a distinct world of its own. The thriving of luxury hotels was linked to general factors like the expansion of tourism and profited from existing concrete circumstances in terms of urban structures and modes of behaviour. The luxury hotel was the location of urban events, it contributed to the urban architecture, to the inner urbanisation of cities and at the same time it was a place of money-making, investment and consumption – until their decline. In addition, luxury hotels were a sphere of innovative urban culture economy until their existence was made practically impossible by the general development of cities in a phase in which tourism intensified – though still not to the extent of post 1960 mass tourism. The example of the luxury hotel as a sphere of a specific urban lifestyle – a phenomenon that has almost totally vanished today – calls into question the one-dimensional phase models and the prevailing ahistoricity of the debate today.

Especially when one views the twentieth century as a whole it becomes clear that phenomena of the cultural economy which are deemed to be contemporary were in fact already being shaped in the early twentieth century. Discussing Venice between 1920 and 1940, Jan Andreas May observes, for example, that ›festivalisation‹ and city marketing are by no means phenomena of the 1980s and later. Art and films were successfully commercialized in the city with a view to stimulating the tourist industry and this occurred in what was effectively a ›global‹ context prior to ›globalisation‹. As May notes, »Venice was one of the first European cities to concentrate its economy primarily on the development of cultural tourism. Supported by the local political leaders and the government in Rome, Venice succeeded in reshaping the historic city into a perfectly organized tourist destination with new infrastructure. [...] Using the city as a stage for the modern arts, that is using locations outside the Giardini, too, supported the festivilisation of the urban cultural policy.«

In their article on ›Swinging London‹ in the 1960s, Breward and Gilbert challenge the assumption – widely held in the academic debate today – that the cultural economy came into existence in the 1980s and 1990s. The authors show on the contrary that new cultural styles and the reorientation of London's economy towards advertising and internationalisation led to a boom in jobs in the cultural economy in the sixties. They describe London in that decade as a »site of a genuinely distinctive and creative urban cultural economy«. In the 1960s – and not in the Silicon Valley age – London was transformed in a direction which still strikes some people as modern today: office-buildings, the development of creative clusters, and the city's reputation as a site of spectacular consumption all began as early as the 50s. One encounters the features of »flexible production and strongly place-specific design-cultures« which are conventionally attributed only to the post-Fordist period. The culture economy of the fifties and sixties was not only a direct precursor and a core part of today's culture economy: it also displayed certain characteristics which are no longer to be found today or which occur to only a limited degree. There was for instance a direct connection and spatial proximity between design and production, for example, designer clothing was produced in London itself. Whereas, in the sixties creative people still regarded themselves as part of a ›scene‹, today the talk is only of ›networks‹; in other words the way creative types see themselves has become much more individualistic and variable. Moreover, at that time the creative milieu was more open to new talents and to new companies, since it was much cheaper in those days to rent and buy real estate than it is now. This last point brings us to a structural precondition which is often neglected: the culture economy can thrive where ›scenes‹ still exist and where the costs of setting up a business are lower, but this is by no means a sure-fire recipe for success. Thus, this article about the 1960s discusses a significant early phase of the urban culture economy which cannot be interpreted as a reaction to ›globalisation‹. The same may be said of the fashion city Milan (Foot 2001).

Following on seamlessly is the contribution by Jörn Weinhold. He discusses urban development, taking as his case study the ongoing project to redevelop the port and waterfront area in Hamburg; he finds that contemporary utilisation of such spaces is determined to some degree by existing traditions and images. It might be assumed that harbour redevelopment projects in the ›post-Fordist‹ age would follow the same aims and plans everywhere, i.e. globally. Yet as the Hamburg example shows, city images cannot be produced just like that: in the case of original structures and sites a utilisation history exists which cannot simply be ignored. Real estate marketing and branding today must take account of historical substance and cannot ride roughshod over local interests and identities. As made clear by the Hamburg harbour case, redevelopment according to the principles of profitable real estate management and the siting of culture industries can come up against firm resistance: this, in Hamburg, ultimately led to the planning of new, more complex projects. Here too, then, urban (cultural) history and political intervention as well as the citizens' own collective memory become factors which play a part in shaping the culture economy that emerges. Hence, Weinhold's paper is concerned with the historicisation of a phenomenon (that is the acknowledgement of an influential prehistory) and also with public policy as a systematic determining factor.

Marjatta Hietala's paper also makes clear how important a city's history is for the development of a cultural economy or for its transformation into an ›innovative city‹. She shows how the characteristics and the fields of the cultural economy in Helsinki have evolved in the two hundred years since the early nineteenth century, and how the emergence of a cultural economy is very much a historical process that is subject to the vicissitudes of time. While in the early nineteenth century nationalistic creative milieus of writers, artists and musicians predominated, in the 1950s a modest policy of festivalisation was initiated. Recently Helsinki has emerged as a high-tech city. The expansion of the cultural sector, comprising science and technology as well as the arts and design, was crucial to Helsinki's evolution from a small shipping town at the beginning of nineteenth century to a city that presents itself today as an innovative city in design, music as well as the high tech industry.

Thus, what is obvious from our case studies is that the project of historicisation is dedicated not to reconstructing (or inventing) a linear process of modernisation, which ends in a modern and now economically most relevant sector of culture economy, but to identifying the differences between earlier formations and the present time. It is very clear that we have to consider the specific historical constellations of global and local factors, which are connected to the emergence of cultural economies in different times. At the same time, of course, urban economies and in particular urban creative milieus are dependent upon concrete historical situations which cannot be made to recur. That was also the implication of the paper on ›Swinging London‹.

However, on one hand we can find micro-historical variations and different constellations, on the other hand one can observe a macro-historical process since 1500 in which service industries, knowledge and cultural products gained importance and in which internationalisation and globalisation, the rising level of productivity and communication set new standards. So we do not speak of an ›origin‹ of cultural economies in early modern times and we do not suggest writing a linear history. Nonetheless, we can distinguish individual phases in which cultural economy gained more importance and visibility. Single situations and unique constellations matter. So Peter Borsay states: »Rather than looking for a single definition of the cultural economy, or engaging in the construction of a progessivist history by which the economy is for ever becoming more and more a vehicle for culture and aesthetics, it may be better to recognize that different types of societies and eras create different forms of cultural economy.«

And Simon Gunn stresses that the »example of Manchester analysed here suggests less a progressive than a cyclical model of the cultural economy in which the key factors are at least as much local as global. According to this analysis, the modern cultural economy was not the creation of late twentieth-century capitalist globalisation or post-modern consumerism. What mattered in the 1880s no less than in the 1980s was the wave of inward investment that resulted in the rapid renovation of the urban fabric of the city centre by both private and public capital [...]. The cultural economy thus appears as the outcome of a periodic interaction between art, the market and the urban environment whose specific features differ historically but whose essential components remain remarkably similar across time.«

Conditions for the Evolution of Cultural Economies in History

When there are actually »remarkably similar components across time« (Simon Gunn), we can try to ask whether certain conditions can be identified which are necessary for the development of an urban cultural economy. Peter Hall's above-mentioned monumental study of the link between creativity and the city considers what the universal conditions for innovations and creativity in cities may be. Despite all the disparities, the particularities and the great degree of divergence between cities, there are nevertheless some circumstances common to creative cities, Hall argues, such as a certain size, a certain degree of prosperity, the existence of communicative networks, of heterogeneity, of foreign elements and outsiders, and the existence of instabilities as a central element of creativity. This can be summed up in the negative formulation: »Conservative, stable societies will not prove creative« (Hall 1998: 286). For natural science and technological ›innovative milieus‹ there is furthermore a need for egalitarian social structures and for competition, which promotes reciprocal learning, Hall claims (ibid.: 494).

Two papers in this volume explicitly emphasize those factors which determine the success, or otherwise, of the cultural economy. Peter Borsay's already mentioned article explores the condition and climate for urban creativity. He defines five conditions for creativity (valorisation of change, circulation of knowledge, incentives, demand, and fashion). Gert-Jan Hospers, who is concerned with ›science cities‹, analyses the factors required for successful creative milieus which are constantly cited in the literature, namely density, diversity and instability. Hospers stresses by contrast, the importance of the *image* of a creative milieu. This is frequently overlooked in contemporary policy-making. People must believe that a creative milieu is creative.

In addition to image, an urban ›climate‹ that welcomes innovation and is favourable to cultural economies is undoubtedly necessary if cultural-economy sectors are to evolve freely, as Sandra Schürmann shows, using the example of Hamburg in the early twentieth century. Her article makes clear that in Hamburg there was not a propitious climate for the development of the advertising industry on account of the restrictive political and cultural conditions prevailing in the city. The advertising industry that nevertheless took root thanks to the business of certain influential enterprises burgeoned, however, only after 1945, and eventually became a major contributor to the local economy in conjunction with the media organisations that were established in the city. Before the Second World War there was a measure of institutional support for the activities of the utilitarian graphic artists and photographers whom Schürmann looks at in the paper – for example in terms of the relationship between graphic artists and art schools. Artistic photography and industrial photography also certainly received support from municipal institutions. Without such institutions, indeed, the private sector art scene would not have been able to develop to the same degree.

Besides these various aspects coming out of our case studies, one aspect is striking. Many case studies make clear that there is obviously a close connection between economic/financial crisis and the rise and promotion of a cultural economy. Thus May shows in his case study of Venice in the 1920s and 1930s that »the Biennale and its accompanying events were used for propagandistic purposes but [...] the binding force behind this was an economic one, a way out of a crisis: tourism was important because it brought in foreign currency«. Höpel points out how cultural policy in German and French cities in the 1920s pertained to a specific situation of economic crisis, which the intensified cultural policy was also intended to ameliorate whereas, Breward and Gilbert underline that »London during the 1960s was clearly in a state of important economic transition. The most obvious features were the decline of the docks, and a collapse of manufacturing industry. [...] Yet while manufacturing in overall was in crisis and the docks were in terminal decline, significant restructuring was taking place«. Many jobs in the cultural economy emerged. Interesting is also a ›counter-example‹, namely Hamburg as a latecomer in terms of urban redevelopment of port cities, as it is described by Jörn Weinhold. Whereas, other ports first introduced urban redevelopment strategies in the 1960s in response to the loss of their traditional function, Hamburg had no such need since its harbour was still functioning well. Therefore, the cultural economy that came to characterize the reconstructed harbour districts of port cities has emerged in Hamburg only recently.

Twentieth Century: The Making of Urban Cultural Economies and Creative Milieus

While we show in this volume that there have been manifold manifestations of the cultural economy since the early modern era, a special observation may be made with respect to the twentieth century. In the twentieth century there is an intensification of efforts to generate creative milieus and to promote the cultural economy of cities. The articles concerned with cultural policy in cities in the twentieth century make this clear. Thus, Thomas Höpel in his study of a systematic sample of four French and German cities reveals the tendency towards the commercialisation and festivalisation of urban culture in the early twentieth century, and it was the cities themselves that contributed to the process institutionally. Going against mainstream research, Höpel demonstrates that the cities' culture policy had an economic function and was targeted at the promotion of a cultural economy. Hence, we can speak of a culturalization of the economy, e.g., through colleges of fine art and applied art which offered the training for the various artistic skills that were required. In Leipzig, for example, a strong link arose between colleges of arts and crafts and the book industry, particularly book graphics. Cultural policy became bound up with image politics: hence a commercialisation of culture took place. By setting up a local radio station, policy makers were seeking to increase cultural diversification and to boost of the image of the location. The idea was to entice visitors and tourists to the city by means of such activities, city marketing and cultural centrality. Höpel's paper thus clearly demonstrates that many components of the culture economy as we know it, already existed in the years 1890 to 1933. Municipal cultural policy led to public subsidy for a cultural sector which had an effect on the economy.

The importance of an active cultural policy is also made clear in the above-mentioned paper by Jan Andreas May on Venice between 1920 and 1940. Historical culture in Venice was effectively ›staged‹ by local and national politicians and by local businesses, and utilized to stimulate a significant new phase in tourism. In the case of Venice – and incidentally Hamburg too, as described by Jörn Weinhold – culture economy turns out to be a variant of urban development policy. The success story of the culture economy of Venice is based politically on the harmonisation of local economic interests with the interests of national cultural policy.

Similarly, Marjatta Hietala's article illustrates the importance of ›public authorities‹ in the development of the culture economy. Especially in the twentieth century, local as well as national elites made considerable efforts to elevate Helsinki in terms of science and culture. In the process Helsinki closely followed the example of other European cities, skilfully adapting their concepts.

The contributors Jan May, Jill Steward and Thomas Höpel show that the culture economy is often used for a city's image. While all three stress the efforts to create an image to attract tourists, Giacomo Bottà focuses on popular music and reveals how music culture in the urban context determines the image of cities – doing so more powerfully and effectively, in his view, than the cities' own official image campaigns. Music represents the city in text and via materiality: sites associated with music help to shape the city's architecture. Through the branding of music the city promotes itself on the international tourism market, Bottà claims with particular reference to advertising professionals and commercial photographers. Bottà shows very clearly that the three music scenes he studied – Manchester, Berlin and Helsinki – owe much to local initiatives for being able to draw on locally generated images and associations. Although pop music may be regarded as a standardized globalised product, on the local level cultural characteristics and initiatives are highly diversified.

Cultural Economies and Failure

While it is not easy to estimate the role of economic effects historically, today as mentioned at the beginning of this introduction, expectations are extremely high that cultural economy should result in economic prosperity. This debate has become something of a hot topic which is already influencing urban policy in spite of the paucity of empirical evidence. So it is necessary to consider to what extent the ›cultural economy‹ and ›creative industries‹ are actually successful in economic terms. Is it not frequently the case that claims of cultural productivity in fact serve to construct an image that is supposed to attract tourists and new businesses? Do efforts to cultivate a city's image have any economic effect at all? What economic advantage can really be ascribed to cultural industries, in the present and in the past?

One problem is that the criteria for the statistical evaluation of the individuals denoted by the terms creative class or cultural economy differ markedly from one another. The differentiation of the 11.7 percent of the working population whom Richard Florida terms the »super-creative core of the creative class« from the 18.3 percent of the »other creative class« is in itself problematic (Florida 2002: 330). What is highly dubious, furthermore, are statistical projections going back into the past. Thus, how shall we know about the number of ›creative‹ employees in the past, since we have to take account of the change in statistical categories and the very real change in job descriptions, the skills required in them and the measure of autonomy and ›creativity‹ in them.

Although it is extremely challenging to measure the economic effects of cultural economies, some case studies give us hints to answer this question: Clemens Zimmermann came to the conclusion, as cited above, that art production and the art trade as well as book-printing and the book trade in eighteenth-century London and Venice were highly significant to the export-oriented economies of the two cities. Martina Heßler shows that the town of Garching did not benefit from the siting and growth of a science city at all, although local politicians had expected a considerable increase in jobs and prosperity.

Birgit Metzger's article can almost be seen as the antithesis to Richard Florida's simplistic and often criticized thesis that alternative milieus (see his thesis of the gay index and immigrants) represent the ideal breeding ground for cultural economies. Metzger focuses on the creative milieu of the Nauwieser district in the southwest German city of Saarbrücken in the 1970s and 1980s. This alternative district was a centre of social experimentation, where people tried out new lifestyles that were politically motivated and chiefly anti-capitalist. She describes the district as a creative urban milieu, and yet virtually no economic effects can be identified, not least on account of the anti-capitalist mentality of many of the inhabitants. She states that »the quarter has also become a location for further cultural products, enterprises and stores constituting small street-level cultural economy, but it never became a centre of cultural economy«. She thus concludes that »the creative vibrancy of the alternative milieu did not continue in a developing cultural economy«.

Alexa Färber offers an unusual celebration of the connection of risk/failure and cultural economy, taking contemporary Berlin as her example, a city which plays coquettishly with its image as ›poor, but sexy‹.

Färber reveals the huge disparity between the high number of creatives, Berlin's image as a creative city, and Berlin's dire economic situation. She analyses the public rhetorical strategies: the vacant city space and the economic stagnation are in stark contrast to the urban ›imageneering‹ which is constantly practiced. The city's image does, in point of fact, contribute significantly to the local economy (which is in deficit). Additionally the Senate is pursuing a strategy to promote creative small businesses. The fact that creative businesses are high-risk is a dark side of the culture economy, which is generally painted in euphoric terms. In this connection Färber presents the history of two initiatives to market designer clothing produced and sold in Berlin. It is probably not at all unusual that one of the initiatives should have failed, while the other is thriving. The article shows explicitly the micro-social constellations of success and failure for such initiatives. The article calls into question the euphoric tenor of culture-economy theories – some statistically based – which seek to occupy the phenomenon for themselves. It also questions the widespread assumption that such shops really only succeed in connection with a particular city district; the strategic alternatives evidently are networks on the municipal level. The article therefore touches on the matter of location as a key factor for the creative milieu – a question which calls for further research.

It has, therefore, become clear that we should not only focus on the history of cultural economies, but that we should also focus more on failure than (eventual) re-writing the history of success stories of creative milieus or cultural economies. Analyzing failure does not only challenge the myth of creative milieus and cultural economies, but could also help to understand better the condition of success stories as well as the historical ›rise and fall‹ of urban creative milieus.

Bibliography

Bell, Daniel (1973). *The Coming of Post-Industrial Society: A Venture in Social Forecasting*. New York.

Borsay, Peter, Gunther Hirschfelder and Ruth E. Mohrmann (eds.) (2000). *New Directions in Urban History: Aspects of European Art, Health, Tourism and Leisure since the Enlightenment*. Münster.

Burke, Peter (2002), »Early Modern Venice as a Center of Information and Communication«. In: John Martin and Dennis Romano (eds.). *Venice Reconsid-*

ered. The History and Civilisation of an Italian City-State 1297–1797. 389–419, Baltimore/London.

Camagni, Roberto (1991). »Introduction: from the local ›milieu‹ to innovation through cooperation networks«. In Roberto Camagni (ed.). *Innovation Networks. Spatial Perspectives,* 1–9. London/New York.

Ethington, Philip J. and Vanessa R. Schwartz (2006). »Introduction: An Atlas of the Urban Icons Project«. *Urban History,* 33, 1, 5–38.

Florida, Richard (2002). *The Rise of the Creative Class.* New York.

Foot, John (2001). *Milan since the Miracle. City, Culture and Identity.* Oxford.

Garfield, Simon (2002). *The Last Journey of William Huskisson.* London.

Gellately, Robert (1993). »An der Schwelle der Moderne. Warenhäuser und ihre Feinde in Deutschland«. In Peter Alter (ed.). *Im Banne der Metropolen. Berlin und London in den zwanziger Jahren,* 131–156. Göttingen/Zürich.

Geppert, Alexander C. T., Uffa Jensen and Jörn Weinhold (eds.) (2005). *Ortsgespräche. Raum und Kommunikation im 19. und 20. Jahrhundert.* Bielefeld.

Goldthwaite, Richard A. (1996). *Wealth and the Demand for Art in Italy, 1300–1600.* New York.

Großbölting, Thomas (2004). »Die Ordnung der Wirtschaft. Kulturelle Repräsentation in den deutschen Industrie- und Gewerbeausstellungen des 19. Jahrhunderts«. In Hartmut Berghoff and Jakob Vogel (eds.). *Wirtschaftsgeschichte als Kulturgeschichte. Dimensionen eines Perspektivenwechsels.* 377–403, Frankfurt am Main/New York.

Guilbaut, Serge (1983). *How New York Stole the Idea of Modern Art.* Chicago/London.

Hall, Peter (1998). *Cities in Civilisation. Culture, Innovation and Urban Order.* New York.

Hartley, John (2005). »Creative Industries«. In John Hartley (ed.). *Creative Industries,* 1–40. Malden/Oxford/Carlton.

Helbrecht, Ilse (2004). »Denkraum Stadt«. In Walter Siebel (ed.). *Die europäische Stadt,* 422–432. Frankfurt am Main.

Heßler, Martina (2002). »Stadt als innovatives Milieu – Ein transdisziplinärer Forschungsansatz«. *Neue Politische Literatur,* 47, 2, 193–223.

Hochreiter, Walter (1994). *Vom Musentempel zum Lernort: zur Sozialgeschichte deutscher Museen 1800–1914.* Darmstadt.

Janik, Allan and Stephen Toulmin (1972). *Wittgenstein's Vienna.* New York.

Kreibich, Rolf (1986). *Die Wissenschaftsgesellschaft. Von Galilei zur High-Tech-Revolution.* Frankfurt am Main.

Läpple, Dieter (2003). »Thesen zu einer Renaissance der Stadt in der Wissensgesellschaft«. In Norbert Gestring (ed.). *Jahrbuch StadtRegion,* 61–78, Opladen.

Landry, Charles (2000). *The Creative City. A Toolkit for Urban Innovators.* London.

Lash, Scott and John Urry (1999). *Economies of Signs and Space.* London.

Lindner, Rolf (2003). »Der Habitus der Stadt – ein kulturgeographischer Versuch«. *Petermanns Geographische Mitteilungen,* 147, 2003/2, 46–53.

Lutz, Burkart (1984). *Der kurze Traum immerwährender Prosperität.* Frankfurt am Main/New York.

Mai, Andreas (2004). »Stadt als Produkt. Werbepolitik für Leipzig 1893–1933«. In Thomas Höpel and Steffen Sammler (eds.). Kulturpolitik und Stadtkultur in Leipzig und Lyon (18.–20. Jahrhundert), 309 – 333 Leipzig.

Matthiesen, Ulf (ed.) (2004). Stadtregion und Wissen. Analysen und Plädoyers für eine wissensbasierte Stadtpolitik. Wiesbaden.

Matyssek. Angela (2002). Rudolf Virchow. Das Pathologische Museum. Geschichte einer wissenschaftlichen Sammlung um 1900. Darmstadt.

Mitchell, William J. (1995). City of Bits: Space, Place, and the Infobahn. Cambridge, Mass.

Oettermann, Stephan (1980). Das Panorama. Die Geschichte eines Massenmediums. Frankfurt am Main.

Peck, Linda Levy (2005). Consuming Splendor. Society and Culture in Seventeenth-Century England. Cambridge.

Perl, Jed (2006). New Art City: Manhattan und die Erfindung der Gegenwartskunst. München/Wien.

Piore, Michael J. and Charles F. Sabel (1984). The Second Industrial Divide. Possibilities for Prosperity. New York.

Rooch, Alarich (2001). Zwischen Museen und Warenhaus. Ästhetisierungsprozesse und sozial-kommunikative Raumaneignungen des Bürgertums (1823–1920). Oberhausen.

Schott, Dieter (1999). »Kunststadt – Pensionärsstadt – Industriestadt. Die Konstruktion von Stadtprofilen durch süddeutsche Stadtverwaltungen vor 1914«. Die Alte Stadt, 26, 277–299.

Schwartz, Vanessa R. (1998). Spectacular Realities. Early Mass Culture in Fin-de-Siècle Paris. Berkeley, Cal./London.

Scott, Allen J. (2000). The Cultural Economy of Cities. Essays on the Geography of Image-Producing Industries. London.

Sheehan, James J. (2002). Geschichte der deutschen Kunstmuseen. München.

Simmel, Georg (1992 [1896]). »Berliner Gewerbeausstellung«. In Georg Simmel, Gesamtausgabe. Soziologische Ästhetik, 197–214. Frankfurt am Main.

Sombart, Werner (1916). Der moderne Kapitalismus, Vol. 1, Second Half. München/Leipzig.

Stehr, Nico (1994). Arbeit, Eigentum und Wissen. Zur Theorie von Wissensgesellschaften. Frankfurt am Main.

Szöllösi-Janze, Margit (2004). »Wissensgesellschaft in Deutschland: Überlegungen zur Neubestimmung der deutschen Zeitgeschichte über Verwissenschaftlichungsprozesse«. Geschichte und Gesellschaft, 30, 189–218.

Vaubel, Roland (2005). »The Role of Competition in the Rise of Baroque and Renaissance Music«. Journal of Cultural Economics, 29, 277–297.

Veblen, Thorstein (1994). The Theory of the Leisure Class (originally published 1899). New York.

Weingart, Peter (2001). Die Stunde der Wahrheit? Zum Verhältnis der Wissenschaft zu Politik, Wirtschaft und Medien in der Wissensgesellschaft. Weilerswist.

Wilson, Bronwen (2006). »Venice, Print, and the Early Modern Icon«. *Urban History*, 33, 1, 39–64.

Wischermann, Clemens and Elliot Shore (eds.) (2000). *Advertising and the European City: Historical Perspectives*. Aldershot.

Zimmermann, Clemens (ed.) (2006). *Zentralität und Raumgefüge der Großstädte im 20. Jahrhundert*. Stuttgart.

1 Cultural Economies in Early Modern Times

The Productivity of the City in the Early Modern Era: The Book and Art Trade in Venice and London

Clemens Zimmermann

Notwithstanding all the differences between various disciplines and authors, there are a number of common premises and at least a minimum of consensus which together define the phenomenon of the urban culture economy with its rapid pace of growth. The first premise is the conviction that certain places – either themselves or the image associated with them – plus a liberal culture and atmosphere are strongly linked to productivity. A further premise is the circumstance that while access to knowledge today, thanks to modern information technologies, is not tied to concrete places, innovation still is. The term cultural economy signifies those branches whose products and services require the input of a higher than usual degree of intellectual competence and artistic impulses. Special knowledge and skills are undoubtedly required by the workforce in these branches. Wherever there is a particularly high rate of innovation in the sphere of culture industries, implicit specialist knowledge and dense local communication may also be found as conditions promoting innovation. Also in the case discussed here, the book and art trade in the early modern era, spatial proximity is crucial to the specialist knowledge, creativity, innovation, the »novelty« in communication required in those branches: »Certain types of« information and knowledge exchange continue to require regular and direct face-to-face contact. [...] The more implicit the knowledge involved, the more important is spatial proximity between the actors taking part in the exchange.« This is so because what always matters in communication is the coordination of social time and because the »communication of implicit knowledge will normally require a high degree of mutual trust and understanding, which is a question not only of language but also of shared values and ›culture‹« (Maskell and Malmberg 1999: 180).

What is more, it may be observed that today businesses active in the culture industry are often relatively small and are located in urban or regional clusters, and they are aided significantly by formal and informal cooperation taking place within the clusters. Relevant information, know-how and technologies are exchanged. Companies from different but related branches in cities or districts of cities make use of particular communications opportunities that arise thanks to the urban environment. However, it is not only local cooperation and communicative networks which characterise the modern urban culture economy, but also non-local networks. While it is locally centred and situated, it is not autarkic. Goods and services are frequently, if not indeed predominantly, sold outside the locality or region where they are produced, particularly in the case of highly specialised products such as those offered by architects' offices or advertising agencies. For this reason the local knowledge economy must be open to productive ideas from outside. Indeed the book and art trade of the early modern era essentially amounted to the circulation of knowledge throughout Europe with individual places attaining pre-eminence as centres of innovation. The ideas and productivity of the cultural economy still originate from the local milieu today, in spite of the supra-local circulation of knowledge. For example, the fashion industry in Paris or Milan is characterised by the close proximity of *Haute Couture*, fashion photography, relevant media like exhibitions, fashion shows and photography, and related industries (such as leather goods), which makes the cultural dynamic and productive progress possible in the first place. These media and industries are connected in an urban culture which with its mass cultural events and tourism already shows a pronounced tendency towards a commercialisation of culture (Camagni 1991a; Camagni 1991b; Priddat 2004; Florida 2002; Heßler 2002; Heßler 2003; Scott 2000a; Scott 2004; Wiesand 2006). The Paris fashion world thrives on the combination of local know-how and an international market. What receives comparatively little attention is the fact that urban culture economies often display a high degree of location continuity, which may be due partly to the success of the branch or cluster itself and partly to the stability of the urban environment. The Paris fashion world is a good example of this. Originating in the royal court, it developed through *Haute Couture* in the nineteenth century, and for the past hundred and fifty or so years has been centred around the Rue St.-Honoré (Camagni et al. 2000; Engert 1997; Foot 2001; Hellmeister 2001; Kauw 1961; Lehnert 1998; Matteaccioli and Tabarriès 2000; Scott 2000b;

Steele 1999). The example of Paris shows that the urban cultural economy does indeed have historical roots contrary to the assumption common in the culture economy debate today. Certainly, Silicon Valley is a relatively new phenomenon – and yet it had its roots in earlier military-technological projects like the Stanford Research institute (Hall 1998: 423–453). It is also certain that today's clusters of technologically orientated businesses came about as a result of political decision-making and their creation was supported by public subsidy. And yet it is no coincidence that 25 percent of all officially registered Italian journalists live in Milan, the publishing capital, where 40 percent of all Italian publications are produced.

The common denominator is an urban milieu with established traditions. Such traditions have often been overlooked because of customary econometric research methods and because of the marginalisation of the concrete conditions of economics. Only in recent years has it been revealed by institutional economics and by the discovery of the importance of consumer markets in urban and economic history just how dynamic such traditions have been for the development of cities, as well as how businesses really function and how economic activity is admitted into social and cultural milieus. With reference to productive urban culture economies as a basis for urban productivity it is too frequently assumed today that it is an entirely new phenomenon: one moreover that offers prospects of growth which are unparalleled in history and are differentiated from those of the declining industrial or Fordist economy. However, a historical perspective reveals that certain phenomena of the contemporary culture economy have occurred before in various sectors; and notwithstanding the fact that the culture economy today is always primarily a sectoral phenomenon, a historical analysis can expose relevant structures and factors for the rise and fall of such economies which would necessarily be missed by studies that are fixated on the present. A historical approach to the phenomenon of urban culture economy seeks to test the premises and criteria of current academic approaches and to clarify particular institutional and urban constellations that allowed culture economies to evolve in history. It poses the question of what is really new about today's culture economy. In particular it asks whether the growth of culture economies is stimulated by the city in general with its mixes, its culture institutions, and the mobility and greater purchasing power of its inhabitants, or whether the phenomena of inner urban milieu formation have any bearing on it. What role was played by internal and external networks? How strong were sales of products and/or services locally and non-locally? How significant were material transfers from the Crown or other state bodies and from patrons? Answers to these questions shall be sought in the following analysis of the cities of Venice and London in the period 1500–1800. The questions are of crucial importance because thus far research into the early modern era has focused on the role of the court as client. It is clear, furthermore, that the society's political and social structure was characterized by its own significant status criteria and by the importance of corporate players: in the urban milieu this is evident in the functions of organised neighbourhoods and guilds. Personal, formalised and acknowledged status determined to a considerable degree one's chances of participating in the exercise of power. These structures may be found in Venice and London, too – although these cities should not be regarded as state entities and although economically progressive practices did evolve there within the framework of traditional institutions and were able to bring about an upsurge in the ›market‹.

The two cities studied here offer decisive structural parallels (albeit not entirely concurrently): their outstanding size, the exceptional importance of foreign trade, their strategic location for transport, the high proportion of prosperous and privileged individuals in society, and the proximity of political power in the urban environment. Beyond any doubt, Venice had a very high status within Italy's polycentric urban structure throughout the early modern era. At its peak the Republic of Venice reigned over considerable territory abroad and became – most clearly in the sixteenth century – a highly capitalised global city with a distinct urban culture. The city state's advance to its position as the foremost trading metropolis in southern Europe began in the thirteenth century, and continued after 1450. The sixteenth century witnessed the first economic and cultural highpoint of an urban history that remains dazzling to this day. The city undertook an extensive building programme, ruled over territory on the mainland, used its strong international political position to expand its foreign trade, and developed a highly differentiated domestic industry in luxury articles. In the seventeenth century Venice was still incalculably wealthy. In spite of unsuccessful military campaigns it was still able to undertake lavish building projects in the baroque style; and innovations like the opera house and the box theatre attest to the city's high artistic productivity. However, its economy began to stagnate on a slightly lower level, though the decline in international trade and political significance was offset by intensified agricultural production on the mainland. The reasons for the economic down-turn in the seventeenth century were Spanish rule and the repressive climate of the Counter Reformation in Italy, a drop in population due the Plague in 1628/1629, the loss of possessions in the Near East, and failing initiative and entrepreneurial spirit. In the eighteenth century Venice survived economically partly from magnificent extravagance and the old sources of revenue, and partly from financial services, tourism, and arts and craft, i.e. still from its culture economy. The intellectual climate of Venice was comparatively free. With a population of nearly 140,000 it was still one of the largest cities in Europe; in Italy (in the seventeenth century) it was the second largest after Naples (Braudel 1989; Pullan 1968; Knittler 2000; Hersche 1999).

London on the other hand, in the early modern era, became the economic centre and principal city of the whole country. While still of fairly modest size in 1500, the city numbered 200,000 inhabitants in 1600, putting it on a level with Venice. There then commenced an extraordinarily dynamic population growth which was stimulated by the concentration of political resources and by maritime trade. Thomas Platter noted in 1599 – and his comment would remain valid for over two hundred years – that »London is the capital of England and so superior to other English towns that London is not said to be in England, but rather England to be in London« (cited after Boulton 2000: 315). In 1700 London had 575,000 inhabitants and was Europe's biggest metropolis – four times as big as stagnating Venice. By the eighteenth century London had become the locus of an unprecedented urban experience where city centre density was combined with mobility and the availability of a wide range of consumer and entertainment goods/services in a municipal area that was constantly expanding. London obviously represented by far the largest market in the country; the majority of the books, newspapers and other printed matter produced there were also sold there. In the system of the European book trade London had a comparable centrality to Venice in the preceding two centuries. Yet in spite of the city's vast scale, direct communication – whether of a formal or informal nature – remained very important to the middle class, which had been emerging since the seventeenth century and differentiating itself according to social criteria.

»Much news and business was conducted by word of mouth [...]. The new Restoration coffee-houses were [...] vibrant places of face-to-face contact, where gossip, news and ideas circulated freely amongst an often surprisingly mixed clientele.

Both the formal and informal institutions of London life also encouraged association, feasting and communication. The guilds and companies of London increasingly [...] became social arenas [...]. Entertainment in the metropolis blended the printed with the spoken or sung word.« (Boulton 2000: 30; see also Brewer 1997: 29–34; Schwarz 2000)

Painting and Art Objects in Renaissance Venice

The Italian Renaissance was characterised by a high degree of innovation and equally by the fact that the building of churches and chapels had great prestige value for the ruling elite. The adornment of churches and other public buildings, *palazzi* and the private residences of the few wealthy families also had high cultural significance and helped bring into being a highly productive arts and crafts industry of great international renown. The »Renaissance« here should be understood not as an autonomous art concept but rather as a distinct material culture. It was characterised by fashionable *objets d'art*, an abundance of works including paintings and liturgical objects, new patterns of consumption as well as by expenditure on public ceremonies and on the prestige buildings of the politically privileged families of the city's ruling class, who attached great value to distinction whilst at the same time being integrated in the urban society and espousing the Venetian ideology of *civiltà*. The prestige value of painting and the interest in collecting went hand in hand with the reproduction of art knowledge, in which the decisive role was played by the printing of graphic art, a technology that at this time was spreading rapidly internationally (Goldthwaite 2004: 177–179).

It is important to regard the material culture of the Renaissance not only in terms of consumption and expenditure. This is in effect a point of view that is rooted in eighteenth century middle class criticism of extravagance and luxury. Material culture should instead be viewed and appreciated as production. A large portion of the fine objects were produced in the city itself and some of them were exported. Venice was the centre of international trade in luxury goods from the Orient and such merchandise was in plentiful supply in the city. Among the Venetian products for export were liturgical paraphernalia like tabernacles, valuable textiles, glass, soap, metalwork, valuable pottery (majolika), paintings and panels partly produced in workshops or schools in standardised fashion, as well as books. Books and paintings are discussed here (ibid.: 1–19).

Characteristic of Venetian society in the early modern era were the confraternities and guilds, in which large sections of the expanding middle classes were brought together by shared religious, social and communicative aims. They were highly relevant to the historical culture economy, as will be shown below. Half of the 100 confraternities, who paraded en bloc in municipal processions, donated up to 1610 altars, most of which were installed in chapels (ibid.: 115–126). These chapels were in many cases not places of quiet devotion, but instead had a public character, functioning as communication forums where the matters discussed could be thoroughly secular. At the same time they represented semi-private spaces for the patriarchal families, for whom decorating the chapels was a priority. By doing so, the families occupied the spaces and secured for themselves access to ecclesiastical networks, benefices and income.

The cult of paintings was not restricted to churches and public buildings, however. There was a general and very considerable trend towards the decoration of spaces with pictorial art – also in workshops and relatively modest households. Appreciation of painting spread – and was criticised in sermons. Pictorial culture had become distinctly secularised since the fifteenth century. Patrician families, and others aspiring to be patrician, decorated walls and ceilings with historical scenes and incorporated references to the family tradition. Public and private buildings were adorned with paintings of religious subjects as well as with individual and family portraits (Roeck 2004: 102–118). Other adornments were *vedute* – pictures of towns (but not the owner's town of residence) and wall maps, which attested to the cosmopolitan and sophisticated character of the owner (Woodward 1996: 76; Wilson 2005: 23–69). Since the sixteenth century paintings had ceased to be part of the furnishings of a house, and everywhere started to appear as distinct and self-sufficient objects (Goldthwaite 2004: 143–145, 212–233). Increasingly they were collected by domestic and foreign nobles, abbots and other members of the clergy, merchants and the less wealthy academics. Collectors developed an interest in foreign art too, especially Flemish. The collecting of paintings, which were increasingly seen as prestige objects, was accompanied by the formation of enthusiasm for the arts and the diffusion of knowledge about art: graphic art and prints, spreading rapidly internationally, enabled collectors to find out about foreign artists, subjects and styles. The secular trend of art collecting as a public, demonstrative practice, no longer dependent aesthetically on the prevailing tastes of the royal court, can also be seen in the fact that the *studiolo*, the scholar's private study or cabinet of art and curiosities (*Wunderkammer*), came to be replaced by the *gallerie*, where several people at a time would gather. In the *porteghi* one showed one's collection to visitors from abroad. By the seventeenth century other *objets d'art* like vases and glasswork were being collected, their commercial value higher than before. There thus arose an urban milieu in which prestige practices were linked with specialised knowledge (Cecchini 2000: 11–23; Fortini Brown 2002: 310; Davis and Marvin 2004: 14–49).

Patrons and the Art Market

In the Venice of the early modern era, the art market differed from today's inasmuch as the great majority – though by no means all – of the paintings executed there were commissioned.

The chief institutional patrons for commissions were:

1) the *scuole* on the basis of religious-social brotherhoods (*confraternitas, confraternita*), of which there were no fewer than 281 in 1663. A distinction is to be made between *scuole grandi* and *scuole piccole*. The *scuole grandi* with up to 600 members amassed a considerable fortune and, from the late fifteenth century, vied with one another unceasingly in the musical life they cultivated, in the processions they organised, the opulence of the decoration of their salons, and the works of art they commissioned (Glixon 2003). In so doing they helped create what was socially a highly diversified public for the arts. The *scuole* functioned as financiers and display windows for the *Serenissima*; they celebrated the city's *civiltà* by linking their social tasks with aesthetic values. Life in the *scuole grandi* involved an impressive amount of music, often performed by the institution's own orchestra. The commissions for paintings were decided by a *banca*, or board, which was chaired by a *guardiano*. The clients often found their place in the painting itself. The artists were selected by competition, and partly by proposals from members of the *banca*. In many cases the paintings were votive paintings offered by members, and they too had to be accepted by the board. The *scuole* preferred

painters who were well known and had a chance of going down in history. An artist was deemed to be popular and recognised if he had obtained prestigious commissions from abroad. Such an artist was Jacopo Tintoretto (1519–1594). This Venetian painter »seized one commission after another« and made full use of the famous *Scuola di San Rocco*'s potential to attract commissions through his personal contacts and skilful entreaties. It was at this *scuola* that he created his life's work of eighty large-format paintings (Ingenday 2007; Hills 1993). The *scuole piccole*, having a more modest clientele, did not have such prodigious resources at their disposal, though they did also commission works of art. They were concerned with religious and social aims and with performing good works »with a view to the next world«. (Ortalli 2001: 17, 31, 44, 48). The criterion of membership would be one's origin (e.g. *scuola dei Milanesi*), profession or the worship of a particular saint. In these *scuole* members of low social status could attain high office. In contrast to the socially exclusive *scuole grandi*, where membership too was exclusive, one could be a member of several *scuole piccole*. The painters and art printers of interest to us did not have their own fraternities or *scuole*, but must have been dispersed among a great many. It can be assumed, however, that some painters were members of merchants' guilds like San Cristoforo. Two *stampadori*, Nicola Jenson and Giovanni di Colonia, are documented in the same *scuola*, the *confraternita di San Girolamo*, in the late fifteenth century; presumably it provided them with a further opportunity to plan projects jointly as members of all *scuole* were obliged to be present regularly.

2) Broadly similar practices were to found at the corporazioni, the professional associations (*arti*) or guilds. It appears that they too possessed buildings, though mostly only meeting rooms – mainly rooms in churches for their funeral services, gatherings and archive storage; these rooms, together with an altar, were decorated at their expense (Kempers 1989: 199f.).

3) Other institutions that commissioned works of art were scientific academies as well as *luoghi pii*, the religious-social institutions, hospitals, foundling hospitals, occasionally schools or institutes for the *poveri vergognosi* (poor people whose status did not permit them to make their impoverishment known). The decoration of the *luoghi pii* was indirectly

financed and organised by rich sponsors; they too gave commissions on the basis of competitions.

In the case of these institutionally commissioned art works, the artist's fee paid was arrived at by negotiation. Pricing thus did not correspond to a strict market principle, but it is true to some degree that individual artists had different market values. Remuneration for panels was based on the material costs plus a subjective assessment of the »value« of the work. The price was consequently the result of an estimation of the artist's *magisterium*, or mastery, an estimation of the merits of the finished work, its prestige value, the social status of the patron and of the artist, and the artist's degree of fame. It has been established that in Florence after 1450 higher and higher sums were paid for works of art as a result of the leading families vying with one another for influence ever more intensely, and increasingly these families had real fortunes at their disposal. There were »unwritten ranking lists of artists, which defined what painters a client may approach with a commission« (Kubbersky-Piredda: 347). The less binding the guilds' ties became, the more these rankings had an influence on the prices paid for art works, and a small group of painters emerged who attracted far higher fees than the average. This ranking system was not fixed, but flexible, and it existed, as already indicated, in a market that was symbolic. In the case of private patrons, who played no great role in Venice, a close tie arose between themselves and the artists, who wished to be well paid for their work but whose social status was not secure. Here, too, it is fair to speak of a price-relevant symbolic market (Checchini 2000: 126–138).

At the same time there was an open art market which operated according to supply and demand, although it was not centred on a specific place such as the auction house of today. Officially art dealers were not permitted. Only locally produced works were allowed to be sold, and were to be sold by the painters themselves, who could also sell the works of other guild members – of whom there were no fewer than 240 in 1530 (Matthew 2003: 255). And yet there were court cases against illegal art dealers between the mid sixteenth and the mid seventeenth century, and their presence is mentioned again in the early eighteenth century. Legal action was also taken against unregistered painters in 1638. Art was produced »illegally« by painters employed by merchants to work clandestinely in the attics of their houses. This even occasioned financial disputes heard in court. Paintings were sold not only in *botteghe*, the artists' official workshops, but also at the fifteen-day-long *fiera dell'Ascensione*, a fair known since the twelfth century on the *Piazza San Marco,* where painters also took commissions. It was incidentally only at this fair that foreign painters were allowed to display their works, on payment of a fee. Albrecht Dürer had to pay a fine of four *gulden* to the *scuola* in 1506 for having worked in Venice without permission for three months. From the middle of the seventeenth century onwards general auctions, known as *incanti,* were important to the art trade. In 1518 the painters' guild sought to prohibit the selling of pictures on the streets: that is outside the official network of workshops. Finally, second-hand dealers or *strazzaruoli* were permitted to sell »used« and less valuable paintings, stolen articles presumably among them. In 1679 a member of the guild of second-hand dealers was accused of having participated in an auction. The auctioning of a deceased's estate and of property pledged as security was widespread, however. The lotteries of Amsterdam, which were a way of getting round strict market regulations, were unknown in Venice, as were sales exhibitions. While officially there were no pure art dealers, merchants did engage – with official sanction – in the export of luxury products, including large-scale works of art by the likes of Flemish painter Daniel Nys or Giacomo Dada the Younger. By the eighteenth century the sale of high quality works abroad was becoming more and more important. In addition, the *Fondego dei Tedeschi* was a centre for the distribution of art objects to Germany. These are all examples of the existence of a partly grey, partly official art market of considerable size and of not only local significance (Checchini 2000: 192–203, 225–235, 250–252; Cecchini 2006: 130; Welch 2003: 286).[1]

And yet it was still a market of commissions, and it was characterised by competitive structures of supply and demand, a variety of types of commission and the differentiation of symbolic capital of the producers and clients. *Scuole* and *corporazioni* played an important role in this, representing at the same time institutions in which local interests could be negotiated directly on a face-to-face basis. The market moreover was by and large an unstructured, discontinuous »open market« governed by the criteria of supply and demand. The commodities on the market were not only works of high quality and high value, but also mass-produced items such as religious souvenirs. It may therefore be assumed that a »multiplicity of intersecting markets, agents and players« existed with regard to paintings (Welch 2003: 291).

---

1   Letter of Albrecht Dürer to Willibald Pirkheimer, April 1, 1506 (Chambers/Pullan 1992: 408f.; Matthew 2003: 254).

Networking in the Milieu of Venice's Fine Artists

While Venetian painters were members of guilds as a rule, they competed freely with one another for commissions and were very flexible in the manner of carrying them out. They employed regular apprentices and took on such other assistants as the workload demanded, and what's more they worked in partnership with other artists, sometimes only on one job, and sometimes for a period of several years. For standard works commissioned from a »school« they would award subcontracts to other practitioners who would finish off not fully completed paintings (Goldthwaite 2004: 428f.). Neither the *collaboratori* nor the *garzoni*, the helpers, were supposed to be creative. Instead they carried out practical preliminary duties and imitated the master's style, often working on serial production in his studio. This, naturally, required great skill, and it provided the opportunity for some to work their way up in the profession. An art production system based on the division of labour, practised in a milieu culturally defined by shared standards and the orientation towards »styles« and local »tastes«, presupposed a reservoir of highly varied artists and artisans – and this existed in Venice in abundance. The networking in the artists' milieu were much more complex in nature than those of a close guild would be. It can be assumed that most of the parties involved were acquainted with one another as a result of a guild membership, and that they also had contacts with other trades like printers and with a broader cultural milieu. Family connections brought the artists into horizontal contact with other social milieus within and beyond their city district.[2] Painters presumably tended to socialise with other painters in preference to other craftsmen. A certain elitism seems to have prevailed among them, and they would engage a colleague from their own profession as best man at their weddings – always a sure indicator of social relationships. It is known that the foreign painters resident in Venice maintained close relations with sculptors and furniture painters as well as with other fellow countrymen who were or had been in the city or whom they knew from somewhere else. These foreigners brought different styles to the city. It is likely that the painters lived relatively scattered, but nevertheless principally in the area between Mark's Square and the Rialto, where is where most of the shops and hence also painters' workshops were located. The urban milieu of fine artists in the

---

2   On the general oral mode of communication, see Muir/Weissman (1989) and Horo-
    dowich (2005).

Venice of the early modern era fluctuated, to be sure, but was still not as locally concentrated as the cultural districts of modern cities are – or indeed was the case with other trades such as the lead-pourers, who were concentrated in the Ghetto, or the tanners in San Marziale. It was present in various places all of them certainly well frequented (Checchini 2000: 162–177; Checchini 2006: 126–129).

Venetian Printers and Publishers
and their Milieus in the Sixteenth Century

From the late fifteenth century onwards Venice was an important centre for the production not only of paintings and luxury artefacts but also of books, possessing a dense cluster of printing works and publishing houses. In terms of Italian *incunabula*, Venice is thought to have produced one third to one half of all 8,000 titles (Richardson 1994: 39). The apogee of the printing industry in Venice was the sixteenth century when the city was home to 493 documented printers, publishers and booksellers and when it produced a documented 17,500 titles and perhaps as many as 20 million copies – well over half the total of published titles in Italy. Venice's printing and publishing sector grew so large because of the quality attained there and because of specialisation in particular fields or types of products. This specialisation was partly a deliberate business strategy and partly due to the cultural resources that happened to be available in the city. The Venetian printing and publishing industry managed to acquire a virtual monopoly over the production and sale of entire genres. In the area of music, for instance, Venice attained a pre-eminent position in the reproduction of manuscripts on account of the wide dissemination of French music culture there and the thriving existence of specifically Venetian religious music (from 1431 the Venetian music school); it also produced works of music theory and possessed a vibrant music press which flourished in the sixteenth century and quite literally set the tone internationally. Two specialised publishing houses came into being – Girolamo Scotto and Antonio Gardani – which produced around 3,000 titles over more than one hundred years and sold them throughout western and southern Europe (Bernstein 2001: 3–4, 10–12). The printing house of the Manuzio family dominated the market in Italy and initially also abroad with their

»rossi e neri« series of devotional books printed in two colours, and with texts in the vernacular. The production of the Giolito publishing house from 1536 to 1606 may also serve as an example. Its production peaked at the time of Gabriel Giolito in around 1555. Four generations worked on the publishing project, despite arguments about power and unequally shared profits. What Giolito published was predominantly secular literature, followed by religious titles, »treatises« of all kinds, and history. With time the target audience of the publishing house came to be general readers. Barezzo Barezzi focused on translations and creative imitations of Spanish novels. Barezzi's unique commercial proposition was founded upon correspondence, but personal mobility was essential too, since he travelled round Spain and established personal contacts with authors while there (Heiler 2000: 31). The fact that Venetian presses specialised in printing translations and foreign-language texts was a consequence of the cultural resources available in what was a highly cosmopolitan city. »The existence of subcultures within Venice made it possible for local printers to act as cultural middlemen more fully than elsewhere.« (Burke 2002: 400–402) With regard to cultural economy, it is impossible to separate printing, publishing and selling; indeed often the functions of printer, publisher and bookseller were carried out by one and the same person. The culture economy was characterised by local and cooperative production, the sale of a large proportion of the books across south and central Europe (through an efficiently organised network of commercial agents abroad, fellow booksellers and even relatives) and the recruitment of foreign authors from far beyond the republic's borders (Bernstein 2001: 10f., 73–90, 154–163; Barbierato 2005). Domestic sales remained an important source of revenue, however, in Venice itself and in its territory, for instance the nearby university town of Padua (Richardson 1994: 42).

The prestige of the various printers was in part the result of their ability to recruit personnel – editors, *correctori* or *poligrafi* – from among the intellectuals. These served as a professional guarantee for other potential authors. The editors were indispensable in the production of reliable texts in the standardised Tuscan language. In the case of popular texts the printer-publishers chose either to rely on themselves or simply to reprint texts. The printer-publisher hence became an agent in intellectual production and in the transfer from writing to printing. He supplied the capital, the equipment, raw materials and the labour; he sought the custom of a geographically dispersed public. Generally speaking the proprietors were personally acquainted with business partners (as in other industries), authors and publishers. These were to be found in Venice and beyond; the secular clergy was also involved in the business. Furthermore the social and geographical origins of the translators and editors were very diverse (Richardson 1994: 5–9). This heterogeneity was a characteristic of the conditions of production in the book trade, as were the forming of networks and local political regulations, which partly restricted business but also partly made it more secure by granting privileges.

In geographical terms, there were a large number of businesses in the same branch established within a relatively small area. In spite of the serious competition that ensued from this, Venice offered five chief advantages as a location for the book trade:

Firstly, it was possible to find out rapidly what other people in the publishing industry were doing, what novelties they were offering; trends could be discerned in their early stages, especially thanks to representatives of foreign businesses and trade fairs. In the city, knowledge about projects, sales channels, the political situation in other countries, possible cooperation with partners and means of payment could be obtained locally, partly through official channels, but also a great deal through conversation.

Secondly, the demand for books in Venice itself was considerable. Great importance was attached to reading and the ownership of books. Appreciation had spread on the basis of hand-written manuscripts. Obviously, however, the 800 or 1000 copies normally printed of a specialist scientific title or the 400 copies of pamphlet of madrigals could not all be sold in the city or the territory of Venice (Fremmer 2001: 67, 114–118, 162–175, 288).

Thirdly, more abundantly than other places Venice possessed the necessary manuscripts and editions, and human resources of appropriate intellectual capacity. One important resource for discursive texts, essays and poetry was conversation at dinners (*cenacoli*) with intellectuals or performances by artists at the houses of the nobility. Book publishers/printers could furthermore get ahead in information and knowledge as a result of the presence of journalists (*scrittori*), who would contribute to weekly publications, whether native or foreign gazettes, reviews or confidential journals, and who consequently possessed up-to-date and not widely known information. The proximity of the Doge's Palace was also most important for this milieu on account of the large number of civil servants, secretaries and clerks working for the central administration. Information could be exchanged at the cafés situated near by. It was there that instructions and dispatches for the cities of the Republic and Venice's embassies abroad were drafted, and there was much to be gleaned from the international missions established in Venice (Bernstein 2001: 15; Infelise 1999; Burke 2002: 397).

Fourthly, one sought to escape the fierce competition by specialising to some degree or other. Securing individual privileges for one's own projects was another way of avoiding this competition. When conflicts arose from the competitive situation, it was common practice to resolve them by means of civil lawsuits and material compensation. There was close cooperation on a territorial basis. While the book trade was not centred in a particular quarter (as in Paris north of the Seine near the university), symbolically it centred round the guild's own chapel in Santi Giovanni e Paolo. The approximately 100 business with a total workforce of about 600 in 1570 were all located north of the Grand Canal in the area where specialised retail as a whole was to be found – namely between *San Marco* and the Rialto or Merzaria and Frezzaria streets, where the printing shops of the cartographers were also situated. The tradespeople cooperated as far as production, financing, sales and distribution were concerned; they formed partnerships, sold or lent typographical and other technical material, and acted as witnesses in contracts for professional colleagues (Bernstein 2001: 12–15, 170; Woodward 1996: 45f.).

A fifth advantage in the first one hundred years was the relatively liberal political climate in Venice. A guild known as the *università delli stampatori et librari* was the last of the Venetian arti to be founded – in 1549. The authorities had been trying to limit the number of producers since the seventeenth century by charging fees, but evidently had not succeeded. In the seventeenth century, in addition to printers licensed in the regular manner, there were also the *forestieri*, who were registered on the payment of higher fees and without requiring the qualification usual since 1671. In spite of some censorship by the church and the state, Venice remained relatively undisturbed by it until about 1560. However, upon the promulgation of the Index of Pope Paul IV and after the Council of Trent in 1564, pre-publication censorship was introduced for works still in manuscript form, and this complicated and slowed down the production process; the editing of academic works was also disrupted, and standards generally fell (Richardson 1994: 141; Pesenti 1983: 93–95; Cattin 1981: 267–277; Gallo 1981; Petrucci 1977: 56–101). It affected sales in Italy altogether, but not the production in Venice itself, because there the Venetian authorities were responsible. The book trade slumped dramatically as a result of harsher censorship in the period 1560–1590 and of the Papal prohibition of the printing of religious works by Venetian printers in 1596 (Infelise 1989: 10).

Venetian Printers and Publishers in the Seventeenth and Eighteenth Centuries

In the seventeenth century, which economic history formerly viewed as a century of decline for the Venetian Republic, the book trade remained very substantial, although at a lower level than in the foregoing century. The causes of the regression were, firstly, that the city largely lost its monopoly position and prices escalated internationally. Also censorship and the intellectual climate of the Inquisition took their toll, as did the resultant weakening of the sciences in Italy. Lastly Venice lost its role as an information centre with the discovery of the New World and the contraction of its presence in the Near East, and Venice found itself increasingly on the margins. Nevertheless, in 1700 the Venetian publishers reached a highpoint in scientific production, and there was another boom in around 1750 (ibid.: 275–294). With 58 *maestri*, a third of whom had no apprentices, the Venetian printing and publishing industry of the seventeenth century was a long way from being able to dominate quality book production in Europe, especially since this had found new locations across Europe now as Humanism took root and universities flourished. Small printers struggled to survive and were unable to pay the guild fees once they were raised in 1666. In 1673 the Venetian authorities divided up the printing of *libri comunali* among the large printers. The wealthy printers invested in real estate and gradually approached in social terms the level of the land-owning class, while some of the poorer licensed printers could only work for them as hired labour. The eighteenth century brought cheap mass-produced wares on to the market in greater quantity than theretofore. This business was dominated by a few publishing houses with a lot of capital (Ulvioni 1977: 93–109; Pesenti 1983: 97–106, 112–123). The functions of bookseller (*librer*) and printer (*stampador*) became more clearly distinct than in former centuries. The advance of capitalisation in the printing trade is evident in the appearance in the eighteenth century of *capitalisti* from outside the profession and the guild (Infelise 1992). The material success of the sector was very considerable in the first half of the century, on a par with that experienced in the sixteenth century. After 1760 competition from the rest of Europe became increasingly fierce; Lyons had established itself as another centre of the book trade since the seventeenth century.[3] At home in Venice the absence of commissions from religious institutions such as the Jesuits made itself felt. And yet as the century drew to a close the readers in Italy, as elsewhere in Europe, began to shun religious and scholarly works, instead preferring novels – which, however, could be published anywhere without significant logistical and technical requirements.

Whereas a century or two earlier printer-publishers in Venice could take their pick from among the manuscripts that were circulating, now they actively sought out unpublished manuscripts, »novelty« having become an even more prized commodity. Ideas and manuscripts circulated more rapidly, and Europe's communication network became denser. In these circumstances Venice was able to become competitive again as a centre of the innovative production of magazines and periodicals, with 30 percent of the 840 titles in eighteenth-century Italy being produced in the city. An advantage was that censorship in the city was comparatively weak in the eighteenth century. All forbidden books could be procured from small booksellers; Voltaire may have been banned, but he was certainly available – which was not uninteresting for the multitudes of tourists (Infelise 1989: 132–147, 162–183, 275–289, 329–353).

Hence one can say the Venetian book trade remained strong in the seventeenth and eighteenth centuries, but it had lost its leading position in Italy and parts of Europe; gone too were its unique business advantage and apparently also any sense of internal solidarity.

---

3   Although in 1789 Lyons had only 13 printing works and 14 bookshops and in 1800 16 printing works and ten bookshops (Varry 2002: 42f.).

London: Producing and Dealing in Art and Luxury Goods in London in the Early Modern Era

The artistic production of the English Renaissance, from statues and sculptures, richly ornamented furniture and paintings to theatres and concerts, was at first closely tied to the court, the centre of high culture (and a kind of microcosm of the kingdom). Increasingly, under the influence of the Puritan revolt and the Glorious Revolution of 1688, with monarchs held on a tighter rein in matters of public spending, art production and trade shifted from the court to the urban milieu (Brewer 1997: 3).

Around 1700, with London a global metropolis and with the rise of the commercial middle class (merchants, and the better-off craftsmen and manufacturers), the demand for pictures grew prodigiously. On the London art market the paintings that were sold were mainly destined for decorative purposes around the house. It is estimated that at this time at least 132,000 paintings adorned the houses of the middle class. It was in the late seventeenth century that an open art market with sometimes spectacular books auctions came into being, and there was an increasing tendency towards internationalisation throughout the eighteenth century. The import restrictions that had been in force were abolished (1695) and the control of the guild known as the Painter-Stainer Company (1708) was substantially curtailed. The guild's influence had lessened anyway because its authority was limited to pre-existing districts of London and not to the constantly expanding suburbs. In the 1690s, auctions had done a roaring trade with some 20,000 items being sold annually, albeit it at modest prices. In the period from 1720 to 1770, by contrast, it is estimated that 25,000 to 50,000 paintings were auctioned in total, about 1,000 (imported) pieces a year. Much more substantial than this was the market for reproductions of art works, with 15,000 items being sold per year in the eighteenth century (Gibson-Wood 2003; Ormrod 2002; Pears 1991: 209; Brewer 1997: 209–223; Cowan 2006).

Auctions were held in certain areas of the city: in the vicinity of Covent Garden, Charing Cross, in the New Exchange (a shopping arcade) on the Strand, where very many booksellers had congregated after 1735 (Maxted 1977; 1984), i.e. to the west of the centre, where the wealthy now began to build their houses; and also at the exclusive Royal Exchange in the City (built in 1570) where all manner of luxury items could be obtained; in coffee houses, and even at popular destinations for an outing like Tunbridge

Wells – hence they were held where a great many middle and upper class citizens were also to be encountered. The commercialisation of art production was of little benefit to English and especially London painters, however. Their paintings generally fetched very low prices. The middle class purchased paintings in order to decorate their rooms. Only in perhaps half of the cases did they know the artists' names. Many of the paintings were old, having been inherited, for example, or they were imports; as a rule it was Italian and Netherlandish art which fetched the highest prices. English artists in many cases made a living by copying masterpieces. By 1730 a network of specialised art dealers had come into being in London, which of course concentrated on the international art trade. Prominent aristocrats would procure a quantity of paintings on their Grand Tour of Europe or they would commission art dealers to assemble entire collections for them. Artists, too, brought paintings home from their travels on the continent and sold them (Stumpo 2006).

Fig. 1: Frans II Francken, Art Dealer in his Shop (1640–1648)

(Source: Neil De Marchi and Hans J. van Miegroet (eds.) (2006). Mapping Markets for Paintings in Europe, 1450–1750. Turnhout: 1)

What kind of contacts the painters maintained with one another has not been researched. There was no clear »artists' quarter«, although in nineteenth century London there were many more artists in the western part of the city, concentrated in the area of Newman Street (Lorente and Targett 2000). Rather than being concentrated in a particular city district, artists would meet at certain coffee houses (as did other professional groups such as printers and authors), in self-organised academies and at social functions. The creative milieu of artists was associated with specific places like Old Slaughter's House in St. Martin's Lane (Brewer 1997: 35), and generally moved in the emerging sphere of the middle class, favouring centrally located districts rather than the fashionable suburbs where the very wealthy had their residences.

Fig. 2: Anon., Interior of a London Coffee-House. Around 1700

(Source: Neil De Marchi and Hans J. van Miegroet (eds.). (2006). Mapping Markets for Paintings in Europe, 1450–1750. Turnhout: 19)

In a society that was becoming both more liberal and more commercialised, the phenomenon of the guild was replaced by free associations of artists and academies (Glanville and Glanville 2004: 18f.; Pears 1991: 107–132), still in rudimentary form, which defended the interests of the members and provided a means for their further training. Painters at this time were undergoing a process of professionalisation. It appears that only a fraction of those who considered themselves artists were involved in the founding of academies. Another location for the self-presentation of London's pictorial artists was the Foundling Hospital on the city's edge in 1764. It can be assumed that at all these sites of the »milieu« there would be talk of commissions, quality criteria, know-how and the situation regarding competition and the market. The great art shows organised by the exhibition societies from the 1760s onwards and by the Royal Academy after 1768 introduced a privileged minority of London's painters to a vast international public. Paradoxically in the context of an increasing commercialisation of indigenous art production and an expansion of public interest, there was a contrary discourse about »fine art« itself. Increasingly it was maintained that a distinction was to be made between fine art on the one hand and utilitarian art, the crafts of the artisans and rational sciences, on the other. Fine art differentiated itself from the »useful« arts and crafts when taste came to be regarded as a matter of distinction among the wealthy. Family portraits and landscapes remained favourite subjects of fine art, and were now joined by »sublime« historical canvases. Hence one can speak of an aesthetic evolution, a specialisation and gradual improvement in status among painters. These had to seek customers actively themselves; the fortunate ones had their own atelier or workshop. Putting oneself in the service of a patron, often from the nobility, was not always worthwhile financially and it was perceived as being undignified (Brewer 1997: 51–70, 87–91, 211–218, 224–228, 237–248). Very few artists, such as William Hogarth (1697–1764), were able to achieve complete independence of clients and to earn a decent living on the strength of their artistic individuality and by dint of engaging in a wide range of activities, for example exploiting the opportunities offered by the market in reproductions.

The art market and the productive activities of painters experienced a very positive evolution in the eighteenth century as part of London's »cultural economy«, the phenomenon going hand in hand with the enormous growth of the city and the expansion of the public sphere. This public sphere was linked to a number of institutions spread across the city, rather than to a particular quarter where the milieu was concentrated. In the course of the eighteenth century the distinct function of the fine arts crystallised. In purely economic terms, though, the material significance of painting production in London in the eighteenth century was less than it had been in Venice in the sixteenth and seventeenth centuries (Mannings 1991: 108–113).

Book Production and the Book Trade in London in the Sixteenth and Seventeenth Centuries

In England as elsewhere in western Europe, the origins of book printing and the book trade lie in the fifteenth century, although the number of titles produced and the extent of the book market in the early decades was very modest compared to major publishing centres such as Venice, Antwerp, Lyons and then Frankfurt and Leipzig. In the British Isles books were produced in certain university and cathedral cities, but by far the biggest share of the production occurred of course in London. It is from there that in the Reformation liturgical, didactic and legitimising texts were disseminated, not without influence by the state authorities (Evenden and Freeman 2004), and this further strengthened the capital's pre-eminent position in the kingdom. From 1557 when the Company of Stationers was founded the sector was strongly regulated; books had to be licensed by the company before they could be printed and sold. Some publishers secured exclusive privileges on certain profitable book genres such as law books. As in Venice there were specialised booksellers, but in the main printers also published books and many booksellers also operated as publishers. An example is Henry Baynneman, who until his death in 1583 owned two bookshops in St Paul's Churchyard – a small area that was nevertheless the heart of the British book trade – in addition to two bookshops in Upper Thames Street. He also operated three printing presses (Handover 1960: 27–31).

As in Venice the Government had a keen interest in controlling religious literature, and yet censorship was less severe than that exercised by both church and state in Venice (ibid.: 40). In the 1630s the Stationers Company is believed to have controlled 80 percent of the publishers in London and the printing works of Cambridge.

Under King Charles II the guild's rights were re-established after 1660, the Company of Stationers recovering the exclusive right to print almanacs and to allocate copyright to certain publishing houses. The number of licensed businesses in the branch was cut from 59 to 20 (ibid.: 65f.), and then the Plague (1665) and the Great Fire (1666) occasioned heavy losses, until towards the end of the century the number of businesses recovered to about 55. 1695 saw the abolition of the Licensing Act, which had vouchsafed London almost exclusive rights to book production in England, and with that all legal restrictions were withdrawn. In 1710 authors were granted copyright for 14 years, abolishing perpetual ownership of book titles by the publishers; yet it would be another fifty years before some prominent writers would be able to live from the proceeds of book sales alone. What is to be noted here is that the milieu of London's printer-publishers in the sixteenth and seventeenth centuries was partly identical with their guild and partly tied to specific localities in the city. In addition, however, there were counter-milieus such as Grub Street which were more or less beyond the reach of state control. Women worked here, too, running small businesses or hawking, selling press products in particular. In the revolutionary period Grub Street represented a thriving network of the illegal or semi-legal book trade, as epitomised by the title of a pamphlet published in 1641: »The Downfall of Temorizing Poets, unlicensed Printers, upstart Booksellers, trotting Mercuries, and bawling Hawkers«. Officially licensed printers, moreover, would secretly print, or smuggle in, non-conformist literature during the reign of the Stuarts (Freist 1997: 85; see also ibid.: 34–46, 80–124; McDowell 1998: 10f., 37, 43, 64–74, 94–118; Peck 2005: 237–240).

In the seventeenth century, there was a concentration of printing works and in particular booksellers, who also sold imported titles, as well as newspaper publishers (partly in personal union) in St Paul's Churchyard. In 1667–1671, after the post-fire reconstruction, no fewer than 45 businesses are documented in the confined space there; most of them had storage capacity and accommodation for the owners, while some were only small stalls leant against the church walls. In the immediate vicinity were 17 other bookshops. This means that at the time approximately 70 percent of England's book trade was concentrated at one spot and the industry dominated a small district including Paternoster Street and Carter Lane. Until 1700 or so it was a closed milieu (Harris 2003; Blayney 1990; Miller 1966).

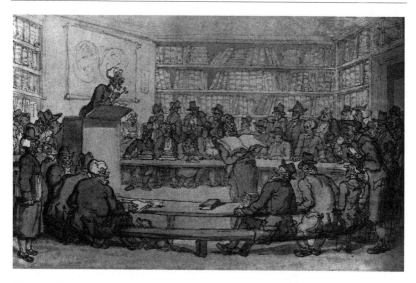

Fig. 3: Thomas Rowlandson. A Book Auction, c. 1805–1815

(Source: John Brewer, The Pleasures of Imagination, London 1997, 134)

Book production itself developed much more dynamically than the institutional organisation, rising from a modest 207 titles in the 1570s – the figure presumably fails to take account of many small publications – to 1,488 in the 1640s; the high-water mark was in 1642 with 2,968 printed works (many of these however were small pamphlets). About two thirds of these titles were first editions (McKenzie 1992: 391–399). We can assume then that at this time each official printer-publisher brought 13 new titles on to the market per year. The bookseller George Thomason managed to collect over 18,000 tracts which had appeared in the years 1640 to 1655; this figure »indicates both the vigour of metropolitan demand and the capacity of the industry to meet it« (Harding 2000: 281). The overlapping of activities persisted essentially until the end of the early modern era. Around the time of the Civil War the related branch of pamphlet-printing boomed, and there was a dramatic expansion of the London press, which was distributed in other regions of the country. Altogether the book industry probably accounted for one percent of all employed inhabitants of London in 1700. Revenue came not only from book sales but also from donations to individual writers from primarily aristocratic patrons, funds which then trickled down into the industry. Typically printers lived from the sale of very few new books (McKenzie 1992: 400–403; Maxted 1977: xxxi, xxxii).

Printers and Publishers in Eighteenth-Century London

In the course of the eighteenth century printer-publishers increased their activities and improved their marketing, which was in keeping with the enormous productivity of the city as a whole and with the different markets that were crystallising. The milieu expanded to incorporate other sites in the growing metropolis. In addition, there were illegal printers beyond the city walls, around West Smithfield and further north-east in Redcross Street, and in Grub Street which in the eighteenth century was still home to publishers and hacks of ill repute (Rogers 1972).

After 1750 the book sector experienced an expansion clearly exceeding that of the population. This is particularly notable in the case of booksellers, the number of establishments doubling from 70 in 1760 to 150 in 1785. By 1814, there were 400 printing works, publishing houses and bookshops in London, three times more than in Venice in its heyday, making it the leading centre in Europe (Raven 2003: 597–602). Hence the London book cluster had emerged as a powerful industry by the end of the early modern era; its growth being stimulated partly by the fact that London was the hub of the country's improved transport network, which among other things aided direct sales to hawkers and to bookshops in commercial centres in the provinces. A contributing factor to the expansion of the book trade in England, more clearly than in Italy, was the printing and publication of literary and political magazines, which could be very lucrative and which made greater use of the capacity of the printing presses (Maxted 1977: xxix).

The magazine business required constant contact with writers and other staff, and demanded a keen sense for evolutions of taste as well as an unfailing supply of new matters to write about. Innovations in literature, now becoming more important, found very fertile ground in this milieu. Art in general found a home in this metropolis, where Pope and Dr Johnson had escaped the comparative squalors of Grub Street and gained admittance to the society of wealthy and noble patrons; where Handel and Haydn secured an independent source of revenue in public concerts; and where a David Garrick not only acted in Shakespeare but also ran a theatre company. It is hardly surprising that Samuel Johnson told his biographer James Boswell on his departure from the capital that no writer is glad to leave London »for there is in London all that life can afford« (Boswell 1981: 246; see also Picard 2001; Clarke 2000).

The biography of the influential bookseller and publisher John Murray, who lived at 32 Fleet Street from 1768 to 1793, is revealing about the establishment of the publishing industry and about business practices. Murray bought part-publications from other publishers and gave them a title page of one's own, or one took over copyright from colleagues. Contacts within the milieu were not enough to ensure commercial success or to keep abreast of developments. Murray made his book business into a club of Scottish authors and politicians, his compatriots. He cultivated a wide network of contacts in his former home town Edinburgh in particular in order to sell books there and to implement common projects (Zachs 1998, Cochrane 1964).

The book trade had localised primarily in Fleet Street. There Murray had »only to look out the window of 32, Fleet Street to see success and failure among his fellow tradesmen. [...] Murray had only to walk down a few doors to meet a fellow tradesman at his shop or in a nearby tavern to transact business. He recognised that a successful business, or its owner, needed to be widely known.« (Zachs 1998: 24) Close cooperation in one of the relevant quarters (St Paul's Churchyard, Fleet Street, the Strand, the Royal Exchange) with a notable preponderance of printing works such as still existed there in the eighteenth century accelerated the execution of big commissions just as accelerated transport, with the result that transaction costs were cut. The close proximity of printers led moreover to the establishment of industry norms and made it easier to monitor pricing and practises among printers. This applies in principle to other trades or industries with local concentrations of production (Winkler 1993: 92–94; Power 1986: 218).

Until 1800 London remained the absolute centre of book production and the book trade in the British Isles (Zachs 1998: 27–41, 81; McKenzie 1992: 404–421; Raven 2003: 590–596). As illustrated by the example of Murray, the centralisation of book production did not proceed any further, although the cluster formation was quite without parallel in the rest of Europe. While London's share of the production of titles in Great Britain amounted to 84 percent in the eighteenth century, nevertheless a few other centres managed to assert themselves as publishing centres, among them Edinburgh (significantly supported by that city's university), which together accounted for five percent of annual sales in the country (Clark and Houston 2000: 596). However it was the vast reading public in the capital which ensured its pre-eminence, and meant that staggering sales figures could be achieved: the *Krünitz Encylopaedia* reports cases in which 14,000 copies of a bestseller were sold, for cash, within two days. In consequence, booksellers in London had such an easy time of it that they – in contrast to German publishing houses – neglected the market in the rest of the country.[4] In London there was still a very high level of mutual acquaintance among those employed in the book industry, in spite of the fact that the sector was giant and labyrinthine, comprising over 900 businesses (Raven 2003: xxiii) – booksellers, printers, sellers of single-page prints, bookbinders and paper-makers (Brewer 1997: 138f.).

Conclusion: Culture, Economy, and the Cities in the Early Modern Era

In this double comparison of two industries and two highly significant cities in the early modern era, we have come across many similarities and many differences to the urban constellations of the modern culture economy.

Firstly, the economy of the early modern era was highly regulated, but in the sectors in question it was already strongly commercialised and internationalised. Secondly, in spite of the huge turnover in the art and book trade, the increased value and employment effects of the branches were limited, especially when compared with the building, textile and food industries. Nevertheless they contributed significantly to the city's foreign trade and their significance for the development of the cultural functions of a major city should not be underestimated. It is evident that in Venice and London in the sixteenth and seventeenth centuries corporations of producers and dealers, other forms of enterprise like brotherhoods, and certain city districts existed side by side, overlapping, all of them relevant for communicative exchange and commercial cooperation in the milieu. Control by guilds should not be viewed only as a negative factor in Venice. In London in the eighteenth century it was done away with altogether. In that city the pluralising of public spheres, the structures of globalised commerce and the subdivision of the milieu into various localities became

4 Compare the article »book« in Johann Georg Krünitz' *Ökonomische Encyklopädie*, vol. 7, 1776, 208.

more apparent than in the preceding centuries, not least on account of the city's expansion in area and population to nearly one million inhabitants. The book sector in both cities was spatially more strictly organised and more institutionalised than painting production, in the case of which it is impossible to talk of an »artists' quarter« or »culture quarter«.

All in all, a number of striking similarities in the constellations of urban culture economy can be observed. Firstly, the physical proximity of producers in an extremely dense urban milieu evidently led to productive effects on the basis of high creative input in work products and on the basis of production by means of genuine private enterprise. Secondly, the competitive and cooperative character of local producers or consolidated companies is noteworthy. The example of the two cities has illustrated the role of a milieu that has evolved throughout history and the relevance of local conditions to cultural products. In consequence, questions that are asked in today's debate about »culture, economy, and the city« are equally applicable and meaningful to the early modern era. Criteria like skilled labour supply, skilled labour demand, learning opportunities, national accessibility, international accessibility, integration of industrial sectors and internationalisation as well as an urban atmosphere were likewise important historically, as they are today (Camagni et al. 2000: 214). Research into the early modern era, for its part, is capable of providing great insight into the complexity and institutional preconditions of culture economies, which so far has been neglected. When comparing the early modern era with the modern era it is clear that the afore-mentioned differences in political structure, the different consumption and demand structures, and the generally lower level of production should not be overlooked. It is also necessary to consider the great diversity of urban societies in the early modern era; in Florence and Rome, for instance, where the courts were dominant, the constellation of the culture economy was rather different to what it was in Venice. On the other hand there was considerable unanimity concerning values and social conduct as well as a high degree of internal communication amongst the European elites in the period before the foundation of modern nation states. The common market order that appears to be establishing itself today as a result of Europeanisation and globalisation did not exist in anything like this form in the early modern era, and yet its absence impeded international trade less than is assumed today. In consequence we cannot talk of any unbroken continuity in the discussed characteristics of the culture economy between then and now. Nonetheless the structures of productive milieus and their communication networks probably were strongly analogous; and in the case of London there is very definite continuity in one significant locality of the culture economy.

Bibliography

Barbierato, Federico (2005). »Giovanni Giacomo Hertz. Editoria e commercio librario a Venezia nel secondo '600«. *Bibliofilia*, 107, 2, 143–170; 107, 3, 275 – 289.

Bernstein, Jane A. (2001). *Print culture and music in sixteenth century Venice.* Oxford.

Blayney, Peter W. M. (1990). *The Bookshops in Paul's Cross Churchyard.* London.

Boswell, James (1981). *Dr. Samuel Johnson. Leben und Meinungen.* Zürich.

Boulton, Jeremy (2000). »London 1540–1700«. In Peter Clark (ed.). *The Cambridge Urban History of Britain*, Vol II: 1540–1840. Cambridge, 315–346.

Braudel, Fernand (1989). *Modell Italien, 1450–1650.* Berlin.

Brewer, John (1997). *The Pleasures of Imagination: English Culture in the Eighteenth Century.* London.

Burke, Peter (2002). »Early Modern Venice as a Center of Information and Communication«. In John Martin and Dennis Romano (eds.). *Venice Reconsidered. The History and Civilisation of an Italian City-State 1297–1797.* 389–419, Baltimore/London.

Camagni, Roberto (1991a). »Introduction: from the local ›milieu‹ to innovation through cooperation networks«. In: Roberto Camagni (ed.). *Innovation Networks. Spatial Perspectives*, 1–9, London/New York.

— (1991b). »Local ›milieu‹, uncertainty and innovation networks: towards a new dynamic theory of economic space«. In Roberto Camagni (ed.). *Innovation Networks. Spatial Perspective*, 122–144, London/New York.

— (2000). »Das urbane Milieu: Voraussetzung für Innovationen und wirtschaftlichen Erfolg«. In Dirk Matejovski (ed.). *Metropolen. Laboratorien der Moderne?*, 292–307. Frankfurt am Main/New York.

— and Milena Galbiati and Tomaso Pompili (2000). »Urban structural dynamics and innovative milieux. The communication and the fashion production system in the metropolitan area of Milan«. In Olivier Crevoisier and Roberto Camagni (eds.). *Les milieux urbains: innovation, systèmes de production et ancrage*, 185–221, Neuchâtel.

Cattin, Giulio (1981). »Formazione e attività delle cappelle polifoniche nelle cattedrali: La musica nelle città«. In Girolamo Arnaldi and Manlio Pastore Stocchi (eds.). *Storia della cultura veneta: dal primo quattrocento al Concilio di Trento.* Vol. 3, 3, 267–296, Vicenza.

Cecchini, Isabella (2000). *Quadri e commercio a Venezia durante il Seicento: Uno studio sul mercato dell'arte.* Venezia.

— (2006). »Troublesome Business: Dealing in Venice 1600–1750«. In Neil De Marchi and Hans J. van Miegroet (eds.). *Mapping Markets for Paintings in Europe 1450–1750.* Turnhout, 125–134.

Chambers, David and Brian Pullan (eds.) (1992). *Venice: A Documentary History, 1450–1630.* Oxford/Cambridge (Mass.).

Clark, Peter and Rab A. Houston (2000). »Culture and leisure 1700–1840«. In Peter Clark (ed.). *The Cambridge Urban History of Britain, Vol II: 1540–1840*, 575–613 Cambridge.

Clarke, Norma (2000). *Dr. Johnson's Women.* London/New York.

Cochrane James A. (1964). *Dr. Johnson's Printer. The Life of William Strahan.* London.

Cowan, Brian (2006). »Art and Connoisseurship in the Auction Market of Later Seventeenth-Century London«. In Neil De Marchi and Hans J. van Miegroet (eds.). *Mapping Markets for Paintings in Europe 1450–1750*, 263–284, Turnhout.

Davis, Robert C. and Garry R. Marvin (2004). *Venice, the Tourist Maze: A Cultural Critique of the World's Most Touristed City.* Berkeley.

Engert, Klaus (1997). *Kunst, Kultur und Kreativität in einer Metropole: stadtgeographische und stadtwirtschaftliche Implikationen einer empirischen Untersuchung in Mailand.* Bremen.

Evenden Elizabeth and Thomas S. Freeman (2004). »Print, Profit and Propaganda: The Elizabethan Privy Council and the Council and the 1570 Edition of Foxe's ›Book of Martyrs‹«. In *English Historical Review*, 119, 1288–1307.

Florida, Richard (2002). *The rise of the creative class.* New York.

Foot, John (2001). *Milan since the miracle. City, Culture and Identity.* Oxford.

Fortini Brown, Patricia (2002). »Behind the Walls: The Material Culture of Venetian Elites«. In John Martin and Dennis Romano (eds.). *Venice Reconsidered. The History and Civilisation of an Italian City-State 1297–1797*, Baltimore/London, 295–338.

Freist, Dagmar (1997). *Governed by Opinion. Politics, Religion and the Dynamics of Communication in Stuart London 1637–1645.* London/New York.

Fremmer, Anselm (2001). *Venezianische Buchkultur. Bücher, Buchhändler und Leser in der Frührenaissance.* Köln/Weimar/Wien.

Gallo, F. Alberto (1981). »La trattatistica musicale«. In Girolamo Arnaldi and Manlio Pastore Stocchi (eds.). *Storia della cultura veneta: dal primo quattrocento al Concilio di Trento Trento.* Vol. 3, 3, 297–314. Vicenza.

Gibson-Wood, Carol (2003). »Picture Consumption in London at the End of the Seventeenth Century«. *Art Bulletin*, 84, 3, 491–500.

Glanville, Gordon and Philippa Glanville (2004). »The Art Market and Merchant Patronage in London«. In Mireille Galinou (ed.). *City merchants and the arts 1670–1720*, 10–24 London.

Glixon, Jonathan (2003). *Honoring God and the City. Music at the Venetian Confraternities 1260–1807.* Oxford.

72 CLEMENS ZIMMERMANN

Goldthwaite, Richard A. (1996). *Wealth and the Demand for Art in Italy, 1300–1600.* New York.

Goldthwaite, Richard A. (2004). »Economic Parameters of the Italian Art Market (15th to 17th Centuries)«. In Marcello Fantoni, Louisa C. Matthew and Sara F. Matthews-Grieco (eds.). *The Art Market in Italy (15th–17th Centuries)*, 423–444, Modena.

Hall, Peter (1998). *Cities in Civilisation.* New York.

Handover, Phyllis M. (1960). *Printing in London from 1476 to Modern Times.* London.

Harding, Vanessa (2000). »Reformation and culture 1540–1700«. In Peter Clark (ed.). *The Cambridge Urban History of Britain*, Vol. II: 1540–1840. Cambridge, 263–288.

Harris, Michael (2003). »Print in Neighbourhood Commerce: the case of Carter Lane«. In Robert Myers, Michael Harris and Giles Mandelbrote (eds.). *The London Book Trade: topographics of print in the metropolis from the sixteenth century.* London, 45–69.

Heiler, Susanne (2000). *Der Pikaro in Italien. Italienisch-spanische Kulturbeziehungen und die Rezeption des pikaresken Romans in der italienischen Literatur des 17. Jahrhunderts.* Habilitationsschrift. Heidelberg.

Hellmeister, Anette (1992). *Die Pariser Haute-couture.* Trier.

Hersche, Peter (1999). *Italien im Barockzeitalter (1600–1750): Eine Sozial- und Kulturgeschichte.* Wien/Köln/Weimar.

Heßler, Martina (2002). »Stadt als innovatives Milieu – Ein transdisziplinärer Forschungsansatz«. *Neue Politische Literatur*, 47, 2, 193–223.

Heßler, Martina (2003). »Vernetzte Wissensräume. Zur Bedeutung von Orten in einer vernetzten Welt«. *Technikgeschichte*, 70, 4, 235–253.

Hills, Paul (1993). »Tintoretto's Marketing«. In Bernd Roeck, Klaus Bergdolt and Andrew John Martin (eds.). *Venedig und Oberdeutschland in der Renaissance. Beziehungen zwischen Kunst und Wirtschaft*, 107–120, Sigmaringen.

Horodowich, Elizabeth (2005). »The gossiping tongue: oral networks, public life and political culture in early modern Venice«. *Renaissance Studies*, 19, 1, 22–45.

Infelise, Mario (1989). *L'editoria veneziana nel' 700.* Milano.

— (1992). »Tra »capitalisti« e corporazione. L'industria del libro a Venezia nel ›700«. In *Produzione e commercio della carta e del libro*, a cura di Simonetta Cavaciocchi, Secc. XIII–XVIII, 475–480. Firenze.

— (1999). »Le marché des informations à Venise au XVIIe siècle«. In Henri Duranton and Pierre Rétat (eds.). *Gazettes et information politique sous l'Ancien Régime*,. Saint-Étienne, 117–128.

Ingenday, Paul (2007). »Jesus ist ein muskulöser Mann. Dem Prado sei Dank: Zum ersten Mal seit siebzig Jahren gibt es Jacopo Tintoretto, den Berserker der italienischen Malerei, in einer Gesamtschau«. *Frankfurter Allgemeine Zeitung*, January 27, 2007, 37.

Kauw Gerda (1961). *Branchenstraßen und -viertel in Paris.* Köln.

Kempers, Bram (1989). *Kunst, Macht und Mäzenatentum. Der Beruf des Malers in der italienischen Renaissance.* München.

Knittler, Herbert (2000). *Die europäische Stadt in der frühen Neuzeit: Institutionen, Strukturen, Entwicklungen.* Wien.

Kubersky-Piredda, Susanne (2002).»Spesa della materia« und »spesa dell'arte«. Die Preise von Altartafeln in der Florentiner Renaissance«. In *Economia e arte*, a cura di Simonetta Cavaciocchi, secc. XII–XVIII. 339–353, Firenze.

Lehnert, Gertrud (1998). *Frauen machen Mode. Modeschöpferinnen vom 18. Jahrhundert bis heute.* Dortmund.

Lorente J. Pedro and Clare Targett (2000).»Comparative Growth and Urban Distribution of the Population of Artists in Victorian London«. In Peter Borsay, Gunther Hirschfelder and Ruth E. Mohrmann (eds.). *New Directions in Urban History. Aspects of European Art, Health, Tourism and Leisure since the Enlightenment*, 65–86, Münster.

Mannings, David (1991).»The Visual arts«. In Boris Ford (ed.). *The Cambridge Guide to the Arts in Britain, Vol. 5: The Augustan Age*,106–147 Cambridge.

Maskell Peter and Anders Malmberg (1999).»Localised learning and industrial competiveness«. *Cambridge Journal of Economics*, 23, 167–185.

Matteaccioli, Anurée and Muriel Tabarriés (2000).»Dynamiques urbaines et milieus innovateurs dans la métropole Parisienne. Les milieus de la finance et de la haute-couture«. In Olivier Crevoisier and Roberto Camagni (eds.). *Les milieux urbains: innovation, systèmes de production et ancrage*, 145–183, Neuchâtel.

Matthew, Louisa C. (2003).»Were There Open Markets For Pictures in Renaissance Venice?«. In Marcello Fantoni, Louisa C. Matthew and Sara F. Matthews-Grieco (eds.). *The Art Market in Italy (15th–17th Centuries)*, 253–261, Modena.

Maxted, Ian (1977). *The London Book Trades 1775–1800. A Preliminary Checklist of Members.* Folkestone.

— (1984). *The London Book Trades 1735–1775. A Checklist of members in trade directories and in Musgrave's »Obituary«.* Exeter.

McDowell, Paula (1998). *The Women of Grub Street. Press, Politics, and Gender in the London Literary Marketplace 1678–1730.* Oxford.

McKenzie, Donald F. (1992).»The Economies of Print 1550–1750. Scales of Production and Conditions of Constraint«. In *Produzione e commercio della carta e del libro*, a cura di Simonetta Cavaciocchi, Secc. XIII–XVIII, 389–425. Firenze.

Miller, William E. (1966).»Printers and Stationers in the Parish of St. Giles Cripplegate 1561–1640«. *Studies in Bibliography*, 19, 15–38.

Muir, Edward and Ronald F. E. Weissman (1989).»Social and symbolic places in Renaissance Venice and Florence«. In John A. Agnew and James S. Duncan (eds.). *The Power of Place. Bringing together geographical and sociological imaginations*, 681–703 Boston.

Ormrod, David (2002).»The Rise of the London Art Market 1660–1760«. In: *Economia e arte*, a cura di Simonetta Cavaciocchi, Secc. XII–XVIII, 303–321. Firenze.

Ortalli, Francesca (2001). »*Per salute delle anime e delli corpi*«. *Scuole piccole a Venezia nel tardo medioevo.* Venezia.

Pears, Iain (1991). *The Discovery of Painting: The Growth of Interest in the Arts in England, 1680–1768.* 2nd edition, New Haven.

Peck, Linda Levy (2005). *Consuming Splendor. Society and Culture in Seventeenth-Century England.* Cambridge.

Pesenti, Tiziana (1983). *Stampatori e letterati nell'industria editoriale a Venezia e in Terraferma.* Vicenza.

Petrucci, Armando (ed.) (1977). *Libri, editori e pubblico nell'Europa moderna. Guida storica e critica.* Roma/Bari.

Picard, Liza (2001). *Dr. Johnson's London.* London.

Power, M. J. (1986). »The social topography of restoration London«. In A. L. Beier and Roger Finlay (eds.). *London 1500–1700. The Making of the Metropolis.* London, 197–223.

Priddat, Birger (2004). »Historische Methode und moderne Ökonomie. Über das Methodische in der Historischen Schule und das Historische in der Neuen Institutionenökonomie«. In Hartmut Berghoff and Jakob Vogel (eds.). *Wirtschaftsgeschichte als Kulturgeschichte. Dimensionen eines Perspektivenwechsels*, 99–116, Frankfurt am Main.

Pullan, Brian (ed.) (1968). *Crisis and Change in the Venetian Economy in the Sixteenth and Seventeenth Centuries.* London.

Raven, James (2003). »Location, Size, and Succession: the bookshops of Paternoster Row before 1800«. In Robert Myers, Michael Harris and Giles Mandelbrote (eds.). *The London Book Trade: topographies of print in the metropolis from the sixteenth century*, 89–126, London.

Richardson, Brian (1994). *Print Culture in Renaissance Italy and the Vernacular Text, 1470–1600.* Cambridge.

Roeck, Bernd (2004). *Das historische Auge. Kunstwerke als Zeugen ihrer Zeit.* Göttingen.

Rogers, Pat (1972). *Grub Street. Studies in a Subculture.* London.

Schwarz, Leonhard (2000). »London 1700–1840«. In Peter Clark (ed.), *The Cambridge Urban History of Britain, Vol II: 1540–1840*, 641–671, Cambridge.

Scott, Allen J. (2000a). *The Cultural Economy of Cities. Essays on the Geography of Image-Producing Industries.* London.

— (2000b). »The Cultural Economy of Paris«. In *International Journal of Urban and Regional Research*, 24, 3, 567–582.

— (2004). *On Hollywood: The Place, the Industry.* Princeton.

Steele, Valerie (1999). *Paris fashion. A Cultural history.* New York.

Stumpo, Enrico (2006). *Between art market and luxury production. Some methodological remarks*, XIV. International Economic History Congress, Helsinki.

Ulvioni, Paolo (1977). »Stampatori e librai a Venezia del Seicento«. In *Archivio Veneto*, 108, 93–124.

Varry, Dominique (2002). »Lyons' printers and booksellers from the fifteenth to the nineteenth century«. In Malcolm Gee and Tim Kirk (eds.). *Printed Matters. Printing, publishing and urban culture in Europe in the modern period*, 30–47. Aldershot.

Welch, Evelyn (2003). »From Retail to Resale: Artistic Value and the Second-Hand Market in Italy (1400–1550)«. In Marcello Fantoni, Louisa C. Matthew and Sara F. Matthews-Grieco (eds.). *The Art Market in Italy (15th–17th Centuries)*. 283–299, Modena.

Wiesand, Andreas Johannes (2006). »Kultur- oder ›Kreativwirtschaft‹: Was ist das eigentlich?«. *Aus Politik und Zeitgeschichte*, 34/35, 8–16.

Wilson, Bronwen (2005). *The world in Venice: print, the city, and early modern identity*. Toronto/Buffalo/London.

Winkler, Karl Tilman (1993). *Handwerk und Markt: Druckerhandwerk, Vertriebswesen und Tagesschrifttum in London 1695–1759*. Stuttgart.

Woodward, David (1996). *Maps as Prints in the Italian Renaissance. Makers, Distributors and Consumers*. London.

Zachs, William (1998). *The first John Murray and the late eighteenth-century London book trade: with a checklist of his publications*. Oxford.

Invention, Innovation, and the »Creative Milieu« in Urban Britain: The Long Eighteenth Century and the Birth of the Modern Cultural Economy

Peter Borsay

An Urban Cultural Economy

Located on the threshold of the so-called »First Industrial Revolution«, eighteenth-century Britain has long been seen as a peculiarly creative economic milieu. Research in recent decades has tended to reinforce rather than undermine this perception. However, it has shifted the emphasis away from technological notions of creativity – spinning-jennies, water-frames and steam engines – to more culturally defined ones, embracing areas such as publishing and printing, architecture, music, art and leisure (McKendrick et al. 1983; Solkin 1992; Brewer and Porter 1993; Bermingham and Brewer 1995; Brewer 1997; Black 2005; Berg 2005; Powell 2005). Underpinning much of this research has been the notion that culture was becoming an increasingly important and market-orientated element within the economy. It was a view pioneered by J. H. Plumb when, in a now celebrated paper, he drew attention »to what seems to be one of the incontestable signs of growing affluence in eighteenth-century British society – the commercialisation of leisure. This can be discerned in the 1690s, and in 1750 and 1760 leisure was becoming an industry with great potentiality for growth.« (Plumb 1973: 3). The »cultural turn« in eighteenth-century historiography has been accompanied and contributed to by a wave of research into the history of towns (Borsay 1990; Clark 2000; Chalklin 2001). This has led many to suggest, explicitly or implicitly, close links between economic, cultural and urban change (Clark and Houston 2000: 576; Ellis 2001: 2, 129). In these circumstances it is tempting to see the creative milieu of the period as an outcome of the fusion of these three factors. This resonates with the emphasis placed on the cultural economy and »creative industries« in western societies today. However, it has to be said that the concept of an urban cultural economy is a problematic one for the historian. It is frequently viewed as a recent phenomenon rather than something with long historical roots. Allen J. Scott has argued that »Cultural products of all sorts constitute a constantly increasing share of the output of modern capitalism, and cultural product sectors represent some of the most dynamic growth industries in the world at the present time. [...] a powerful convergence is occurring between the economic and cultural spheres in contemporary society« (Scott 2000: x). Is it then plausible to talk of an urban cultural economy before the late twentieth century? There is also the key issue of definition. Does the term »urban« mean exclusively cities, or are *all* towns embraced? Is it possible to distinguish between cultural and non-cultural, economic and non-economic phenomena? Even if the answer to this last question is positive, how are objects, institutions and forms of behaviour which mix cultural and non-cultural, economic and non-economic elements to be categorized? What is meant by »culture«? Does it encompass simply »high« culture and the arts – classical music, theatre, painting, etc. – or can popular pleasures and pastimes, and indeed politics, science and technology be included? Can features of towns which support the cultural economy, such as infrastructural elements, be incorporated? There is no simple answer to these questions. However, it will be argued that the notion of the urban cultural economy remains a valuable heuristic tool with which to explore the creative milieu of eighteenth-century Britain.

In the first part of the paper I will identify a sample of urban-based inventions and innovations, developed in eighteenth-century Britain, that possess strong cultural and economic resonances. The second part will explore the conditions and climate which brought these phenomena into being. The third part will focus specifically on the extent to which this climate flourished in the city and town, and address the question how far a dynamic urban sector was the engine behind the creative environment of eighteenth-century Britain. The final part of the paper will attempt to historicize the cultural economy, by posing the question: to what extent did the long eighteenth century see the birth of the modern cultural economy?

Inventions, Innovations, and Creativity

A Working List

Below is a working list of predominantly urban inventions and innovations of the eighteenth century, categorized under broad headings, which shared significant cultural and economic associations:[1]

(i)   technological infrastructure – oil street lighting; piped water systems (Falkus 1976);

(ii)   information systems – street numbering and naming; printed directories, guides, urban histories, two-dimensional maps and prospects; the circulating library; the newspaper and journal press (Corfield and Kelly 1984; Sweet 1997; Elliot 1987: 57–66; Hyde 1985; Kaufman 1967; Cranfield 1962; Wiles 1965; Black 1987);

(iii)   Architecture – the uniform street terrace; classical multi-dwelling units (the square, the crescent and circus); style (urban classicism) (Girouard 1990; Ayres 1998);

(iv)   commercial institutions – the modern shop with glass windows and internal display facilities; the merchant exchange; the customs house; the specialist cloth hall (Cox 2000: 76–115; Stobart 2007);

(v)   recreational institutions and forms – the commercial concert, opera, and the musical festival; assemblies (for dancing and socializing); the public promenade and pleasure garden (Fawcett 1979; Weber 1992; McVeigh 1993);

(vi)   social institutions – the club and society; coffee houses (Clark 2000a; Ellis 1956; Ellis 2004);

(vii)   political institutions – the urban improvement commission, voluntary societies engaged in social and political reform (Jones and Falkus 1990);

(viii) urban types – the spa and seaside resort (Hembry 1990; Walton 1983; Corbin 1994; Borsay 2000a);

(ix)   modes of behaviour and thought – civility; politeness; sociability; improvement (Carter 2001; Langford 1989: 424–435; Borsay 2002).

Two initial observations may be made about this list. First, it could be objected that the items included are not new phenomena. Elements of classical design, for example, had been available in English towns since at

---

1   Many items in the list are discussed in Borsay (1989) and Brewer (1997).

least the early seventeenth century, town centre streets had long possessed retail outlets of a sort, and people had for many centuries gathered together in social institutions like guilds and fraternities. However, the argument here is not that the new phenomena do not have precursors: rather, it is either that this is the point in which they are introduced on a large scale and become dominant forms (like urban classicism); or that they take on a qualitatively new form (like the street, the shop and the club/society). Second, it could be argued that several of the items listed are only marginal to the cultural economy. Street lighting and piped water supplies, for example, could be defined as essentially infrastructural, parts of the working machinery of the town, and lacking in symbolic, aesthetic or economic value. Yet such pieces of urban infrastructure were tightly linked to the cultural economy, and were critical to its operation. For example, street lighting – once installed on a significant scale – permitted a reconstruction of the urban notion of time and daily routine, which turned night time into an active as opposed to passive phase and supported novel social institutions like the assembly, the coffee house, the concert and the club, that were themselves the mediums through which new modes of behaviour such as politeness and sociability were cultivated. The inventions and innovations catalogued here were part of a seamless web. Moreover, it is arguable that street lighting was as much a cultural as a technological phenomenon. The banishing of darkness resonated closely with the idea of Enlightenment, and the introduction of the new oil lamps represented a powerful symbol of the culture of improvement. In these circumstances there is an argument for taking a broad view of what constituted the »cultural economy«.

Invention or Innovation?

What conditions encouraged invention and innovation? There is, of course, a distinction between the two terms. By invention is conventionally meant the creation of something new, by innovation the introduction and dissemination of that novelty. George Sorocold of Derby appears to have been the inventor of the rising and falling water wheel in the 1690s, a device which varied its position according to the level of the river, and, using the force of the current to drive a pump, was able to deliver a more consistent supply of water into the piped water systems that increasingly serviced the better off of in towns. Though he acted as an entrepreneur in his own right, the widespread introduction of piped water systems in general, and the new technology in particular, depended ultimately upon other engineers (Williamson 1936). John Wood the elder and younger, architects in Georgian Bath, were the first to construct the multi-dwelling urban residential units known as crescents and circuses, but it was other architects who spread these fashionable forms beyond Bath when they built in locations as varied as Brighton, Bristol, Buxton, Edinburgh, London, Tunbridge Wells and Wisbech (Summerson 1949; Cruickshank 1985). Both inventors and innovators are part of the creative milieu. In practice the distinction is a somewhat simplistic and misleading one. Few, if any, inventors create something *de novo*. Most inventions draw upon ideas already in circulation. Urban piped water supplies in England date back to the medieval systems that supplied monastic houses, and sometimes also benefited the towns in which they were based (Schofield and Stell 2000: 377–378); and the late Tudor and early Stuart period piped systems were being introduced to service private customers in a number of the larger provincial towns (Slack 2000: 367, 369). The Woods' King's Circus and Royal Crescent at Bath were strikingly novel building forms, but there were historical precedents, and they reflected a range of developments in urban design that had been long underway. More to the point might be John Wood the elder's first major building project in Bath, Queen Square. When this was built in 1728–1736, classical squares had been part of the British urban landscape for about a century, since they were introduced by Inigo Jones at Covent Garden in London in the 1630s (he, in fact, drew upon Continental models) (Summerson 1966: 83–96). But Queen Square, Bath, included a dramatic new feature, the so-called palatial façade, by which the entire front of one side of the square was constructed to look like the façade of a palace or country house, even though it concealed a number of separate dwellings. It has been suggested that Wood acquired the idea in London, where it was projected for the north side of Grosvenor Square, but not properly implemented (Summerson 1949: 91; Mowl and Earnshaw 1988: 66–68). If so, then it is arguable that Wood was not so much the inventor as the innovator. What further challenges the inventor/innovator distinction is the fact that many of the phenomena in the working list have no obvious originator. Indeed, to ask the question who invented the coffee house, the assembly, the improvement commission, never mind modes of thought and behaviour like politeness and civility, is a misguided exercise. They are forms which grow out of a general *Zeitgeist*, and the key figures are those who introduce, disseminate, evolve and modify the models. Even men like Joseph Addison and Richard Steele, authors of the hugely influential early eighteenth-century journals *The Tatler* (1709–1711) and *Spectator* (1711–1712), and closely associated with the cults of politeness and sociability, were essentially broadcasters and propagandists rather than inventors of ideas.

Five Conditions of Creativity

To question the heroic notion of invention is not, however, to challenge the importance of creativity, of an environment in which such a condition flourished, or indeed the role of individuals in promoting cultural change. What, then, were the conditions which stimulated individuals and groups to invent and innovate in Britain in the long eighteenth-century? First, there needed to be a general recognition that change *per se* was acceptable and even desirable. This is not to say that everyone wanted change, simply that a novel practice or form would not be ruled out automatically because it was new, as it may be in so-called »traditional« societies. Critical was the attitude of the national and local state in late Stuart and Georgian Britain in not, as a matter of course, discouraging and blocking change, and in providing the legal framework through which others – if not necessarily themselves – could patent inventions, raise capital and introduce improvements. Also vital was the way that novelty and change were valorized through the increasingly influential ethos of improvement, in which change and the pursuit of progress became a moral duty (Borsay 2002: 185; Spadafora 1990). Second, there was the rapid circulation of knowledge (defined in its broadest sense to include not just intellectual ideas but taste and fashion), without which there would not be the material with which to invent and innovate. It was to a large extent the volume and variety of knowledge, and the velocity with which it circulated that stimulated change. Knowledge was the oxygen which fuelled the minds of inventive and innovative people. In providing the mechanisms for the spread of knowledge of particular importance was the emergence of a permanent newspaper and journal press, the expansion of the book trade, the growth in letter writing allied to the development of the postal service, the efflorescence of clubs and societies, and the development of tourism, travel and resorts. Third, there needed to be some incentive for those who promoted change. Inventors and innovators were not altruistic boffins, but had to be able to make money and acquire social esteem from their enterprise. Of especial importance was the opportunity to pursue status. The relatively open social structure of eighteenth-century Britain and the importance of non-genetic factors in defining gentility were an undoubted help in this respect (Heal and Holmes 1994: 6–10, 38–42; Rosenheim 1998: 180–181). It was possible, if not common, for enterprising individuals of relatively lowly birth, to make dramatic advances in their economic and social position. Of the three so-called »inventors« of Georgian Bath, the premier spa town in Britain – men who made their fortunes and reputations during the city's early boom – Wood the architect, who probably attended the Bath Blue Coat charity school, was the son of a local builder; Ralph Allen, Bath's enormously wealthy postmaster and quarry owner, the son of a Cornishman, possibly a labourer or innkeeper; and Richard Nash, the fabled master of ceremonies, the offspring of a small businessman who shared the ownership of a glass works in Swansea (Mowl and Earnshaw 1988: 10; Boyce 1967: 1–2; Connely 1955: 2–3). Fourth, to make money, there had to be a demand for inventions and innovations. This depended at the simplest level upon wealth, and in particular surplus wealth that could be directed into new products which were often over and above the necessities of life, and had a strong »cultural« content. Such »luxury« items were the outcome of a process which, for a latter period, Scott Lash and John Urry have called the »aestheticisation of material objects« (Lash and Urry 1994: 4). The growing prosperity of Britain in the long eighteenth century was fundamental in this process, as was the expansion of a middling order with spare resources and a taste for novelty. Fifth, in shaping demand for »the new« a critical factor is fashion. Fashion depends not so much upon inherent content, as upon the kudos attached to novelty itself; to be in fashion depends upon possessing and displaying the *latest* designs, and behaving in a way that reflects the most *up-to-date* tastes. Fashion is also essentially a cultural construct. It was the eighteenth-century's passion for fashion, the craving for novelty that created an endless and insatiable stream of demand for new culturally-dense products, institutions and modes of behaviour.

Towns, Cities, and the Climate of Creativity

The items in my working list of inventions and innovations are predominantly urban in character and location. In this section of the paper I want to address the question, to what extent were the city and town forcing-houses of change? Commentators have often portrayed the urban world in these terms. Fernand Braudel declared »The towns are so many transformers. They increase tension, accelerate the rhythm of exchange and ceaselessly stir up men's lives.« (Braudel 1974: 373). In his monumental study of *Cities in Civilisation*, Peter Hall asserts that »every great burst of creativity in human history« was »an urban phenomenon«, and at the outset of the book poses the question »Why should the creative flow burn so especially, so uniquely in cities and not the countryside?« (Hall 1999: 3). In this paper I will explore how far the five factors identified here that contributed to a creative cultural milieu – a valorisation of change, the circulation of knowledge, incentive, demand, and fashion – were concentrated in the urban sector.

Valorisation of Change

It would be naïve to assume that eighteenth-century towns always welcomed change. The forces of conservatism were invariably very powerful. Even in dynamic cities like London and Bath change could be resisted. Despite figures like John Evelyn, Robert Hooke and Christopher Wren producing impressive plans, the great opportunity provided by the Fire of London in 1666 to remodel the commercial core of the metropolis along the lines of an international capital like Rome – to invest, as it were, in image – was largely wasted. Practical impediments, such as matters of finance and compensation, were a major disincentive to radical change, but it is likely that equally important was resistance to change a ground plan whose topography provided the physical and mental foundations on which citizens lives and businesses had been built (Reddaway 1951; Porter 1996). For much of the first half of the eighteenth century the corporation at Bath was lukewarm to expansion, resisting some new developments beyond the city walls and failing to release its own considerable extra-mural properties for development (McIntyre 1981: 222–237). John Wood's fractious relationship with the ruling body in Bath, and – as he saw it – their wilful attempts to thwart his plans for the city, might suggest that corporations in general were inherently conservative bodies that acted as a brake on urban development. Much of the historiography on the eighteenth-century corporation, portrayed conventionally as moribund and corrupt, would point in this direction. However, as ongoing research on Georgian urban government has revealed, the story is much more complicated than this (Sweet 1999: 141–161; Innes and Rogers 2000). It is unlikely that town governments resisted change as a matter of course. Invariably there were good practical reasons to do with finance, risk taking and loss of civic control, in addition to the threat posed to established interests that prompted a cautious approach to development. Moreover, viewed not through the distorting prism of the 1835 Municipal Reform Act, but in terms of what was practically achieved at the time, the role of eighteenth-century urban government as a supporter and promoter of change is quite creditable. Many corporations used the machinery of the central state, in the form of Parliament, to obtain local acts to improve road and river access (through turnpiking, navigation and bridge-building schemes), to enhance street paving, and to introduce piped water supplies and oil street lighting. Some corporations saddled themselves with heavy debts to pay for a new town hall or market hall. Most impressive are the innumerable small decisions – the shaving off of a street corner to improve the turning lock for a coach or cart, the donation of a race prize to enhance the appeal of the local race meeting, payment to establish a tree-lined promenade – that collectively were remodelling the character of the town and repositioning its image (Borsay 2003: 5–6). There is a persistence of intention here, an accumulative agenda of improvement that is easy to miss. In York, for example, there were efforts to introduce a small but significant piece of street widening in the 1720s, so as to improve access for coaches to the projected new assembly rooms; though frustrated at the time, the scheme was resuscitated in the 1740s when an opportunity to solve the problem, and overcome the initial objections, fortuitously arose (York City Archives, House Book, October 29, 1729; June 14, 1745; April 29, 1747). This is not to suggest that councils did not face difficulties, and the introduction of improvement commissions, largely from the middle of the century, was indicative of the need for a more focused body of authority with the power to raise money and enforce change, as well as being a way to provide more effective governmental structures for towns which were unincorporated. The establishment of the commissions was a sign of urban local government's ability to adapt to cope with the problems and expectations gener-

ated by urban growth; and more broadly of a cultural and political milieu
that accepted the need to, and encouraged the process of change.

Circulation of Knowledge

Piped water supplies, classical town halls and assembly rooms did not
autonomously and spontaneously plant themselves in towns. They were
part of a body of new ideas about urban living that circulated rapidly
through a system in which towns were constantly engaged in competitive
emulation. After the port of Bristol obtained an impressive new Merchants' Exchange 1741–1743, its great west coast rival, Liverpool, felt
obliged to employ the same architect to construct it an Exchange 1749–
1754 (Mowl and Earnshaw 1988: 149–168). It is difficult to imagine that
Warwick's decision to construct a baroque town hall in the late 1720s was
not prompted by the building of a hall by its neighbour and rival county
capital at Worcester earlier in the decade (Gomme 2000: 441–450). It was
not just a question of competing civic egos. Both halls contained assembly
rooms, and this reflected the fact that both towns were eager to exploit the
lucrative gentry market, where expectations as to what towns offered in
terms of environment, shopping and recreational facilities were escalating
rapidly. For civic bodies and individuals with an enterprising turn of mind,
it was easy to pick up details of new fashions, pastimes or types of business
projects – such as setting up a newspaper or opening a bookshop – where
there was the potential for accessing or creating a niche in the market.
Towns were the engines of the knowledge system, creating, collecting and
circulating ideas and information. It was to the town that people came to
not only to trade in goods, but also knowledge. The inn and alehouse had
for centuries served the role of information centre, but during the long
eighteenth century a range of other urban-based institutions emerged, such
as the coffee house, newspaper press and club, to further facilitate the
exchange of knowledge. Frequently these institutions interconnected; so,
for example, coffee houses and inns often took newspapers and journals,
multiplying their readership, and accommodated clubs, including groups
which were dedicated to the exchange of knowledge, such as book clubs,
and debating and antiquarian societies (Borsay 1989: 144–146). Even institutions with less overtly serious purposes, like the assemblies, provided
arenas for intensive conversation and gossip, during which social information would be exchanged. Moreover, it was not just a matter of transferring

a given body of ideas; the very acts of talking and debating would mean that knowledge was constantly being reconstituted. In addition it should also be remembered that acquiring information could be as much a visual as an oral exercise. Changes in clothing fashion or ways of bodily deportment would be transmitted more by what people saw, than what they heard, at the assemblies or on the public walks.

Incentive

Inventors and innovators need incentives. There must be some prospect that if they take a risk and run with a new idea that there is a reasonable expectation of a return. Though this can be measured crudely in economic terms, a social return may be even more important. The town possessed several advantages, in comparison to the countryside, in this respect. The social structure was likely to contain a wider variety of gradations, and in particular there would be a substantial and growing middling order. The consequence was that there was no unbridgeable chasm between top and bottom, and there was a reasonable prospect for the successful entrepreneur of turning economic gain into social advancement. This was reinforced by the fact the very nature of urban economies meant that for townsmen engaging in business and trade did not carry the social stigma that it might among the rural gentry. This is not to claim that towns were completely open societies with no barriers to social mobility. But for those with a will, and preferably some capital, it was possible to introduce a novel enterprise and to use this as a platform for business success and the acquisition of social status. Only fragments are known of the career of James Keating, who introduced the first newspaper into Stratford-upon-Avon in 1749, capitalizing on the closure of a publication in a neighbouring town. The paper only appears to have operated until 1753, but Keating continued to run what would seem to have been a successful bookshop and printing business that gave him a more than local reputation – his death in 1793 was mentioned in the *Gentleman's Magazine* – and to judge from the description of him as a ›banker‹ on his tombstone, projected him into the higher echelons of the Stratford bourgeoisie (Morgan 1947–8: 57–59). Francis Smith (1672–1738) was the son of a substantial Staffordshire bricklayer. At the age of twenty two he moved to Warwick, after the major fire of 1694, to take advantage of the greatly enhanced opportunities for building work. His elder brother William was appointed one of the two surveyors to regu-

late the rebuilding – no doubt opening up opportunities for Francis – and
in 1697 William and Francis were appointed contractors to rebuild St
Mary's church. By the time of his death Francis had established in the town
one of the leading provincial architectural and building practices in Britain,
carrying classical architecture to innumerable country houses in the region.
He himself became mayor of Warwick on two occasions, and was designated on at least one inscription as a »gentleman architect« (Colvin 1995:
882–890: Gomme 2000). The career of the architect John Carr (1723–
1807), the son of a stonemason, follows a not dissimilar pattern to that of
Smith, eventually carrying him to the office of Lord Mayor of York in
1770. John Wood the elder of Bath's career path differed not so much in
his social background or his economic and social success, as in his failure
to join the city council – a product of his tetchy relationship with it – and
his greater focus on urban building. For all three architects towns provided
fruitful environments in which to contribute to the cultural economy and
make personal social and well as economic progress.

Demand

The success of figures like Keating, Smith, Carr and Wood depended upon
there being a demand for their services. The rising levels of wealth and
disposable income of the period that underpinned this demand were not
exclusively urban.[2] However, with urbanisation not only was a growing
proportion, if still a minority of the population located in towns, but the
middling order – a key element in the market, and a major beneficiary of
the new prosperity – were predominantly an urban-based group (Holmes
1982; Barry and Brooks 1994; Glennie and Whyte 2000: 183–185). Moreover, and probably the critical issue, the town, because of its role in the
sale of goods and services, represented the interface between producer and
consumer. Even if goods were produced in the countryside, it was generally through urban markets they would have to pass to reach the consumer.
The consequence was that the town was the best point for an inventor or
innovator to be located. Though in the case of Francis Smith and John
Carr their clients were predominantly country gentlemen, the optimum

---

2   For rising level of wealth and disposable income, and a ›new context‹ in the economy in
    the century or so after the Restoration, see Pollard and Crossley 1968: 153–173; Cole-
    man 1977: 91–201.

location from which to operate was the county town, because this was the place where the local rural elite gathered to transact administrative and political business, shop and recreate themselves. The town's role as a meeting place also made it the natural point at which to introduce and develop the new social institutions – such as assemblies, public promenades and coffee-houses – designed to facilitate sociability. Indeed, there was seen to be an inherent relationship between sociability, politeness and urban living, and it was this that made the town as a whole the appropriate environment in which to promote these modes of behaviour. Such was the demand that it led to the making of a quite new type of town, the spa and seaside resort, devoted to intensive socializing. The coastal resort constituted a particularly innovative and influential urban type, of which there was no real precedent before its emergence – at Brighton, Scarborough, Margate and Weymouth – in the early to mid-eighteenth century.

Fashion

Towns may be focal points of demand, but they were not just passive locations. Crucially, they had the capacity to shape that demand. Fashion was the key mechanism in structuring consumers' aspirations, and it was towns that in large measure controlled this mechanism. Fashion set the standard in product design, forms of behaviour and such like, that consumers had to follow; and, because of its unstable nature, and its emphasis upon novelty and innovation, fashion varied and changed that standard at intervals that could be remarkably short. Setting the standard depended not so much upon the inherent qualities of the product as the simple process of display. What was fashionable was to a large degree what the right people were wearing and doing in the right places. It was the town that provided these social catwalks, or high kudos show spaces, such as public promenades, pleasure gardens, assemblies and theatres. To these must be added shops. In the larger towns and resorts a new type of prestigious retail outlet, often clustered together along a main street – such as the Rows in Chester, the Pantiles in Tunbridge Wells, the Orange Grove and later Milsom Street in Bath (Stobart 1998; Brown 1999: 95–113; Fiennes 1947: 133–134; Fawcett 1990; Fawcett and Inskipp 1994; Borsay 2000b: 3) – was emerging, architecturally designed, outdoors and indoors, to display goods in the most favourable light. In the 1720s Daniel Defoe described how »it is a modern custom, and wholly unknown to our ancestors […] to have tradesmen lay out two-thirds of their fortune in fitting up their shops. By fitting up, I mean, in painting and gilding, in fine shelves, shutters, pediments, columns of the several orders of architecture and the like; in which, they tell us now, it is a small matter to lay out two or three, nay, five hundred pounds, to fit up what we call the outside of a shop.« (Defoe 1970: 205) Consumers would turn to the shop windows to discover what was in fashion, because it was the very presence of an object in the window that defined the latest fads. Spaces, therefore, shaped fashion, and it was urban spaces that moulded consumer demand.

The above analysis has focused on the positive features of the town as an agent of cultural change, and avoided the inevitable corollary to the argument, that the countryside was by comparison an environment less conducive to change. Defining the urban sector as progressive and the rural sector as backward fails to recognize the degree of change that was occurring in the countryside – where, for example, many new industrial and agricultural processes, alongside innovative aesthetic trends in gardening, were being pioneered – and the level of interconnection between sectors that were in most essential respects integrated. Nonetheless, it is reasonable to argue that comparatively speaking the town constituted an environment more inclined to promote creativity and cultural change than the countryside, and that Britain's dynamic urban sector in the eighteenth century was critical to its success as a creative milieu. It is not simply a matter of accident that the inventions and innovations listed at the start of this paper originated predominantly in the town. There is also the point that over the last three centuries those societies which have accommodated economic change most successfully have also been those that have most effectively embraced the process of long-term, large-scale urbanisation.

Towns or Cities?

Urban and rural comparisons apart, there remains the question, to what extent did the urban sector as a whole constitute a creative milieu? The urban system was a highly variegated and in many respects increasingly differentiated one. It would seem absurd to imagine that a country town like Ludlow or Leominster offered the same climate for innovation as a dynamic industrial centre such as Manchester or Birmingham. The distinction is an important one because the Ludlows and Leominsters were far more typical of the urban system than the industrial super novas. In 1700 about 92 percent of the 1005 towns in mainland Britain had populations of under 2,500 people (Langton 2000: 463). Nonetheless, it would be dangerous to write off these small towns as sterile backwaters. The evidence from detailed research into small towns over the last decade or so – not least that undertaken by Peter Clark and Alan Dyer – is that the they were a remarkably buoyant group of settlements, perfectly capable of absorbing and contributing to the processes of change going on around them (Clark 1995; Clark 2000c; Corfield 1987; Dyer 2002). The widespread introduction of shops and modish classical architecture and pastimes to many of these smaller settlements suggests that they could be highly receptive to new tastes and ideas, and that the urban network was closely interconnected, allowing new fashions to course rapidly through the system. However, though the smaller towns were effective in introducing new ideas, it is likely that the real work in terms of invention and innovation was focused elsewhere in the urban system. Peter Hall has referred to the »unique creativity of great cities«, and the presence of London in particular – a mega metropolis of half a million people in 1700 and a million by 1800, and one closely connected to national, imperial and global networks – was critical (Hall 1999: 7). It provided the access to new influences, and the sort of concentrated market of well off consumers, that provided the ideal breeding ground for cultural inventors and innovators. It was London that pioneered, tested and disseminated many of the new developments in the working list which opened this paper (Borsay 2001: 170–178). We may be inclined to dwell on the failure of the capital to adopt a model baroque town plan in the wake of the Great fire of 1666. But it may be more percipient to note the extraordinary way in which London responded to the loss of perhaps 80,000 people in the plague of 1665 and 13,200 properties in the conflagration of the following year, by becoming the most vibrant and creative capital in late seventeenth-century Europe (Porter 1994: 84; Porter 1996: 70).

The Birth of the Modern Cultural Economy?

The towns of long-eighteenth-century Britain possessed economies that both encouraged and manifested cultural invention and innovation. This is a period and a place when it is seems plausible and appropriate to talk of a creative milieu in towns and of the cultural economy that it spawned. To what extent the long eighteenth century was special in this respect is a matter of debate. It would be naïve to argue that a creative milieu and cultural economy did not exist in British towns before the late seventeenth century. Late medieval towns were home to clusters of craftsmen producing works of religious art; they engendered a sophisticated guild system that supported lavish public ceremonial, such as that at Corpus Christi and Whitsun, which included miracle plays; and they constructed a wealth of religious fabric, which housed sacred music and shrines that could attract huge numbers of pilgrims-cum-tourists. The Reformation dealt a serious blow to this cultural heritage and threatened to undermine the town's role as a centre of cultural production. Revival of a sort is evident in late Tudor and early Stuart London, which accommodated a series of flourishing theatres and supported an outstanding group of innovative playwrights (Gurr 2004; Hall 1999: 114–158). However, outside the metropolis, which was quite exceptional is size and influence, creativity and the cultural economy were less evident, and in this context the urban cultural renaissance of the long eighteenth century, which affected a wide range of towns,[3] looks impressive. But did it mark a watershed in laying the foundations for the modern urban cultural economy, or at least represent the beginnings of a process that was to culminate in this? On the face of it the evidence is persuasive. First, there was the sheer volume of new cultural output in the eighteenth century, and in forms that we would find recognizable today, such as theatre, musical concerts and sports. Second, much of this was delivered on a new-found commercial basis, leading to the »economizing« of cultural production and the growth of the overtly cultural sector in the urban economy. Third, print culture expanded very rapidly, and included the establishment of a permanent newspaper press and growth in educational literature in the broadest sense. This provided not only a source of cultural consumption in its own right, but also – through its role in advertising, reporting and informing – stimulated and structured the nature of cultural consumption as a whole, and anticipated the role of the media in this respect in modern society. Fourth, the emergence of the shop not just as a point of sale but also display and resort, highlighted not only the growth in the number of luxury items on sale with a large »cultural« content, but also the role of retail outlets in giving meaning to products, and

---

3   For the debate on how widespread see Borsay and McInnes 1990: 189–202; Sweet 1999: 251–255.

the development of shopping as a recreation in its own right. This could be said to have foreshadowed several of the innovations in retailing of the nineteenth century, including the emergence of the department store and what has been called »shopping for pleasure« (Rappaport 2000). Fifth, transformations in the built environment of towns introduced a style of architecture, classicism, that emphasized the cultural content of buildings – partly through the use of printed pattern books – and was internationalist in perspective, anticipating the globalisation of culture. Sixth, the creation and spatial dissemination of cultural products was critically facilitated by the emergence of London as a mega-metropolis and truly global capital (Ogborn 1998). Much of this rested on its role at the centre of a rapidly developing British state and empire. Seventh, forms of urban culture began to emerge in British towns, based on heritage, tourism and absorption of the countryside, that presaged developments in recreational travel and leisure associated to day with the so-called »cultural industries« (Borsay 2006: 167–191). Eighth, a new form of town emerged devoted to health and leisure, the spa and seaside resort. This reflected a growing differentiation in urban function between and within towns, and it could be argued was part of a process that sought to separate leisure from work, and cultural from non-cultural forms of activity. Finally, many of the changes outlined here were underpinned by an ethos that might broadly be associated with the notion of Enlightenment, with its emphasis on civility and sociability, improvement, secular values and universalism. To the extent that the Enlightenment is to be seen as the cradle of modernity (Lyon 1996: 19; Hollinger 1994: 1–20), and the Enlightenment was an urban phenomenon, then the eighteenth-century town was a forcing-house for developments of a long-term significance.

However, we should not get carried away in this pursuit of the modern. There was an urban cultural economy in Britain before the late seventeenth century, and many of the so-called innovations had precedents. Indeed, the forces of the past continued to exert a considerable presence in the long eighteenth century, and some observers have argued that the factors that underpinned the ›old society‹ in England *strengthened* in the period (Clark 1985). Each of the points made drawing out the connections with the modern cultural economy could be easily critiqued, and the sheer scale of changes ahead – as a consequence of intensive urbanisation and industrialisation – brought new dimensions to the notion of a cultural economy. Moreover, the changes which I have been describing were in the eighteenth century concentrated in a fairly narrow sector of society, so that arrival of modernity – if that is what is being witnessed – was socially selective. The concept of modernity and its chronology are highly debateable issues (Ogborn 1998: 1–38). The argument is further complicated by the fact that for some commentators the cultural economy only truly came of age in the late twentieth century under the impact of post-Fordist economics and *post*-modernism. Lash and Urry have argued that »What is increasingly produced are not material objects, but *signs*. These signs are of two types. Either they have a primarily cognitive content and are post-industrial [...] Or they have primarily an aesthetic content and are what may be termed postmodern goods.« (Lash and Urry 1994: 4) However, rather than looking for a single definition of the cultural economy, or engaging in the construction of a progressivist history by which the economy is for ever becoming more and more a vehicle for culture and the aesthetic, it may be better to recognize that different types of societies and eras create different forms of cultural economy (reflecting, for example, variations in social and political structure, levels and distribution of wealth, and attitudes towards religion, magic, and science), and to focus on the conditions and milieus – such as the growth of cities and towns – that shape the processes of creation.

Bibliography

Ayres, James (1998). *Building the Georgian City*. New Haven/London.
Barry, Jonathan and Christopher Brooks (eds.) (1994). *The Middling Sort of People: Culture, Society and Politics in England, 1550–1800*. Basingstoke.
Berg, Maxime (2005). *Luxury and Pleasure in Eighteenth-century Britain*. Oxford.
Bermingham, Ann and John Brewer (eds.) (1995). *The Consumption of Culture: Word, Image and Object in the Seventeenth and Eighteenth Centuries*. London.
Black, Jeremy (1987). *The English Press in the Eighteenth Century*. Beckenham.
— (2005). *A Subject for Taste: Culture in Eighteenth-century England*. London.
Borsay, Peter (1989). *The English Urban Renaissance: Culture and Society in the Provincial Town, 1660–1770*. Oxford, 1989.
Borsay, Peter (ed.) (1990). *The Eighteenth-Century Town: A Reader in English Urban History 1688–1820*. Harlow.
— (2000a). »Health and leisure resorts 1700–1840«. In Peter Clark (ed.), *The Cambridge Urban History of Britain*, Vol. II, 775–803. Cambridge.

— (2000b). *The Image of Georgian Bath 1700–2000: Towns, Heritage and History*. Oxford.
— (2001). »London, 1660–1800: a distinctive culture?«. In Peter Clark and Raymond Gillespie (eds.). *Two Capitals: London and Dublin 1500–1840*, Proceedings of the British Academy 107, 167–184, Oxford.
— (2002). »The culture of improvement«. In Paul Langford (ed.). *The Short Oxford History of the British Isles: the Eighteenth Century*, 183–210. Oxford.
— (2003). »Politeness and elegance: the cultural re-fashioning of eighteenth-century York«. In Mark Hallett and Jane Rendall (eds.). *Eighteenth-Century York: Culture, Space and Society*, Borthwick Text and Calendar 30, 1–12. York.
— (2006). *A History of Leisure: the British Experience since 1500*. Basingstoke.
— and Angus McInnes (1990). »Debate: the emergence of a leisure town: or an urban renaissance?«. *Past and Present*, 126, 189–202.
Boyce, Benjamin (1967). *The Benevolent Man: A Life of Ralph Allen of Bath*. Cambridge, Mass.
Braudel, Fernand (1974). *Capitalism and Material Life 1400–1800*, transl. M. Kochan. London.
Brewer, John (1997). *The Pleasures of the Imagination: English Culture in the Eighteenth Century*. London.
— and Roy Porter (eds.) (1993). *Consumption and the World of Goods in the Seventeenth and Eighteenth Centuries*. London.
Brown, Andrew (ed.) (1999). *The Rows of Chester: The Chester Rows Research Project*. London.
Carter, Philip (2001). *Men and the Emergence of Polite Society: Britain 1660–1800*. Harlow.
Chalkin, Christopher (2001). *The Rise of the English Town 1650–1850*. Cambridge.
Clark, Jonathan C. D. (1985), *English Society 1688–1832: Ideology, Social Structure and Political Practice during the Ancien Regime*. Cambridge.
Clark, Peter (ed.) (1995). *Small Towns in Early Modern Europe*. Cambridge.
— (2000a). *British Clubs and Societies, 1580–1800: the Origins of an Associational World*. Oxford.
— (ed.) (2000b). *The Cambridge Urban History of Britain*, Volume II, 1540–1840. Cambridge.
— (2000c). »Small towns 1700–1840«. In Peter Clark (ed.), *The Cambridge Urban History of Britain*, Vol. II. , 733–773, Cambridge.
— and R. A. Houston (2000). »Culture and leisure 1700–1840«. In Peter Clark (ed.). *The Cambridge Urban History of Britain*, Vol. II, 575–613. Cambridge.
Coleman, Donald C. (1977). *The Economy of England 1450–1750*. Oxford.
Colvin, Howard (1995). *A Bibliographical Dictionary of British Architects 1600–1840*. 3rd edition, New Haven/London.
Connely, Willard (1955). *Beau Nash: Monarch of Bath and Tunbridge Wells*. London.
Corbin, Alain (1994). *The Lure of the Sea*, trans. J. Phelps. Cambridge.

Corfield, Penelope J. and Serena Kelly (1984). »»Giving directions to the town«: the early town directories«. *Urban History Yearbook*, 22–35.

— (1987). »Small towns, large implications: social and cultural roles of small towns in eighteenth-century England and Wales«. *British Journal for Eighteenth-Century Studies*, 10, 125–138.

Cox, Nancy (2000). *The Complete Tradesman: a Study of Retailing, 1550–1820*. Aldershot.

Cranfield, G.A. (1962). *The Development of the Provincial Newspaper 1700–1760*. Oxford.

Cruickshank, Dan (1985). *A Guide to the Georgian Buildings of Britain and Ireland*. London.

— and Neil Burton (1990). *Life in the Georgian City*. London.

Dain, Angela (2001). »Assemblies and politeness 1660–1840«. Ph.D thesis, University of East Anglia.

Defoe, Daniel (1970). *The Complete English Tradesman*, first published 1725–1727, 1745 edition reprinted, New York.

Dyer, Alan (2000). »Small market towns 1540–1700«. In Peter Clark (ed.). *The Cambridge Urban History of Britain*, Vol. II, 425–450. Cambridge.

— (2002). »Small towns in England, 1600–1800«. In Peter Borsay and Lindsay Proudfoot (eds.). *Provincial Towns in Early Modern England and Ireland: Change, Convergence and Divergence*, Proceedings of the British Academy 108, 53–67. Oxford.

Elliot, James (1987). *The City in Maps: Urban Mapping to 1800*. London.

Ellis, Aytoun (1956). *The Penny Universities: A History of Coffee Houses*. London.

Ellis, Joyce M. (2001). *The Georgian Town 1680–1840*. Basingstoke.

Ellis, Markman (2004). *The Coffee House, a Cultural History*. London.

Falkus, Malcolm E. (1976). »Lighting in the Dark Ages of English economic history: town streets before the Industrial Revolution«. In Donald C. Coleman and A. H. John (eds.). *Trade, Government and Economy in Pre-industrial England*, 248–273. London.

Fawcett, Trevor (1979). *Music in Eighteenth-Century Norwich and Norfolk*, Norwich.

— (1990). »Eighteenth-century shops and the luxury trade«. *Bath History*, 3, 49–75.

Fawcett, Trevor and Marta Inskipp (1994). »The making of Orange Grove«. *Bath History*, 5, 24–50.

Fiennes, Celia (1947). *The Journeys of Celia Fiennes*, edited by Christopher Morris. London.

Girouard, Mark (1990). *The English Town*. London/New Haven.

Glennie, Paul and Ian Whyte (2000), »Towns in an agrarian economy 1540–1700«. In Peter Clark (ed.). *Cambridge Urban History of Britain*, Vol. II, 167–193. Cambridge.

Gomme, Andor (2000). *Smith of Warwick: Francis Smith, Architect and Master-builder*. Stamford.

Gurr, Andrew (2004). *Playgoing in Shakespeare's London*, 3rd edition, Cambridge.

Hall, Peter (1999). *Cities in Civilisation: Culture, Innovation and the Urban Order.* London.

Heal, Felicity and Clive Holmes (1994). *The Gentry in England and Wales, 1500–1700.* Basingstoke.

Hembry, Phyllis (1990). *The English Spa 1560–1815: a Social History.* London.

Hollinger, Robert (1994). *Postmodernism and the Social Sciences: A Thematic Approach.* London.

Holmes, Geoffrey (1982). *Augustan England: Professions, State and Society, 1680–1730.* London.

Hyde, Ralph (1985). *Gilded Scenes and Shining Prospects: Panoramic Views of British Towns 1575–1900.* New Haven.

Innes, Joanna and Nicholas Rogers (2000). »Politics and government 1700–1840«. In Peter Clark (ed.). *The Cambridge Urban History of Britain,* Vol. II, 529–574. Cambridge.

Jones, Eric L. and Malcolm E. Falkus (1990). »Urban improvement and the English economy« in the seventeenth and eighteenth centuries«. In Peter Borsay (ed.). *The Eighteenth-Century Town: A Reader in English Urban History, 1688–1820,* 116–158. Oxford.

Kaufman, Paul (1967). »The community library: a chapter in social history«. *Transactions of the American Philosophical Society,* new series, 57, 7.

Langford, Paul (1989). *A Polite and Commercial People: England 1727–1783.* Oxford.

Langton, John (2000). »Urban growth and economic change: from the late seventeenth century to 1841«. In Peter Clark (ed.). *The Cambridge Urban History of Britain,* Vol. II, 453–490. Cambridge.

Lash, Scott and John Urry (1994). *Economies of Signs and Space.* London.

Lyon, David (1996). *Postmodernity,* reprinted. Buckingham.

McIntyre, Sylvia (1981). »Bath: the rise of a resort town, 1660–1800«. In Peter Clark (ed.). *Country Towns in Pre-industrial England,* 198–249. Leicester.

McKendrick, Neil, John Brewer and J. H. Plumb (1983). *The Birth of a Consumer Society: The Commercialisation of Eighteenth-Century England.* London.

McVeigh, Simon (1993). *Concert Life in London from Mozart to Haydn.* Cambridge.

Morgan, Paul (1947–1948). »Early booksellers, printers, and publishers in Stratford-upon-Avon«. *Transactions of the Birmingham Archaeological Society,* 67 (1947–1948), 55–70.

Mowl, Tim and Brian Earnshaw (1988). *John Wood: Architect of Obsession.* Bath.

Ogborn, Miles (1998). *Spaces of Modernity: London's Geographies, 1680–1780.* New York/London.

Plumb, J. H. (1973). *The Commercialisation of Leisure in Eighteenth-century England.* Reading.

Pollard, S. and D. W. Crossley (1968). *The Wealth of Britain 1085–1966.* London.

Porter, Roy (1994). *London: A Social History.* Harmondsworth.

Porter, Stephen (1996). *The Great Fire of London.* Stroud.

Powell, Martyn J. (2005). *The Politics of Consumption in Eighteenth-Century Ireland*. Basingstoke.

Rappaport, Erike Diane (2000). *Shopping for Pleasure: Women in the Making of London's West End*. Princeton/Oxford.

Reddaway, T. F. (1951). *The Rebuilding of London after the Great Fire*. London.

Rosenheim, James M. (1998). *The Emergence of a Ruling Order: English Landed Society 1650–1750*. London.

Schofield, John and Geoffrey Stell (2000). »The built environment 1300–1540«. In David Palliser (ed.). *The Cambridge Urban History of Britain*, Vol. I, *600–1540*, 371–393. Cambridge.

Scott, Allen J. (2000). *The Cultural Economy of Cities: Essays on the Geography of Image-producing Industries*. London.

Slack, Paul (2000). »Great and good towns 1540–1700«. In Peter Clark (ed.). *The Cambridge Urban History of Britain*, Vol. II, 347–376. Cambridge.

Solkin, David H. (1992). *Painting for Money: The Visual Arts and the Public Sphere in Eighteenth-century England*. New Haven/London.

Spadafora, D. (1990). *The Idea of Progress in Eighteenth-century Britain*. New Haven/London.

Stobart, Jon (1998). »Shopping streets as social space: leisure, consumerism and improvements in an eighteenth-century town«. *Urban History*, 25, 1998, 3–21.

— (2007). *Spaces of Consumption: Leisure and Shopping in the English Town, c. 1680–1830*. Abingdon.

Summerson, John (1949). »John Wood and the English town-planning tradition«. In John Summerson. *Heavenly Mansions*, 87–109. London.

— (1966). *Inigo Jones*. Harmondsworth.

Sweet, Rosemary (1997). *The Writing of Urban Histories in Eighteenth-century England*. Oxford.

— (1999). *The English Town 1680–1840: Government, Society and Culture*. Harlow.

Walton, John K. (1983). *The English Seaside Resort: A Social History 1750–1914*. Leicester.

Weber, William (1992). *The Rise of Musical Classics in Eighteenth-century England: A Study in Canon, Ritual and Ideology*. Oxford.

Wiles, R. M. (1965). *Freshest Advices: Early Provincial Newspapers in England*. Columbus, Ohio.

Williamson, F. (1936). »George Sorocold, of Derby: a pioneer of water supply«, *Journal of the Derbyshire Archaeological and Natural History Society*, new series, 10, 57, 43–93.

Wollenberg, Susan and Simon McVeigh (eds.) (2004). *Concert Life in Eighteenth-century Britain*. Aldershot.

Wragg, Brian (2000). *The Life and Works of John Carr of York*, edited by Giles Worsley. York.

Wroth, Warwick (1979). The London Pleasure Gardens of the Eighteenth Century, reprinted. Michigan/London.

2   The Nineteenth and Twentieth
    Century: The Question of
    Anticipation of Today's Cultural
    Economies

»How Manchester is Amused«: The Cultural Economy of the Industrial City, 1860 – 1920

Simon Gunn

»We might deck ourselves out resplendently and visit Mr Hallé at the Concert Hall; we might sit up aloft in the gallery at the Queen's, or settle ourselves in the somewhat dusty and fusty stalls at the Theatre Royal; we might be ›free and easy‹ in the regions of Rochdale Road or Deansgate [...] For there are amusements and Amusements, and every type of entertainment will claim, in its turn, the attention of the FREELANCE.« (The Manchester Freelance, founding editorial, December 22, 1866, p. 5)

Like other provincial cities in Britain, cultural activity has played a major part in the social and economic regeneration of Manchester since the 1980s; »Madchester«, the gay village, the construction of the new Bridgewater Concert Hall and the Urbis museum are testaments to this cultural rejuvenation. The costly makeover of the city centre stands in ambivalent relationship to Manchester's past; while it gestures to certain aspects of the city's heritage – industrial, musical, and so on – its purpose is also to draw a line under that past, to detach a present of dizzying consumerism from a long history of economic decline and perceived cultural marginality (Deas 1999; Mellor 1997; Taylor I. et al. 1996). Such a stunted perspective, however, raises questions about the origins of the cultural economy in cities like Manchester. In this chapter I shall argue that the renaissance of the last two decades of the twentieth century had its antecedents in the emergence of a night-life and a »cultural quarter« in Manchester in the last third of the nineteenth century, between the 1860s and the early 1900s. In important respects recent attempts at culture-led regeneration have, wittingly or not, replicated certain features of an earlier historical phase of urban culture, even as they have worked to erase other aspects of Manchester's past.

Why might this case be of interest beyond the shores of Britain, in a European context? Firstly, the size and scale alone of late Victorian Manchester rendered it significant. The city that Friedrich Engels had consecrated as the »first manufacturing city of the world« in the 1840s did not cede its pre-eminence easily: with a population of over one and a quarter million in 1900, it was the sixth biggest city in Europe, and the largest that was not also a capital (Engels 1987: 92; Hohenberg and Lees 1996: 11). Throughout the mid- and later Victorian decades it continued to represent the quintessential city of the industrial revolution, not least abroad where the neologism *Manchestertum* evoked a whole ethos.[1] *Kultur* did not form part of this ethos, of course; in England as elsewhere, industrialism and art were assumed to be antithetical. Thus a reviewer for *Blackwood's Edinburgh Magazine* in 1821 professed astonishment at the book of Manchester poetry he had been sent: »There is something in the very name which puts to flight all poetical associations«.[2] That this charge was wide of the mark, that the industrial bourgeoisie of cities like Manchester were involved in the patronage of all types of culture, has been demonstrated by a succession of studies over the last twenty years. Painting, sculpture, architecture, interior design, literary fiction, choral and symphonic music were only some of the art forms that flourished in Victorian Manchester (Archer 1985; Kennedy 1960; McLeod 1996; Seed 1988; Vicinus 1973). Nevertheless, »culture« has normally been studied in segmented ways, »high« or »popular«, and in relation to specific forms, such as music, fine art and literature. In this respect as much as in the separation of »culture« from »economy« historical studies have reproduced the hierarchies and disciplinary divisions of the later nineteenth century. This chapter consequently marks a departure from the norm in attempting to understand public culture as an integrated whole and to assess its spatial and economic dimensions.[3] My concern is with the emergence of a »cultural economy« defined as a coherent, public commercialized sphere of art and entertainment run predominantly on capitalist lines, entry to which was based on cash payment. Elements of this formation had existed at an earlier period in Britain, in places such as eighteenth-century London, but they were not capitalized at the same level, did not encompass such wide sections of the urban population as paying consumers, and did not occupy such a distinctive spatial and financial place within the urban economy (Brewer 1997). Although the main focus will be on the

---

1 The term *Manchestertum* seems to have been coined in Germany in the 1850s, evoking (usually negatively) the Cobdenite combination of free trade, *laisser faire* and (non-patriotic) pacifism. In socialist discourse especially it seems also to have stood for the bourgeoisie.

2 »Manchester poetry«. *Blackwood's Edinburgh Magazine*, IX, April 1821, 64.

3 Though recent studies of leisure (as opposed to culture) have also sought to eschew the high/low division: see for example Borsay 2006.

formative period between 1860 and 1900, in the conclusion I shall attempt to follow through trends over a longer period to gauge change and persistence in the cultural economy over time.

The Origins of the Cultural Economy

As we have just observed, prior to the mid-nineteenth century Manchester was not noted for its cultural life. Even W. Cooke Taylor, generally taken to be an apologist both for Manchester and the factory system, reported in 1842:»It is essentially a place of business, where pleasure is unknown as a pursuit, and amusements scarcely rank as secondary considerations« (Cooke Taylor 1842: 10). In this regard Manchester was little different from other towns and cities outside London, where polite culture ranked relatively low in the order of priorities behind business, often being confined to particular groups (the gentry, urban notables) and times of year (festivals, the »season«) (Borsay 1999; Money 1977). At Taylor's time of writing there existed nevertheless an established network of institutions and associations of polite culture in Manchester. They included scientific and learned societies, concerts and assemblies, subscription libraries, social clubs and art exhibitions (Kargon 1977; Seed 1988; Stancliffe 1938). More dense still, of course, was the undergrowth of institutions of popular culture, from the »free and easy« to the temperance association (Hewitt 1996; Joyce 1994). In 1849 the journalist Angus Bethune Reach noted how the streets around the Apollo music saloon were filled with the sounds of itinerant musicians, organ grinders and ballad singers, while »the melodious burst of a roaring chorus, surging out of the open windows of the Apollo, resounds loudly above the whole conglomeration of street noises« (Kidd 1996: 52).

However, if we restrict our perspective to bourgeois or »high« culture before the 1850s, then three characteristics are evident. Firstly, the associations of culture were private or semi-private: access could only be obtained by election and/or subscription. Of the Gentleman's Concerts in the early 1850s the musician and impresario Charles Hallé observed in his *Autobiography*, they were »an exclusive society. None but subscribers were admitted and no tickets sold« (Kennedy 1972: 138). Secondly, such bodies were non profit-making, albeit separate from rather than opposed to the market.

Thirdly, the majority of cultural associations tended to have no dedicated building or physical space; meetings were peripatetic, taking place in hotels or even pubs.[4] Especially in its more respectable and bourgeois manifestations, then, culture remained for the most part a private and exclusive affair. Hence Richard Cobden's celebrated attack on Manchester's unreformed government in 1838, in the name of the »shopocracy«, extended from the city's political to its social and cultural institutions: »The tone which has so long prevailed in the government of the town has naturally enough pervaded all our institutions [...] and the retailer would find it, probably, almost as difficult to obtain admission to our clubs and our concerts, as he might to obtain the privilege of *entré* to the Queen's court« (Cobden 1838). Consequently, it is difficult to speak of a cultural economy in anything more than a very partial and limited sense in Manchester in the early and mid-nineteenth century.

From the early 1860s, however, this situation began to change. The Manchester Art Treasures Exhibition of 1857, the fine arts equivalent of the Great Exhibition of 1851 and attracting over a million visitors, is often taken to be the catalyst but its effects were transitory (Finke 1985). More important locally, and arising out of the Art Treasures event, was the foundation of the Hallé concerts which were to become a regular feature of Manchester cultural life by the 1860s. The Hallé was the first permanent, professional orchestra in Britain and its annual season of grand concerts, held during the winter months, rapidly became »one of the institutions of Manchester«, as a local periodical put it in 1868, a miraculous conjunction of high culture and high society: the concert hall on Hallé night was reported to be »the most gorgeous and dazzling sight that is anywhere to be seen in Manchester at one glance«.[5] It was a position at the peak of the city's cultural life that the Hallé was to maintain for the next half-century and it helped to ensure that as early as 1861 the city possessed the largest number of professional musicians of any urban place outside London (Russell 2000). The Hallé attracted new audiences to the classical music concert, clerks, teachers and even manual workers on occasions such as the annual *Messiah*, alongside the elite families of the city and region.

---

4   This was not the case with some bodies such as the Royal Manchester Institution (1823), the Gentlemen's Concert Hall (1830) and the Manchester Athenaeum (1835) but even here the buildings tended to be multi-purpose, not the home of a single association.

5   The Freelance, January 5, 1867 and January 4, 1868.

Fig. 1: Theatreland. Peter Street in 1890

(*Source: Manchester Central Library Collections*)

But as the quotation from *The Freelance* which prefaces this paper suggests, the expansion of »amusements« in the 1860s, both high and low, went well beyond the Hallé. Two new theatres, the Prince's and the Queen's, joined the Theatre Royal, the Gentlemen's Concert Hall and the Free Trade Hall in Peter Street. Music halls, including large-scale, purpose-built venues, such as the Alexandra and the London, likewise opened in the central area; in 1868 it was estimated that some 15,000 people flocked to these new »palaces« on any one night, not to mention the myriad small and generally less respectable halls in working-class districts. Factory workers, warehousmen, counting-house clerks and shop workers were all reported as making up the audiences for the new commercial entertainments.[6] From the late 1860s, moreover, substantial new club-houses were under construction in Manchester, some political, others purely social, each with memberships ranging from several hundred to several thousand (Anon. 1888; Mills 1921). Connected to these or independent, there had also

6   Freelance, 25 January 1868.

sprung up a growing number of restaurants and dining rooms.[7] As a result, by the 1870s it was possible for the first time to view Manchester as having a night life. In this chronology Manchester did not necessarily lag behind European capitals like London, Paris and Berlin that were themselves only developing the institutional infrastructure of a night life in these years (Nead 2000; Schlör 1998; Spang 2002).

The public culture that emerged from the 1860s differed from that which preceded it in several respects. Firstly, it was based on cash payment rather than election or subscription. Contemporaries noted the shift, commenting favourably for example on the contrast between the Hallé, where tickets could be purchased for individual concerts, and the older Gentlemen's Concerts, where entrance was only available through membership and ballot.[8] Secondly, activity tended to be located in purpose-built premises, such as palaces of variety, club-houses, theatres and concert halls. Much popular entertainment continued to be conducted on the street, of course, from music-making to the institution of the Sunday night »monkey parade«, but even this became part of the city's living panorama for bourgeois »bohemians« no less than for workers and the poor.[9] By the 1870s, indeed, all sections of the city's population seem to have become habituated to a weekly routine of entertainment: Thursday night was »Hallé night«, Friday the fashionable theatre night, Saturday and Sunday evenings the pre-eminent times for popular amusements and street revelry. Entertainments were classified by status and taste, of course, but the boundaries between them were less rigid in practice than in theory; factory hands swelled the ranks of the »shilling freeholders« at the Hallé concerts while »bohemians« and »swells« revelled in Manchester's proletarian street life. When one considers that audiences at concerts and theatres could themselves run into many thousands, quite apart from those at the musical hall and social clubs, the numbers involved in Manchester's cultural economy by this period were very substantial, the city acting as a magnet for the region. In institutional terms, too, culture and entertainment mushroomed in these years. Around 1890 it was estimated that the city contained some 400 licensed music halls and over 3,000 licensed drinking establishments[10],

7   See for instance »The dining rooms of Manchester«. *The Freelance*, February 16, 1867;
     »Dining in town«. *City Lantern*, October 30, 1874.
8   »On Union club snobbery«. *City Jackdaw*, March 15, 1878, 143.
9   »Sunday night in Oldham Street«. *Comus*, February 14, 1878; Eva 1996.
10   *Manchester Guardian*, September 9, 1892.

while the city guides and directories listed over twenty theatres (ranging from variety to Shakespeare), two concert halls and eleven social clubs (Anon. 1888; Tomlinson 1887). In effect, in the three decades after 1860s it is possible to see something like a modern cultural economy developing in Manchester, public, mass-based and increasingly organised according to the precepts of the capitalist market.

The Cultural Quarter and the Cultural Economy

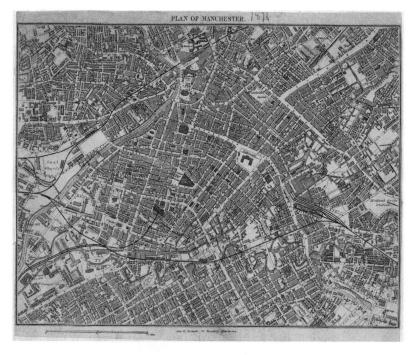

Fig. 2: Map of Central Manchester, 1876 by J.T. Cornish

(Source: Manchester Central Library Collections)

Manchester's burgeoning »culture industry« had a distinct spatial locale from the later 1860s. It was situated within the rectangular heart of the city which had been recognised by commentators such as Engels and Faucher as the central area in the 1840s, and whose extent was to remain virtually unchanged for more than a century thereafter (Engels 1987: 53; Faucher 1844: 17). The main site of theatres, concert halls and some of the larger music halls was Peter Street and Oxford Street, on the central area's western boundary. These streets had access to three of the city's main railways stations, Central, Victoria and Oxford Road, linking the emergent cultural quarter to the wealthy Cheshire suburbs such as Bowdon, Altrincham and Alderley Edge to the south and the Lancashire cotton towns like Bolton, Blackburn and Oldham to the north. As it took shape the cultural quarter was close to the headquarters of banking and business in King Street and Spring Gardens and to the locus of fashionable shopping in St. Ann's Square and the upper end of Deansgate. It was also contiguous with »clubland«, an area based in and around Mosley Street. At its lower end Oxford Street turned into Oxford Road, where another significant cultural institution, Owen's College, later the Victoria University of Manchester, was sited from 1873.

There were historical antecedents for the activities associated with each of these urban locales. But the functional specialisation of Manchester was augmented in the 1860s by escalating investment in the urban infrastructure of the central area. Some measure of the scale of this investment – contemporaneous with the radical reconstruction of central London but unprecedented in the provincial centres at any earlier period – is suggested by evidence of soaring land values. Estimates at the time indicated that both annual rental and rateable values in the township of Manchester – the heart of the city – rose by 40 percent in the single decade 1861–1871 (Baker 1873). Taking a slightly longer term view, government statistics show the rateable value of property in the combined boroughs of Manchester and its satellite, Salford, as rising by 324 percent between 1847 and 1882. By the latter date Manchester and Salford had the highest gross valuation of any urban area outside London.[11] These rises were not simply the product of industrial and commercial property. While the imposing new warehouses in the southern district of the central area undoubtedly contributed to a substantial part of the increase, mills and industrial works were mostly sited outside this area by the period. The remainder of the rise was thus accounted for by investment in the public, retail and broadly cultural institutions that came to characterize central Manchester.

---

11 *British Parliamentary Papers*, vol. lvi (1886), 377–378.

As Arthur Redford, one of the earliest authorities on Manchester's history, recognised, the prosperity of the decades after 1850s represented an »Age of New Gold«, the most striking testament to which was the regeneration of the city centre (Redford 1940). Renovation extended from the construction of lavish new buildings, including the new Royal Exchange (the »parliament of the lords of cotton«), churches and club-houses, to the makeover of whole streets, such as Deansgate. Much of the building was funded privately: the Royal Exchange, the Free Trade Hall and the political club-houses, for instance, were private concerns, run by tight syndicates of Manchester businessmen motivated by a mixture of profit and »public spirit«.[12] The occurrence of specialisation, without any trace of Haussmannian planning, was widely noted at the period, the *Manchester City News* commenting on the »clustering of trades in particular areas of the city«, barristers in St. James' Square, bankers in King Street, silk mercers and other »ladies shops« in St. Ann's Square.[13] Especially significant was the proximity of the cultural quarter to what by the later 1860s was already being proposed as Manchester's civic heart, Albert Square, complete with memorials, statuary and, from 1877, the massive neo-Gothic town hall. For while the Corporation benefited from informal association with the Hallé, chief emblem of Manchester's urban culture, the larger music and variety halls were crucially dependent on the city magistracy for licences to show entertainment and sell drink (Waters 1986). The civic-cultural complex of the later Victorian period was thus a specific form of public/private partnership comprising, in broadly equal measure, profit-led investment, elite patronage and Corporation initiative. It was from these elements that an urban public sphere was created at the heart of Victorian cities, in tandem with a modern cultural economy.

The emergence of a cultural economy in Manchester during the 1860s and 1870s, therefore, was closely linked to other contemporaneous domains of symbolic and financial investment: in consumerism (shops, department stores), in transport (new and upgraded railway stations, special »Hallé trains«) and in the civic (the provision of public libraries and, from 1882, of a municipal art gallery). It was likewise intimately connected to the growth of the local press as a mass medium, in which the discussion of culture and leisure became a staple theme. By the early 1860s concert pro-

---

12 The development of building projects can be followed in the Victorian periodical, *The Builder*.

13 *Manchester City News*, March 16, 1872; see also *Freelance*, November 2, 1867.

moters were sending free tickets to the editors of the city's three daily newspapers, to ensure reviews in the following morning's edition.[14] The emergence of the Manchester periodical press in the late 1860s and early 1870s, featuring titles as *The Sphinx*, *Comus* and *City Jackdaw*, was itself premised on the opening up of a new world of urban leisure on which the journals thrived.

Typical was the *Freelance*, which styled itself »a Journal of Humour and Criticism, Political, Municipal, Social, Literary and Artistic«, but whose priorities were announced in its first issue in December 1866 with the start of a weekly feature, »How Manchester is Amused«. By the late 1880s Manchester boasted four daily papers, one evening and 26 weeklies, and had become the major press and publishing centre outside London.[15]

The local press, the periodicals especially, was fascinated with the cultural life of the city, exhibited in institutions and public places. Figures such as the »urban rambler«, the »street philosopher« and the »bohemian« all featured routinely in reportage, which covered the kaleidoscope of urban events from the Christmas *Messiah* at the Free Trade Hall to the weekly promenades on the city's squares and streets (Gunn 2000: 66–78). The effect of such criticism was ambiguous. On the one hand, it worked to classify cultural forms, to elaborate a hierarchy of »high« and »low«, the »sublime« qualities of the Hallé, for instance, contrasted with the »vulgarity« of the singing saloon and the »viciousness« of the working-class tavern (Gunn 1997: 219–221). On the other hand, by reporting the variety of »amusements«, including the music hall and the singing saloon, and describing them in picaresque and sometimes lurid detail, the journals inevitably ended up promoting them and the domain of culture, both »high« and popular, as a whole. Tensions between moral puritanism and bohemian toleration were thus played out in the columns of the local papers, and even within individual articles (Huggins and Mangan 2004). At the same time, the city press was an integral part of the cultural economy, which it indeed helped to bring into being.

How, then, was culture financed? In the case of »high« culture, the idea of art as sealed off from and antithetical to the values of the market was

14 *Minutes of the Concert Hall General Committee*, February 9, 1863, Henry Watson Music Library, Manchester.
15 *Freelance*, December 22, 1866: 1 and 6; figures from Anon. 1888.

vociferously promulgated by artists themselves and the press.[16] But this was always a partial view. Fine art, it was true, had long been supported by private subscriptions and public patronage, and the tradition was continued with Corporation-sponsorship of the City Art Gallery opened in 1882 in Mosley Street on the edge of the cultural quarter, funded by gifts from private benefactors, cotton magnates like Henry Lee and professionals like the architect Thomas Worthington, and the rates (Manchester City Art Gallery 1984; Seed 1988). Music on the other hand was left largely to the market. The Hallé concerts were Hallé's private property, though underwritten in case of losses by a group of guarantors including members of the German merchant elite, such as Salis Schwabe and Gustav Behrens, together with industrialists like the cotton spinner and Conservative MP Sir William Houldsworth. But the accounts show the concerts to have continuously made profit from the 1862 through to Charles Hallé's death in 1895. Hallé himself always considered the orchestra a commercial enterprise, employing agents to market the concerts and to set up rigorous nationwide touring schedules.[17] Unsurprisingly, music hall was organised on still more commercial lines, with a handful of impresarios like George Edwardes backed by a large number of small investors; increasingly, too, the halls and »palaces of variety« moved from being private ventures to limited liability companies by the 1890s (Earl 1986: 37–39; Kift 1996). Theatre likewise used the format of an actor-manager or impresario supported by business capital; entertainment was known to be a risky enterprise. The Prince's Theatre in Oxford Street was opened in 1864, for instance, using Charles Calvert as actor-manager with initial capital of £20,000 provided by local businessmen; the Theatre Royal in Peter Street, opened in 1844, under the auspices of the entrepreneur John Knowles and remained Manchester's premier theatre throughout the later Victorian period, becoming a limited liability company in 1875 (Wyke and Rudyard 1994). Characteristically, Knowles was closely connected with the city's business bourgeoisie, sitting on the boards of a variety of joint-stock companies and leaving personal wealth of £60,000 on his death in 1880.[18] It

---

16 Plentiful examples are to be found in the regular reviews of classical music in the *Manchester Guardian*. For useful insights on art and the market more generally see Bourdieu (1993).

17 »Hallé programmes and concert accounts«, mss, Henry Watson Music Library, Manchester.

18 Obituary of John Knowles, Manchester Central Reference Library cuttings, 920.0427301.

was not just music halls that were becoming highly commercialized by the 1870s and 1880s; classical music and drama were also run on strict »business lines«.

Fig. 3: Roof Garden, Midland Hotel, Manchester 1905

(Source: Manchester Central Library Collections)

As this indicates, the development of Manchester's cultural economy was financed for the most part from within the city and Lancashire – external, predominantly London-based funding could prove controversial, as in the case of the Palace of Varieties in 1890–1891 (Waters 1986). More research remains to be done, but the examples cited here suggest that while the individual artist-impresario or entrepreneur remained an important frontman for cultural ventures, he (and it was largely »he«, at least before the advent of Annie Horniman's celebrated Gaiety Theatre as home to England's first permanent repertory company in 1908) was invariably implicated in wider local networks of financial, social and political support. As such, the early cultural economy was a hybrid, located between an older tradition of voluntary association and private subscription, and a newer model of cutting-edge business enterprise epitomised by the use of shareholder capital and the limited liability form. The increasingly confident relationship between culture, consumerism and business by the end of the nineteenth century was strikingly manifested in the construction of the Midland Grand Hotel. Built on Peter Street in the middle of the cultural quarter and opened in 1903, the Midland was Manchester's largest, most modern and lavish hotel. Within it was a purpose-built theatre, seating 1,000 people, where some of the earliest of Annie Horniman's productions were staged as well as variety and opera. The Midland also featured a roof garden, so that in summer it was possible to take tea while listening to the strains of a violin quartet and gazing out over the smog-ridden city. By 1900, one could say, culture was built into the very fabric of consumerism in the industrial metropolis.

Conclusion: The Cultural Economy and the Mechanisms of Change

However, changes were afoot by the early 1900s, the most significant being the dilution of the spatial and social concentration of culture. Between 1900 and 1910 the largest new entertainment venues were built for the most part not on Peter and Oxford Streets but outside the central area altogether, particularly in the large working-class districts to the south and east of the city. They included the Ardwick Green Empire (1904), the Hulme Hippodrome (1905) and the King's Theatre, Longsight (1905), all combining occasional touring theatre shows with a staple diet of variety and music hall; theatres were also established in middle-class suburbs such as the Chorlton Theatre and Winter Gardens (1904), offering »high-class promenade concerts every evening at 7.45« (Wyke and Rudyard 1986: 21). Reviewing Manchester's »amusements« in 1907, the former actor Robert Courtneidge was ambivalent in his verdict, acknowledging the city as a »centre of culture« but criticizing the lack of diversity and innovation in what was on offer. Yet he was still able to list twenty-five »places of amusement« including twelve theatres, eight music halls and two concert halls (Coutneidge 1907: 199–203).

In other respects, however, a major shift did occur in the status and profitability of an older »high« culture in the decades after 1910, apparent in the declining fortunes of some of the city's most celebrated institutions. Annie Horniman's Gaiety Theatre, a standard-bearer for new and avant-garde drama nationally as well as locally, was sold in 1920 and re-opened as a cinema; and laments were made between the wars that even the Hallé concerts had waned in attractiveness and fashionability: »only here or there one of the old guard appeared with a satin or velvet cloak or a white shirt-front« (Gooddie 1990; Chorley 1950: 144). Cultural variety was reduced, as elsewhere, by the rapid spread of cinema with halls and theatres being taken over, especially in the 1920s and early 1930s. In overall terms the numbers of theatres and music halls listed in the directories fell by more than half between 1920 and 1945. The same years also saw the effective dissolution of »clubland«, with shrinking membership, ageing facilities and the closure of many of the more select establishments of the late Victorian period, such as the Bridgewater and Princes clubs. Small wonder, then, that even so sympathetic an observer as the historian A. J. P. Taylor could describe the city as progressively becoming »provincialized« in cultural terms during the first half of the twentieth century, while London reasserted its position as the arts and entertainment capital of the nation (Taylor 1957: 9). This pervasive sense of cultural decline in industrial cities like Manchester was underscored by the material evidence of economic recession in manufacturing after 1918 and, more contentiously, by suggestions of a loss of »natural leadership« as former elites drifted away from local politics and civic engagement (Gunn 2000: 187–197; Hunt 2004: 343–350; Chorley 1950: 138–139).

Fig. 4: The Gentleman's Concert Hall in 1900

(Source: Manchester Central Library Collections)

Extending the timescale of analysis in this way is useful in underlining that there was no linear growth in the cultural economy of English industrial cities like Manchester. Instead, the movement tended to be cyclical, investment in culture and entertainment occurring in waves over particular time-periods and alternating between the tendency to concentration in a specialised cultural quarter and dispersal to sites closer to the populations who comprised the bulk of audiences. Longitudinal statistics for levels of investment in city centre development are limited. However, the impression of later Victorian Manchester is that the city centre underwent a building boom in the 1860s and 1870s, followed by a steady phase in the decades to 1914, with a definite downturn in investment in the inter-war period. This pattern is given some support supported by historical geographers such as J. W. R. Whitehand who have investigated the urban land market in the nineteenth and twentieth centuries. Whitehand, for example, found that although there was some evidence for a later Victorian boom in public and commercial building in British cities, investment in these types of building was generally flatter and more stable over time than that in housebuilding (Whitehand 1987). Such categories, of course, are too broad to allow for specific examination of the cultural and entertainment sectors, but the case of Victorian Manchester strongly suggested that the cultural economy expanded alongside and in tandem with investment in other types of urban infrastructure in the city centre, from railways to civic and business institutions. It was part of a generalized renovation of the city centre. Equally, although economic and political conditions were very different in the 1980s the revitalisation of the cultural economy in late twentieth-century Manchester went hand in glove with a much larger surge of investment in offices, shops and transport (the revived tram system), conducted under the aegis of the Urban Development Corporation (Deas 1999; Mellor 1997).

To conclude, then, the beginnings of Manchester's cultural economy are to be found in the last four decades of the nineteenth century, contemporaneous with both the creation of a bourgeois public culture, hierarchically ordered and based on cash payment rather than subscription, and the development of a »traditional« working-class culture closely aligned with the growth of a capitalist leisure industry (Gunn 2000; Hobsbawm 1984). This simultaneity of developments in high and popular culture is important, indicating the strong economic relationship between »art« and »amusement« in the late Victorian period, even as cultural categories hardened to distinguish between them, not least via the columns of the critics in the press. Moreover, the spatial location of the cultural quarter around Oxford and Peter streets suggested its interaction with other burgeoning domains of consumption, from retail to hotels, as well as with the civic authorities and the iconic image of the city. Though waning for much of the twentieth century, this area remained the focus of Manchester's »theatreland«. Significantly, when the city's new landmark concert hall, the Bridgewater Hall, was built in the 1990s it was in sight of the home of the Hallé, the Free Trade Hall, and the former Gentleman's Concert Hall in Peter Street. The wider programme of culture-led regeneration in the 1980s, it is true, was situated not in this earlier cultural quarter but in the derelict warehouses on the southern edge of the city centre. But as in the previous century it mixed cultural forms, art galleries jostling with bars and dance clubs, and made central Manchester a cultural cynosure for the outer suburbs and satellite towns of the region. Once again, »Madchester« was to presage the return of night-life to England's provincial cities and to challenge, if briefly, the persistent cultural hegemony of London.

What does this tell us more generally about current understandings of the cultural economy? The example of Manchester analysed here suggests less a progressive than a cyclical model of the cultural economy in which the key factors are at least as much local as global. According to this analysis, the modern cultural economy was not the creation of late twentieth-century capitalist globalisation or postmodern consumerism. What mattered in the 1880s no less than in the 1980s was the wave of inward investment that resulted in the rapid renovation of the urban fabric of the city centre by both private and public capital. This was contemporaneous and interlocking with the remaking of the category of »culture« itself, indicated by its new institutional forms, its ability to attract new audiences and its localisation in a particular area of the city. The cultural economy thus appears as the outcome of a periodic interaction between art, the market and the urban environment whose specific features differ historically but whose essential components remain remarkably similar across time.

Bibliography

Anon. (1888). *Manchester of Today*. Manchester.
Archer, J. (ed.) (1985). *Art and Architecture in Victorian Manchester*. Manchester.

Baker, H. (1873). »On the growth of the commercial centre of Manchester«. *Transactions of the Manchester Statistical Society*, Manchester.

Borsay, P. (1999). *The English Urban Renaissance: Culture and Society in the Provincial Town, 1660–1770*. Oxford.

— (2006). *A History of Leisure*. Basingstoke.

Bourdieu, P. (1993). *The Field of Cultural Production*. Cambridge.

Brewer, J. (1997). *The Pleasures of the Imagination: English Culture in the Eighteenth Century*. London.

Chorley, K. (1950). *Manchester Made Them*. London.

Cobden, R. (1838). *Incorporate Your Borough*. Manchester.

Cooke Taylor, W. (1842). *Notes of a Tour in the Manufacturing Districts*. London.

Courtneidge, R. (1907). »The amusements of Manchester«. In C. W. Sutton (ed.). *Manchester of Today*. Manchester.

Deas, I. et al. (1999). »Rescripting urban regeneration, the Mancunian way«. In R. Imrie and H. Thomas (eds.). *British Urban Policy*. London.

Earl, J. (1986). »Building the halls«. In P. Bailey (ed.). *Music Hall: The Business of Pleasure*. Milton Keynes.

Engels, F. (1987 [1844]). *The Condition of the Woirking Class in England in 1844*, edited by V. Kiernan. London.

Eva, P. (1996). »Popular song and social identity in Victorian Manchester«. unpublished PhD diss., University of Manchester.

Faucher, L. (1844). *Manchester in 1844*. London.

Finke, U. (1985). »The Art Treasures exhibition«. In J. H. G. Archer (ed.). *Art and Architecture in Victorian Manchester*. Manchester.

Gooddie, S. (1990). *Annie Horniman: A Pioneer in the Theatre*. London.

Gunn, S. (1997). »The sublime and the vulgar: the Hallé concerts and the constitution of ›high culture‹ in Manchester, c.1850–80«. *Journal of Victorian Culture*, 2, 2, 208–228.

— (2000). *The Public Culture of the Victorian Middle Class*. Manchester.

Hewitt, M. (1996). *The Emergence of Stability in the Industrial City: Manchester, 1832–1867*. Aldershot.

Hobsbawm, E. J. (1984). »The remaking of the working class 1870–1914«. In *Worlds of Labour. Further Studies in the History of Labour*. London.

Hohenberg, P. and Lees, L. (1996). *The Making of Urban Europe*. Cambridge, Mass.

Huggins, M. and J. A. Mangan (2004). *Disreputable Pleasures*. London.

Hunt, T. (2004). *Building Jerusalem*. London.

Joyce, P. (1994). *Democratic Subjects*. Cambridge.

Kargon, R. (1977). *Science in Victorian Manchester*. Baltimore.

Kennedy, M. (ed.) (1972). *The Autobiography of Charles Hallé*. London.

— (1960). *The Hallé Tradition: A Century of Music*. Manchester.

Kidd, A. (1996). *Manchester*. Keele.

Kift, D. (1996). *The Victorian Music Hall*. Cambridge.

Manchester City Art Gallery (1984). *A Century of Collecting, 1882–1982*. Manchester.

McLeod, D. S. (1996). *Art and the Victorian Middle Class*. Cambridge.

Mellor, R. (1997). »Cool times for a changing city«. In N. Jewson and S. Macgregor (eds.). *Transforming Cities*. London.

Mills, W. H. (ed.) (1921). *The Manchester Reform Club, 1871–1921*. Manchester.

Money, J. (1977). *Experience and Identity: Birmingham and the West Midlands, 1760–1800*. Manchester.

Nead, L. (2000). *Victorian Babylon*. London/New Haven.

Redford, A. (1940). *History of Local Government in Manchester. Volume II: Borough and City*. Manchester.

Russell, D. (2000). »Musicians in the provincial English city: Manchester, *c*.1860–1914«. In C. Bashford and L. Langley (eds.). *Music and British Culture, 1785–1914*. Oxford.

Schlör, J. (1998). *Nights in the Big City*. London.

Seed, J. (1988). »Commerce and the liberal arts«: the political economy of art in Manchester, 1775–1860«. In J. Seed and J. Wolff (eds.). *The Culture of Capital*. Manchester.

Spang, R. (2002). *The Invention of the Restaurant*. Cambridge, Mass.

Stancliffe, F.S. (1938). *John Shaw's Club, 1738–1938*. Manchester.

Taylor, A. J. P. (1957). »Manchester«. *Encounter*, 8, 3, March 1957, 1–9.

Taylor, I. et al. (1996). *A Tale of Two Cities. Global Change, Local Feeling and Everyday Life in the North of England: A Study in Manchester and Sheffield*. London.

Tomlinson, W. (1997). *Bye-Ways of Manchester Life*. Manchester.

Vicinus, M. (1973). »The industrial muse: poetry in Victorian Manchester«. In H. J. Dyos and M. Wolff (eds.). *The Victorian City: Image and Reality*. London.

Waters, C. (1986). »Manchester morality and London capital: the battle over the Palace of Varieties«. In P. Bailey (ed.). *Music Hall: The Business of Pleasure*. Milton Keynes.

Whitehand, J. W. R. (1987). *The Changing Face of Cities: A Study of Development Cycles and Urban Form*. Oxford.

Wyke, T. and N. Rudyard (1994). *Manchester Theatres*. Manchester.

Advertisers, Commercial Artists, and Photographers in Twentieth Century Hamburg

Sandra Schürmann

Hamburg has traditionally been known as the leading German harbour city and a centre for overseas trade. However, especially in recent years, it has developed a reputation as a city of the press and media, of advertising and photography. Nowadays, these ›creative‹ branches are considered important components of the city's economy as a whole. The presence of big advertising agencies as well as photography studios is referred to by politicians and officials as proof of their city's economic potential. I will try to historicise this development and show that the key phenomena of cultural economy – i.e., a close interplay of arts and economy – had developed already in the early twentieth century. The economic importance of advertising and photography nonetheless, were not considered self-evident at this early stage. Advertising held an uneasy position in German society in general and especially in Hamburg. Artists and advertising professionals thus perceived Hamburg as a difficult or even hostile environment; even commercial photographers found it hard to earn their living.

So far, historians have rarely investigated creative milieus in Hamburg or linked findings on the development of advertising to their urban settings. The aim of this essay is thus to contextualise local sources and the history of German advertising in order to provide a basis for further research.

The field of work examined underwent various transformations during the twentieth century with regard to techniques and media as well as to the professionals' self-definitions and their public perception. This is also reflected in Hamburg's address books, where advertising professionals offered their services under various headings. Sections for *Reklame* or *Werbung* (both to be translated as advertising), which only emerged on their own in the late 1920s, became an integral part of the yellow pages by the 1930s.

The advertising industry, commercial art and commercial photography developed from older services and the visual arts under the influence of industrialisation. In Hamburg, the latter was invigorated by the city's integration into the German Reich in 1888. Within a few years, it became the second largest industrial region of the German Reich and thus a market for new cultural techniques. Additionally, apart from working for the industry and commerce, creative professionals contributed to the urban economy by providing images for the city's advertising and tourism industry. Advertising and commercial arts are thus examples of a culturalisation of urban economy by means of the production and use of images, while culture on the other hand was economised, when art school graduates increasingly earned their living in the economic sphere.

Advertising and Urban Space

As pointed out by Clemens Wischermann, until the rise of an industrial economy, a moral underpinning in most European economies had posited that ›honourable merchants‹ did not entice customers (Wischermann 2000: 1). The rise of industrial mass production of consumer goods between the 1850s and 1880s had then initiated a »breakthrough period for advertising as a force in competition and consumption« (Wischermann 2000: 9). The example of Hamburg will demonstrate that it took much longer until advertising was widely accepted as a part of the economy and everyday life, not to mention before it was considered a prestigious aspect of urban cultural economy. The ›honourable merchant‹ habitus turned out to be very persistent and influential, at least during the first half of the twentieth century. Many authors referred to this when complaining about poor working conditions for commercial artists in Hamburg.

As public advertising fundamentally changed the appearance of European cities, it became an essential part of the modern city as such. Discourses of urbanity and advertising were closely linked: In the mind of its opponents, advertising was an aspect of uncontrollable urban growth, chaos and over-stimulation. It was denounced for »defacing« the urban scenery with posters and signs. Such statements often expressed »an admixture of incipient environmental awareness and anti-modern hostility to the city« (Wischermann 2000: 12), combined with ideas of *Heimatschutz* (homeland preservation) which were becoming increasingly popular throughout Germany. They could also be heard in Hamburg: As Bärbel

Hedinger wrote, advertising had conquered public space since 1880 »firstly the facades and then also the attics«, the latter via roof letters (Hedinger 1996: 94). Until around the turn of the century, this had been accepted by the general public, probably because it was perceived as reflecting the period of promoterism. When eventually »the facades threatened to disappear behind advertising posters« (ibid.) – i.e., when advertising reached an extent that it was seriously changing the urban scenery – public debate intensified. One outcome was the passage of a building code for Hamburg (*Hamburger Baupflegegesetz*) in 1912. It was widely discussed all over Germany and considered a landmark as »one of the few codes in which the aspects of *Heimatschutz* and modern forms of advertising were coordinated« (ibid.: 94). It is remarkable that leading members of the city's cultural elites took part in the formulation, for example Albert Lichtwark, the Director of the Arts Museums who had dedicated much of his work to the aesthetic education of the public, as well as Justus Brinckmann, the Director of the Arts and Crafts Museum (ibid.: 98). Additionally, the will to ›educate‹ advertising was expressed in seminars for painters and varnishers as well as in an essay published in the journal *Das Plakat* (The Poster). In the essay, which was part of a special issue in 1921 on Hamburg, the city's building authorities promoted their aesthetic norms and educational agenda (Rolffsen 1921).

Unsurprisingly, activities following the building code started in the Alster Arcades right in Hamburg's architectural centre (Hedinger 1996: 99). The arena for the next conflict about advertising and the city was also symbolic: Between 1924 and 1928, Hamburg's newspapers were full of articles about two hotels at the Jungfernstieg (the central boulevard along Alster Lake) which had illuminated their facades contrary to a decision made in 1915 banning such lighting. According to a commentator at the time, the building authorities expressed their wish to protect »the charm of the changing scenery against the strong glare of artificial light«, while their opponents considered this attitude »unprogressive« and demanded a »metropolitan character«. Moreover, both sides believed they were serving tourism which had become an important source of income and prestige in the 1920s (Harbeck 1930, quoted in Hedinger 1996: 101). The case was finally resolved by an arrangement that limited advertising within a certain zone and permitted exceptions upon application (ibid.).

Such debates over advertising in Hamburg brought competing interests to the surface: While business people and advertisers fought against restrictions, political elites and sections of the public tried to preserve their idea of a proper use of urban space. This was not specific to Hamburg, although discussions were based on and enforced by the traditional ›Hanseatic‹ habitus of the local educated middle class (*Bildungsbürgertum*) who put special emphasis on decency and understatement. Cultural and political elites were eager to avoid any obtrusiveness, both in personal behaviour as well as in their city's representation.

In general, German advertisers were able to work in a »relatively laissez-faire atmosphere« during the Weimar Republic (Berghoff 2003: 129). This changed when the National Socialist regime adopted the ›commercial advertising law‹ in September 1933 and created the *Werberat* (advertising council), in order to control all advertising activities (ibid.: 133–134; Wischermann 1995: 376–377). By prohibiting ›ostentatious‹ and ›disparaging‹ advertising, the regime appealed to older discourses (Berghoff 1995: 135) while the exclusion of Jewish and foreign artists as well as the artistic avant-garde from the federation of advertisers (*Reichsverband der Werbetreibenden*) led to a creative decline. After the Second World War, the Central commission of advertising (*Zentralausschuss der Werbewirtschaft*) was established as a mediator between advertisers and society (Wischermann 1995: 378).

The social and political status of advertising in urban space remained controversial after the Second World War – as was reflected in the report from a conference for advertisers' in Hamburg in 1951. For example, in his opening address, the mayor Max Brauer elaborated on the »defacing of the urban scenery« and pointed out that in many German cities tensions were caused by the advertisers' activities. According to Brauer, German cities in general should make sure that their beauty was not destroyed by advertising. Hamburg in particular had a tradition of education in arts and therefore demanded that advertisers – whose profession was »so closely connected to art« – should follow such principles. He also pointed out the need for restrictions: »Go to underdeveloped countries, even go to America, and look at the small towns. Part of their sceneries are completely ruined by senseless and bad advertising.« At the end of his address, Brauer spoke less critically and pointed out the economic relevance of advertising for Hamburg: »We want it to support our exports, our tourism, and our national economy that stimulates our industry.« (Brauer 1951: 34) Another speaker at the same congress acted as Brauer's opponent: John Schlepkow, who had been working as an advertising consultant in Hamburg since the

1920s, complained that building authorities in Germany traditionally had a »hostile attitude towards advertising and economy«. According to him, the history of public advertising in Hamburg had been a »fight over space« and the building code of 1912 had been »ruthlessly« implemented. Now, after the »deprivation« during Nazi Germany and the Second World War, he expected the matter to be handled with more cooperation. Pointing out that advertisers had turned away from »sledgehammer tactics«, he asked the Hamburg senate to change its »defensive« and »intolerant« attitude (Schlepkow 1951: 158–160).

To sum up, the tone of the debate was remarkably aggressive and illustrated how Hamburg's political elites did not embrace advertisers despite being interested in their assumed economic benefits. It also reflected the elites' ambiguous attitude towards advertising which continued to influence this field of cultural economy in Hamburg. Today's myth of the creative class and their role in urban society is indeed an answer to a specific historical situation, and conditions that were still quite different in 1950s-Hamburg.

The Advertising Industry

The first advertising departments in Germany were established after the turn of the century, mostly by brand name companies. Their activities mainly consisted of engaging artists who designed posters, advertisements or packaging and offered a chance to engage in both economy and art. This was an attractive field of work especially for companies' heirs who had received a humanistic education or studied arts (Haas 1995: 81). Younger leading employees, who had been influenced by the experience of industrialisation, mass media and consumption and who realised the outdatedness of their predecessors' belief in the ›self-advertising quality‹ of commodities also took initiatives (Reinhardt 1993: 27).

After a break and regression due to the First World War, advertising departments were (re)established in most German brand companies during the following decade (Reinhardt 1993: 91). At Reemtsma, a company that moved to Altona near Hamburg in 1921 and became the leading German cigarette producer in the following years, one of the two young owners took over the advertising and branding responsibilities. In 1919, he asked various commercial artists to send brand design proposals and finally chose one by Wilhelm Deffke, a famous commercial artist from Berlin. During the following decades, the Reemtsma company regularly employed commercial artists from Hamburg as well as from Berlin, Munich and abroad. The niece of Bruno Karberg – one of the better-studied and most productive commercial artists in Hamburg before the Second World War – said in an interview that »an order by Phoenix [a producer of vulcanised rubber] or Reemtsma always put us in the black again« (Matthes 2005: 7). Reemtsma is also an example of advertising as a part of the rationalisation strategies in German companies during the 1920s. Lintas (Lever International Advertising Service), another advertising department founded in Hamburg in 1929 by the Unilever Corporation, later became independent and entered the growing regional and international market. As a whole, it is apparent that among brand producers in Hamburg, economic strategies became increasingly culturalized when producers started to equip their products with aesthetic values.

External advertising services in Germany were initially offered by *Annoncen-Expeditionen*, i.e., agents who arranged newspaper advertisements. The first was located in Altona near Hamburg, *Ferdinand Haasenstein* founded in 1855. Advertisers in today's sense were scarce in the nineteenth century: Any customer looking for *Reklame* in the address books was referred to artisans who produced signs, labels or posters.

By the turn of the century, around thirty *Annoncenexpeditionen* could be found in Hamburg, as well as twenty *Reklame-Institute* (advertising companies). The difference between the two was not entirely clear in the early years, and many companies were listed in both sections. Generally, *Reklame-Institute* claimed to be more objective and less linked to newspapers, offering a wider range of services such as the circulation of posters, signs and other advertising media. Some of these also ran their own design studios. Prior to the First World War, the number of such companies had grown to sixty, most located in the western or south-western city centre, i.e., close to the centre of commerce and newspaper publishing companies.

Advertising agencies in today's sense – i.e. offices that planned and designed whole campaigns for their customers – did not exist in Germany before the mid-1920s, and most of them closed down soon after during the economic depression. In Hamburg, a company called *German American Reklame Agency* was listed among *Reklame-Institute* in the address book in 1914 and also from 1918 to 1921, but the services it offered were not specified any further. Following the First World War, an increasing number of *Reklame-Institute* indicated the growing market for advertising. Again, most offices were located near the city centre – in 1923, an advertisement agent pointed out its »prime location in the busy city centre«. It thus seems as if a proximity to traditional urban business and service centres was considered more prestigious than being close to places of industrial production or the harbour: Despite Hamburg's position as a leading centre for oversees trade and industry, having a ›good address‹ meant being located in the centre.

During the 1920s, some *Reklame-Institute* in Hamburg began to promote services similar to today's advertising agencies (see also Reinhardt 1993: 126–127), arranging newspaper advertisements as well as »planning complete advertising campaigns« (»*Planung ganzer Werbefeldzüge*«). Only a few of them also offered strategic consulting (e.g., »*Beratung in allen Werbefragen*« by the Wilkens Company in 1921). During this same period, a number of initial steps towards a specialisation of advertising services were taken: In 1926, John Schlepkow exclusively named his field of work as »*Werbeberatung*« (advertising consulting) in the address book. Three years later, six competitors were doing the same, and by 1930, one of them was listed in a section of his own. Previous research on advertising in Germany suggests that those early freelance advertisers could scarcely make a living from their work, because companies were not yet ready to pay suitable fees (Reinhardt 1933: 126). However, the field's expansion became obvious during the 1930s: In 1934, ten *Werbeberater* (advertising consultants) and thirteen *Reklame-Fachleute* (advertising specialists) were listed in the address book, and the numbers grew even further during National Socialism.

Agencies modelled on American examples finally started to dominate Hamburg's advertising industry in the 1950s. Economical and psychological knowledge was now considered crucial for an advertiser's work, while the artistic background was almost completely repressed. The Hamburg address book of 1950 listed four pages with 23 specifications of advertisers, subdivided into »assistants and agents«, »media« and »material«. Whereas, the number of *Reklame-Institute* had dropped to 14, *Werbehelfer* (advertising assistants) and *Werbungsmittler* (advertising agents) formed a growing group of professionals. In 1952, 100 of them were listed and the number grew to about 200 during the next decade. The larger offices were still mainly situated around the city centre, but smaller offices spread over most of the more or less bourgeois parts of the city, near the university and west or north of Alster Lake.

Above, I mentioned that advertising generally did not enjoy a high public esteem in Germany during the twentieth century. As Rainer Gries put it, common perception was that »advertising shouts where the decent trader's moral ends« (Gries 1999: 260). This discourse, as also noted previously, had a strong cultural base among Hamburg's bourgeois elites. Many German advertisers of the early twentieth century thus »nursed an inferiority complex and harboured social-climbing ambitions« (Berghoff 2003, 129). As a result, they tried to declare their profession an art or a science. Hans Domizlaff (1882–1971) is the most prominent example of this type of German advertisers. He moved to Hamburg in 1923. Acting as a bohemian, philosopher and artist, he has been called the »prototype of a German freelance advertising consultant« (Gries et al. 1995: 47) and the »Urfaust in management, advertising and marketing thought« (Dale 1967: 147). Between 1921 and 1955, he was an associate and advertising consultant for Reemtsma. In 1933, he also began working for Siemens (among others), becoming the head of the main advertising department in 1938. Two volumes of his Handbuch der Markentechnik (handbook of brand technique, Domizlaff 1939/41 and 1951) were published in Hamburg. In 1954, Domizlaff founded the Institut für Markentechnik (Institute for Branding Technique) in Hamburg, which existed up until his death. The generation of advertisers who followed was more pragmatic and less eager to prove their artistic or philosophical background, but were still affected by common criticism and persisting opinions that a good commodity could sell itself (Schindelbeck 1995: 237; Schröter 1997: 96).

Hartmut Berghoff has shown that the German advertising industry welcomed the National Socialist regime, because it used modern advertising methods and raised expectations for prestige and power, while regimentations were considered necessary to solve the structural problems of the industry (Berghoff 2003: 134). The increase in advertising consultants in Hamburg after 1933 might indeed indicate some positive effect on this field of work. Ultimately however, hopes remained unfulfilled: »By the end of the National Socialist era, perversion, self-denial, and decay were the hallmarks of German advertising« (Berghoff 2003: 144). After the war, Americanisation and professionalisation led to a growing acceptance, but the public perception remained much more critical than elsewhere, for example, in America (Schröter 1997: 114). It was only towards the end of the twentieth century that advertising and mass culture seemed to be far less criticised than in previous decades. Stefan Haas also stated that the advertisers' self-conception shifted back to a more ›artistic‹ one reminiscent of older views, combined with a general aestheticisation (Haas 1995: 88).

Commercial Art

Before 1890, commercial art as such did not exist within Germany. Newspaper advertisements were designed within the limitations of letter cases, and artists' self-conceptions did not allow them to accept orders from companies – »only the less gifted art school graduates at times had to work in this field for breadwinning« (Reinhardt 1993: 49). This slowly changed when poster art developed in France and artists like Henri de Toulouse-Lautrec and Jules Chéret became popular in Germany (ibid: 52) This advancement was also echoed in Hamburg: In 1893 Justus Brinckmann, the director of the Arts and Crafts Museum in Hamburg *(Museum für Kunst und Gewerbe)* and head of the art school *(Hochschule für bildende Künste)* hosted the first poster exhibition in Germany. In his opening address, he praised French poster art and voiced the hope that German artists produce such work in the future (Reinhardt 1993: 53). During the next decade, posters were primarily used to promote exhibitions or stage performances in Germany as well as in Hamburg (ibid.: 59). Commercial art thus developed without a direct economic influence, but through the volition of young artists who »converted the city into one big art exhibition«, brought art into the street, freeing it from the museum and expanding its role to everyday life (Haas 1995: 81). Ultimately, this also encouraged a new relationship between the arts and the economy, because it was no longer objectionable from the outset to work for somebody other than museums and galleries (Haas 2000: 60).

It could be said that market mechanisms barely influenced the production of cultural goods at this early stage. Advertising designs reflected the artist's style rather than the commodity or company it was promoting. Apart from their aesthetic value, an economic use was not directly perceivable – which is probably one of the reasons why business people were still not interested. This changed as companies began to take advertising more seriously and commercial art increasingly opened itself to economic pur-

128

SANDRA SCHÜRMANN

poses. In 1914, a commercial artist wrote that he and his colleagues were »all business-like« and knew »that advertising needs experienced professionals and artisans rather than artists with ideas« (quoted in Reinhardt 1993: 61).

In Hamburg's address books before the First World War, only a minority of artists or illustrators referred to advertising in their self-promotion. *Reklame* (advertising) was most frequently mentioned by sign-painters/writers and producers of labels as well as by printers and draughtsmen. The address book from 1910 listed ten »advertising painters« separately from artistic painters, although some of the names appear in both categories. The growing market was mirrored in the presence of artists in the new field: During the inter-war period, the section advertising painters consistently listed between twenty and thirty names. Numbers grew during the 1930s reaching 55 *Gebrauchsgrafiker* (commercial artists) and six *Entwerfer* (designers) in 1938, and in 1949, 79 and 13 respectively. By the 1950s and 1960s there were consistently around two hundred. It can thus be deduced that advertising increasingly became a considerable source of income for artists.

During the inter-war period in Germany, the *Verein der Plakatfreunde* (poster friends' association), a union of artists and business-people that edited the journal *Das Plakat*, acted as an influential mediator between the cultural and economic realm (Reinhardt 1993: 61). The previously mentioned special issue of *Das Plakat*, featuring Hamburg in 1921, reflected the ongoing debates about commercial art in the city. For example Paul Etbauer, who promoted his »advertising art« (»*Werbekunst*«) in that year's address book, asked his fellow artists not to avoid commercial art but to »carry art […] onto the streets« and to »not wait for patronage«. Furthermore, he pointed out that Hamburg lacked commercial artists, because the city's elites had no clear position about their status and thus discouraged young artists (Etbauer 1921: 429). In the same volume, Gustav Schiefler complained about »the conservative Hamburg« (Schiefler 1921: 421), and Fred Hendriok accused the city's bourgeois middle-class of treating arts like a »poor cousin«. According to Hendriok, although the economy in general had flourished, the situation for the commercial artist in Hamburg was still »unenviable«, and innovative design could not succeed when mediocrity was generally preferred (Hendriok 1921: 379–381). Notwithstanding, Hendriok named a considerable number of commercial artists whose work he considered being of high quality.

The importance of such statements is hard to measure. It is obvious that there were still reservations, but it can also be deduced that as opportunities grew, more and more artists earned their living in this field. By 1925, the German Association of Commercial Artists (*Bund deutscher Gebrauchsgrafiker*) listed 37 members in Hamburg. Taking into account that some artists were not members of such associations, the market would have already been quite competitive (Matthes 2005: 41).

There are not many sources available describing the everyday and professional life of commercial artists in Hamburg before the Second World War, but what little material exists suggests that it was in some ways comparable to the situation in the late twentieth century: Bruno Karberg for example, whose posters and packages were used by museums and theatres as well as by companies like Phoenix and Reemtsma, was recommended in a commission by Maria Brinckmann, a teacher at the Arts Academy and the daughter of the first Director of the Arts and Crafts Museum. In the end, the project was not realized, but obviously – as is the case today – personal relations around the academy of arts contributed to working opportunities (Matthes 2005: 10). Nonetheless, it serves to demonstrate how a network of creative professionals provided a base in a field of work that was yet to be clearly defined. Conflicts with competitors on the other hand, indicated the difficulties and social frictions in a freelancers' sphere (Matthes 2005: 42).

At first sight, the Art Academy would have seemed an ideal centre for a cultural milieu in Hamburg. It had been founded on the initiative of the »Society for the Promotion of Practical Arts and Crafts« (*Hamburgische Gesellschaft zur Beförderung der Künste und nützlichen Gewerbe/Patriotische Gesellschaft von 1765*) in 1767 and began as a school for technical drawing. When the School of Applied Arts became independent in the 1880s, its curriculum was extended to sculpture, free and applied graphics, typography, and since 1913, photography. The Director of the Arts and Crafts Museum, founded by the same society in order to promote ›good taste‹, held the office of Director of the Academy. When opportunities for training in cultural and artistic techniques diversified after the Second World War, the *Hochschule für bildende Künste* remained the most important art school in Hamburg and one of the most prestigious ones in Germany despite the competition with new private academies and an Academy of Applied Arts.

Regardless of its long tradition, there is little enthusiasm in historical sources about the status of the arts academy in Hamburg's society. For example, in 1956 its director Gustav Hassenpflug began his introduction to a school's chronicle by quoting a colleague who had warned him six years before against moving to Hamburg: »In this city of trade and merchants there is neither the ground nor the atmosphere that an academy of arts needs to gain any significance. As head of this academy, you will have nothing but trouble [...].« Hassenpflug had, nevertheless, come to Hamburg. He said that at the time he had considered it obvious that an important merchants' and harbour city also had to be a centre of the arts; he had simply not imagined that the situation could possibly be different in Hamburg. Hassenpflug continued saying he »still« had »this same belief in the essential togetherness of trade, economy and arts – although recent events did justify the above warning«. In conclusion, Hassenpflug pointed out that trade, crafts and arts needed to be »deeply connected«, because alone they were incomplete and could not flourish without the others (Hassenpflug 1956: 6).

To the present day, the echoes of such historical complaints over the elites' indifference or even hostility towards arts and creativity can still be heard in Hamburg. Leaving the question of truth or prejudice aside, it is clear that this representation influenced the self-perception of artists and creative workers in Hamburg during most of the twentieth century. As the examples of big brand producers like Reemtsma, Phoenix and Unilever, or the growing number of commercial artists as well as Bruno Karberg and his competitors show, there was nevertheless a base for commercial art in Hamburg as early as the 1920s. As with advertising however, there was little enthusiasm for the ›creative class‹, ›creative milieus‹ or their assumed benefit for the city's economy.

Commercial Photography

When photography was invented in the middle of the nineteenth century, the new medium met huge public interest in Hamburg. Supposedly one of the world's first press photos shows the ruins around the Jungfernstieg after the Great Fire of 1842 – a symbolic picture since the fire destroyed most of the old city centre initiating a reform in town planning and infrastructure. In this manner, the use of the modern medium in terms of documentation corresponded with the onset of modernism in Hamburg.

During the following decades, the first photographers opened their studios in Hamburg. Like other creative professionals, most of them were located in the centre of the town, at the Jungfernstieg or near the university. Portraits of the urban elites and their families were an important source of income. Some photographers, such as Rudolf Dürkhoop and his daughter Minya Diéz-Dührkoop, even achieved a certain stardom and presented their work abroad. The production of images for the city became a profitable new field of work, especially after the First World War: Publications and postcards not only showed landmarks like the Michel Church, Alster, Jungfernstieg and the harbour, but also the premises of the important local industrial firms and shipyards. It is remarkable that two of the best-known photographers in the 1920s and 1950s had their studios in the Art Museum or the Arts and Crafts Museum, both located in prestigious buildings near the city centre and the main station. At least in some cases, such spatial proximity corresponded with a social nearness of photography and art. Stephen Bann has argued that early photography was seen as being related to drawing and painting while at the same time competing with reproductive engraving (Bann 2001: 49). ›Artistic photography‹ (*Kunstphotographie*, as opposed to ›applied photography‹) was very popular in Hamburg around the turn of the century and was encouraged by Alfred Lichtwark, director of the art museum. Tradition has it that his regular photography exhibitions in the museum were quite inconceivable for some of the audience. As Lichtwark said, it was »as if a natural scientists' congress held a meeting in a church« (Kempe 1976: 8). He himself promoted a close connection between the ›applied‹ and ›free‹ arts. Generally speaking though, it seems that the status of photography was far less controversial than that of advertising and commercial art. This may have been because it was not considered an art in the first place, but rather was perceived as an integral aspect of ›modern times‹ and their fascinating new techniques.

From its very beginnings, commercial use contributed to the development of photography. Similarly, advertising would not have developed and diversified to such an extent without the impact of photography (Schmalriede 1996: 5). Unlike artists who had to decide between ›free‹ and applied work, professional photographers rarely specialised in one genre before the Second World War. Instead they worked as portraitists, industrial or press photographers, according to the orders they received.

Photography quickly became popular as a medium of self-presentation for industries, because it appeared to be ideal for demonstrating the modernity of production and the »authenticity« of its representation. The first examples of industrial photography in Hamburg can be found in the late nineteenth century – a few decades later than in the Ruhr area, where Alfred Krupp had become famous for his detailed instructions concerning photographs of his premises in the 1860s (Rahner 1999: 8). The archives of companies in Hamburg contain thousands of images of production sites and employees as well as still-life arrangements of products, for example by the photographer Carl Friedrich Timm who worked in Harburg (an industrial town incorporated in Hamburg in 1937). He started working for Phoenix in 1910 and produced two large albums depicting the fabrication and products. Whereas the older album (finished in 1912) follows a tour through the company and its departments as is typical for this period, the second (taken in 1925) shows rain hats or bathing caps worn by alluringly smiling women. Those pictures were not used in advertising campaigns, but are just one step before the use of photography in advertising.

In the 1920s, photography in Germany profited from the increasing professionalisation of advertising. Although photography had been used before, due to its assumed objectivity, it was now considered the ideal medium to gain public acceptance (Schmalriede 1996: 4) and was used in campaigns that ›documented‹ production and quality standards. However, this use of photography was less popular during National Socialism and in the immediate post-war years. On the one hand, this was in part due to internal design and art trends (i.e. a dominance of a graphic and reduced style with drawings and comical figures). On the other hand though, the use of an ›objective‹ medium might have conflicted with the collective will to forget about the past and reality: »There was seldom a place for photography since reality was not relevant.« (Schmalriede 1996: 7) In the last third of the century, when new advertising concepts stressed the importance of emotional address and experience, photography was once again considered the medium of choice to provide lifelike images.

In Hamburg, only a few photographers specialised in industrial or commercial photography before the Second World War. Wilhelm Schäfer, who characterised himself as a specialist for »technical photography« and »advertising and propaganda« in the address book of 1929, is an exception; he also offered the »arrangement of complete albums of large industrial companies in order to create the most effective propaganda etc.«. His colleague Franz Rompel, head of the local photographers' guild, is an example of a creative professional whose position was rooted both in economical and cultural spheres. He worked mainly as a portraitist of the ›better-off‹ and as a teacher at the academy of arts in Hamburg before becoming a freelance resident photographer for Reemtsma in the 1920s. Many of his pictures were directly used for advertising campaigns – especially for a cigarette brand called *Ova* whose advertising was based on demonstrative objectiveness (Kosok and Rahner 2003).

Three decades later, when the photographer Ralph Kleinhempel was at the peak of his career, this field of work had changed considerably. Kleinhempel had been trained in Hamburg and started his first studio during the Second World War. After the war, he opened a new studio in the art museum where he worked as a reproductionist. His main income, however, was derived from his industrial and commercial photographs which could be found in the archives of nearly all important companies in Hamburg during the 1950s and 1960s. Unlike many of his colleagues, Kleinhempel specialised early on in one genre and was able to sustain a living from it (see Kosok and Rahner 2003). It should be noted though, that in 1961, there were still only a few photographers who offered industrial photography in Hamburg's address book. During the following decades however, industrial photography ended in the sense that commercial photographers no longer documented the production and premises of companies. Instead photographers worked for advertising agencies that in turn produced images representing a lifestyle and emotional qualities of a product.

Conclusion

After exploring the developments of advertising, commercial art and commercial photography in Hamburg since the late nineteenth century, it is revealed that some phenomena considered typical for creative economies and their urban milieus of the late twentieth century had already developed decades earlier. The overall view shows some continuities and discontinuities in terms of self-conception and public perception: During the twentieth century, advertising as well as commercial art and photography underwent processes of professionalisation and specialisation while their stature within society and economy remained disputed.

The importance of this field of work for a city's economy as a whole had been pointed out by members of different social and political groups by the early twentieth century – although with less effect than some decades later. It can be said that the phenomenon itself did by no means only commence in the late twentieth century, but accompanied urban development since the beginning of industrialisation and urbanisation.

On the other hand, at least during the first two thirds of the twentieth century none of today's euphoria for creative milieus and their assumed influence on a city's attraction can be found in sources from Hamburg. This might be explained by the close relationship between advertising and the discourses of the modern city: Since advertising was perceived as an essential aspect of urbanity, wide-spread anti-urban positions had an effect on it. Advertising thus also profited from the posited ›renaissance of the city‹ in recent years. That is, as urbanity and urban life became attractive to a growing number of people, it also changed the public status of an essentially urban phenomenon like advertising.

As for the urban setting of creative milieus in Hamburg, a detailed mapping was found to be beyond the scope of this essay. Eventually it became clear that institutions and places – like personal relationships (in the environment of an art school) or spatial (and social) closeness to publishing houses and cultural institutions – played an important role in the expansion and definition of this field of work. Creative networks in Hamburg existed long before the recent rise of certain districts which present themselves as places famous for young creative milieus (and the resulting gentrification).

Bibliography

Anatoff, Roman (1982).»Die Gestaltung durch Werbefotografie«. In Bruno Tietz (ed.). Die Werbung. Landsberg.
Bann, Stephen (2001). Parallel lines. Printmakers, painters and photographers in nineteenth-century France. New Haven/London.
Berghoff, Hartmut (2003).»Times change and we change with them‹: The German advertising industry in the Third Reich – between professional self-interest and political repression«. Business History 45, 1, 128–147.
Brauer, Max (1951). »Zum Reklame-Kongreß am 17. Mai 1951«. In Paul Kettel (ed.). Werbung überbrückt Ländergrenzen. Reklamekongreß Hamburg,. 31–34, Hamburg.
Dale, Ernest (1967). »Begegnungen«. In Paul M. Meyer (ed.). Begegnungen mit Hans Domizlaff. Festschrift zu seinem 75. Geburtstag, 147–148. Essen.

— (1939/1941). *Die Gewinnung des öffentlichen Vertrauens. Bd. 1: Lehrbuch der Markentechnik.* Hamburg.

— (1941). *Die Gewinnung des öffentlichen Vertrauens. Bd. 2: Beispiele aus der Markenartikel-Industrie.* Hamburg.

Domizlaff, Hans (1951). *Die Gewinnung des öffentlichen Vertrauens. Lehrbuch der Markentechnik.* Hamburg (revised and shortened version of the 1939/1941 editions).

Etbauer, Theodor Paul (1921). »Kunst heraus!«. *Das Plakat.* 7/8, 429–430.

Gries, Rainer, Volker Ilgen and Rainer Schindelbeck (1995). »Stilgedanken zur Macht. ›Lerne wirken ohne zu handeln!‹ Hans Domizlaff, eines Werbeberaters Geschichte«. In Rainer Gries, Volker Ilgen and Rainer Schindelbeck. (eds.). ›*Ins Gehirn der Masse kriechen!*‹*: Werbung und Mentalitätsgeschichte*, 45–73, Darmstadt.

Gries, Rainer (1999). »Zum Selbstbild westdeutscher Werbeunternehmer in der Nachkriegszeit. Eine ideologiegeschichtliche Bestandsaufnahme«. In Günther Schulz (ed.). *Geschäft in Wort und Meinung. Medienunternehmer seit dem 18. Jahrhundert*, 251–274. München.

Haas, Stefan (1995). »Psychologen, Künstler, Ökonomen. Das Selbstverständnis der Werbetreibenden zwischen Fin de Siècle und Nachkriegszeit«. In Peter Borscheid and Clemens Wischermann (eds.). *Bilderwelt des Alltags. Werbung in der Konsumgesellschaft des 19. und 20. Jahrhunderts*, 78–89, Stuttgart.

— (2000). »Visual discourse and the metropolis: Mental models of cities and the emerge of commercial advertising«. In Clemens Wischermann and Elliot Shore (eds.). *Advertising and the european city. Historical perspectives*, 54–78, Aldershot.

Hassenpflug, Gustav (1956). *Geschichte der Kunstschule in Hamburg.* Hamburg.

Hedinger, Bärbel (1996). »Las Vegas an der Alster oder Der Hamburger Reklamestreit«. In Susanne Bäumler (ed.). *Die Kunst zu werben. Das Jahrhundert der Reklame. Katalog zur Ausstellung im Altonaer Museum in Hamburg, 18. September 1996 bis 12. Januar 1997.* Köln.

Hendriok, Fred (1921). »Die Hamburger Reklamegraphik«. *Das Plakat* 7/8, 376–406.

Kempe, Fritz (1976). *Vor der Kamera. Zur Geschichte der Photographie in Hamburg.* Hamburg.

Kosok, Lisa and Stefan Rahner (2003). *Industrie und Fotografie. Hamburger Arbeitswelt 1863–2002*, CD-Rom. Museum der Arbeit, Hamburg.

Matthes, Olaf (2005). *Bruno Karberg. Gebrauchsgrafiker in drei Epochen.* Hamburg 2005.

Rahner, Stefan (1999). »Glanzbilder. Die Ausstellung ›Industrie und Fotografie‹«. In Stefan Rahner and Lisa Kosok (eds.). *Industrie und Fotografie. Sammlungen in Hamburger Unternehmensarchiven, Ausstellungskatalog Museum der Arbeit*, 8–13. Hamburg.

Reinhardt, Dirk (1993). *Von der Reklame zum Marketing. Geschichte der Wirtschaftswerbung in Deutschland.* Berlin.

Rolffsen, Hans (1921). »Stadtbild und Außenreklame«. *Das Plakat*, 7/8, 435–441.

Schiefler, Gustav (1921). »Das konservative Hamburg«. *Das Plakat*, 7/8, 421–422.

Schindelbeck, Dirk (1995). »Asbach Uralt« und ›Soziale Marktwirtschaft‹. Zur Kulturgeschichte der Werbeagentur in Deutschland am Beispiel von Hanns W. Brose (1899–1971)«. *Zeitschrift für Unternehmensgeschichte*, 4, 235–252.

Schmalriede, Manfred (1996). *Deutsche Werbefotografie 1925–1988. Ausstellungsserie Fotografie in Deutschland von 1850 bis heute.* Bonn.

Schröter, Harm (1997). »Die Amerikanisierung der Werbung in der Bundesrepublik Deutschland«. *Jahrbuch für Wirtschaftsgeschichte, 1*, 92–116.

Schlepkow, John (1951). »Städtebild und Außenwerbung«. In Paul Kettel (ed.). *Werbung überbrückt Ländergrenzen. Reklamekongreß Hamburg 1951*, 155–161. Kongreßbericht Hamburg.

Westphal, Uwe (1989). *Werbung im Dritten Reich.* Berlin.

Wischermann, Clemens (1995). »Grenzenlose Werbung? Zur Ethik der Konsumgesellschaft«. In Clemens Wischermann and Peter Borscheid (eds.). *Bilderwelt des Alltags. Werbung in der Konsumgesellschaft des 19. und 20. Jahrhunderts*, 372–407, Stuttgart.

— (2000). »Placing Advertising in the Modern Cultural History of the City«. In Clemens Wischermann and Elliot Shore (eds.). *Advertising and the European Ccity. Historical perspectives*, 1–31. Aldershot.

Life on Stage: Grand Hotels as Urban Interzones around 1900

Habbo Knoch

Grand hotels remind us of a past which is most likely reduced to a pseudo-aristocratic life-style of the late nineteenth and early twentieth century. Novels and movies have represented these places as spheres of exclusiveness, elegance, and almost ceremonial rituals, but also as sites of erotic temptation and moral disorder (Becker 2000; Künzli 1996; Seger 2005; Seger and Wittmann 2007; Matthias 2006). But they were neither as aristocratic nor as timeless as they want themselves to be seen. Since the 1850s urban grand hotels were central for the dynamic change of urban geographies and social topographies. Hotels as well as department stores or railway stations followed and initiated a fundamental transformation of city zones and spatial arrangements of public and private life. They were symptomatic for modern interzones of entertainment, social interaction, and consumption. Between the conventional public sphere and private rooms, hotels in particular offered a transitory and transitional zone at central locations of the city's web.

Thus, urban hotels were deeply embedded into the fabric of modern city life. Decorations, advertisements, and perceptions doubled the material space of the luxury hotel by relying on a specific semantic of illusions and dream-worlds. Within the constraints of urban space the luxury hotel placed itself as a spatial vehicle for shifting experiences. In turn, they were created as social spaces by guests, formal and informal gatherings, meetings, and dances as well as the interaction of employees. But creating such a space for the redefinition of cultural practices and social relations turned more and more into a strictly economical task – the hegemony of social elites for the definition of cultural styles and social rules was questioned and overruled by the enormous impact buildings like modern hotels have had on the urban infrastructure.

Offering an imaginative space, hotels served as observation platforms for modernity as such. It was the impression of an exceptional everydayness which animated many observers to their creative perceptions of modernity when using hotel-life (or, more specifically in some prominent cases, the hotel-hall) as one of its prisms.

Urban hotels in particular, due to their close connection with industrial, commercial, and entertainment developments were stages of modern life without the attribute of artificiality like in theatres and the fictionality of artistic representations. They provided a privileged scenery for modern life-styles: the main hall, a number of rooms and spaces with different social functions, the distinction between front and back area, representative staircases or seating arrangements drew their fascination from a staged theatrality though being real at the same time. Significantly, rooms were constantly equipped with mirrors, wall paintings, and art collections.

It would be mistaken and a consequence of the imaginary world of the »grand hotel« itself to ignore the social functions for the transformation of urban elites around the turn of the century. It was precisely the period between the 1880s and 1910 which made the modern luxury hotel not an accident or just an outcome of economic profitability. Profound changes and erosions in the social arrangements of upper-class »societies« – which were framed by and locked into a polarisation of aristocratic and bourgeois moral and social codes before – gained their spaces in modern hotels. They were definitely not class-blind, but a much more neutral mixed zone of social entanglement than many other urban institutions. Here, money levelled traditional social barriers and created new ones: exclusivity and distance within spatial proximity. The inclusion by educated habits was replaced by the mascerade of changing styles. Nevertheless, beside its exclusions and its exclusive atmosphere the modern hotel provided the modern society at least with a dream of a creative destruction of classified, gendered, and restricted spaces.

The following argues in four steps that the urban hotel was the product of a specific period of transformations of spatial, social, and economic relations since the end of the nineteenth century (I). The modern hotel was dynamically linked to urban space, but transcended it into non-urban areas. Thus, via commercial spaces like modern hotels urbanity expanded and fostered, in turn, the establishment of resort-like spaces within the city itself (II). The image of a »city in itself« was an integral part of the perception and function of the modern hotel. It reflects proximate spatial as well as functional relations of the modern hotel with urban economics (e.g. food markets, cultural events, tourists). Likewise, it includes a specific difference in that the hotel was idealized as a functional organism and shelter which perfectly linked its guests with its own interiors and the city space (III). Though social elites especially in Europe were not immediately in favour of this new space of social intercourse, hotels became stages for urban social life. The dynamics of technological innovations, economic rationalisation, and social agenda-setting developed its own creative potential which, in turn, translated tradition into transition and local belonging into spatial imagination (IV). Thus, due to the economic effects and social attractions of urban life, precisely between the 1880s and 1910s high culture in terms of music, art, or building styles became commodified and served as a means to support the well-being of guests. Intertwining economy and culture by creating dream-worlds and imaginative spaces within an urban context, modern hotels served as training grounds for social interactions beyond enclosed societies and anonymous street scenes. Neither imitation nor distinction are sufficient in order to explain these effects. Social spaces, like in particular the modern hotel, which offered and defined spaces of interaction on a medium range between anonymity and intimity were most important for both, the transformation and structuring of a bewildering city space and for the integration of the growing element of transitoriness into the social fabric of the »liquid modernity« (Bauman 2000).

»A Depth of Six Miles«:
The Invention of the Modern Hotel, 1880–1910

Although early examples of the »modern hotel« differing from »Gasthaus«, »Inn«, or »Tavern« were built or opened between around 1800 and 1830, the main foundations for later developments were layed during the three decades thereafter. Particularly the 1850s served as a watershed in terms of size, location, management, and style. A number of huge Broadway hotels in New York (Hutchins 1902), railway and semi-aristocratic hotels in London, which defined the urban hotel topography of the town (Borer 1972; Taylor 1974; Taylor 2003), the first-time so called »Grand Hotel du Louvre« in Paris 1855, or extensions of first-class hotels in Swiss towns like

Geneva, Zurich or Interlaken, set a new stage for public intercourse and a temporary participation in or retreat from »urban life« (Flückiger-Seiler 2001; Ott 1990; Schmitt 1982). Predominant among the differences between European and American hotels until the turn of the century were the degree and form of their publicness. American hotels were much more a product of urban life or, rather, the result of agglomerations and concentrations of people, commerce, and travel options. At the same time, due to the rapid growth of some commercial centers like New York the local social life was neither fully rooted in traditions of private sociability, nor could the sociospatial demands for a »Society« of European style be fulfilled. Since the 1830s, hotels were seen as »public palaces«, located in the centre of the town and its theater or shopping district (White 1968). Large entrance halls for everyday, local visitors quoted former Exchange houses and reflected a gendering of the public sphere: Separate entrances for married or unmarried women allowed them to avoid the bustling, exclusively male entrance scenario. European first-class hotels like the Swiss family hotel or the West End hotel in London were much more influenced by private accomodations of aristocratic or upper-class nature and style. Distance from the »public«, the retreat character, and the importance of personal service were specific traits.

Modern hotels, in particular in America, focussed on technical equipments of the latest kind and a perfect organisation (Denby 1998). In July 1889, the *Los Angeles Times* published a description of »The hotel of the future«, originally printed in a Berlin newspaper. It envisioned a new hotel at St. Augustine, Florida, with »a frontage of three English miles long, and a depth of six miles«. 500 balloons »will always be ready to take visitors up to their rooms« in the 77-floor-building, with tables in the dining-room four miles long, served by waiters on horses, and with 1000 billiard tables. Instead of room waiters, a most important sign of European hotel standards at that time compared to American hotels, the article let its reader dream of a »newly patented automatic« in every bed-room doing all shaving or shampooing »by a very simple and ingenious mechanism«. This vision of a future high-tech, but completely anonymous hotel reflects the beginning of both, the growth of the modern hotel and the intensification of transnational perceptions of and transfers between hotels in the 1880s. The article exaggerated developments of the American hotel business which tended towards much larger and extensive buildings than in Europe.

Though differences remained, since the middle of the nineteenth century a number of hotels in urban environments, most of all in metropolitan spaces, were transformed into an international and pace-making class of establishments in terms of size, equipment, and supply (Denby 1998; Watkin 1984).

Obviously, this development of the modern hotel was interlinked with modern urbanisation as well as travel infrastructure and transregional business relations. More specifically, a number of forces and factors supported this development: *First*, due to the expansion of railways and the discovery of travelling by the upper- and, increasingly, upper middle-classes temporary accomodation of a distinct quality and much extended quantity was required and offered. While this is commonly associated with Switzerland, the Riviera or Saratoga Springs, in particular metropolises like London, Paris or New York became crossing-points of the international travelling public. Exhibitions, in particular the World Exhibitions in London, Vienna, or Paris in the second half of the nineteenth century, served as driving-forces for both, the inrease of travellers in numbers and the improvement of infrastructure in quantity and quality. *Second*, industrialisation and increasing commercial relations were accompanied by the rise and growth of social groups which requested modern, albeit not necessarily luxurious hotel accomodations, e.g. travelling salesmen with expanding networks of commercial contacts, international bankers, and new professions which gained significant profits from the improvement of salaries and life-styles. While the traditionally leading strata of society had to reorganize themselves due to an increase in numbers and a decrease in former local cohesion, their attempts to distinguish themselves by style and topography were paralleled by increasing demands for temporary luxurious living spaces to which access was made possible by wealth instead of rank and tradition.

Third, cities as hot-spots of modern developments as well as centres of civilisation and history developed into cultural shopping-windows. The invention of museums, the expansion of theatres and entertainment places, and the commercialisation of shopping experiences turned the centres of big cities into attractive travel destinations. Immensely rising numbers of tourists in the decades before the First World War put pressure on the infrastructure. Shopping itself became a cultural event of utmost economic importance for the city as the development of London's West End exemplifies. In turn, *fourthly*, these cities began to include the new phenomenon of town vacations and city travelling into their image policies. Non-governmental and commercialized at the beginning, these policies relied on self-advertisements of hotels and travel-agencies, guide-books and press reports, but since 1900 the value of city marketing gained more support and was much further developed in the 1920s. *Fifth*, hotels themselves were presented and idealized as representations of the importance and economic strength of the city. To have sufficient and well-established first-class hotels as well as accomodations for the travelling public was used as a main argument to foster the development of this market. Hotels drew on this in order to underline their general importance for the common wealth and the image of the city. In London or New York, these images of hotels as microcosms of the city itself were closely tied to the image of an imperial or prosperous nation leading in the world. Hosting an exclusive world, hotels were seen as interchangeable representations of the life-standard of the upper-classes, the city, and the nation.

Sixth, beside the travelling public which visited the cities home-coming vacationers and travellers imported and transferred expectations between hotels in resorts and cities. Certain demands for social space in a distinct and luxurious environment grew because even among the top ten percent of the society space for larger social gatherings was sometimes rare. Special occasions, semi-public events, and formal dances helped to establish hotels as social centres for the upper classes though a certain social distance remained. Since 1910 the informality, which hotel spaces allowed, made them even more attractive for social contacts beyond the »at home« etiquette. Its rules were set by owners and staff, but basically they had to be invented and adapted (Gruber 1994; Vehling 1910). Thus, grand hotels were not only important links between other entertainment zones, but also catalysators for a fundamental moral change within and beyond upper-class elites. *Seventh*, within the range of modern consumer spaces urban luxury hotels offered settings for a commercialized culture of fascination. Guests were expected both, to feel »at home« and to experience memorable impressions beyond the routines of their daily lifes. In a very symptomatic and self-generating way, the modern (urban) hotel occupied, widened and transformed the space of experience between »private« and »public« life, routine and exceptional moments.

Eigth, outward displays of grandeur and style which quoted historical styles in building and interior decoration were inventions of the late nineteenth century (Schmitt 1982; Wenzel 1991). Since the 1880s transfers in both directions improved European hotels in terms of equipment and administration, while a large fraction of newly built American first-class hotels were remodelled alongside the reinvention of former aristocratic styles of public display. Thus, the »private«, socially more distinct European hotel became more »public«, the American »public palace« became more distinct and differentiated in terms of its social and spatial organisation. But, *ninethly*, in order to survive economically, most of the »mammoth hotels«, as they were called by mid-century travellers, had to provide a large number of rooms for travellers and guests of middle-class origin. Regularly, large-size hotels included, among other features, an extensive amount of social and public rooms, a spacious entrance hall and offered a number of specialized services. Due to the social widening of guests and the growing differentiation of standards, hotels became subject to internal classifications. Architects, travel guides, or hotel associations used their own categories, but accompanied by hotel advertisements and travellers' experiences luxury, first-, and second-class hotels could be identified (Borocz 1992; Koshar 1998; Palmowski 2002; Tissot 1995). Distinctions of this kind were part of a powerful movement to establish certain standards and to improve the quality of housing, service, and food. In turn, this required a more elaborate form of marketing, administration, and knowledge about the expectations of guests. They were also meant to direct guests towards their appropriate class of hotels. Thus, temporary hotel societies were structured according to the social status of their guests.

Though a large number of public articles, brochures, and advertisements tried to convince future guests of the safe, personal, and comfortable character of the modern hotel (Bien and Giersch 1988; Mai 2003; Wobmann 1982), its invention around 1900 was accompanied by a swelling critique against the impersonal and anonymous atmosphere (»too little homeliness«), as an English traveller remarked 1900 for example under the heading »The modern hotel – A grumble« (Anon. 1900: 19). While the lack of standards and comfort of any modern kind had dominated the perception between 1850 and 1900, now uniformity on the one side, too much luxury on the other side were the most prevalent reasons for public critique. Would it not be the case that in particular really luxurious hotels were flourishing until the 1910s, one could get the impression that hotel owners and advertisers on the one hand, guests on the other were constantly talking at cross-purposes.

Travelling Modernity: Luxury Hotels and Urban Spaces

Compared to England and the United States, until the final quarter of the nineteenth century the hotel sector in continental Europe was dominated by resort and spa hotels (Bajohr 2002; Blackbourn 2002; Knoll 2006; Kolbe 2005; Mittelstädt 1985; Steward 2002). But also Wiesbaden or Nizza are important examples for the fact that even resort hotels were profoundly influenced by urbanisation processes around 1900 (Niess and Lorenz 2004; Schaller 2006). Beyond its territorial, demographic, and administrative aspects, »urbanisation« included a transformation of life-styles which basically took place in the growing metropolises. But it was by no means restricted to it, nor that geographically urban spaces had been »urbanized« completely (Lenger 2002; Trentin-Mayer 2000). Vertical and horizontal unevenness were natural around 1900, and the modern hotel one element of it.

The innovative character and the high standard of some hotels in resorts and spas, which advertised themselves to a translocal, often urban elite, show that »urbanity« and »modernity« were not tied exclusively to a restricted urban space. Civilized manners and comfortably equipped surroundings which drew a lot from technological innovations were realized within a network of places and spaces throughout Europe, consequently extended towards Asia and Egypt (Meade 1987). They guaranteed living standards which the travelling elite knew from their own homes and urban amusement sites. Beside their comfort it was their relatively quick accessibility and the combination of retreat and modern entertainment which made mountain resort hotels attractive for an urban clientele. Their guests were not looking for something opposite to their regular life-style, but for its continuation or extension on a higher level in terms of comfort and social prestige.

Instead of juxtaposing »city« and »countryside«, these retreats should be seen as an attempt to realize a kind of modern life which was based on the live within urbanized communities. Thus, a debate about the relation of culture, economy, and the city cannot restrict itself to a specific »city space«, but should take the interrelations and growing penetrations of space by urban life-styles into account. The modern hotel is but one example for this process. At resorts and spas, modernity and urbanity was neither ignored nor fought against. Rather, they were intrinsically interwoven into the regime of industrial and urban life. This relation between urbanity and resort spaces was, of course, not one-dimensional. They were proto-typical spaces for liberations from ceremonial procedures where enter-tainment, fashion, and social relations could be lived up to a certain extent with relaxed moral attitudes. Likewise, hotels offered their guests a realm of retreat from the city-life which might be interpreted as an attempt to deeconomise the hotel space – though the winter, palm or roof gardens with their oriental decorations represented social distinction at its best. At the beginning, a resort culture like in Europe was rarely present in America (Franklin Tolles 2003). Since modern hotels developed here as centres of industrial and commercial cities, they found prominent repre-sentations in travel guides and city maps or panoramas much earlier than in most European cities. Embodying the republican and anti-aristocratic tradition and fueled with local city pride they were a natural part of the city's image and were perceived as »culture« – even without any tradition. Their economic progress was translated into a symbolical language of local pride. In Europe, until the 1880s city sights and cultural objects were kept more or less as a secret for travelling upper-classes. Thus, their economic value was less important than their importance as spatial markers for one's belonging to the elite. Luxury hotels in American cities, in particular in New York, invested heavily into cultural objects and authentic decorations as a means of economic expansion. These interior objects served as signs of quality and superiority; the value of collections was transferred into and projected on the imagined space of the hotel so that its transitory character was furnished with an international semantics of luxurious distinction. Difference and distinction were the result of investments, selections, and perceptions of cultural objects which were de- and recontextualised to serve an economic and a social purpose.

In the middle of the nineteenth century European observers were con-fused and annoyed about the behaviour in American first-class hotel en-trance and hall areas. The public character aroused feelings of cultural superiority which had already been a main part of many travellers' mental luggage. In addition, especially British observers were not used to partici-pate in social gatherings in semi-public spaces. While hotels in New York and other American cities like Boston or Philadelphia were meeting-points of the town's elites like the »salon« in Europe, in cities like London or Berlin, for different reasons, hotels and, more or less until the 1900s, even luxurious modern hotels were seen, at best, as second-class places for so-cial conviviality. For some time, the second-rate ranking even of luxury hotels in the hierarchy of social city spaces was further confirmed by a general refusal against commercial buildings in the European architectual tradition. In America, hotel buildings were not only leading buildings in the cityscape at least between the 1850s and 1900s, but the erection of buildings for commercial purposes in itself was a matter of local and national pride. Nevertheless, the difference between the republican and the more private type in America and Europe should not be overstressed: At least at the end of the nineteenth century in American as well as in European societies the most representative and distinctive way to show off one's wellbeing and social status was to give a ball »at home« and, increasingly, to spend a lot of time in »country houses« or at the urban periphery.

When it was announced that the famous Palais Redern in Berlin would be replaced by a hotel, a number of citizens protested against it. They referred to examples of hotel buildings which had been built in an ostentatious and eclectic style. But the Adlon, when it opened in 1907 with its well-structured and decent façade, convinced even the critical intellectual public of Berlin (Demps 2004; Jansen-Fleig 1997; Gruber 2000). While it appeared modest from outside, it copied the practice of a very rich interior design from its predecessors since the early 1890s. Expensive, opulent, and colourful period rooms, art objects and collections, furniture of exceptional quality and craft – this very selective arrangement, common among the international luxury hotels at this time, allowed its guests to travel in space and time, as far away as into the Italian renaissance or a stylized contemporary China. At the same time, these hotels tried to pass the elite's homes in terms of splendour and modern equipment. Here, attributes and symbols of culture served as an over-compensation for the lack of tradition, history, and social standing. It was a costly, effectful, and successful attempt to counter the long-standing reputation of a non-private, socially even dangerous site. To provide guests with private art collections belonged to an economic strategy but served the improvement of its owner's prestige as well. Cultural objects, which less luxurious hotels presented as imitations, set virtual sceneries and revalued a city space for demands of public entertainment beyond ceremonial and social rules.

Thus, the style of hotel-living travelled beyond the given city or hotel scape and aimed at illusionary effects. They stood in stark contrast to the more and more rationalized spatial organisation of the hotel itself. Urban hotels had to calculate their space more efficient than resort hotels. The main task for an architect since the 1880s was to adjust the length and width of rooms and floors so that a balance between the economic needs of the hotel and the expectations of guests concerning roominess was found. Luxury and calculation or rationalisation became intrinsically interwoven although it remained part of the policy of first-class hotels to pretend that there were no limits and nothing too costly. That was part of their attraction: Guests, well-off or of limited means, expected almost unlimited space, a multidimensional world of floors, rooms, and spaces which had to be discovered as well as a luxurious interior. In terms of calculation, this included a permanent dilemma: Growing prices for land and building required strictly rationalizing measures, while guests expected to be welcomed by spaciousness, a smooth atmosphere of personal service, and quiet surroundings. Constant complaints of guests even of first-class hotels about noise and odor show that urban hotels had to struggle in order to cover the tensions or contradictions between the hotel as an inner-city retreat and the sensual hardship which modern city-life meant to nervous contemporaries.

In order to fulfill their expectations, modern hotels provided their guests and visitors with opportunities to travel within virtual arrangements. Nevertheless, within the urban area, hotels marked specific places and geographies of commercialized entertainment. The urban topography of hotels varied from city to city due to specific circumstances and developments, but some elements were similar: *First*, the modern urban hotel in Europe, including Great Britain, was closely linked to the development of railway lines and stations. In London, in the 1850s and 1860s explicitly hotels owned by railway companies defined a circular border around the inner city space in connection with the main railway stations. During the following decades, smaller private hotels were established in the vicinity of the railway stations so that hotel quarters could be identified. Similarly, in Berlin the Friedrichstraße or the Potsdamer Platz were main locations for modern hotels (Huscher 1931). *Second*, in Europe and England luxurious hotels were built in a certain distance to the bustling streets of the modern entertainment areas, at least at the beginning. In London, for example, semi-aristocratic hotels of the 1860s were located in connection with parks and upper-class living quarters.

Nevertheless, in the 1880s the Gordon Hotels at Northumberland Avenue and, most prominent, in 1889 the Savoy were very close to the main amusement and theatre area. Until the end of the nineteenth century only hotels for guests of moderate means had been located here. This

proximity even of first-class hotels to entertainment areas was imported
from American cities. It was a *third* element of the hotel topography, first
of all typical for hotels in New York: They neighboured theatres and department stores, the shopping and amusement zones at Broadway. While
this element was transferred to Europe, since the 1880s hotels in New
York also moved towards residential areas close to the Central Park or
flocked around the major railway stations Pennsylvania and Grand Central.
In any case, the mobility syndrome of traffic, travel, and temporary movement were of indisputable importance for the topography of hotels in the
modern metropolis: first, either by proximity or by distance from the major
traffic points and aims, then as a matter of attraction for a thriving location. Hotels close to theatres, the opera, or shopping areas served as an
important recreation and entertainment interzone, connecting all the other
spaces by offering food, drinks, and shelter.

Living Organism: Hotels as Entrepreneurial City Spaces

Transatlantic perceptions and increasing transfers contributed to a convergence of hotel styles and features. This convergence was part of a larger
process to establish an urban culture of commercialized sociability and
retreat. Between the 1880s and 1910, central spaces of inner city areas were
transformed into interrelated and connected mono- and multifunctional
zones of gatherings, amusements, and commercial activities. Their experience and social character shifted from total anonymity towards recurring,
ritualized, or informal ways of personal contacts. Beside hotels railway
stations, department stores, and cinemas were the most prominent places
of this modern urban life. Compared to those places, hotels were specific
in some points, most of all: At none of the other places mentioned, the
intimate sphere of sleeping, eating, and everyday life was so close to and
intertwined with the semi-public or intermediary sphere of social life like
public dining, wedding breakfasts, and dancing balls. This combination of
private and public spaces, creating a spatial frame for shifting boundaries
between them required a large amount of investment capital, entrepreneurial standing or foresightness, and advertising.

Since demands were expanding, including a drive towards »conspicuous
consumption«, as Thorstein Veblen called it in 1899 (Veblen 2004), not

only the sheer and growing size of hotels alone required immense amounts of money. Beginning with English railway hotels in the 1850s, modern hotels in central urban or retreat locations, of big size and modern style were financed by investment companies or syndicates. A few exceptions of individual personal investments remained: William Waldorf Astor and his cousin John Jakob Astor III in New York were responsible for three luxury hotels each, most prominent the Waldorf-Astoria (1893/97) which was divided among them (Dearing 1986; Hungerford 1925; Kaplan 2006). Lorenz Adlon was the founder of a hotel in Berlin bearing his name, though the latter would not have been successful without the financial and political support of Wilhelm II (Gruber 2000). Nevertheless, in the 1920s there were only about fifty limited companies among more than 20,000 hotels in Germany.

Still, by far the most hotels were of smaller scale, belonged to families, and offered much less comfort than the larger und luxurious ones. The model of individuals or families as main or sole owners could also be found among medium-sized or larger hotels: It was a promising but difficult perspective for headwaiters and porters to rent or buy their own hotel after a while. At least ten years and a lot of international experience were the minimum requirements for hotel entrepreneurs – or, money and reputation which had been earned differently. Since the latter case was more common in America, it was usual to find a proprietor who then was responsible for everything at least from the interior design onwards. In Britain, the investment companies employed managers who were much more dependend on the decisions of the company's board while in Germany the image of the innkeeper as »Hausvater« remained to be most important.

Large city hotels required modern systems of administration, technical organisation, food control, and staff management (see e.g. Bigelow-Paine 1903). They functioned as powerful economies within the city's and nation's economy. In particular, food and house equipments like carpets or dishes created an important market for the local industry and commerce. In particular luxury goods and speciality food found its privileged partners in hotel companies; newspaper reports about American hotels stressed this local economic importance in quoting incredible numbers of amounts of beef, bread, or oysters which were used and processed day by day. In turn, the amount of expensive goods made costly investments into technical equipment and the development of modern household utilities and machines even more important – as well as the development of rationalisation and contral mechanisms in order to prevent theft, personal profiting, and black marketing by hotel employees.

While guests consumed luxury goods without limits, the hotel management had to rely on tools of exactness, calculation, and control. Although booking systems were invented in Europe and America nearly at the same time, it was definitely the American modern hotel culture which was founded on organisation and hierarchical administration. Visitors from abroad were irritated by the fact that European hotels lacked the kind of internal structure American hotels were using (Bennett 1984). While internal mechanisms of a rationalized hotel economy developed within the walls of buildings with pseudo-historical fronts, extensive descriptions in America as well as in Europe provided the public with images of the modern hotel as a kind of living organism, which was linked internally by miles of electrical wires and tubes, controlled by an almost omnipotent and genius-like manager whose abilities as well as the organic character itself were illustrated by detailed observations of the extremely differentiated workforce. »A grand hotel«, readers of an American intellectual magazine were informed in 1897, »is really a government in itself«. In order to understand this »small town«, it was said to be »necessary to go beneath the surface« (Parks 1897, 397). Numerous walks into the »underworld« of modern hotels, mainly the kitchen, cellars and engine-rooms, revealed a hidden world, which guaranteed a perfect service and experience upstairs.

Drawn from those texts, writers as well as readers seem to have been obsessed with a desire to illuminate and discover the structures of the modern hotel not only to understand its mechanism but to solve the mysteries and problems of the modern city as well, sometimes including anticipations of a future destruction. Quite often, the hotel was presented and read as a miniature city and either as an example for the dangerous temptations of modern city-life, or for perfect solutions for the problems modern urban societies created. Fascination and fear, both due to the technical innovations, merged into a pars-pro-toto perception and projection of modern life into modern hotels and vice versa. The link between the modern world, city, and hotel worked in both directions: William Hutchins, an architectural critic, resumed in 1902 that the difference between old and new hotels was constituted by the fact that »the mechanism of a modern hotel is an expression of the most ingenious planning in the world« (Hutchins 1902: 462). The next step within this pattern was to proclaim city and hotel as almost interchangeable when companies advertised their hotels as a »city in little«.

Public Stages: Luxury Hotels and Urban Social Life

Since the early 1890s some modern urban hotels played an important role for the public entertainment in urban cultural economies. Imagination, promise, and decoration were intended to create distinct spheres of social intercourse. Though separation was never complete and international guests perforated ideals of private noble or bourgeois life, hotel spaces became part of the growing network of popular culture. Still, music halls and cabarets were different, but the pervasive nature of popular music, theatre, and dance did not leave the serene scenery of modern hotels unimpressed. To the contrary, luxury hotels offered transient spaces for informal intercourse which could be used for acts of emancipation, for the loosening of gender relations and moral codes, and as savety-valves for generational conflicts within families. Smoking women, dancing young women, and flirting couples made ample use of the surroundings in hotel spaces, especially since around 1910 the »dance craze« developed in America and was transferred to Europe via London.

At the same time, the social life of city elites underwent a dramatic change. Certainly, public dining had been a strong feature of city life in Paris since the eighteenth century. But hotels like the Savoy in London, the Waldorf in New York or the Bristol in Berlin (1893), the latter on a smaller scale though, included noble restaurants which were explicitly established to attract local high societies for regular, public, and informal gatherings. Lead by some members of aristocratic circles or leading families, hotel restaurants provided the local elite with a representative space and a luxurious surrounding which served perfectly to the demonstrative consumption patterns of a modern »leisure class« (Veblen 2004). Nevertheless, if these spaces of distinguished conviviality – in most hotels, but to a differing degree, separate dining-rooms were offered beside larger restaurants and halls – would not have been used for commercial relations, business matters, and social relations of business partners and their families they would never have been as successful as they were.

Hotel restaurants were a kind of door-opener for the growing social acceptance of hotels as city spaces against their aura of privatism, especially in London. In different degrees and styles, modern urban hotels, in particular first-class hotels, offered their own ball-rooms and other rooms for private celebrations or social gatherings. While it is not possible to quantify how many weddings, anniversaries, or family meetings took place in hotels, their advertisements allow to assume that it was a stronghold of their existence at least after 1900. Especially since around 1910, and even more so in the 1920s these ball-rooms and the hotel-halls were more frequently used for balls, dances, kinds of varieté or cabaret, thus developing the hotel into a scenery of social contacts which could only be partly controlled. On the other side, hotels were much better controlled than ordinary vaudevilles, other public houses, cinemas, or zones of entertainment the modern city culture offered. The limited informality of a private ball at a city hotel was a price upper-class families had to pay since they themselves could no longer offer a continuous social life at home. To a certain extent, luxury hotels served here as a safety-valve for generational and social conflicts while they provided the local elites with a city space which, at least, promised to limit informality by its own standards of »civilisation«, rules of behaviour, and social exclusiveness. Thus, balls which were held at first-class urban hotels in London or Berlin were part of the regular court »seasons« and open only for subscribers and on invitation.

Partly as a consequence of this social activities after 1900 – public dining, private festivities, informal dancing – the hotel hall gained growing attraction. Imported from American hotels, modern luxury hotels around 1900 transformed their entrance spaces and exchange halls into designed areas of transition into the hotel world – liminal spheres, in which private and public, home and town, intimacy and anonymity turned into each other and where guests changed their habits. These limimal spaces were particularly decorated in an attractive way, which represented the main character and classification of the hotel. Size, layout, design, and furniture served as more or less exact signs for the standard and quality of the hotel. Spacious areas, more than one entrance, transparent, no steps from outside, accompanied by cafés or less ostentatious restaurants opening towards the street, shops – since 1910 a hall like this most certainly would be found in a hotel even for travellers, by-passers and of middle-class origin. An important part of the continuous process of inner distinction within the class of modern hotels was that certain new ones like the Ritz-Carlton in New York by separating the entrance sphere as a rather small space and the true hotel hall which was placed more to the centre and luxuriously decorated.

Luxury hotels like the Waldorf-Astoria included all the general features of hotel halls – but here, the quality of its decoration, the size, and the value of the furniture made the difference. They could play on the standard model by offering innovative solutions with regard to travel connections, street entrances, or restaurant guests. The Ritz in London (1906) invented a different, less transparent type of hall than the American example (Binney 2006; Montgomery-Massingberd 1989). Combining the style of luxury interior with the privacy of English aristocratic family hotels, the two entrances of the Ritz – one for hotel, the other for restaurant guests – were both guarded by a number of porters and separated the guests according to their desirability in the eyes of the front employees. Entering from different sites, hotel and restaurant guests met in an oval space at the crossing of the two entrance passages. Thus, architecture supported the social constitution of an »inner circle« and their self-induction of representability even before they entered the much more refined restaurant itself.

The Ritz in London as well as the Ritz-Carlton in New York were symptomatic for another important trend around 1910: the convergence of hotel architecture and interior decoration towards a more simplified yet still expensive style. It was much less eclectic and not aimed at the artistic reconstruction of a specific early modern style. They relied on a new elegance as such – with forms simpler, colours brigther, ornaments lacking, and furniture more pragmatic within and outside one's hotel room. Sanitary devices were important for this trend, but most of all the main addressee of the hotel business changed: Women, either single or married, turned into the yardstick for the true quality of hotels. Advertising brochures, posters, and texts in professional hotel journals reflected this shift towards female interests and desires shortly before the war. It was accompanied by the beginning of public balls, tea dances, and private tea parties which replaced the afternoon »at homes«. Urban hotels were transferred into an informalizing space of gender relations: Women entered for some retreat from the shopping world, afternoon dancing and dinner with music gave female and male guests the chance to meet accidentally or deliberately, breakfast, lunch, or dinner invitations offered more formal opportunities for couples, friends, or business partners to convene. Although private invitations still remained to be an important part of the social reputation, to a certain extent the private space at home could be confined to more intimate meetings. The »Jazz age« of the 1920s with hotel halls as dancing floors for the middle-class women goes back to the final years before the First World War (Lamonaca 2005).

Conclusion

Modern hotels promised their guests to situate them safely and comfortably within their own temporary private space and the semi-public space of temporary sociability. They were presented and experienced as a shelter against the impact of city-life as well as a starting-point to discover it by day or night. The hotel experience itself was a matter of choice, money, and time. It played creatively on the modern urban experience with its attractions and dangers. Many luxury hotels were proud to offer everything the city itself would have, and even guests who decided to leave the hotel were most welcome to recover from their urban experience. Driven by a need to house increasing numbers of translocal and international guests – most of them commercial travellers –, the modern hotel presented itself as the fulfillment of modernisation dreams and the incarnation of a profound dissonance with modern urban life.

Modern hotels were setting the scene for a cultural revolution: They played a dynamic and inherent role within a fundamental transformation of social relations in the age of a commercialized public culture. Modern, in particular luxury hotels developed into institutions, centres and front signs of their cities (Kiecol 2001). As a receiver and distributor of commercial und consumerist elites and due to their general attraction, they were important parts of a growing travel and social industry in the modern city. They were used and served as liminal zones of entertainment. Here, liberalizing effects in terms of gender relations, social border-crossing, and temporary transgressions could be exhibited in a controlled setting. That this space, in turn, produced erosions of moral rules was part of its complex position between upper-class morality, the moral temptations of urban social life, and the otherness of the hotel which was tied up with the imagination of danger, erotic adventure, and personal crises. Luxury hotels, therefore, were of central importance for the transformation of the urban fabric into a space of imagination and temptation, supported by a culture of mass media representation which made it more and more difficult to distinguish between hotel-life reality and its image.

Bibliography

Anon. (1900). »The Modern Hotel – A Grumble«. *The Hotel*, May 1900, 19.

Bajohr, Frank (2002). *»Unser Hotel ist judenfrei«. Bäder-Antisemitismus im 19. und 20. Jahrhundert*. Frankfurt am Main.

Bauman, Zygmunt (2000). *Liquid Modernity*. Cambridge.

Becker, Sabina (2000). »Großstädtische Metamorphosen. Vicki Baums Roman ›Menschen im Hotel‹«. *Jahrbuch zur Literatur der Weimarer Republik*, 5, 167–194.

Bennett, Arnold (1984 [1902]). *The Grand Babylon Hotel. A Fantasia on Modern Themes*. Leicester.

Bien, Helmut M. and Ulrich Giersch (1988). *Reisen in die grosse weite Welt. Die Kulturgeschichte des Hotels im Spiegel der Kofferaufkleber von 1900–1960*. Dortmund.

Bigelow-Paine, Albert (1903). »The Workings of a Modern Hotel«. *The World's Work*, 5, March 1903, 3171–3187.

Binney, Marcus (2006). *The Ritz Hotel, London*. London.

Blackbourn, David (2002). »Fashionable spa towns in nineteenth-century Europe«. In Susan C. Anderson (ed.). *Water, leisure and culture. European historical perspectives*. 9–21, Oxford/New York.

Borer, Mary Cathart (1972). *The British hotel through the ages*. Guildford.

Borocz, Jozsef (1992). »Travel-Capitalism. The structure of Europe and the advent of the tourist«. *Comparative Studies in Society and History*, 34, 4, 708–741.

Dearing, Albin Pasteur (1986). *The elegant inn. The Waldorf-Astoria Hotel, 1893–1929*. New Jersey.

Demps, Laurenz (2004). *The Hotel Adlon*. Berlin.

Denby, Elaine (1998). *Grand Hotels. Reality & Illusion*. London.

Flückiger-Seiler, Roland (2001). *Hotelträume zwischen Gletschern und Palmen. Schweizer Tourismus und Hotelbau 1830–1920*. Baden.

Franklin Tolles, Bryant (2003). *Resort hotels of the Adirondacks. The architecture of a summer paradise, 1850–1950*. Hanover.

Jansen-Fleig, Claudia (1997). *Das Hotel Adlon*. Weimar.

Gruber, Eckhard (2000). *Das Hotel Adlon*. Berlin.

— (ed.) (1994). *Fünf Uhr-Tee im Adlon. Menschen und Hotels*. Berlin.

Hungerford, Edward (1925). *The story of the Waldorf-Astoria*. New York/London.

Huscher, Reinhold (1931). *Das Berliner Hotelgewerbe im Rahmen des Fremdenverkehrs der Stadt Berlin*. Diss. Berlin.

Hutchins, Williams (1902). »New York Hotels I + II«. *The Architectural Record*, 12, 5, 459–471; 6, 621–635.

Kaplan, Justin (2006). *When the Astors owned New York. Blue bloods and grand hotels in a gilded age.* New York.

Kiecol, Daniel (2001). *Selbstbild und Image zweier europäischer Metropolen. Paris und Berlin zwischen 1900 und 1930.* Frankfurt am Main.

Knoll, Gabriele M. (2006). *Kulturgeschichte des Reisens. Von der Pilgerfahrt zum Badeurlaub.* Darmstadt.

Kolbe, Wiebke (2005). »Strandurlaub als liminoider (Erfahrungs-)Raum der Moderne? Deutsche Seebäder im späten 19. und frühen 20. Jahrhundert«. In Hans-Jörg Gilomen (ed.). *Freizeit und Vergnügen vom 14. bis zum 20. Jahrhundert,* 187–199. Zürich.

Koshar, Rudy (1998). »What ought to be seen«. Tourists' guidebooks and national identities in modern Germany and Europe«. *Journal of contemporary history,* 33, 3, 323–340.

Künzli, Lis (1996). *Hotels. Ein literarischer Führer.* Frankfurt am Main.

Lamonaca, Marianne and Jonathan Mogul (eds.) (2005). *Grand hotels of the jazz age. The architecture of Schultze & Weaver.* Miami Beach/New York.

Lenger, Friedrich (2002). »Building and perceiving the city. Germany around 1900«. In: Friedrich Lenger (ed.). *Towards an urban nation. Germany since 1780,* 87–105. Oxford/New York.

Mai, Andreas (2003). »Neue Welten. Werbung für Sommerfrischen im 19. Jahrhundert«. In Habbo Knoch and Daniel Morat (eds.). *Kommunikation als Beobachtung. Medienwandel und Gesellschaftsbilder 1880–1960,* 101–111. München.

Matthias, Bettina (2006). *The hotel as setting in early twentieth-century German and Austrian literature. Checking in to tell a story.* Rochester, N.Y./Woodbridge.

Meade, Martin (1987). *Grand oriental hotels. From Cairo to Tokyo, 1800–1939.* New York.

Mittelstädt, Fritz-Gerd (1985). »Der Badeort Norderney im 19. Jahrhundert als gesellschaftliche Fiktion der Oberschichten. Ein Beitrag zur Historischen Sozialgeographie«. *Berichte zur deutschen Landeskunde,* 59, 2, 461–493.

Montgomery-Massingberd, Hugh (1989). *The London Ritz. A social and architectural history.* London.

Niess, Wolfgang and Sönke Lorenz (eds.) (2004). *Kult-Bäder und Bäderkultur in Baden-Württemberg.* Filderstadt.

Ott, Thierry (1990). *Palaces. Die schweizerische Luxushotellerie.* Yensur-Morges.

Palmowski, Jan (2002). »Travels with Baedeker. The Guidebook and the middle classes in Victorian and Edwardian England«. In Rudy Koshar (ed.). *Histories of leisure,* 105–130. Oxford/New York.

Parks, Fred Warren (1897). »A study in California hotel management«. *Overland Monthly and Out West Magazine,* 29, 172, 1897, 396–409.

Schaller, Detlef (2006). *Kaiserzeit. Wiesbaden und seine Hotels in der Belle Epoque. Ein Bildband.* Wiesbaden.

Schmitt, Michael (1982). *Palast-Hotels. Architektur und Anspruch eines Bautyps 1870-1920.* Berlin.

Seger, Cordula (2005). ›Grand Hotel. Schauplatz der Literatur. Köln.

Seger, Cordula and Reinhard G. Wittmann (eds.) (2007). Bühne der Literatur. München.

Steward, Jill (2002). »The culture of the water cure in nineteenth-century Austria, 1800–1914«. In Susan C. Anderson (ed.), Water, leisure and culture. European historical perspectives, 23–35. Oxford/New York.

Taylor, Derek (1974). The golden age of British hotels. London.

— (2003). Ritzy. British hotels, 1837–1987. London.

Tissot, Laurent (1995). »How did the British conquer Switzerland? Guidebooks, railways, travel agencies, 1850–1914«. Journal of Transport History, 16, 1, 21–54.

Trentin-Meyer, Maike (2000). »Die Anfänge des Alpinismus als urbanistisches Phänomen«. In Thomas Busset (ed.). Ville et montagne = Stadt und Gebirge, 229–240. Zürich.

Veblen, Thorstein (2004 [1899]). The Theory of the Leisure Class. New York.

Vehling, Paul (1910). Die Moral des Hotels. Tischgespräche. New York.

Watkin, David (1984). Grand Hotel. The golden age of palace hotels. An architectural and social history. London.

Wenzel, Maria (1991). Palasthotels in Deutschland. Untersuchungen zu einer Bauaufgabe im 19. und frühen 20. Jahrhundert. Hildesheim.

White, Arthur S. (1968). Palaces of the people. A social history of commercial hospitality. London.

Wobmann, Karl (1982). Schweizer Hotelplakate 1875–1982. Luzern.

Anticipations of the New Urban Cultural Economy: Fashion and the Transformation of London's West End, 1955 – 1975

Christopher Breward/David Gilbert

The late Arthur Marwick, writing in his book *The Sixties,* described the period as a modern renaissance. While some of his claims for the significance of the period may be over-stretched, it did undoubtedly mark an important moment in the history of the interrelations between culture, economy and certain key cities. Nowhere was this more the case than in London, where developments in popular music, fashion, art and youth culture seemed to many to presage a rebirth of the city. *Time* magazine's famous *London: The Swinging City* issue of April 1966 helped to establish enduring stereotypes of 1960s London. Its editorial deftly itemized the distinctive character of the new London, stating that:

»In a decade dominated by youth, London has burst into bloom. It swings; it is the scene. This spring, as never before in modern times, London is switched on. Ancient elegance and new opulence are all tangled up in a dazzling blur of op and pop. The city is alive with birds and Beatles, buzzing with minicars and telly stars, pulsing with half a dozen separate veins of excitement.« (*Time,* April 15, 1966: 32)

The most common interpretation of the ›Swinging London‹ phenomenon focuses primarily on cultural change. In this reading, London was a central site in transformations of lifestyles, social attitudes, intergenerational relationships and forms of consumption that were to be important across the western world and beyond. Marwick's account is the most comprehensive ›culturalist‹ account of these changes, but this is also a feature of more popular accounts of the period. At its most hyperbolic this perspective argues that what the new creative forces of London achieved was nothing less than the remaking of the modern world. As Shawn Levy puts it, »in London for those few evanescent years it all came together: youth, pop music, fashion, celebrity, satire, crime, fine art, sexuality, scandal, theatre, cinema, drugs, media – the whole mad modern stew. [...] Within three miles of Buckingham Palace in a few incredible years, we were all of us born.« (Levy 2003: 6) Understandably much of the emerging historical work on London in the 1960s has attempted to challenge or at least complicate this view of radical, seemingly overnight, change. Some have emphasised the limits of the Swinging London phenomenon, stressing its short-lived and elitist character, and calling for an end to histories and memoirs of the period »ploughing over the same old turf, gamely pretending that Swinging London changed the world« (Cohn 2006: 130; see also Green 1999; Sandbrook 2006. For detailed consideration of the mythologies of Swinging London see Gilbert 2006a.).

Fig. 1: Carnaby Street. Guide produced for the boutique. ›I was Lord Kitchener's Valet‹ by David Block, c. 1970.

(Source: Private Collection)

An alternative response has been to provide a firmer contextualisation of the changes that took place, stressing the continuities with earlier periods in London's history. Both Mary Quant, the designer most often associated with 1960s fashions, and Carnaby Street, now forever remembered and mythologised as the heart of Swing London, started out much earlier than might be expected, given their strong identification with the high sixties. Quant's first shop *Bazaar*, opened in Chelsea in 1955, while the opening of Basil Green menswear store *Vince* in 1954 is often taken as the beginnings of the men's boutique scene. This contextualising strategy has been pushed further in recent studies of London's fashion history, that have interpreted emergence of new designers, boutiques and forms of street-style in the sixties as a further phase in a long tradition of London-based demotic styles that have emphasised the edgy, playful and experimental (Breward 2004; O'Neill 2007).

This essay is a rather different response to urban creativity in London during what might be described as the long 1960s. Here the emphasis is neither on the 1960s as cultural revolution, nor on the period as another twist in a long tradition of urban creative activity, but rather on the way in which many of the elements of what has been described as the new cultural economy of cities were anticipated in the developments of the period. Our primary focus here reflects our interests and research into the development of the fashion industry and broader fashion culture of the West End in the post-war period, but our more general argument applies to a wider range of cultural industries that developed in the city during the period. Examining the history of London in the 1960s alongside consideration of the new urban cultural economy literature can help to achieve three outcomes. First, this analysis of the urban creative economy that developed in London from the late-1950s onwards complicates what has become a dominant reading of the periodisation of the interrelations between culture, economy and certain key cities. We consider this periodisation model in the following section. Secondly, ideas developed from the urban cultural economy literature can contribute new perspectives to our understanding of London in the 1960s. Finally, this exercise can also be used to reflect on contemporary developments, indicating some of the specificities and limitations of claims about contemporary urban creative sectors.

Periodising the New Cultural Economy of Cities

Much of the literature about the new cultural economy of cities emphasises that a major turning point took place in the 1980s and 1990s. Such changes were variously associated with the emergence of post-Fordist production systems (Piore and Sabel 1984), and with a decisive shift towards industries whose principle products consisted of images, signs and symbols (Crane 1992, Lash and Urry 1994). The most systematic expression of these ideas comes in Allen Scott's work on the cultural economy of cities (Scott 2000a, 2000b, 2001, 2005). Scott makes a number of basic claims about the cultural economy, concerning the sectors of the economy producing goods and services »whose subjective meaning, or, more narrowly, sign value to the consumer, is high in comparison with their utilitarian purpose.« (Scott 2005: 3) First, Scott argues strongly that the late twentieth century saw the appearance of a distinctively post-Fordist cultural economy in the advanced capitalist societies, associated with a »vast extension« of craft, fashion and cultural-products industries and a »great surge in niche markets for design- and information-intensive outputs.« (Scott 2000a: 6) Scott's second argument is that this shift towards post-Fordist flexibility has fostered new geographies of economic organisation. While Fordism was seen as a force breaking up industrial regions and making production ever less place dependent, post-Fordism has seen resurgent spatial agglomeration. One strand of analysis of the economic geography of post-Fordist flexibility has concentrated on the emergence of neo-Marshallian industrial regions like Silicon Valley or the Third Italy. However, Scott argues that the great expansion of commercialized cultural production since the mid-1980s has been very largely based in major urban centres, particularly so-called ›world cities‹ like New York, Paris, Berlin, Tokyo, Los Angeles and London (Scott 2005: 6).

There is within the new cultural economy literature, therefore, a strong argument that changes of the 1980s and 1990s formed a redefining set of transformational processes in the metropolitan cores of major world cities (Hutton 2004: 106). There are a number of key elements often identified with this new urban formation. First and foremost of these is the growth of what have become known as creative clusters – concentrated districts of creative, knowledge-based and technology-intensive industries, often found within old de-industrialised parts of the metropolitan core (Pratt 1997; Hutton 2004). Key examples of such clusters include Manhattan's ›Silicon‹

Alley‹ in the Tribeca and SoHo districts, and London's Hoxton and Clerkenwell. Secondly such clusters, and the urban creative economy more generally, are characterised by dense networks of strongly interdependent small- and medium-sized firms (Scott 2000: 12). Thirdly, often drawing upon the distinctive profile and traditions of major world cities (what Molotch (1996: 229) describes as a kind of monopoly rent that adheres to places) and using new media to disseminate product, these highly localised cultural economy clusters come to have increasingly globalised recognition and markets. Fourthly, the new urban cultural economy is marked by considerable hybridity of industries and firm types, combining new design-orientated advanced-technology industries (such as software authoring, web design), with established creative industries (themselves increasingly shaped by new technologies) such as graphic design, architecture and fashion design, alongside arts organisations and studios. These zones are marked by a relatively open labour market for creatively skilled workers, who may cross sectors relatively easily.

Finally, the urban creative economy literature places great store on the concept of urban milieu, emphasising the overlaps between economic and social networks. For Allen Scott, these are places »where qualities such as cultural insight, imagination, and originality are actively generated from within the local system of production« (Scott 2001: 9). In Richard Florida's controversial arguments about the emergence and significance of a ›creative class‹, this idea of urban milieu is pushed much further, to include a much wider urban cultural infrastructure and ambiance, emphasising the significance of environments that attract, stimulate and retain young affluent creative professionals. (Florida 2002)

As this collection demonstrates, there is clearly a need to historicise these debates over the cultural economy of cities, and particularly to question the assertion that the last 25 years have seen a marked disjuncture in the nature of major cities. We need, however, to move beyond the straightforward assertion that cities through their history have often been crucibles of creativity. The new cultural economy model, with its component elements of post-Fordist flexibility, geographical clustering, dense networks of relatively small firms, local-global connections, hybridity, and creative urban milieu, provides the basis for more a effective historical periodisation that compares the details of particular urban formations.

Some responses to claims about the newness of the new urban cultural economy have worked in just this way. In particular, it has been argued that a combination of flexible production and strongly place-specific design cultures has long been a feature of certain sectors and certain world cities. (Gilbert 2006b) Nancy Green argues that the fashion and garment industry (in Paris and New York) demonstrated »flexible specialisation before the term was coined« (1995: 4). Green's and Sally Weller's work on the significance of copyright and licensing arrangements in the geographies of twentieth century fashion also indicate both the longevity of issues concerning the symbolic economy in a pre-digital age, and the extensive reach of Parisian fashions as both material objects and as symbolic goods (Weller 2004; 2007). There are indeed places in Scott's work, particularly in his writings on Paris, where he recognises the importance of long-running continuities in some features of urban creative economies, particularly in Paris (Scott 2000b). While Scott holds to his model of decisive transition, much of his writing on the development of the Parisian creative economy implicitly indicates the difficulties of applying the crude categories of Fordist and post-Fordist to the economies of established major urban centres. Cities like New York, Paris and London have long been characterised by flexibility, clustering, close inter-firm interdependencies, hybridity of economic activity, and creative milieus. To describe urban formations in eras prior to the take-up of digital technology in creative sectors as ›pre-Fordist‹, ›craft‹ or ›artisanal‹ risks imposing a false teleology of economic activity, and missing some key continuities in urban creativity.

Swinging London as New Urban Cultural Economy

While the Swinging London period has been recognised both for its general creativity (particularly in popular music, fashion design and the visual arts) and, despite some of the counter-cultural rhetoric of the period, in terms of new forms of entrepreneurialism, it has not been treated as an important antecedent or anticipation of the formation that developed from the mid-1980s. The oil crisis and recessions of the 1970s and very early 1980s (combined with what might be described as urban crises in key centres of the global cultural economy, notably New York City) have served to disconnect this period from discussion of earlier changes, over-emphasising the newness of urban creative economies in the 1980s.

London during the 1960s was clearly in a state of important economic transition. The most obvious features were the decline of the docks, and a collapse of manufacturing industry. Between 1961 and 1973 manufacturing employment in Greater London fell from 1.6 million to under 1.0 million for the first time in the twentieth century (falling further to 0.68 million by 1981 and 0.36 million in 1991) (Wood 1978: 38; Hamnett 2003). This process of deindustrialisation was a key issue for policy makers and planners – particularly in the Greater London Council (GLC) – and for contemporary academics, who also highlighted the accelerating depopulation of central districts (Keeble 1976; Clout and Burgess 1978).

Yet while manufacturing overall was in crisis and the docks were in terminal decline, significant restructuring was taking place. One measure of this was that between 1969 and 1973, even as overall manufacturing employment declined, *vacancies* in manufacturing employment grew by 27 percent in London, with the highest rates in inner London, indicating substantial skills shortages (Wood 1978: 48). Significant growth in key creative industries such as advertising took place in the late 1950s and 1960s and crucially, the period also saw the beginnings of significant redirection towards international markets. Taken together the ›boom businesses‹ of fashion, design and music, together with photography, modelling, magazine publishing and advertising added »nearly a quarter of a million jobs in London during the decade« (Porter 1994: 363). As early as 1964, advertising was a £0.5 billion industry, employing around 200 000 people in Britain, and was heavily concentrated in London's West End (Pearson and Turner 1965: 323). Public relations also took-off in the period with around 300 agencies based in the West End by the mid-1960s. (Pearson and Turner 1965: 224)

London had experienced an office-building boom during the late-1950s and early 1960s, associated with planning deregulation and aggressive property speculation. There were expressed concerns about London's landscapes, but also about what was described by local government as the »relentless squeeze« on »all the other activities essential to the life of the metropolis«, such as »theatres, clubs, hotels and residences« (Robson 1965: 11). While office development did make fundamental alterations to the character of central London, and contributed to both urban depopulation and the demolition of some mixed-use areas, it was also an important factor in restructuring. As geographer Gerald Manners noted, reviewing the developments of the 1960s, while many relatively routine office jobs were decentralised;

»in contrast the office jobs that have stayed and expanded have tended to involve more specialised activities and the application of higher skills. In addition, of course, central London's retail trade, entertainments, cultural activities and tourism have all grown in importance as creators of wealth and sources of employment in the centre. In recent years they have added considerably to the diversity and economic strength of the centre of London.« (Manners 1978: 13)

This new office world was a fundamental influence on the development of Swinging London. The new office workers provided a large group of younger consumers, who had disposable income and were increasingly fashion-conscious. By the early 1960s there were also six women to every four men employed in office work in the capital, which provided a significant new stimulus for certain sectors of the creative industries (Humphries and Taylor 1986: 66). The independent young woman, with an income of her own, sometimes sexistly stereotyped as the ›dolly-bird‹ secretary or ›girl Friday‹ was in many ways the primary target of the new fashion sector, and a driving force for change in wider consumption patterns (Gilbert 2006b: 9–10).

What, in the language of the new urban creative economy school, would be described as creative clusters were important features of the geography of 1960s London. This geography was strongly shaped by the pre-existing geographies of economic activity, and particularly by what Peter Hall described as the ›Victorian Belt‹ of inner London industrial districts (Hall 1962). The surviving belt in the 1950s was characterised by: a predominance of small workshops; complex inter-firm production networks; dependence on specialised local facilities; and as a consequence, clustering of production into a number of specialised ›quarters‹, such as the Shoreditch furniture quarter, Hatton Garden jewellery quarter in Clerkenwell, and the printing district around Fleet Street. (Wood 1978: 40)

After near complete collapse by the late-1980s some of these districts formed the sites for the new creative quarters in the 1990s. However in the late-1950s and 1960s, the connections between economic innovation and the established industrial sectors were much closer. Carnaby Street was an important example of this. Although its history had a strong element of serendipity, its geographical position was highly significant, just off the main shopping thoroughfare of Regent Street, but also in a district of mainly Jewish tailoring workshops. It was also close to an area of wholesale garment warehouses to the north of Oxford Street, which connected the district to flexible supply chains reaching to East End factories and beyond. Carnaby Street rose from an unexceptional bomb-damaged backstreet in the early 1950s, to become one of the best-known addresses in the world by 1966. This came about through a combination of newly emancipated young consumers, with the economic and cultural power to force the pace of change, entrepreneur-designers who were able to experiment with short-runs of often highly outré fashions in cheap materials, and a finishing and supply industry that proved highly flexible (not least because of the sweated wages and conditions in many of the workshops.) (Breward 2006) The fashion boom of the 1960s proved to be the last period of sustained growth for some of the traditional industrial clusters of the Victorian belt.

The 1960s have perhaps been under-recognised in terms of the development of creative industries because it was hard for contemporaries, particularly within the government, media, and academia to take this new urban milieu seriously. The most visible aspects of the transformation of 1960s London – youthful fashion and popular music – also seemed the most transient and frivolous. A view was shared by many on both right and left that the development of fashion, music and other parts of the creative economy were essentially trivial, a sideshow in a longer story of metropolitan decline. Reactionary critics such as Christopher Booker argued that this youthful world was too dominated by the attitudes of the ›neophiliacs‹ – those in love with newness itself, who paid scant attention to the realities of life beyond their narrow, myth-infused metropolitan concerns. He considered the whole ›swinging scene‹ to be a solipsistic mirage and was not alone in holding such opinions (Booker 1969). At the close of the decade even John Lennon, speaking from a rather different position in the cultural politics of the period, famously claimed that »the whole bullshit bourgeois scene is exactly the same, except that there are a lot of middle-class kids with long hair walking around London in trendy clothes [...] nothing happened except that we all dressed up.« (Quoted in Green 1999: 256)

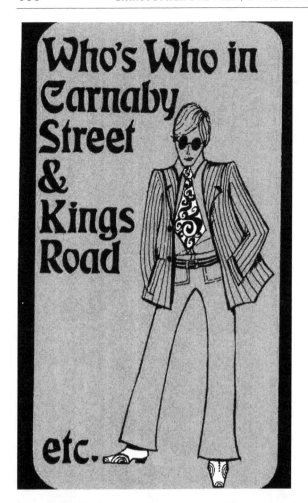

Fig. 2: Who's Who in Carnaby Street and The King's Road. Anonymous retail guide, c.1969

(Source: Private Collection)

This extended to the discourse of those contemporaries who were more enthusiastic about the developments of the period. The oral histories of fashion designers and entrepreneurs from the period often emphasise the ›amateurishness‹ and chaotic nature of inter-connections between key players, firms and sectors in the city during the 1960s. This exchange between

Marion Foale and Sally Tuffin, key designers of the period who ran a boutique just off Carnaby Street, is typical of such discussions:

»Marion Foale: [...] then I went to Art School and got to the Royal College of Art at the same time as Sally and Sylvia and at the end of Royal College I knew I didn't want to go and work for those boring, boring firms doing the most awful things. We'd had a talk by Alexander Plunket Greene just before the end and it really impressed me, and Bazaar was open and I thought, ›Well, if they can do it, we can!‹ And that's basically it – I wasn't going to go and work for these – nah!«

Sally Tuffin : »We used to have tea break downstairs and hatched out these plans didn't we? I'm not going to do this, I'm not going to do this, I'm better than everybody else!« (Marion Foale and Sally Tuffin: interview with Sonia Ashmore and Jenny Lister, Victoria and Albert Museum, April 4, 2006)

By the 1980s the culture and language of creative business in the city had changed – the idea of ›the scene‹ had been replaced by a much more purposive rhetoric of contacts and networking. This switch in the language of the socioeconomic interactions of the urban cultural economy is deceptive. Although the ›classless‹ rhetoric of 1960s London was clearly overplayed (despite the rise of significant working class figures such as the photographer David Bailey and the model ›Twiggy‹ – ›the scene‹ was still highly class-stratified), there is also substantial anecdotal evidence of a strongly interconnected creative economy, one in movement between different sectors was relatively common. The hat-designer and milliner Jimmy Wedge recollected his sudden and successful move into fashion photography at the end of the 1960s:

»SA: What happened after you closed the shop?
Jimmy Wedge: I became friendly with Terence Donovan and David Bailey, but mostly with Terence Donovan and I think it was his lifestyle that persuaded me! He was always driving around in a Rolls Royce with a beautiful model on his arm and I thought I'd like to do that! So anyway I thought it would be quite nice to be a photographer and there was an actress who used to buy her clothes from Top Gear and she had a camera that she bought for her husband, and he didn't want it and she sold it to me, and I thought right this is a sign so I thought I'd go into photography.« (James Wedge: interview with Sonia Ashmore and Jenny Lister, Victoria and Albert Museum, February 2, 2006)

The creative sectors of 1960s London were clearly marked by geographical clustering, by new hybrid firms (the Beatles' Apple Corps was the most famous, if not the most successful of these), by fluid opportunities for privileged members of a creative ›class‹ to flirt between different sectors, and by strong overlaps between social and economic networks. The period was also marked by rather stronger synergies between what might be described as pre-Fordist industrial sectors and new ›symbolic‹ industries than was the case in the late twentieth century. There are a number of other useful comparisons and contrasts to be made between urban economic creativity in the 1960s and in the past twenty years.

Firstly the late 1950s and 1960s were characterised by relative entrepreneurial openness, and by relatively low entry costs and starting capital, certainly for a ›World City‹ and certainly in comparison with the later period. What comes across very strongly in oral history interviews and in contemporary reports from the period is an often-repeated claim that ›anything was possible‹. Stripped of the mythologizing of the self-proclaimed ›special‹ sixties generation, much of this sense of possibility was about a combination of cheap available property and generational money. London in the period was marked by established family money being used to open businesses in what might be seen as high-risk sectors. Mary Quant's pathbreaking opening of the boutique Bazaar in Chelsea in 1955 depended on a combination of fairly cheap premises outside the established shopping districts and the family money of husband, Alexander Plunkett Green. Scott discusses the way that »vibrant agglomerations of cultural products industries become magnets for talented individuals from other areas« (2005: 7). There are however differences in circumstances and an important distinction between places and periods where such agglomeration is likely to take place with a structure dominated by existing firms, or where there will be significant opportunities for new entrepreneurialism.

Related to this is an issue about the relative spatial openness of the city to new creative industries. 1950s and 1960s London was effectively still a post-war city, with significant remaining bomb damage, and was characterised by what we might describe as urban interstices, affordable premises available in central locations. The best of these like Carnaby Street, were just off established centres of consumption in the city. There are strong connections here with Angela McRobbie's discussion of »a mixed economy of fashion design« in the 1980s and 1990s where young fashion designers were able to find niches in the city through college shows, markets and in small shops outside the established shopping areas (McRobbie 1998). This kind of small-scale urban creativity has become increasingly difficult in the hypercapitalised London property market of the 2000s. In some ways Carnaby Street has become symbolic of this. In the late 1950s and early 1960s, it was a cheap opportunity for fashion entrepreneurs like Basil

Green, John Stephen and Warren Gold to gain a foothold in the heart of the West End. In 1997 the property company Shaftesbury purchased most of the leases in Carnaby Street and adjacent streets in Soho. The area is now branded as the Carnaby Village, but while it trades on a kind of urban memory of an older Carnaby Street, with an emphasis on street fashion, limited special editions and short-run designs, it is dominated by major international brands like Puma and Diesel (Gilbert 2006b). The openness of the 1960s must be contrasted with the creative clusters of the 1990s and 2000s. In London, and in other major world cities, such interstices have almost been completely removed from central city areas, and property values even in inner city marginal zones like Hoxton, Shoreditch and Clerkenwell are prohibitively expensive for small-scale start-up businesses.

A second contrast to be drawn concerns the role of consumers in the urban creative economies of the 1960s and more recent times. It is easy to over-romanticise about the performance of fashion and other forms of urban creativity in the past, and our approach to the fashion culture of the 1960s has emphasised the back-regions of rag-trade production and distribution as a more firmly contextualised counter-balance to more sensationalist accounts of a ›youth-quake‹ (Breward 2006). Nonetheless, the fashion culture of London in the late-1950s and 1960s saw the development of highly active and creative consumers who were able to shape trends. A vital part of the urban milieu of the period came from the wearing and display of clothes on key streets in the city. This often provoked a direct response on the part of entrepreneurs. Writing in 1970, Tom Salter, owner of ›Gear‹ on Carnaby Street, described the working methods of one of his competitors:

»If a girl liked his style, but could find nothing suitable, he would pretend to have a larger stock and ask her to come back in an hour, to give him time to sort out something from his ›other stockroom‹. Eyeing her closely, he would run up something […] before her return.« (Salter 1970: 13–16)

This is indicative, not just of the extreme flexibility of Carnaby Street's businesses, but also of its responsiveness to street-style, and of the demanding, discriminatory nature of its consumers. The male consumers of the early ›mod‹ movement were particularly active, pushing tailors to tighter fitting suits, narrower trousers, thinner lapels, and experimenting with coloured fabrics (Chenoune 1993). This should be contrasted with the characteristics of the kinds of urban spaces and associated with Richard Florida's celebration of the new creative classes. The policy effects of Florida's arguments often have the effect of limiting urban consumption to a rather limited repertoire (mostly obviously through outlets of global chains of coffee bars and ›designer‹ clothing), and have often been accompanied by greater restrictions and controls on public space.

Sensing the Creative City

A final theme that we might take from 1960s London is to stress a closer engagement with the materiality of creative practices than is common in much of the creative economy literature. John Lennon's casual dismissal of ›dressing up‹ belies the importance of materiality and experience. The very process of dressing-up, however, engendered a powerful sense that the design, manufacture, retailing and wearing of new clothes constituted a key component of cultural, economic and physical change in the city, grounding myth in everyday experience – and this understanding has played a pivotal role in our research on the urban creativity of London in the 1960s. With its emphases on the digital and the symbolic recent writing on the urban creative economy has often distanced itself from the material realities of creative urban environments. The idea of the urban milieu is usually addressed either through a rather generalised sense of attractive consumption spaces, as in Florida's work, or else in the more specific sense of dense networks sometimes conceived in terms of social or cultural agglomeration (see Moulaert and Gallouj 1993, Thrift and Olds 1996). More recent work in urban theory tries to understand the city as a creative experience, that engages the senses as well as providing commercially useful connections (Etherington and Meeker 2002). However, there are only limited examples of direct connections being made between the city as a locus of sensory experience and stimulation and the development of the creative economy (Amin and Thrift, 2002).

Counterintuitively, it has often been historical work that has most vividly demonstrated the significance of the experienced city for creativity. In searching for evidence about past contexts of creativity the historian may turn to material evidence. In own work we have worked closely with the surviving clothes of the period, which reveal ways in which versions of the Swinging Sixties were encountered on the body and in space. They challenge the historian to engage with the period through a consideration of what it *felt* like to change appearances with the times, to enjoy, for women especially, a novel freedom of choice and movement, and to appropriate the highly specific ›look‹ of the time and place. In their very materiality such items constitute a complex version of the ›Swinging Sixties‹ that is in some ways more compelling and convincing a record of the times than the clichés of the *Time* editorial. Examination of actual garments also prompts us to alter our notions of creativity in the city – a dress is not simply about the creativity of designers, advertisers and boutique retailers, but also crucially about the urban creativity of consumers.

Consider, for example this Hessian dress, produced by Mary Quant in 1965. With its short skirt and deceptively simple line, utilizing an extended belt to form a halter neck fastening with a large buckle worn high on the chest over a polo-neck sweater, the ensemble points to the multi-faceted version of an avant-garde fashionable femininity promoted by Quant and her generation of London-based designers. It was clearly easy to wear and maintain, well adapted to the increased pace of modern city-living. But stylistically it moved beyond comfort and practicality to suggest bohemian revolt (in its emphatic use of black), graphic sophistication (in its play with texture, form and bold accesorisation) and sexual provocation (the dress, whose form tends to narrow the hips, was worn with a schoolboy cap in matching linen material). It tells us a great deal more then about the lifestyles and aspirations of the habitués of Chelsea's King's Road than many other contemporary sources.

Fig. 3: Pinafore Dress. Natural hessian with silk trim.
Designed by Mary Quant, 1965 (remade 1973).

(Source: Given by Mary Quant. V&A: T.110–1976)

Yet there is also admittedly also something rather reducible about the Quant dress and its modish signifiers that belies the layered contexts in which it was produced. Like all such artefacts, the object is positioned in a series of relationships between processes of production and consumption that economist Ben Fine has famously termed »systems of provision« – systems whose workings help to »explain the mechanisms that lead to the introduction of entirely new commodities, the disappearance or transformation of old ones, or the prolonged survival intact of some inveterate goods« – though its chic surfaces rather disguise this (Fine 2002: 83). Quant's innovations would have gained little purchase without the older, relational networks of London's longstanding culture of fashion making and distribution. In order to understand the dynamics that produced both a haptic and metaphorical sense of Swinging London, we need to place the garment in an understanding of the city as a complex creative economy. In considering this formation we need to think about the ways that the city's reputation as a site of spectacular consumption, with its celebrated experience of shopping and fashion performances its certain key spaces, sat alongside more mundane geographies of intensive production clusters.

Conclusion

Writing just as *Time* was lauding Swinging London, the industrial geographer John Martin described the city's economy in terms that anticipated almost precisely the lexicon of the urban cultural economy school. For Martin, what made London unique was its status as a centre of »enterprise and linkage, contact and flexibility« (Martin 1966: 261). But Martin also noted that the city was also a centre of »style and fashion«, qualities that crucially extended beyond the dynamism of businesses in London to include the urban creativity of its shoppers, streets and everyday life. There is a danger of slipping into easy mythologizing about Swinging London when looking back and comparing its ›scene‹ with later examples of the creative urban economy. Nonetheless such comparisons when used carefully can be instructive, particularly in countermanding some of the stronger claims of the urban cultural economy school.

Allen Scott has argued that the recent growth of urban cultural economies in major world cities has been a force for diversification, a counter-tendency to the homogenising imperatives of globalisation, potentially producing what he describes, as a »global but polycentric and multi-faceted system of cultural production« (Scott 2000a: 211). This prognostication for the twenty-first century is based upon claims that major cities are usually marked by quite dissimilar traditions and cultures of production, and also »from the theoretical proposition that the long-run economic vitality of any centre is apt to be dependent on its ability to offer real alternatives to products originating in competing centres« (Scott 2000a: 211).

Such theoretical propositions are hard to test, but the longitudinal study of one world city throws this dynamic into question. While London's industrial structure has undoubtedly shifted towards the cultural industries, there must be severe doubts that it has become more distinctive or more creative since the 1960s. The competition between major cities for symbolic distinctiveness may be one imperative of the contemporary global economy, but there are contradictory forces that stifle urban individuality and creativity, particularly in the hyper-capitalisation of property markets, and the increasing power of global corporations in a vastly expanded luxury goods sector. The connections between new symbolic industries and older craft traditions were much stronger in the post-war epoch than after the massive deindustrialisation of the 1970s and 1980s. Within fashion in particular there is a danger that the kind of dynamic urban formation found in cities like London, New York, Paris and Milan in the post-war decades, characterised by creative networks, flexible production and vibrant consumer culture, has been replaced by what we have described as ›Potemkin cities‹ of fashion, increasingly left with little more than the corporatised surface sheen of fashion culture (Gilbert 2006: 30). Beneath its own surface myths of ›birds and Beatles‹, sixties London had far fewer people engaged in its ›urban creative economy‹ than the city of today. Nonetheless, through its openings for new entrepreneurs, its legacy of craft industries, its relatively affordable urban interstices and its new consumer culture, sixties London was a site of a genuinely distinctive and creative urban cultural economy.

Bibliography

Amin, A. and N. Thrift (2002). *Cities: Reimagining the Urban*. Cambridge.

Booker, C. (1969). *The Neophiliacs. The Revolution in English Life in the Fifties and Sixties.* London.

Breward, C. (2004). *Fashioning London: Clothing and the Modern Metropolis.* Oxford.

— (2006). »Fashion's front and back: ›rag trade‹ cultures and cultures of consumption in post-war London c. 1945–1970«. *The London Journal,* 31, 1, 15–40.

Chenoune, Farid (1993). *A History of Men's Fashion.* Paris.

Clout, H. and J. Burgess (1978). »Central London«. In H. Clout (ed.). *Changing London,* 49–60. Slough.

Cohn, N. (2006). »It was 40 years ago today …« *GQ Magazine,* April 2006, 130–138.

Crane, D. (1992). *The Production of Culture: Media and the Urban Arts.* Newbury Park, Cal.

Ethington, P. and M. Meeker (2002). »Saber y Conocer: the metropolis of urban enquiry«. In M. Dear (ed.). *From Chicago to LA: making sense of urban theory.* London 403–420.

Fine, B. (2002). *The World of Consumption: The Material and Cultural Revisited.* London.

Florida, R. (2002). *The Rise of the Creative Class: and how it's transforming work, leisure, community and everyday life.* New York.

Gilbert, D. (2006a). »›The youngest legend in history‹: cultures of consumption and the mythologies of Swinging London«. *The London Journal,* 31, 1, 1–14.

— (2006b). »From Paris to Shanghai: the changing geographies of fashion's world cities«. In C. Breward and D. Gilbert (eds.). *Fashion's World Cities.* Oxford.

Green, J. (1999). *All Dressed Up. The Sixties and the Counterculture.* London.

Green, N. (1997). *Ready-to-Wear and Ready-to-Work: A Century of Industry and Immigrants in Paris and New York.* Durham, NC.

Hall, P. (1962). *The Industries of Greater London since 1861.* London.

Hamnett, C. (2003). *Unequal City: London in the Global Arena.* London.

Humphries, S. and J. Taylor (1986). *The making of Modern London 1945–85.* London.

Hutton, T. (2004). »The New Economy of the inner city«. *Cities* 21, 2, 89–108.

Keeble, D. (1976). *Industrial Location and Planning in the UK.* London.

Lash, S. and J. Urry (1994). *Economies of Signs and Space.* London.

Levy, S. (2003). *Ready, Steady, Go! Swinging London and the Invention of Cool.* London.

Martin, J (1966). *Greater London: An Industrial Geography.* London.

Marwick, A. (1998). *The Sixties: Cultural Revolution in Britain, France, Italy, and the United States c. 1958–c. 1974.* Oxford.

McRobbie, A. (1998). *British Fashion Design: Rag Trade or Image Industry?* London.

Mouaert, F. and Gallouj, C. (1993). »The locational geography of advanced producer service firms: the limits of economies of agglomeration«. In P. Daniels, S. Illeris, J. Bonamy and J. Philippe (eds.). *The Geography of Services,* 91–106. London.

O'Neill, A. (2007). *London: After a Fashion.* London.

Pearson, J. and G. Turner (1965). *The Persuasion Industry.* London.

Piore, M. and C. Sabel (1984). *The Second Industrial Divide: Possibilities for Prosperity.* New York.

Porter, R. (1994). *London: A Social History.* London.

Pratt, A. (1997). »The cultural industries production system: a case study of employment change in Britain, 1984–1991«. *Environment and Planning A*, 29, 11, 1953–1974.

Robson, W. (1965). »The heart of Greater London: Proposals for a policy«. *London School of Economics: Greater London Papers*, No. 9.

Salter, T. (1970). *Carnaby Street.* Walton-on-Thames.

Sandbrook, D. (2006). *White Heat. A History of Britain in the Swinging Sixties.* London.

Scott, A. (2000a). *The Cultural Economy of Cities.* London.

— (2000b). »The Cultural Economy of Paris«. *International Journal of Urban and Regional Research*, 24, 567–582.

— (2001). »Geographical foundations of creativity and innovation in the cultural economy«. Paper presented at the ESRC Cities Competitiveness and Cohesion Programme Workshop on ›Innovation and Competitive Cities in the Global Economy‹, March 28–30, in Worcester College, Oxford.

Scott, A. (2005). *On Hollywood: The Place, the Industry.* Princeton.

Thrift, N. and K. Olds (1996). »Reconfiguring the economic in economic geography«. *Progress in human Geography*, 20, 311–337.

Weller, S. (2004). *Fashion's influence on garment mass production: knowledge, commodities and the capture of value.* Unpublished Melbourne University PhD.

— (2007). »Fashion as viscous knowledge: fashion's role in shaping trans-national garment production«. *Journal of Economic Geography*, 7, 1, 39–66.

Wood, P. (1978). »Industrial changes in inner London«. In H. Clout (ed.). *Changing London*, 38–48. Slough.

Port Culture: Maritime Entertainment and Urban Revitalisation, 1950–2000

Jörn Weinhold

»The HafenCity is the largest urban project in Hamburg. […] The city extends to create a quarter with a metropolitan mixture of housing, culture, entertainment, trade and commerce. This allows for a continuous and long-term increase in value, providing stabilizing effects for the urban economy. […] The waterside location close to the harbour and Elbe offers the opportunity for the development of a distinctive, maritime milieu.« (Master Plan Concept 1999: 6f.)

Introduction: Culture-Led Revitalisation at the Urban Waterfront

The way the *HafenCity* project in Hamburg is described in this quotation from its *Master Plan Concept* might easily be applied to many waterfront regeneration projects in major seaport cities of the world. The current project of revitalising a large part of its historic port, therefore, only adds Hamburg to a long list of cities, which already underwent similar transformations in the last five decades. Culture and entertainment were and – as the remarks from the *Master Plan Concept* illustrate – still are considered to be vital factors in redeveloping the urban waterfront. By setting up cultural institutions and events in the former harbour area, the goals of the public private partnership between the Hamburg Senate and the *HafenCity* developers are two-fold: In addition to making the new neighbourhood more attractive, so that the area's real estate value will increase and the economic success of the revitalisation project will be guaranteed, they are also trying to foster the tourist sector as one of the most dynamic parts of the city's overall economy. The redevelopment projects in former port areas thus constitute a rich object for research in the discussion of the relationship between culture, economy and cities. The way maritime cultural landscapes of seaport cities were used or created for revitalisation processes is especially pertinent.

Indeed, one might argue that the policy of investing in culture in order to support urban regeneration played a key role in the early debate on the cultural economy of cities. This is indicated by the large number of groundbreaking and often cited publications (Bianchini et al. 1988; Wynne 1992, Bianchini and Parkinson 1993; Bassett 1993), which approached the question of the relationship between culture and the economic performance of a city by focusing on urban revitalisation projects.[1] The issue of cultural policy and urban regeneration has remained a highly disputed aspect of the broader discussion on culture and its interrelation with the urban economy ever since (Kunzmann 2004). Thus, Steven Miles and Ronan Paddison introduced their article quite appropriately with the title *The Rise and Rise of Culture-led Urban Regeneration* describing the strategy as the »new orthodoxy by which cities seek to enhance their competitive position« (Miles and Paddison 2005: 833). In this context revitalisation projects at the urban waterfront appear merely as a specific variation of urban regeneration. However, not only were examples for waterfront redevelopment such as Bilbao – even before it became famous for Gehry's Guggenheim-Museum and its so-called Bilbao effect (Gonzalez 1993) – introduced early into the academic discussion. But it is precisely because of their unique histories as seaport cities with an assumed ›maritime culture‹ that cases of urban regeneration at the waterfront are prime exemplifications for addressing major questions in the debate: In which ways was and is culture applied for image producing identities of cities and for the selling of places?

The notion of ›cultural planning‹ that is used by scholars who explore how culture and urban economies are intertwined is often quite vague. As Bianchini puts it:

»Its central characteristics are that it rests on a very broad, anthropological definition of ›culture‹ as ›a way of life‹, and that it integrates the arts into other aspects of local culture and into the texture and routines of daily life in the city. Its field of action ranges from the arts, the media, the crafts, fashion and design to sports, recreation, architecture and townscape, heritage, tourism, eating and entertainment,

---

1   The amount of academic attention given to this topic appeared to have been so prominent in the 1990s that Allen Scott even felt the need »to go beyond – though not to abandon entirely« this understanding of the cultural economy of cities (Scott 1997: 325; Scott 2000: 5).

local history, and the characteristics of the city's public realm and social life, its identity and external image.« (Bianchini 1993: 209)

It is the strength of such an all-embracing understanding of culture that it takes into account the complexity and multiplicity of how culture can be utilised for urban regeneration. At many waterfront revitalisation projects, in fact, the whole repertoire of cultural implementations suggested by Bianchini can be found.[2] The definition also opens up the possibility to notice changes in the way these cultural strategies are applied. Thus, as Lily Kong (2000) observes in her review, since the 1990s there has been a remarkable turn towards ›popular culture‹ at the expense of ›high culture‹ or the arts in conceptualising cultural policy for urban redevelopment. This shift of attention towards forms of popular culture seems especially appropriate in the case of projects at the waterfront. In their rhetoric, developers and investors repeatedly refer to a specific maritime port culture to promote their revitalisation projects. ›Culture‹ in this context is usually used within the same line as terms such as ›entertainment‹, ›leisure‹ and ›tourism‹.[3] Therefore, it is in many ways popular or mass culture that is presented by waterfront developers as – what I will call here – ›maritime entertainment‹ to attract not only citizens, but also tourists with money to spend.

Of course, this does not mean that high culture, i.e., art and science, did not play a major role for revitalisation projects at the urban waterfront. Quite the opposite is true: It was and is a common feature of regeneration processes in former harbour areas to include an opera house, a concert hall or an art museum. The Sydney Opera House, the mentioned Guggenheim-Museum in Bilbao, the new Copenhagen Opera House and Hamburg's planned Elbe Philharmonic Hall to name only a few, are well known examples. They do not just offer high culture, but as buildings designed as

2 By focussing on the media, design, fashion etc. and adding the trend to install universities into redevelopments at the waterfront one could also consider the role of the creative classes in this context as it was done recently for the Arabianranta project in Helsinki by Mervi Ilmonen and Klaus Kunzmann (2007). This would, however, go beyond the scope of this short article. I will therefore only hint at some plans of this kind for the case of Hamburg without elaborating on them.

3 As in the case of Hamburg's *HafenCity* project: »HafenCity provides a unique opportunity to equip the city centre with a new and enhanced infrastructure that will support retail, entertainment, leisure, culture, and tourism. [...] The goods and services offered will place an accent on international flair, port and waterside atmosphere, which will attract a large number of daytime visitors.« (HafenCity Hamburg 2000: 29)

landmark architecture by world famous architects they are pieces of art themselves. Very often these buildings or examples of public art, such as Gehry's sculpture Pez de Oro (golden fish) at Barcelona's waterfront, function as symbols for the whole revitalisation projects. Whereas, high culture has undisputedly had an impact on many revitalisation projects at the urban waterfront, it is more often forms of popular culture, such as harbour spectacles and festivities, museums presenting the maritime tradition of a city as well as urban historic fabric and architecture documenting a seaports' urban heritage, which are supposed to define the city and its waterfront project as a unique maritime place for both its citizens and tourists.

A Latecomer: Hamburg as a Case Study

It is through this aspired »distinctive, maritime milieu« as put forward in the quotation from the Master Plan Concept that the *Hamburg HafenCity GmbH* wishes to differentiate the *HafenCity* from other urban regeneration projects. Avoiding cultural uniformity by stressing the place specific culture of a city in order to achieve competitive advantages on national and international markets is a major concept in the discussion of the cultural economy of cities (Scott 1997: 324f.). However, the diction used by the Hamburg developers to illustrate their strategy barely differs from the descriptions used already for other waterfront projects in the past. Therefore, among the existing literature on revitalisation projects,[4] the way in which many cities seem to just follow the same kind of redevelopment model which originates in early American projects of the 1960s is strongly criticized. According to the critics, many local authorities, developers and investors tend to reproduce kitschy imitations of a port culture by focussing on marinas, aquaria, maritime museums and artefacts of the harbour history and mixing these with restaurants, shops and events to please the trend of successful city tourism (Schubert 2001: 57f.). Proponents of this school of thought like Peter Hall (1988), David Harvey (1988) or Jan Goss (1996), however, have been just as strongly criticized for one-sidedness and

---

4   With the growing number of waterfront revitalisation projects all over the world during the last 50 years the literature on this topic has increased enormously. An excellent, regularly updated bibliography has been put together by Dirk Schubert (see Schubert, »Bibliographie«).

oversimplification. By concentrating on commercialized elements of regeneration projects only they are ignoring, according to Uta Hohn (2000), that many revitalised waterfronts are much more functionally diversified and are the outcome of quite specific planning cultures. She therefore rejects the allegations of »sameness« at the waterfront.

Maritime entertainment conceived as a cultural tool for the *HafenCity* project is a good object to explore how an urban image is produced in order to raise the perspectives of a city's real estate and tourist economy at the waterfront. In pursuing this question it is important to assess, the way in which Hamburg as a current and late example of waterfront revitalisation is still following a model developed half a century ago, or, whether there are peculiarities in the relationship of Hamburg to its port that differentiate this case from other waterfront redevelopments. By investigating the history of maritime entertainment as a cultural strategy used for the interest of urban regeneration I will try to contribute to the task of historicising the phenomenon of cultural economies of cities as Martina Heßler and Clemens Zimmermann outlined in the introduction to this book. Contextualising the case study of Hamburg as a latecomer in the worldwide process of regeneration projects at the urban waterfront offers the opportunity to put the questions of urban cultural strategies, urban regeneration and place selling into a historical perspective as K. Bassett (1993: 1773–1775) and Stephen Ward (1998) have done to discover precedents for the 1980s' cultural economy of cities. Culture – understood as a ›way of life‹ and the expression of everyday practices as discussed not only by Franco Bianchini, but others as well (Miles and Paddison 2005: 834; Miles 2005: 892) – allows a closer look at actors beyond local governments, investors and developers engaged in revitalisation projects in order to understand the participation of different social groups and individuals in the dynamic and long-lasting cultural process of producing an urban image, developing maritime entertainment and constructing a local identity.

In their contribution to the early debate of cultural policy and its impact on urban development Jürgen Friedrichs and Jens Dangschat (1993: 132) concluded that »the advantages of Hamburg have yet to be discovered«. According to them, due to an inadequate policy the city fared less well as a tourist destination than other German cities in the 1980s. Compared to Berlin and Frankfurt, which had promoted themselves through aggressive marketing campaigns, Hamburg lacked the tools for selling the city and its image. As I will argue here, the absence of a coherent cultural policy in

Hamburg is probably just part of the story. Instead, the example of maritime entertainment as practised in Hamburg based on the everyday reconstruction of local harbour identities reveals how contested the urban image of Hamburg as a seaport city with a specific port culture already was, when the plans to redevelop the city's waterfront started. Social groups as diverse as the organisers of harbour boat tours, curators of maritime museums, owners of souvenir shops and quayside bars as well as ship's chandlers, mongers at the fish market or members of traditional harbour professions like *Quartiersleute*[5] or sailors were just as much part of and profiting from maritime entertainment industries as the recent collaboration between local authorities and developers at the urban waterfront. To understand the competition of this wide spectrum of social actors for defining the urban image of Hamburg as a seaport city one also has to take into account the spatial context of maritime culture and waterfront revitalisation.[6] While the *HafenCity* project, which is claiming to add an area of c. 115 hectare to Hamburg's downtown district, appears to be the natural focus of attention in the discussion, I will try to show that reproducing a maritime atmosphere in its urban setting is spatially much more complex, taking place at sites in Hamburg which are hardly related to the area of the planned *HafenCity*.

Maritime Excitement:
Sailortown and Harbour Spectacles up until the 1960s

Hamburg has had the reputation of a city in which commerce and trade means everything, while culture and fine arts means relatively little for a long time. In this tradition, museums, theatres, libraries and concert halls were initiated by rich individuals or families acting as patrons of the arts rather than by Hamburg's Senate as the head of local government. These cultural interventions by the Hamburg bourgeoisie appear to have not been very satisfying. Travel guides to Hamburg in the late nineteenth and early twentieth century stressed the lack of sights and tourist attractions (Evans

---

5 Stock keepers in the harbour's warehouse complex *Speicherstadt*.

6 Ilse Möller (1999: 134–137), for example, questions the way the term *Hafenrand* (harbour's edge) is used to describe the different developments along the river Elbe as urban waterfront revitalisation projects.

1990: 36; Klessmann 2002: 489–502; Möller 1999: 159). Instead, visitors turned to the port and its notorious sailortown to find some excitement and amusement. Harbour boat tours especially became popular not only for tourists, but for citizens alike many years before a maritime nostalgia emerged. In fact, it was the excitement of the ever increasing and busy harbour that allured people to explore the port area around the St. Pauli Landungsbrücken[7]. Shipping agents fostered the interest in the harbour by publishing guides for the boat tours (Botsch 1928). Visitors to the city thus had the chance to admire windjammers, watch the construction of new ships in the dockyards or observe the unloading of foreign goods like coffee, tea, and spices.

Fig. 1: Harbour boat tour, paddle-steamer and Stülcken-dockyards, c. 1954

(Source: www.bildarchiv-hamburg.de)

St. Pauli as Hamburg's most famous harbour district emerged during the nineteenth century as a popular sailortown around Spielbudenplatz and Reeperbahn, which had attractions to offer far beyond the work routines of the port to be watched during a harbour boat tour. In the heydays of the sailing-ships, waterfront neighbourhoods around the world appeared to be

---

7   The St. Pauli *Landungsbrücken* are well known piers in Hamburg within the St. Pauli habour district and are frequently referred to as simply the *Landungsbrücken*.

very much alike. Each with their urban fabric structured by the shops and business establishments closely linked to sailors' and marine interests such as houses of ship chandlers, marine surveyors, ropewalks, sail lofts, but also taverns, tattooing parlours, music halls, souvenir shops, bars and brothels (Rudolph 1980: 31–36; Fischer 1927). Due to their exotic and at times dangerous appearances, sailortowns, as amusement districts of seaport cities with excitements like dance halls, wax figure cabinets or ghost trains, became popular among the middle classes and were soon turned into tourist sites. With the restructuring of the harbour work and the decline of the sailing merchant marine in the first half of the twentieth century the transformation of the sailortown phrased by Wolfgang Rudolph as the »Retreat from the Reeperbahn« went along: »All over the world, the streets of Sailortown had been thrown wide open to tourism and the hordes of affluent inland visitors, thirsting for amusements [...]; wherever you looked – in Liverpool, London, Antwerp, Hamburg, Copenhagen, Marseilles or Naples, it was the same« (Rudolph 1980: 178f.). From the 1930s onwards a number of ›St. Pauli-movies‹ with popular ›sailor songs‹ were produced indicating a growing maritime nostalgia with the alleged vanishing of the sailortown as it used to be (ibid.: 179f.).

The sailortowns obviously played an important role for the port culture images of people living and working in the neighbourhoods adjacent to the commercial, industrial or naval harbours, but also in the public imagination of a maritime culture. Therefore, Dirk Schubert stresses the cultural role of sailortowns in the process of the changing relationship between seaport cities and their ports which ultimately led to the rediscovering of the urban waterfront and its revitalisation after the 1950s. This transformation has been described according to Brian Stuart Hoyle's port evolution model with five stages: The first stage of the so-called primitive city-port is characterised by ports which function till the mid-nineteenth century mainly as places of commerce and for storing goods. The harbours with their emerging sailortowns were at that time integrated into the urban fabric of the cities. The stage of the expanding city-port, which then extended up until the early twentieth century, describes the introduction of steamships and the widening of harbour basins. While the mixture of functions such as living and working in harbour districts were gradually disintegrating, a specific subculture of dock workers came into being. Following that, the modern industrial city-port illustrates the stage during which the working processes in harbours were increasingly mechanized during the interwar years. The industrialised harbours and the disappearance of sailing ships led to the beginning of a maritime nostalgia and the early examples of maritime museums. Sailortowns were turning gradually into nightlife districts appealing for citizens and tourists alike. Starting after the middle of the twentieth-century, especially in the 1960s to 1980s, the retreat of cities from their waterfronts is marked as the fourth stage by the deindustrialisation of many harbours and the abandonment of port areas close to downtown areas in major seaport cities. This was due in large to the changes in transport technologies. Especially the introduction of containers in the harbour economy demanded new, larger harbour areas usually some distance from the urban core. Finally, during the time period spanning between the 1970s and 1990s the by then open spaces in the traditional harbour areas close to the city centres were rediscovered and the worldwide movement for the redevelopment of the waterfront was under way (Hoyle 1988: 3–19; Schubert 2001: 14–36).

David Hilling (1994) pointed out that the »rise and fall« of the sailortown within the changing relations of the city to its port has to be considered as a vital factor in the discussion of the revitalisation of urban waterfronts. However, as his example of Cardiff shows, with too much of the original fabric of the maritime quarter removed as a result of post-war redevelopments, the possibility for a waterfront revitalisation project to take up elements of this former culture to invoke a sailortown atmosphere is extremely limited. This is true also for the development of the Reeperbahn, where the transformation of the former sailortown into a night-life district was completed with the arrival and success of the Beatles in the 1960s. The image of a sailortown vanished, while in addition to its role as the notorious red-light district the neighbourhood flourished as a place for music and dance halls. One might even wonder whether the importance ascribed to restored sailortowns as part of a cultural strategy to support urban regeneration is exaggerated in the research done so far. While historically it was without doubt a major part in the creation of a port culture, it remains questionable whether the image of crime and prostitution – always linked to sailortowns as well – is exactly what developers have in mind when they try to establish maritime entertainment. Furthermore, with the emphasis that many scholars of the history of seaport cities put on the similarities of sailortowns' culture (Rudolph 1980:31) or of the dockers' culture (Andersen 1992: 154) the function of culture as a tool for pointing out the unique identity of a place and its distinctiveness in competition with other waterfront projects is considerably weakened.

Interestingly, in one of the earliest examples of waterfront developments the sailortown also played an insignificant role: In Boston the old, run-down sailortown at Scollary Square was converted into a government complex including the New City Hall in the 1950s, thus abandoning the immigrant and maritime image of the neighbourhood (Hall 1993: 16).

Early American examples like those of the development projects of the ports in Boston and Baltimore have been – according at least to some researchers – taken as models for other seaport cities ever since. It is here, where the leisure and tourist oriented strategies in waterfront revitalisation projects were first developed in the late 1950s and early 1960s (Turnbridge 1993: 290–296). The introduction of festival marketplaces as a key concept to this approach of waterfront developments was of vital importance (Schubert 2001b). Between 1971 and 1985 more than 80 festival marketplaces were built, many of them by the Rouse Corporation. It was in Boston, where James Rouse – also involved in the waterfront project in Baltimore as a founder of the Greater Baltimore Council – refurbished the former Quincy Market as Faneuil Hall Market in the mid-1970s. Before being turned into the first waterfront enterprise of the Rouse Corporation, the two eighteenth century market halls located close to the shoreline were about to be demolished. Since then the Faneuil Hall Market is regarded by many as the prototype of a festival marketplace, a »synonym for the port renaissance« (ibid.: 342). It functions as a link in the urban fabric connecting the Government Centre and the CBD of Boston with the city's waterfront (»walkway to the waterfront«). Later the opening of the New England Aquarium at Central Wharf in 1969, the building of a ferry port, the restoration of historic warehouses and the introduction of the Boston Harborwalk in 1984 were supposed to add to the maritime attractiveness of the place. While ›yuppie food‹ and retailing were important aspects of the festival marketplace, it was the number of activities and events taking place at the Faneuil Hall Market which made it an important element of downtown waterfront revitalisation projects.

The case of Hamburg diverges from the general pattern described by Hoyle's evolution model and the early waterfront redevelopment projects in North America. Although the first containership arrived in Hamburg as early as 1968 (Engel and Tode 2007: 123)[8] – an occurrence, which is usually taken as the indication for the economic and technological changes that made a restructuring of the port necessary – this did not yet lead to the retreat of traditional harbour companies from the waterfront areas close to the Speicherstadt and Hamburg's city centre (Möller 1999: 136f.). Instead the harbour in Hamburg remained in many ways an active port and an important part of Hamburg's economy, though not without fluctuations. The distinctive port culture was thus shaped over the years by what might be called ›harbour spectacles‹, which people already enjoyed at the beginning of the twentieth century during the harbour boat tours. In the 1960s and 1970s, long before the arrival of the ocean liner Queen Mary II started to attract huge crowds in our times, many spectators in Hamburg were regularly watching the arrival and departure from cruise liners like the Queen Elizabeth II in 1972 at the Landungsbrücken. Thousands of people were also lured to the waterfront when supertankers with a length of 350 meter stayed in one of the docks (Grobecker 2004: 119). In the decades after WWII, therefore, the everyday incidents of harbour activities constituted the port culture in Hamburg. Smaller businesses like souvenir shops and organisers of harbour boat tours used these spectacles for their income and at the same time contributed to the daily reproduction of maritime entertainment.

This applies also for urban retreats like the Schulau Ferry Station on the western border of the city of Hamburg. In 1952 Otto Friedrich Behnke established the »ship welcoming station«, which since then has been greeting every larger incoming ship with welcoming words and the ship's national anthem. Soon after, the café at the ferry station became a popular weekend destination for families from Hamburg. Another place on the western beaches along the river Elbe that invites its guest to ship-spotting is a small, informal looking café called *Strandperle* (›pearl of the beach‹). Opening right at the beach as *Lühr's Gaststätte* in 1949 it was at first only known to local people in the Övelgönne neighbourhood, such as the owners of sailing boats, harbour pilots and pensioners. Due to the opening of a hiking trail in the early 1970s, however, it became a favourite place to watch the incoming and outgoing container ships (Gall 2007). While in other parts of the world modes of maritime entertainment were invented to attract people to the former neglected urban waterfront and to install

8   Other sources are dating this event in the year 1966 (Rüttgerodt-Riechmann 2000: 6).

businesses to earn money by selling stereotypes of a port culture, the allure of the river and the city's harbour had been a Hamburg obsession for quite a while. As the result of largely uncoordinated private initiatives the maritime culture in Hamburg was far from the festivalisation organised around the festival marketplaces at North American waterfront developments. However, these everyday activities constituted a maritime atmosphere that was ready to be taken on.

Maritime Celebrations: Festivalisation and a ›String of Pearls‹ in the 1970s and 1980s

The occasion for greater events and celebrations was soon to come. Already in 1964 the Hamburg Senate grasped the opportunity to commemorate the harbour's 775th anniversary. What till then was traditionally organised every year as a small, exclusive *Überseetag*[9] was transformed now into a large popular festival lasting for three days. About 100,000 citizens and visitors celebrated along the shoreline of the river Elbe between Blankenese and Övelgönne as well as in the harbour area, enjoying the alleged world's greatest fire works arranged on barges in the middle of the river. The official character of the celebrations was demonstrated by a series of events, such as receptions at the town hall and ecumenical services for official guests, arranged from May till the end of the year. The Senate seized the chance for a comprehensive marketing campaign in order to strengthen the resurgent harbour economy and to build up new trading links (Grobecker 2004: 85). It took, however, more than another decade till the local authorities used the harbour anniversary regularly as a form of image production to support not only the harbour development, but also the tourist sector of Hamburg's economy. It was in 1977 that the senator of economic affairs Wilhelm Nölling initiated the idea to organise the anniversary as a public event through the city's official tourist office. While it started as a rather small celebration with only a couple of carnies at the Landungsbrücken it changed into a major annual event, the 800th anniversary in 1989 marking a climax with an estimated three million visitors. The festival programme, nevertheless, linked up with the SAIL'89, another

---

9   A day which celebrates Hamburg's overseas tradition.

mega-event, concentrated again on ship spotting as the foremost attraction of the harbour (ibid.: 174f.). The official interpretation of the maritime culture to be used in the cultural policy thus did not actually have anything new to offer (except in magnitude), instead it firmly relied on what had already been established by Hamburg's citizens in the past decades.

For many decades after the war, arriving in Hamburg with a cruise ship meant being confronted with a »façade of ugliness« (ibid.: 65). The waterfront west of the Landungsbrücken between Neumühlen and St. Pauli was still marked in many places by demolitions resulting from the war or by areas which had fallen into disuse. This part of Hamburg's northern waterfront had a very different appearance than that of the areas east of the Landungsbrücken – close to the Speicherstadt – with its historic warehouses or the southern areas of the harbour with their container terminals and dockyards. This is due to the fact, that the district to the west, Altona, was a city on its own up until 1937 and unlike Hamburg not a commercial harbour, but rather mainly a fishing and timber harbour. Whereas in other major seaport cities waterfront revitalisation projects were already underway on a large scale (especially in, for example, the docklands in London), the small strip along the northern riverbank turned out to be the starting point for such endeavours in Hamburg during the 1980s. A task force was set up in 1984 to devise a development plan for 6 kilometers of waterfront between Neumühlen in the west and the Speicherstadt in the east. Egbert Kossak, the head of the Hamburg building authority and a strong proponent of the regeneration along the northern riverbank, came up with the metaphor of a ›string of pearls‹. The idea was to generate single projects – instead of a master development concept – to interpret the specific context of each site and create an appropriate solution (Perlenkette 2000: 93). In the general planning guidelines of 1987, which explicated the mixed use development approach, he stressed the cultural factor of the concept right in the first point: »New nodal points are to be created for culture, shopping and amusement on the northern riverbank of the Elbe having a simultaneous positive effect on the Reeperbahn and the area between the Reeperbahn and the northern riverside« (ibid.: 96).

The formulation of the planning guidelines was preceded by the Hamburger Bauforum 1985, which was initiated as a symposium by the Hamburg building authority to gather international architects, urban designers and urban planners to stimulate the discussion in Hamburg with their ideas. The discussions and presentations of the Bauforum took place in the historic Fischauktionshalle, located quite centrally in the area to be developed as a ›string of pearls‹ (II. Hamburger Bauforum 1985). The Fischauktionshalle, itself an object of the planning process, was indeed an important part of the maritime milieu created in this section of Hamburg's waterfront. With the adjacent Fischmarkt it symbolised a significant aspect of Hamburg's role as a port city for which it is known beyond its city borders, due to national marketing campaigns for the »Hamburger Fischmarkt«. Built in the years 1895/1896 the Fischauktionshalle was heavily damaged during the war. Poorly restored in the post-war years the market hall fulfilled its function only until the 1970s, when its demolition was discussed in order to provide more space for the fishmongers of Sunday's fish market. However, the commitment of a local architect helped to save the building and after a decision by the Hamburg senate in 1982 the Fischauktionshalle was reconstructed and reopened in 1985 (Fischer 1986, 207–209; Perlenkette 2000: 71; Historische Stadtrundgänge 1988: 11). The restoration of the Fischmarkt and the use of the Fischauktionshalle got very mixed reviews. While some criticized the historicising redevelopment of the square and the market practices as a stage design attractive only for tourism (Historische Stadtrundgänge 1988: 10; Schubert 1996: 145), others appraised the result as a successful alignment of new and old buildings (Möller 1999: 136). What is clear though, is the noticeable tendency towards festivalisation[10] in this planning process. With its alternate utilisation for a great variety of events the Fischauktionshalle is indeed reminiscent of a festival marketplace (although without shops for souvenirs, yuppie food etc.). Thus the second Bauforum – one might argue puckishly – functioned as an early event in the restored market hall. This impression is even strengthened considering Egbert Kossak's explicit reference to earlier examples of waterfront developments in Boston, Baltimore, New York, San Francisco and London (Perlenkette: 29), which in the 1980s were the obvious examples to look into.

---

10 The term festivalisation usually used in relation to Olympic Games or world exhibitions might at first appear exaggerated considering the examples discussed here. However, it is the notion of a festival-led policy that is at the core of the concept of festivalisation and therefore I think it is also appropriate here (Häußermann and Siebel 1993: 7).

Fig. 2: Second Hamburg Bauforum in the Fischauktionshalle, 1985

(Source: Staatsarchiv Hamburg)

The Bauforum and the planning for the ›string of pearls‹ received broad media coverage and through that raised attention to the project even outside of Hamburg. At the same time, however, both also became subjects of intense criticism. The results of the Bauforum were described as a colourful mixture of different approaches to architecture, the event itself as a spectacle (Schubert 1996: 140). Critics from the political environment of the Hafenstraße squatting milieu even described the planning at the urban waterfront as the continuation of plans Hitler had ordered to be developed for Hamburg's waterfront (Grolle 2005: 153f.). The allegation, though completely far fetched, does show the political circumstances of the 1980s, when the Hafenstraße as a squatted street made national news. The conflict around the Hafenstraße, as part of the proposed regeneration project, reflects the social problems linked to the housing market at that point in time. With too little focus on affordable housing and a strong bias in favour of offices and shops for media and design related companies in order to attract the new creative classes, the planning for the ›string of pearls‹ not surprisingly aroused considerable opposition (Schubert 1996). The cultural aims of this waterfront project, like the instalment of a museum and the inclusion of a museum ship into the ›string of pearls‹, gained less attention in this situation. However, the regular occurring routine events like the fish market or the harbour anniversary, which were firmly established in this period, are clear indications of a public cultural policy supporting the waterfront redevelopment in Hamburg through maritime entertainment.

Maritime Legacy: Speicherstadt and Harbour Museumisation in the 1980s and 1990s

Whereas the harbour spectacles and the port's festivalisation cherish the present maritime atmosphere of a seaport city, urban heritage as documented by historic buildings and museums is supposed to show visitors and citizens that the city's maritime culture is authentic, deeply rooted in the past. In this sense the Speicherstadt is probably the prime symbol for Hamburg's history as a major commercial port. This might be surprising, since the building of the warehouse complex did not start before 1883. Considering the long history of Hamburg's harbour one could wonder, whether there are no older and more spectacular buildings which could function as the major heritage sites in the port. Moreover, due to the social history of its building process in which the Senate ›ruthlessly‹ let a whole neighbourhood be torn down without taking much concern for the former 24,000 inhabitants the Speicherstadt still seems to bear negative connotations for some scholars (Schubert 1996: 148; Lafrenz 1994: 323; Seemann 1997: 69f.). The popularity of the Speicherstadt could also be questioned, because although it was visible, as part of the Freihafen (free trade zone) it was not freely accessible for everybody for a long time, due to the customs regulations. Finally, the restructuring of the harbour economy in recent decades has lead to the traditional usage of the warehouses declining, which may in turn have also caused a lack of interest in the complex. Despite all these reasons for possible reservations or disinterest towards the Speicherstadt as a symbol for Hamburg's maritime past, a conflict in the late 1980s established its position in the urban heritage of the city durably. While converting the warehouses had already been considered in the 1970s and early 1980s, the Senate's announcement in 1988 that it was planning to sell the Speicherstadt took many people by surprise. The assumption that the Hamburg Senate was trying to seize the occasion for a profitable commercialisation of the warehouse complex to deal with its budget problems soon led to the emergence of a public resistance movement (Lafrenz 1994: 329–331; Seemann 1997: 71). The concern that offices for new media would evict the traditional companies from the Speicherstadt was especially omnipresent. Revitalisation projects at Hamburg's waterfront were, therefore, closely linked to the tendency of attracting the ›creative classes‹ (Wilkens-Caspar 2004), an idea that was opposed by owners and the workforce of the traditional harbour related companies as well as preservationists of historic port buildings.

Some of the movement's groups were organised as voluntary associations, such as the »Speicherstadt Hamburg e.V.«. They were able to make their objections public through the support of newspapers like the powerful *Bild* tabloid. In one of these publications Karl-Ludwig Mönkemeier, the former harbour director, representing especially the view of the companies still using the warehouses to store their goods demanded: »Hände weg von Speicherstadt und Freihafen!«[11] (Krüger 1991). On the one hand, by emphasising the advantages of storing commodities like spices, coffee, tea or carpets he stressed the point that for many companies and customers the usage of the warehouses made economic sense. On the other hand, he also showed that through these everyday trading practices the Speicherstadt remained a lively part of Hamburg's maritime culture. In 1991 the movement's groups met with success – the warehouse complex was added to the listed buildings. Jürgen Lafrenz pointed out that the image factor linked to the Speicherstadt by then could indeed have an economic value for the city (Lafrenz 1994: 338). It can also be assumed that the significance of this factor was even increased in combination with the so-called Kontorhausviertel (office building district) (Hipp 1986; Historische Stadtrundgänge 1989). This district within the city centre of Hamburg, separated from the Freihafen by only the Customs Canal, was mainly built in the 1920s and 1930s, though there were also examples of *Kontorhäuser* built at the same time the Speicherstadt was erected. Due to its commercial purpose the Kontorhausviertel contributed to the image production of the Speicherstadt just across the canal, reproducing the representation of Hamburg as a major commercial seaport city.[12] Thus the port related self-conception did

---

11 »Hands off the Speicherstadt and the harbour's free trade zone«.
12 In 1999, the Hamburg local authorities submitted an application requesting that the Speicherstadt in combination with the Kontorhausviertel be listed as cultural world heritage.

not stop at the boundaries of the harbour, but instead transcended into the adjacent downtown areas.

There are of course other historic buildings or elements of the harbour fabric in Hamburg's seaport area that are worth discussing (Bohnsack et al. 1989) including a few architectural monuments left in the area south of the Speicherstadt, where the HafenCity is now being built. The *Kaispeicher A*, however is being turned into a concert hall as Hamburg's new architectural landmark, the *Kaispeicher B* is being converted into a new maritime museum and the Sandtorhafen, originally the first modern basin of Hamburg's port, is supposed to be transformed into a museum harbour. In 1986 Karin Maak very strongly stated that the best way to experience architectural monuments like the Speicherstadt is by keeping the function it was built for, aiming at the authentic life of working practices taking place in the Speicherstadt instead of altering it to a museum (Maak 1986: 123f.). Since then, nevertheless, the museumisation of the harbour has transformed the ways of experiencing the waterfront. The Speicherstadt itself became the subject of an exhibition which was shown in one of the warehouses in 1988/1989. The initiative to establish a permanent exhibition in the Speicherstadt led to the opening of the Speicherstadtmuseum in 1995 as a private branch of the Museum of Work in Hamburg run by Henning Rademacher. Rademacher, was already involved in the 1988 exhibition and was previously a member of a maritime profession himself. The Museum Harbour Övelgönne also originated from private enthusiasm for the historic maritime world. A voluntary association (Verein Museumshafen Övelgönne) was founded in 1976 and was able to exhibit the first ships in the museum harbour's basin already in 1977. Since then the museum has extended its number of ships to 30 including numerous sailing boats, a fishing cutter and a light vessel.

Therefore, the museumisation of Hamburg's harbour started as early as the 1970s and many new museums emerged during the 1980s and 1990s. In the Speicherstadt area alone three more museums were founded alongside the Speicherstadtmuseum: the Customs Museum opened in 1992, the Hot Spice Museum in 1993 and the Afghan Museum in 1998 (Küpper 1999) covering a huge variety of topics related to maritime trade. Central to every maritime entertainment and, therefore, major attractions along the waterfront between Övelgönne and the Speicherstadt are two museum ships. The MS Cap San Diego was built in 1961 by the Deutsche Werft AG in Hamburg and designed by the marine architect Cäsar Pinnau. It finally returned to Hamburg in 1986 to be converted into a museum ship after serving as a cargo vessel. One year later the windjammer Rickmer Rickmers found its mooring close to the MS Cap San Diego and the Landungsbrücken. Again, both ships were run as museums not by the Hamburg state, but by two foundations. The historic maritime atmosphere thus created is, however, not linked only to museums along the waterfront. The Museum for the History of Hamburg and the Altonaer Museum have both possessed and regularly exhibited maritime collections for a long time (Plagemann 1989: 64). It follows from all this that the resources in Hamburg for historic elements of maritime entertainment became extremely rich over the years, not only in the form of architectural urban heritage, but also as a museum-landscape of Hamburg's maritime life. The popularity and success of each as part of the port's maritime entertainment was very dependent on the agency of people who started a new museum or who struggled for the preservation of the harbour's material urban heritage.

Conclusion: The *HafenCity* Project between Past and Future Port Culture

A diverse port culture borne by both private and public initiatives existed and was growing, when in 1997 »Hamburg's mayor had a vision« (Sack 1997)[13]: During a high profile event the mayor announced in the presence of the prestigious merchant association the Übersee-Club and the Federal President of Germany his plans for the then so-called *Hafen-City*. The project, which had been prepared in secrecy for about five years through numerous activities in order to avoid building speculations, was supposed to »return the city centre to the waterfront«. The hoped for profit the city would gain from this project could then be reinvested in the southern harbour extension. The mayor imagined a service centre for »finances, media, image producing tourism and culture for the Hafen-City«. This time, however, with many failed urban planning projects in Hamburg in mind, housing was to be firmly included in the project and not only for the rich.

---

13 The following quotations from *DIE ZEIT* are my own translations.

The journalist Manfred Sack of the weekly *DIE ZEIT* remained sceptical alluding in his article to the fact, that the mayor's vision was in fact an old idea: Egbert Kossak had already envisioned a similar scenario in 1989 during another Bauforum (ibid.), which, with the shortcomings of the London dockland development presenting a negative example by that time, was not well received. The frustration the former head of Hamburg's building authority felt (Kossak 1999: 138) and the ›lateness‹ of Hamburg in the international process of waterfront revitalisation reflects the fact that the process is not a one way road as Hoyle's model could be misunderstood or even a »worldwide urban success story« (Breen and Rigby 1996) as some scholars on waterfront redevelopment suggest.[14] This is especially true for the ›culture-led‹ concept of many of these projects. The model of the festival marketplace as applied first in Boston and Baltimore was developed to provide »the function of entertainment« to the revitalised urban waterfront in order to attract as many visitors as possible. In urban planning thinking »the function of entertainment« is still repeated in today's redevelopment projects and defined roughly by »cultural, leisure, tourism, markets, museums, public places and exhibition halls« (Kossak 1999: 137).

The festival marketplaces as conceived in the late 1950s and early 1960s were in this respect introduced as »strategic central approaches« (Schubert 2001b: 319) for the planning of waterfront redevelopment schemes to guarantee their economic success. In Hamburg such entertainment entities did not have to be invented for the waterfront revitalisation, because the harbour's maritime entertainment based on the idea of local port cultures being used for tourism was well established. The example of Hamburg's attempts to redevelop its waterfront shows that when the local authorities in cooperation with developers and investors nevertheless tried to implement a maritime entertainment the way it has been planned for other places before, they stirred huge criticism and opposition. While the case of Hamburg therefore questions the allegations of global homogeneity at the waterfront, one should at the same time not overestimate the local forces in creating a specific port culture ready to be utilized for the local economy in terms of real estate and tourism. The conflicts concerning the ›string of pearls‹, the Hafenstraße and the Speicherstadt illustrate how contested the

---

14 To be fair one has to say that Breen and Rigby do not forget to discuss some failures as well. Nevertheless, their evaluations as well as those of other researchers are at times astonishingly positive, frequently concentrating on the economic and design aspects of the projects.

definition of the Hamburg's waterfront as an urban neighbourhood with a distinctive port culture was. There was not one local maritime culture in Hamburg and it was not even always envisaged in the harbour area. In this situation a coherent cultural policy for urban regeneration beyond the Hafengeburtstag or the Fischmarkt was difficult to conceive. The urban image of Hamburg as a seaport city with a specific maritime culture was thus the result of continuing negotiations between different players, which took place in the context of interwoven local and global processes. World-wide technological changes in the harbour economy, the deindustrialisation of large urban areas, and the decline of traditional working and living structures at the waterfront, boosted tendencies of industrial romanticism and maritime nostalgia, which had already been part of maritime entertainment in Hamburg for many decades. For Hamburg as a latecomer in the global process of waterfront revitalisation one can argue, that since events like the *Hafengeburtstag* in the 1970s/1980s, institutions such as museums which present Hamburg's maritime past and interest in preserving the architectural heritage of the harbour started to flourish. All these developments were adding significantly to the already existing port culture as an expression of local identities and as a cultural tool to attract and entertain more tourists in times of growing competition between cities.

Thus, the local authorities, developers and investors of the HafenCity project could rely on a substantial variety of events and institutions as well as a long history of practices of maritime entertainment when they started the redevelopment project in the late 1990s. Since then, however, they have been proceeding with an apparently inconsistent strategy. By incorporating local initiatives of the image production of Hamburg as a major seaport city they were trying to point out a place-specific culture which could help to avoid the ›sameness‹ at the waterfront and thereby strengthen Hamburg's competitive position on real estate and tourist markets. At the same time, nevertheless, just like during the planning of the ›string of pearls‹ the local government in cooperation with the HafenCity developers were again looking to the well known examples of waterfront revitalisation to apply similar strategies in Hamburg. It is thus planned that the Hafen-City will add two more museums and an ›edutainment centre‹ to enhance the maritime character of the project even more: the »Traditional Ship Harbour« at the Sandtorhafen, the »International Maritime Museum Hamburg« in Kaispeicher B and the »Hamburg Maritime Centre« including an aquarium and science centre. While the rhetoric of the *HafenCity* was already interchangeable with other waterfront developments right from the beginning of the project, these new plans are reminiscent of similar cultural installations in waterfront projects and might, contrary to their intentions, endanger the place-specific images of Hamburg as a traditional commercial port which the grown structure of maritime entertainment in the city so far had mainly produced.

Fig. 3: HafenCity construction site with Kaispeicher B and Speicherstadt, 2007

(Source: www.bildarchiv-hamburg.de)

Conflicts about Hamburg's peculiar maritime cultures and how these are used in terms of the cultural economies of the city as well as debates on the reproduction of Hamburg's image as a seaport city will certainly continue. The different status and influence of actors in this processes can be illustrated by the artistic representation of the *HafenCity* under construction: While on the one hand the construction site of the *HafenCity* soon became a favourite motif for many competing photographers in the city, only a few artists had the privilege of being invited with the support of the influential Körber foundation to inspire the area through their art installations during the building process (Körber-Stiftung 2006). It is even more important in this context to closely observe how private initiatives in the construction of a maritime image are supported by local authorities as the conflict over

Peter Tamm's controversial marine collection for the »International Maritime Museum Hamburg« shows. His collection will be exhibited in the Kaispeicher B with the support of 30 million Euros from the city of Hamburg, but was accused of presenting a militaristic maritime culture (Schellen 2005). The role of the Hamburg authorities in their cultural policy towards the revitalisation project therefore raises the question of social inclusion or exclusion in the process of the image production. Considering the spatial urban impact it should also be questioned, whether this policy favours the *HafenCity* over other parts of Hamburg, because traditionally the maritime culture in Hamburg was the outcome of activities at quite different parts of the city, sometimes not even at the waterfront.

Today the *HafenCity* is a key-element of Hamburg's disputed general guiding principle »Hamburg – a growing city« (Altrock and Schubert 2004) and the transformation of the urban waterfront, with the help of maritime entertainment to achieve an even better competitive position, is far from over. »The idea of the ›leap across the Elbe‹ encompasses the urban arc extending from today's city centre, Speicherstadt and *HafenCity*, over the Veddel district and Wilhelmsburg right through to Harburg« (HafenCity Hamburg GmbH 2006: 101). Pioneers of a maritime culture in these parts of the city will again be two museums, demonstrating once more the ongoing process of the museumisation of Hamburg's port: the BallinStadt Museum, illustrating the city's history as a port of emigration, and the Hafenmuseum as another branch of the Museum of Work. Whether urban regeneration and Hamburg's overall economy will profit from this cultural policy is yet to be seen and in general difficult to measure.[15] The *HafenCity Hamburg GmbH* (2006: 46–49, 105) is optimistic that its cultural highlights will attract many visitors thereby contributing to Hamburg's tourism as one of the city's largest growth sectors. The most recent »Hamburg Maritim« (2007), the official guide to Hamburg's places of maritime interest, puts in return the *HafenCity* – still mainly a construction site – on top of the list of recommended sightseeing tours, ahead of places such as the Speicherstadt, the Landungsbrücken or the Fischmarkt.

---

15 The problem of evaluating this policy is pointed out by Graeme Evans (2005). A sceptical point of view as to quantitative evidence is taken by D. A. Pinder (1993).

Bibliography

Altrock, Uwe and Dirk Schubert (2004). *Wachsende Stadt: Leitbild – Utopie – Vision?* Wiesbaden.

Andersen, Svend Aage (1992). »Dockers' Culture in Three North European Port Cities: Hamburg, Gothenburg and Aarhus, 1880–1960. A study of subcultures and their social contexts«. In Poul Holm and John Edwards (eds.). *North Sea Ports and Harbours. Adaptations to Change*, 133–158, Esbjerg.

Bassett, K. (1993). »Urban cultural strategies and urban regeneration. A case study and critique«. *Environment and Planning A*, 25, 1773–1788.

Bianchini, Franco (1993). »Culture, conflict and cities. Issues and prospects for the 1990s«. In Franco Bianchini and Michael Parkinson (eds.). *Cultural policy and urban regeneration. The West European experience*, 199–213. Manchester.

Bianchini, Franco et al. (1988). *City Centres, City Cultures. The Role of the Arts in the Revitalisation of Towns and Cities.* Manchester.

— and Michael Parkinson (eds.) (1993). *Cultural policy and urban regeneration. The West European experience.* Manchester.

Bohnsack, Gabriele et al. (1989). »Bau- und Technikdenkmale im Hamburger Hafen«. In Jörg Haspel and Juliane Kirschbaum (eds.). *Aspekte und Perspektiven der Hafendenkmalpflege*, 72–92. Bonn.

Botsch, Hermann (1928). *Kennst Du den Hamburger Hafen? Eine Rundfahrt unter fachmännischer Führung.* Hamburg.

Breen, Ann and Dick Rigby (1996). *The New Waterfront: A Worldwide Success Story.* Singapore.

Engel, Sandra and Sven Tode (2007). *Hafen Stadt Hamburg. Von der Alster an die Elbe – Hafenentwicklung im Strom der Zeit.* Hamburg.

Evans, Richard J. (1990). *Death in Hamburg. Society and Politics in the Cholera Years 1830–1910.* London.

Fischer, Hans Erasmus (1927). *Sittengeschichte des Hafens.* Wien.

Fischer, Manfred F. (1986). »Der Hamburger Hafen als Ort technischer Kulturdenkmale. Probleme und Möglichkeiten der Denkmalpflege«. In Jürgen Ellermeyer and Rainer Postel (eds.). *Stadt und Hafen. Hamburger Beiträge zur Geschichte von Handel und Schiffahrt*, 202–209. Hamburg.

Gall, Insa (2007). »Abschied vom Zauberfluss«. *Die Welt*, 12, March 25, HH3.

Goll, Joist (2005). »Der Hamburger Hafenstraßenkonflikt und der Geisterkrieg um die Vergangenheit«. *Zeitschrift des Vereins für Hamburgische Geschichte*, 91, 133–158.

Gonzalez, Julia M. (1993). »Bilbao: culture, citizenship and quality of life«. In Franco Bianchini and Michael Parkinson (eds.). *Cultural policy and urban regeneration. The West European experience*, 73–89. Manchester.

Goss, Jon (1996). »Disquiet on the Waterfront. Reflections on Nostalgia and Utopia in the Urban Archetyps of Festival Marketplaces«. *Urban Geography*, 17, 3, 221–247.

Grobecker, Kurt (2004),. *Hafen Hamburg. Sechs Jahrzehnte Erfolgsgeschichte.* Hamburg.

Häußermann, Hartmut and Walter Siebel (1993). »Die Politik der Festivalisierung und die Festivalisierung der Politik«. In Hartmut Häußermann and Walter Siebel (eds.). *Festivalisierung der Stadtpolitik. Stadtentwicklung durch große Projekte*, 7–31. Opladen.

HafenCity Hamburg – The Masterplan (2000), edited by the HafenCity Hamburg GmbH. *Reihe Arbeitshefte zur HafenCity 6*, Hamburg.

HafenCity Hamburg GmbH (2006). *The Birth of a City*. Hamburg.

Hall, Peter (1988). *Cities of Tomorrow*. Oxford.

— (1993). »Waterfronts. A new urban frontier«. In Rinio Bruttomesso (ed.). *Waterfronts. A New Frontier for Cities on Water*, 12–20. Venice.

II. Hamburger Bauforum (1985), edited by the Baubehörde Hamburg. Hamburg.

Hamburg Maritim (2007), edited by Hamburg Tourismus GmbH. Hamburg.

Harvey, David (1988). »Voodoo cities«. *New Statesman and Society*, 1, 17, 33–35.

Hilling, David (1994). »Socio-economic change in the maritime quarter. The demise of sailortown«. In B. S. Hoyle et al. (eds.). *Revitalising the Waterfront. International Dimensions of Dockland Redevelopment*, 21–37. Chichester.

Hipp, Hermann (1986). »Heimat in der City. Die Wandlung des Stadtbildes in der Hamburger Innenstadt um die Jahrhundertwende«. In Jürgen Ellermeyer and Rainer Postel (eds.). *Stadt und Hafen. Hamburger Beiträge zur Geschichte von Handel und Schiffahrt*, 127–141. Hamburg.

Historische Stadtrundgänge. Altonaer Hafen – Fische & Fabriken (1988), edited by the Museum der Arbeit, Hamburg.

Historische Stadtrundgänge. Kaufmannshäuser, Speicher und Kontore – von der Deichstraße zur Speicherstadt (1989), edited by the Museum der Arbeit, Hamburg.

Hohn, Uta (2000). »Stadtumbau an der metropolitanen Waterfront hoch industrialisierter Staaten. Grundmuster und planungskulturell bedingte Variationen«. In Hans H. Blotevogel et al. (eds.). *Lokal verankert – weltweit vernetzt*, 247–256. Stuttgart.

Hoyle, Brian Stuart (1988). »Development dynamics at the port-city interface«. In B. S. Hoyle, D.A. Pinder and S Husain (eds.). *Revitalising the waterfront*, 3–19. London.

Ilmonen, Mervi and Klaus R. Kunzmann (2007). »Culture, creativity and urban regeneration«. In *Arabianranta. Rethinking urban living*. Helsinki.

Klessmann, Eckart (2002). *Geschichte der Stadt Hamburg*. Hamburg.

Körber-Stiftung (ed.) (2006). *Kunst und Kultur in der Hafen City*. Hamburg.

Kong, Lily (2000). »Culture, economy and policy. Trends and developments«. *Geoforum*, 31, 385–390.

Kossak, Egbert (1999). »Visionen für ein neues Jahrtausend«. In Jörgen Bracker et al. *Die Hafenkante. Menschen, Geschichten, Visionen. Övelgönne bis Meßberg*, 132–142. Hamburg.

Krüger, Horst (1991). *Speicherstadt. Kein Verkauf der Speicherstadt*. Hamburg.

Küpper, Anke (1999). »Schmuggel, Gewürze und Elbe 3 – Museen und Kultur an der Hafenkante«. In Jörgen Bracker et al. *Die Hafenkante. Menschen, Geschichten, Visionen. Övelgönne bis Meßberg*, 54–59. Hamburg.

Kunzmann, Klaus R. (2004). »Culture, creativity and spatial planning«. *Town Planning Review*, 75, 4, 383–404.

Lafrenz, Jürgen (1994). »Spekulationen zur Speicherstadt in Hamburg in Vergangenheit und Gegenwart«. *Die alte Stadt*, 4, 1994, 318–338.

Maak, Karin (1986). »Die Speicherstadt im Hamburger Freihafen. Eine Stadt an Stelle der Stadt«. In Jürgen Ellermeyer and Rainer Postel (eds.). *Stadt und Hafen. Hamburger Beiträge zur Geschichte von Handel und Schiffahrt*, 115–126. Hamburg.

Master Plan Concept (1999), edited by the Hamburg Port Area Development Corporation. Reihe Arbeitshefte zur HafenCity 2, Hamburg.

Miles, Steven (2005). »Interruptions. Testing the Rhetoric of Culturally Led Urban Development«. *Urban Studies*, 42, 5/6, 889–911.

— and Ronan Paddison (2005). »Introduction: The Rise and Rise of Culture-led Urban Regeneration«. *Urban Studies*, 42, 5/6, 833–839.

Möller, Ilse (1999). *Hamburg*. Gotha/Stuttgart.

Perlenkette – Hamburgs Hafenrand. Die Revitalisierung des nördlichen Elbufers (2000), edited by the Freie und Hansestadt Hamburg. Hamburg.

Pinder, D. A. (1993). »Waterfront Revitalisation and the Cityport Economy«. In Rinio Bruttomesso (ed.). *Waterfronts. A New Frontier for Cities on Water*, 159–166. Venice.

Plagemann, Volker (1989). »Der Hamburger Hafen – ein Nationaldenkmal der maritimen Industriekultur«. In: Jörg Haspel and Juliane Kirschbaum (eds.). *Aspekte und Perspektiven der Hafendenkmalpflege*, 60–65. Bonn.

Rudolph, Wolfgang (1980). *Harbor and Town. A Maritime Cultural History*. Leipzig.

Rüttgerodt-Riechmann, Ilse (2000). »Hafen Hamburg«. In Dirk J. Peters and Hartmut Bickelmann. *Hafenlandschaft im Wandel*, 75–86. Bremerhaven.

Sack, Manfred (1997). »Dicht am Wasser. Der Hamburger Bürgermeister hat eine Vision: Die City wieder zurück an die Elbe zu führen«. *Die Zeit*, 21, August 9, 1997.

Schellen, Petra (2005). »Schiffemuseum versenken«, *die tageszeitung*, July 2, 2005.

Schubert, Dirk (1996). »Neues von der Wasserkante‹ – Chancen und Probleme nachhaltiger Stadt(teil)entwicklung und Stadterneuerung am nördlichen Elbufer«. *Jahrbuch Stadterneuerung*, 133–155.

Schubert, Dirk (2001). »Revitalisierung von (brachgefallenen) Hafen- und Uferzonen in Seehafenstädten – Anlässe, Ziele, Ergebnisse sowie Forschungsansätze und -defizite«. In D. Schubert (ed.). *Hafen- und Uferzonen im Wandel. Analysen und Planungen zur Revitalisierung der Waterfront in Hafenstädten*, 14–36. Berlin.

— (2001b). »Festival Market Places als Revitalisierungsstrategie für brachgefallene Hafen- und Uferzonen in Baltimore, New York, Boston und Seattle. ›Learning from North-America and see you in Disneyland?‹«. In D. Schubert (ed.), *Hafen-*

und Uferzonen im Wandel. Analysen und Planungen zur Revitalisierung der Waterfront in Hafenstädten, 319–360. Berlin.

— (2002). »Revitalisierung von brachgefallenen Hafen- und Uferzonen. Transformationsprozesse an der Waterfront«. *Raumforschung und Raumordnung*, 60, 1, 48–60.

— »*Bibliographie. Transformationsprozesse in Seehafenstädten – Revitalisierung von (brachgefallenen) Hafen- und Uferzonen*«. August 20, 2007. http://www.tuharburg.de/b/kuehn/themen/wfb.html.

Scott, Allen J. (1997). »The Cultural Economy of Cities«. *International Journal of Urban and Regional Research*, 21, 2, 323–339.

Scott, Allen J. (2000). *The Cultural Economy of Cities. Essays on the Geography of Image-Producing Industries*. London.

Seemann, Agnes (1997). »Historische Entwicklung des Hamburger Hafenrandes und der Speicherstadt seit dem frühen 19. Jahrhundert«. In *Altstadt – City – Denkmalort*, 67–71. Hamburg.

Turnbridge, John (1993). »The Tourist-Leisure Dimension. North American Waterfronts in Comparative Perspective«. In R. Bruttomesso (ed.). *Waterfronts. A New Frontier for Cities on Water*, 290–296. Venice.

Ward, Stephen V. (1998). *Selling Places. The Marketing and Promotion of Towns and Cities 1850–2000*. London.

Wilkens-Caspar, Nicola (2004). »Kreativität an der Hamburger Waterfront – Die Bedeutung von Werbung und Neuen Medien für die Stadt- und Wirtschaftsstruktur«. In: A. Priebs and R. Wehrhahn (eds.). *Neue Entwicklungen an der europäischen Waterfront*, 117–138. Kiel.

Wynne, Derek (1992). *The Culture Industry. Arts in Urban Regeneration*. Aldershot.

3   The Role of Cultural Policy: City
     Images, Media, and the Cultural
     Economy in the Nineteenth and
     Twentieth Century

»Queen of the Arts« – Exhibitions, Festivals, and Tourism in Fascist Venice, 1922–1945

Jan Andreas May

Introduction

At the 52nd International Art Exhibition of the Venice Biennale in 2007, seventy-eight countries officially participated and the city was full of contemporary art. In September of the same year, the International Film Festival, today an integral part of the Biennale, took place for the 64th time. Set up 75 years ago, it is the oldest and still one of the most important film festivals in Europe. Within the international art and film scenes, Venice has long established itself as the location of two of the most important events: the International Art Exhibition, established in 1895, and the International Film Festival, first organised in 1932. Both events found numerous imitators: Currently, there are more than a hundred biennales and film festivals all over the world. Venice – also referred to as The Queen of the Adriatic Sea or La Serenissima – has long been one of the touristiest cities in the world. In the following, I will examine the critical role that both its art exhibition and its film festival play in the city's touristic history. Looking at the historical development of the cultural economy of cities in Europe, Venice provides an extraordinary example of how a city in decline succeeded in giving itself a new image by becoming a stage for the modern arts.

In my text I want to focus on the most important period of these developments which lies in the fascist era – a time when Venice was modernized and reshaped for the purposes of the tourist industry. Venice stands for romanticism, beauty and love, however, behind that stands Italy's strongest economic power: the tourism industry. Culture is the most important magnet for visitors. Further research on Venice's clever strategy could support the growing number of studies in the field of culture, economy and the city, which is examined in this volume.

In the early 1990s, Häußermann and Siebel coined the term of the »festivilisation« of urban politics, describing it as a new phenomenon. This view, however, does not take into account the long tradition of festival strategies by civic and private actors in many European cities, as I want to demonstrate with the example of Venice (Häußermann and Siebel 1993). In Europe, series of exhibitions or festivals for music have existed for many decades. Although Venice was not the first city to host art exhibitions, music, opera or theatre festivals or other traditional festivities, its history and fame has a firm root in its festival culture. In the eighteenth century, Venice was the hotspot for decadent carnival life, all year round. But the fall of the Republic marked the beginning of the most wretched century in the history of Venice: When Napoleon put an end to the Venetian Republic in 1797, the city's total cultural and economic decline began. Soon the ruin of a former metropolis, Venice became a symbol for death and decline, as captured for instance by Byron and Ruskin (Plant 2002). The only industries which survived, though on very small scale, were glass, mosaic and lace. In its search for new business sectors, the city turned towards tourism: »Venice was perhaps the first European city to recognize the newly emerging tourist industry as a saving grace and to develop it systematically« (Forssmann 1971: 11). In the beginning, this turn towards tourism was a positive development, but these days it has become a dangerous element for the future of Venice (Van der Borg 1992; Isman 2000; Davis and Marvin 2004).

This text will focus on the important period of urban development in Venice from the 1920s to the 1940s, when Venice organized its tourism professionally and became a favoured cultural tourist destination for an international elite of travellers and art lovers. Venice was one of the first European cities to concentrate its economy primarily on the development of cultural tourism. Supported by the local political leaders and the government in Rome, Venice succeeded in reshaping the historic city into a perfectly organized tourist destination with new infrastructure. In these decades, the city was modernized with the help of the Italian state and created its image as one of the most important exhibition and festival cities in Europe. This period was the foundation for the big success which began after 1945 and continues until this day.

The following paragraphs will examine how the cultural heritage of Venice was used for tourist purposes. How did the fascist leaders support the development? Which new attractions were added in the 1930s? And who developed them? The text will then look at organisational and financial questions. How were the events financed? And which role did the concept of »public-private partnership« (PPP) play in developing the infrastructure for the International Film Festival at the Lido? PPP is generally regarded as a concept that emerged in the late 1970s, but the example of Venice proves its existence at a much earlier time. Finally, the text will address promotion and marketing strategies in Venice.

Cultural Tourism as an Industry in Italy

Italy is a country with one of the longest traditions as a travel destination. Starting in antiquity, the tradition continued throughout the Middle Ages, until the seventeenth and eighteenth centuries when the country became the main destination for travellers doing the Grand Tour. Based on this tradition, the travel industry was developed in the nineteenth century as one of the most important economic sources for the country. Until the First World War, tourism was organized mostly by private companies from foreign countries: Thomas Cook, Wagons Lits, Hapag Lloyd and others (Dawes 2003). Then the state recognized its importance for national wealth, and in 1919 voted for a law to create a national tourism agency (Bosworth 1996; Paloscia 1994; Paloscia 2004; Syrjämaa 1997; Brilli 2006). In 1922, the Ente Nazionale Italiano del Turismo (ENIT) was founded to focus on the professionalisation of tourism organisation and marketing; it still exists today.

The ENIT defined a unique image of Italy abroad for an international market. Periodicals were published in several languages and ENIT maintained offices in all important capitals in Europe and America.[1] In fascist

---

1 ENIT published several books and guides in different languages. Today it is still the most important institution for promoting Italy as a tourist destination. See *Statistica del turismo: bollettino mensile dell'Ente nazionale industrie turistiche*, 1929–1934. Rome; *Reiseland Italien: Monatsschrift der ENIT und der Staatsbahnen für Reise & Verkehr*, 1933–1936. Rome; *Italia: rivista turistica mensile dell'ENIT e delle ferrovie dello Stato*, 1935/1936–1943. Rome; Ente nazionale industrie turistiche (1937) (ed.). *Viaggio di nozze in Italia*. Milan/Rome.

Italy this industry played a very important role and the state supported the economic factor of cultural heritage. It restored, recreated and reshaped historic attractions for the growing tourist industry like no other country had ever done. Research in the last years has shown that the fascist state used antique, medieval, renaissance or baroque buildings, festivities or traditions not only for national propaganda, but also for the most part in order to optimize the tourist schedule. Among the most innovative cultural events organized in Tuscany during the regime were festivals such as the *calcio* in Florence and the *palio* in Siena which had their roots in medieval events. As Medina Lasansky and other scholars have shown in their case studies, many cities created new images based on their cultural heritage (Lasansky 2004; Crum and Lazzaro 2005).

I want to describe the example of Venice in order to show the ideas and concepts which were used for optimizing tourism, largely by way of adapting other successful models. Before 1900, when Venice was an attractive travel destination in Europe, the first entrepreneurs to make a profit on travellers were private hoteliers (Cosulich 1990). With the historic centre and the fashionable seaside resort of the Lido di Venezia, it combined the wishes of the upper and middle class travellers going to Venice. During the nineteenth century, more and more private palaces were converted into hotels or the property of antique dealers (Bierbaum 1900). Focusing on the history of Venice during the fascist period, I want to show how the city optimized the organisation of cultural heritage and spectacle for economic reasons (Bosworth 1999; Fincardi 2001). The most recent research on this subject is the PhD thesis *Culture, tourism and Fascism in Venice 1919–1945* by Stefania Longo (2005) who has examined some of these aspects closely and came to parallel results.

»Venezia Moderna« – Industrialisation and New Infrastructure

Fascist politicians from Venice, including Count Giuseppe Volpi di Misurata and Giovanni Giuriati, used their influence in Rome to support the economic and cultural development in their hometown (Romano 1982; Brunetta 1986; Reberschak 2002). The first important step in modernizing Venice was the creation of some important infrastructural elements. On the surface, the city seems to have preserved its historic shape, but on closer examination the elements built in the 1920s und 1930s become visible. Venice is an example for the synthesis of antiquity and modernity that was promoted by the fascist state to create a modern country. Other cities like Rome and Florence are mainly famous for their historic sites. The modern elements of fascist politics in combination with the economic growth and the cultural heritage created a unique destination (Ben-Ghiat 2001).

The experienced colonial politician Count Volpi treated the city as a business project whose wealth was based on urban development. From 1917 onwards, he oversaw the creation of the new industrial port area Porto Marghera near Mestre on the edge of the lagoon. The settlement of electric, chemical and petrol industry combined with a modern port made the Veneto region one of the fastest growing industrial regions in Italy. In 1933, Porto Marghera was Italy's second largest port after Genova.

Until 1933, this economic growth supported mainly the wealth on the mainland, but with the realisation of an old plan which involved building a second bridge linking Venice to the mainland industrial area, the historic centre also became an integral part of this modernisation (Zucconi 2002). »La Grande Venezia« – as it was called now – consisted of three main parts: the historic centre of Venice, the industrial area Porto Marghera/Mestre and the seaside resort Lido di Venezia. The 1933 inauguration of this bridge, the Ponte del Littorio, which was part of the motorway between Milan-Padova-Trieste, made Venice reachable by car. The bridge leads directly to the western edge of the historic centre and was an important element of the rebirth of the *Serenissima*.[2] Supporting the railway station as the main entry, the starting point for visiting Venice or the Lido now was Piazzale Roma with a huge public garage for more than 2,000 cars (Farinati 2002). Water traffic was also modernized with new vessels and the Rio Nuovo shortened the distance from the station or Piazzale Roma to Piazza San Marco. The last big project was the new Riva dell'Impero (1938) which connects the historic centre and the Giardini of the Biennale at the eastern edge of the city. The last part of the modern traffic infrastructure was the construction of a new terminal for the Aeroporto San Nicolo (1934) at the Lido with direct flights from Rome, Munich or Vienna.[3]

---

2   »Road to Venice«. *Time Magazine*, May 1, 1933.
3   *AMV, Determiniazioni Podestarili, Aeroporto Lido. Costruzione di una stazione passaggeri*, trim. II, 1934, n. 1162.

»*I call upon Venice as a witness*«, proclaimed the famous architect and urban planner Le Corbusier when he talked about the modern aspects of its urban structure (Le Corbusier 1924: p. 71).[4] The division of the transport systems into separate spheres for cars, boats, planes, trains and pedestrians – as realized in Venice – underlined his urban ideals. Generally, the whole transport system is still currently based on these developments and demonstrates its enormous capacity with the ever growing number of tourists. Like a modern amusement park you could reach Venice by train, bus, car or plane and all this was possible without destroying the unique character of the historic centre. It is this rigorous, yet gentle modernisation which forms the key for Venice's success on the tourism front.

»Venezia Antica« – Economising the Glorious Past

Today, there is no doubt that Venice itself and its artistic treasures represent a unique heritage world-wide. However, in the early 1920s, the situation of the museums, palaces and collections was not comparable to the contemporary situation. Since the seventeenth century, the art of the city had been sold in large quantities to royals, museums, collections and art dealers all over the world. Most of the palaces were empty and in some cases it was impossible to imagine the richness of the past. The treasures of the Ducal Palace, the Accademia Gallery or the Museo Correr had numerous voids. The cultural state of Venice after the fall of the Republic, could to a certain extent, be described as a stage without actors. The goal now was to remedy that situation in order to make culture profitable.

During the 1920s, Venice also optimized its cultural infrastructure in the historic centre. The restoration of buildings and the creation of new museums were accompanied by a series of newly inaugurated cultural events. These included, for example, the *Regatta Storica*, and the religious *Salute* or *Redentore* festivities. This made the city more and more attractive for visitors. An anachronistic guild like that of the gondoliers only survived because of tourism.

---

4   See Le Corbusier, Charles (1935). In Institut International de Coopération Intellectuelle (ed.). *L'art et la réalité. L'art et l'état. Conference given in Venice in July 1934*, 73–86. Paris; Le Corbusier (1934). *La Ville Radieuse*, 24. Paris.

After the collapse of the tourist industry during the First World War, Venice continued to reshape the historic centre. Travellers came to Venice because they wanted to find the romantic dream city of the past and wanted to see the treasures in San Marco, the Palazzo Ducale, several churches and the famous Accademia Gallery. The inception of a new cluster of state or civic museums was intended to capitalize on the linkage between the arts and cultural tourism. Private property was given or sold to the city with the aim to make Venice more attractive. This period started in 1920 with the Italian royal family of Savoy who gave several royal palaces to the cities. A large part of the Procuratie Nuove at Saint Mark's square was also given to the City of Venice. It was then possible to move the Civic Museum Correr from the Fondaco dei Turchi to the centre of the city. In 1922, the museum opened its new building and immediately attracted a great number of visitors. In January 1927, the gallery at the Palazzo Ca'd'Oro opened. The gallery had been given to the state by the private art collector Giorgio Franchetti. The Gallery of the Accademia and the Ducal Palace, which were still the most successful museums in Venice, were also renovated at this time. Under the presidency of Count Giuseppe Volpi di Misurata, the next step for increasing the number of civic museums was the city's acquisition of the enormous eighteenth century Palazzo Ca'Rezzonico and the private Collection from the Palazzo Michiel dalle Colonne. This became the main museum for eighteenth century fine and decorative art. The Casa Goldoni was also donated to the city during this period. The idea of developing the island of S. Giorgio Maggiore with its monastery buildings into to a cultural and research centre also originated in the late 1930s. Therefore, in less than ten years the city received three new museums widening the cultural spectrum for art lovers coming to Venice. This was, nevertheless, still below the museum standard of most of the European cities.

The city needed new methods and ideas to attract more visitors. Thus, under the presidency of Count Volpi the civic museums decided to organize large loan exhibitions in order to create »ephemeral museums« (Haskell 2000). These types of temporary art shows were not an Italian invention, but had proved very successful in a great exhibition on seventeenth and eighteenth century art in Florence in 1922. In the 1920s, these events became more and more popular – today they are still the most important sort of exhibitions in the museum world. The main problem at the time was insuring the travelling art treasures. In the case of Venice, however, it was easily resolved by Count Volpi's good business contacts to the main insurance companies in Italy. Starting in 1929 with the eighteenth century art exhibition, *Settecento Italiano*, put together in cooperation with several international museums and collections and shown in the Exhibition Palace in the Giardini, the city had found a new successful instrument for promoting itself through cultural heritage.[5] Included in the exhibition program were guided tours to villas in the Veneto, which turned it into a major cultural tourism event. Mayor Pietro Orsi's hopes that the event »would contribute to increasing tourism to the lagoon«[6] were fulfilled when over 350,000 visitors came to see the show. The exhibition had »served the purpose of enhancing Venetian typical products in a joint celebration of cultural tourism and local economy« (Longo 2005: 183).

These large-scale loan exhibitions were a relatively new type of art event and some traditional institutions did not participate for conservation reasons. As Haskell has described in his book on »ephemeral museums« though, the Italian state had no limits in loaning even the rarest and most unique pieces of art to London or Paris, for instance. The old masters were instrumentalized for the promotion of the fascist state abroad. The art historian Nino Barbantini, curator of an exhibition celebrating the anniversary of Ariosto in Ferrara in 1933, refined this exhibition concept. An important decision was the idea to run huge loan exhibitions with the ›biggest names‹ in Venetian art history: the painters Titian, Tintoretto and Veronese. There was little need for advertising such well-known artists who had already been the focus of interest for museums and private collections in Europe and the U.S. as well as for scholars, art lovers and tourists from all over the world for centuries. In Venice, Barbantini was able to work with the best pieces from other Italian museums, although the director of the Uffici in Florence protested against losing his most important pieces like the *Venus from Urbino* by Titian during the high travel season. In 1935 more than 100 oil paintings were shown in the palace Ca' Pesaro and there is no doubt that this show was one of the most important Titian exhibitions ever.

Opened on St. Marks Day, April 25, 1935 and accompanied by a ceremonial appearance of the king, the Titian exhibition demonstrates how the

5   See ACS, PCM, 1934–1936, 14.1.2826, Sottofasc. 1, *Roma – Mostra del 700 Italiano* (1929); ASAC, Serie Scatole Nere, b. 50, *Mostra del Settecento* 1929; AMV, 1941–1947, IX.11.2, *Minuta di Processo Verbale di determinazione presa dal Podestà*, June 20, 1928.
6   AMV, Determinazioni Podestarili, *Mostra del'700 Italiano*, trim. II, 1929, n. 1086.

fascist state resolutely exploited its artistic heritage for its own propaganda. It was a dreamlike situation for all curators, because in no other state was it possible to get as many good exhibits as in fascist Italy. Once Mussolini had officially approved a loan, every museum, palace or church had to comply. Later shows on Tintoretto (1937) and Veronese (1939) were also mostly as successful in terms of their research impact, public echo and financial gains. This is indicated by the countless articles in art journals all over the world,[7] such as the one in *Art News* from New York:

»Such great shows as the Titian Exhibition held two years ago at the Palazzo Pesaro in Venice and the current magnificent Tintoretto display are milestones in this new scale of evaluations.« (Frankfurter 1937: 9).

These traditional cultural institutions were supported by a new festival policy with which the city exploited traditional festivities like the Regatta, Redentore or Salute in order to celebrate its glorious past as the Queen of the Adriatic Sea in the same manner Florence or Siena had done. Shows in the museums, such as *Feste e maschere a Venezia* in Ca'Rezzonico, supported the rebirth of the traditional carnival.[8] The renovated opera house La Fenice and open air classic concerts on Saint Mark's Square were further important parts of this economic strategy.

Biennale di Venezia – Staging Modern Culture

In contrast to other historic cities like Florence or Rome, Venice developed a second image as a centre for the modern arts. The most important instrument for reshaping the cultural economy was the existing Interna-

7   See *Il Settecento italiano: catalogo generale della mostra e delle sezioni*. Venice 1929; Norris, Christopher (1935). »Venetian regrets«. *Time Magazine*, May 13, 1935; »Titian: notes on the Venice Exhibition«. *The Burlington Magazine*, 67/1935, 127–131; Von der Bercken, E. (1937). »Die Tintoretto-Ausstellung in Venedig«. *Pantheon*, 20/1937, 229–254; Von der Bercken, E. (1939). »Die Paolo-Veronese-Ausstellung in Venedig«. *Pantheon*, 24/1939, 247–258.
8   See Goering, Max (1938). »Feste e maschere a Venezia, Venezianische Feste und Masken: zur Ausstellung von 1937 im Ca' Rezzonico in Venedig«. *Zeitschrift für Kunstgeschichte*, 7/1938, 41–52.

tional Art Exhibition of the city of Venice, better known as the Biennale.[9] Since its foundation in 1895 it became one of the most prestigious international art events in Europe, with 15 countries participating in 1928. The new general secretary of the Biennale, Antonio Maraini, had big plans for the future of this cultural institution. Starting in the late 1920s, Count Volpi and Giuriati lobbied in Rome for a stronger financial support and official acknowledgement from the state. Finally in 1930, the Biennale became an autonomous body controlled by the state with Count Volpi as its president. I do not intend to explain the organisational structure of the Biennale as an organisation in this text, however I do want to show its multifaceted character by focusing on the economisation of modern forms of entertainment.

The world economic crisis and the accompanying decline of the number of visitors to Venice lead the people responsible for the Biennale to an expansion in other contemporary arts sectors. With financial support from the state, the patronage of the House of Savoy and Benito Mussolini, the Biennale started to organize new festivals for contemporary music, film, poetry and theatre. Using the city as a stage for the modern arts, that is using locations outside the Giardini too, supported the festivilisation of the urban cultural policy.

The location for many events was the seaside resort Lido di Venezia which, since the end of the nineteenth century, had been developed into an elite resort with mostly wealthy customers. The numerous new hotels, holiday houses and public baths from that time demonstrate the Lido's importance for the city. Some of the most prestigious hotels in Venice were owned by the Compagnia Italiana dei Grandi Alberghi (CIGA) since 1908. The biggest hotel was the Excelsior Palace, a 600 room hotel, which was finished in 1908. The decadence of Lido life is best illustrated by Thomas Mann's novel *Tod in Venedig* (Death in Venice). After the interruption by the First World War, the Lido re-conquered its prestigious position with international sport and entertainment events. The *Evening Standard* noted in 1932 that it »has become the most beautiful and fashionable bathing resort in Italy«.[10]

9   See also my doctoral thesis on this issue: *La Biennale di Venezia. Continuity and Change in the Venetian Exhibition Policy 1895–1948*, Technical University Berlin, which was defended in June 2007 and will be published soon. See also Stone (1998).
10 »Venice surprise. Italian resort that set the fashion«. *Evening Standard*, June 26, 1932.

One of the most successful feats of Venetian cultural marketing, however, was the invention of the International Cinematographic Art Show (Mostra Internazionale d'Arte Cinematografica), the first international film festival in the world.[11] Under the patronage of Benito Mussolini, the show was organized by the Biennale in cooperation with the International Institute for Educational Cinema (ICE) in Rome.[12] In great parts financed by the hotel company CIGA, it was run like a private business on the terrace of the Hotel Excelsior Palace. It had enormous synergy effects for the local tourist industry, the international film industry and the Italian state. The press stated that »it was a great financial success and a great asset to Venice as a means of attracting tourists« (Pasinetti 1934: 14).

After only two successful festivals it became an integral part of the Italian film strategy under the leadership of the newly formed Ministero della Cultura Popolare (MinCulPop). Nonetheless, it was more than a stage for fascist propaganda: it was planned from the very beginning to be an international meeting point for the film industry. European and American studios used Venice as a stage for their struggle for dominance in the important and growing European film market. This was dominated, like today, by the big studios in Hollywood (Higson and Maltby 1999). The show in Venice only stood to gain from this situation because it became the official festival of the newly founded International Film Chamber. Initiated by the German propaganda minister Joseph Goebbels, the European film industry was to compete with Hollywood, with the aim to create an independent European film industry. This rivalry guaranteed that the U.S. and Europe sent major productions, including their actors and directors, to Venice and that there were always many journalists to report about these events. Walt Disney, Jack Warner, Greta Garbo, Marlene Dietrich, Clark Gable were only a few of the celebrities who came to the lagoon in the 1930s.

The festival created a »win-win-situation« for all participants. The advantage was its openness to all kinds of movies without strict censorship. The ideological openness is best illustrated by the variety of films screened in Venice: from Hollywood films to Russian propaganda and French intellectual films as well as the first German propaganda movies. It is not fitting

---

11 See Paulon, Flavia (1950). *2000 film a Venezia: 1932–1950*. Venice; Paulon, Flavia (1971). *La dogaressa contestata: la favolosa storia della mostra di Venezia: dalle regine alla contestazione*. Mestre; *Venezia 1932. Il cinema diventa arte*. Exhibition Catalogue, Venice 1982.
12 The ICE was created in 1927 as a body of the League of Nations to develop educational cinema. See Taillibert (2000).

to speak about fascist propaganda when British warships in the Bacino S. Marco accompanied the première of the film *Victoria the Great* in 1939, for example. In combination with the attractiveness of the location, Venice could claim to be a tolerant and international place without national animosity. The fascist film policy failed to compete in quality and quantity with the established Hollywood studio system, but with the creation of the studio complex *Cinécittà* in Rome in 1937, it was able to increase the number of films produced. Nevertheless, even Italian film critics stated that there was still a long way to reach the international standard of film production – purely propagandistic movies from Italy played a minor role in this period.

The intelligent concept had one main winner – Venice: The Lido and the CIGA hotels were fully booked, the restaurants packed and the beaches crowded. At the same time, the appearance of politicians and film stars made the festival more popular in the world. The fact that 50,000 tickets were sold in 1935 further shows the economic importance of this event. Moreover, its costs were relatively low compared to the music or theatre festivals. When in 1937 the new film palace opened next to the Excelsior, its high technological standard made it one of the most modern movie theatres in Italy.[13] Here, films could be shown even in bad weather and it could be used as a multi-purpose hall for conferences, festivals, and concerts outside of festival times.

Based on the model of Venice, there were other international film festivals during the World Expositions in Brussels (1935) and Paris (1937) and another one in Moscow (1935). The film festival's program was full of variety up until 1939. With the implementation of new racist laws and the beginning of the Second World War though, this changed and many American studios owned by Jews were prevented from showing their movies. Nonetheless, the Venice Festival was without any real rivals in Europe until 1939 when French, English and American studios began thinking of starting another festival in Cannes. However, this idea was first realized in 1946. The seven film festivals of the 1930s were the first successful series of international events of this kind in the world. They helped to promote new films in many different countries and were an important meeting place for the film industry. It was only after the war that Cannes (1946), Locarno

---

13 Passarella, O. L. (1937). »Innovazioni al Lido di Venezia. Il Palazzo del Cinematografo Internazionale«. *Illustrazione Italiana*, 32, August 8, 1937, 910–911.

(1946), Berlin (1951) and Moscow (1958) started their own international film festivals also following the model of Venice.

Modern Business and Marketing Methods

What was new about the methods organizing culture in Venice during Fascism? And how were all these events financed? As we have seen, the leading figure within most of these activities was Count Volpi, whose entrepreneurial experience and network in Italy and abroad played a major role. In his position as president both of the Biennale as well as of the Civic Museums, he professionalized the organisation of cultural events. With the help of creative cultural impresarios like Nino Barbantini, Antonio Maraini and later Rodolfo Pallucchini he achieved his aim: the economisation of culture in Venice.

Operating like a private company, Venice's perfectly organized cultural machinery launched products such as an international art exhibition, an international music festival, an international film festival, an open air theatre festival, and the big ›Old Master‹ shows, thus shaping a new image of the city in order to attract an international audience and remain one of the top European tourist destinations. Although it was well organized, the cultural expansion was quite expensive. Hence, it was seriously impacted by the financial crisis in the mid-1930s. The Art Exhibition earned its money not from sales commissions, but from the combination of train and entrance tickets sold in cooperation with the state railway company. To run a film festival is much cheaper than the organisation of a music or theatre festival: Only a projector and a screen are required and there is no need to pay for hundreds of members of an orchestra, stage decoration etc. When the Biennale slid into a financial crisis, Count Volpi contemplated suspending the prestigious, but very costly, music and theatre festivals.[14] A report from the appointed commission for the Ministry of National Education (MEN) described the substantial problems of the Biennale activities.[15]

---

14 See AMV, 1931–35, IX.13.4, EA, Letter from Count Volpi to Minister Alfieri, May 13, 1936.

15 ACS, MPI, AABBAA 1929–1960, div. III, B. 281, Giuseppe Volpi/Ugo Ojetti/F. Pantaleo/F. Stroppa, Relazione a S. E. Il Ministro dell'Educazione Nazionale, August 1936.

In 1938, accompanied by the reform of the institutional and financial organisation of the Biennale, the city of Venice and private investors developed new methods of financing the cultural events.[16] The main winner of the film festival was the hotel company CIGA. It co-financed the modern film palace, which was directly linked with a tunnel to the Hotel Excelsior Palace (Longo 2005: 227–232). The technology was donated by sponsors, among them the projector producer *Cinemeccanica* from Milan and the film company *Kodak*.[17] The film festival was, in summary, a commercial venture dictated by the economic interests of the local and international economy (Longo 2005: 230). It was established with the purpose of attracting the international, wealthy elite travelling to Venice and its Lido. This in turn was of great interest to the CIGA as the main accommodation provider.

Like many other cities at the time, Venice set up a new municipal casino in 1936 as a reliable and important source of income with which to finance culture. Cities at the Côte d'Azur or traditional spa towns have shown the large amount of money that could be made through casinos. A casino for Venice had been controversially discussed since the early 1920s (Barizza 1988; Longo 2005: 233–244), but despite the moral doubts about profiting from gambling the city and the Fascist Party decided to establish one. It was run by a private consortium which had a license for 20 years. For Venetians it was »officially« forbidden to gamble in the casino, but this was not very strictly controlled. The state was pushing the city to use the casino profits for supporting the cultural events or the renovation of eminent cultural venues like the Teatro La Fenice.

Thus, Venice was able to create public-private partnership projects in two different cases within the cultural sector. As illustrated in Gunn's text about Manchester or in Höpel's about France and Germany, the private sector has played a very prominent role in culture ever since the 1920s. But, in contrast to these cities, Venice was developed under the rule of a dictatorship – a situation which guaranteed a coordinated exhibition and festival calendar including events of national importance. All the above events were included in this calendar, therefore, official support was guar-

---

16 See for the new Statutes ACS, PCM, 1940–42, 14.1.730, Sottofasc. 1–2, R. Decreto-legge, 21. Juli 1938 – XVI-Nuovo ordinamento dell'Esposizione biennale internionale d'arte di Venezia.

17 The company CINEMECCANICA from Milan was founded in 1920 and is still one of the leading companies for projectors.

anteed. The centre of attention were the Biennale and the Old Master shows which alternated from year to year, followed and accompanied by the theatre, music and film festivals. These attractions were supported by modern marketing methods throughout the world. Supported by the ENIT, the Venetian municipality created a special campaign for promoting the image of Venice in the world. The so-called »Venetian Summer« was invented to attract travellers coming to Venice from early spring to autumn.[18] This »Venetian Summer« included art exhibitions, film festival, but also the traditional festivities like Redentore or Salute.

The Biennale worked together with important influential media partners on a local, national and international level. Beginning in 1922, the city published the *Rivista di Venezia* in order to report about the efforts and cultural events in Venice.[19] In 1925, the CIGA started to publish *Venice*, an English language, travellers magazine, which was transformed into *Le Tre Venezie* published by the Venetian branch of the Partito Nazionale Fascista (PNF).[20] Right from its initial inauguration the Biennale was connected to the most important national periodical on art and culture, *Emporium*. On an international level the exhibition of art journals in 1932 reflected the importance of these media partners.[21] In these publications you could find extensive articles on cultural events in Venice. For example: when the International Music Festival was started in 1930, the *Rivista di Venezia* published an issue on the tradition of music in Venice throughout the centuries. Articles in international journals, mostly written by the organizers, were a successful advertising instrument. Publicizing the city and its festivals to a larger audience strategically enabled the organizers to accelerate the development of tourism.

As mentioned above, Venice was not unique in pursuing this strategy. A coordinated marketing strategy in cooperation with the art journals also

18 See for example *Venedig und Umgebung*, Grieben Reiseführer 106, Berlin 1939.
19 Comune di Venezia. Ufficio Statistica (1922–1935) (ed.). *Rivista Mensile dell'Città di Venezia*. Venice.
20 See *Venice*. Published by the »Federazione per gli interessi turistici della Venezia« (1925), from 1926 *Le Tre Venezie/Venice. Rivista mensile illustrata di propaganda turistica* published by Federazione Provinciale Fascista di Venezia till 1943.
21 See catalogue 1932, p. 56–67: Italy: *Arte, Dedalo, Domus, Casa bella, L'Eroica, Emporium, Poligono, Rassegna dell'istruzione artistica, Vita d'arte, Architettura*; France: *Cahier d'art, Art et décoration, La Renaissance de l'art, L'amour de l'art, Formes*; Germany: *Deutsche Kunst & Dekoration, Kunst und Künstler, Die Kunst, Innen Dekoration, Farbe und Form, Moderne Bauformen*; Great Britain: *The Studio, Commercial Art, Apollo, The Orbit*.

included the publication of guidebooks such as the series *Cities of Art*, co-published by ENIT. Advertising campaigns offered cheaper fares for air and train travel throughout Europe and the USA. Early on, National Socialist politicians like Joseph Goebbels recognized their role as an integral part of a publicity campaign when visiting Venice:»Graf Volpi shall go and advertise the Lido on his own.«[22] Despite further big events like the shows for Tintoretto and Veronese, further art exhibitions and film art shows, the success was in decline. When in 1940 Italy entered the Second World War at the side of Nazi Germany the glorious »last years of the Lion« ended for Venice (Damerini 1988). Even these political events, however, did not stop the cultural activities in Venice. Whereas up to 1939, the city had tried to maintain the international character of its art events, this attempt was doomed to failure with the outbreak of the Second World War: All events between 1940 and 1942 were used as propaganda for the fascist regime and the Italo-German axis.

Only when Rome was occupied and all film production was halted there, did Venice became the centre of Italian film production once more, though on a small scale. Some pavilions were rearranged to host studios, laboratories and offices for the production of films, forming the so-called »Cinevillaggio«, named after the »Cinecittà«, the big studio complex in Rome – the »film city« had now become a little »film village«.

The long term effects of the cultural development can still be seen today. The developments of the 1930s formed the basis for the growing international success after 1945. The negative side was that this was the beginning of today's mass tourism. Taking into account that the city's infrastructure – the number of bridges, vessels etc. – is still almost identical to what it was in the 1930s, the long term concept of this policy becomes evident. And yet, the festival hype has had surprisingly little impact on a creative scene in Venice. For instance, only very few private galleries exist or existed in Venice. Although this year will see the 75th anniversary of the International Cinematographic Art Show, there is just one cinema left in Venice. On the other hand, the Istituto Universitario Architettura di Venezia (IUAV) was born in this international milieu, in a city with very few building projects.

---

22 Goebbels' diary, September 9, 1937. Response to a report by von Lehnich, see Bundesarchiv, R 43 II, 389, letters from Lehnich to Goebbels, August 22, 1937 and September 6, 1937.

Conclusion

As I have demonstrated, Venetian cultural heritage was used as a base for the development of new events and festivals; the city became a unique stage for the events. Like in an entertainment park, the supply was optimized. The comparison with the fake ›Venices‹ built as amusement parks around 1900 in Vienna, London and Los Angeles lies at hand, and it is quite possible that the actual Venice was inspired by the strategies of these fairgrounds when reshaping the city for mobile tourists from all over the world. Venice is now suffering the success of its own strategies: with over 13 Million visitors per year the success is destroying the city. The cultural politics in Venice mainly supported the success of Venice as an important tourist destination. Using the historic city as a stage for hosting the modern arts it created a new image to attract new audiences. The Biennale and its accompanying events were used for propagandistic purposes, but, like Longo I want to support the opinion that the binding force behind this was an economic one, a way out of a crisis: tourism was significant because it brought in foreign currency. Today, this is still the basic reason behind all the efforts and the entire development is based on the institutions/infrastructures founded during the two decades between 1920 and 1940:

1) Intelligent networking in Rome helped the city to modernize the traffic infrastructure with the motorway bridge, new canals and new embankments.

2) The glorious past with all its arts, attractions and festivities was reactivated for tourist purposes as we have seen in the example of the Old Master blockbuster shows and the exploitation of traditional festivals and the carnival. The past was economisized by creating »ephemeral« museums with Titian, Tintoretto and Veronese.

3) At the same time the authorities responsible for the Biennale succeeded in bringing the international elite of artists and filmmakers to the Lagoon to show their new art and films. This was not so successful in the 1930s and 1940s, but during that time the infrastructure was created for after 1945.

4) All events were organized and financed like private businesses with most modern methods such as public-private-partnerships and up-to-date marketing methods involving media partners, cooperation with the train company etc.

The parallels between the cultural economy strategies implemented in fascist Venice and today's methods are clearly discernable. Nevertheless, the main advantage for the success in the 1920s to 1940s was the centralized, dictatorial organisation.

Bibliography

Barizza, Sergio (1988). *Il Casino Municipale di Venezia. Una Storia degli Anni Trenta.* Venezia.

Ben-Ghiat, Ruth (2001). *Fascist Modernities. Italy 1922–1945.* Berkeley/Los Angeles/London.

Bierbaum, Otto Julius (1900). *Eine empfindsame Reise im Automobil.* Berlin.

Bosworth, Richard J.B. (1996). *Italy and the wider world, 1860–1960.* London.

— (1999).»Venice between Fascism and international tourism, 1911–45«. *Modern Italy. Journal of the Association for the Study of Modern Italy*, 4, 1, 5–24.

Brilli, Attilio (2006). *Il viaggio in Italia: storia di una grande tradizione culturale.* Bologna.

Brunetta, Ernesto (1986).»L'egemonia di Volpi sul fascismo veneziano«. In Emilio Emilio Franzina (ed.). *Venezia*, 166–170, Roma.

Cosulich, Alberto (1990). *Viaggi e turismo a Venezia dal 1500 al 1900.* Venice.

Crum, Roger J. and Claudia Lazzaro (ed.) (2005). *Donatello among the Blackshirts: history and modernity in the visual culture of Fascist Italy.* Ithaca.

Damerini, Maria (1988). *Gli ultimi anni del Leone. Venezia 1929–1940.* Padova.

Davis, Robert C. and Garry R. Marvin (2004). *Venice. The tourist maze. A cultural critique of the world's most touristed city.* Berkeley/Los Angeles/London.

Farinati, Valeria (2002).»Il terminal automobilistico«. In Guido Zucconi (ed.), *La grande Venezia. Una metropoli incompiuta tra Otto e Novecento*, 80–89. Venice.

Fincardi, Marco (2001).»Gli ›anni ruggenti‹ del Leone. La moderna realtà del mito di Venezia«. *Contemporanea*, 4, 3, July 2001, 54–78.

Forssmann, Erik (1971). *Venedig in der Kunst und im Kunsturteil des 19. Jahrhunderts.* Stockholm.

Frankfurter, Alfred M. (1937).»The splendor of Tintoretto in Venice«. *Art News*, September 18, 1937.

Haskell, Francis (2000). *The ephemeral museum: old master paintings and the rise of the art exhibition.* New Haven, Connecticut.

Häußermann, Hartmut and Walter Siebel (eds.) (1993). *Die Festivalisierung der Stadtpolitik.* Opladen.

Higson, Andrew and Richard Maltby (1999).»*Film-Europe*« and »*Film-America*«: cinema, commerce and cultural exchange, 1920–1939. Exeter/Trumpbour.

Isman, Fabio (2000). *Venezia, la fabbrica della cultura. Tra istituzioni ed eventi.* Venice.

Longo, Stefania (2005). *Culture, tourism and Fascism in Venice 1919–1945*. PhD thesis, University College London, London.

Medina Lasansky, D. (2004). *The Renaissance Perfected. Architecture, Spectacle, and Tourism in Fascist Italy*. University Park/Pennsylvania.

Paloscia, Franco (1994). *Storia del turismo nell'economia italiana. Biblioteca di cultura del viaggio e del turismo: Documenti*. Città di Castello.

— (2004). *Il turismo nell'economia italiana: dall'unità d'Italia a oggi*. Rome.

Pasinetti, P. M. (1934). »66 films in a Lido hotel«. *Cinema Quarterly*, 3, 1, Autumn 1934, 14–16.

Plant, Margaret (2002). *Venice. Fragile City. 1797–1997*. New Haven/London.

Reberschak, Maurizio (2002). »Gli uomini capitali: il »gruppo veneziano« (Volpi, Cini e gli altri)«. In Mario Isnenghi and Stuart Woolf (eds.). *Storia di Venezia. L'Ottocento e il Novecento*, 1255–1311. Rome.

Romano, Sergio (1982). *Giuseppe Volpi et l'Italie moderne; Finance, industrie et État de l'ère giolittienne à la 2. Guerre mondiale*. Rome.

Stone, Marla Susan (1998). *The Patron state. Culture and politics in Fascist Italy*. Princeton.

Syrjämaa, Taina (1997). *Visitez l'Italie: Italian State Tourist Propaganda Abroad, 1919–1943: Administrative Structure and Practical Realisation*. Turku.

Taillibert, Christel (2000). *L'Institut International du cinématographe éducatif. Regard sur le role du cinéma éducatif dans la politique internationale du fascisme italien*. Paris.

Van der Borg, Jan (1992). »Tourism and urban development: the case of Venice«. *Tourism Recreation Research*, 17, 2, 45–56.

Zucconi, Guido (2002). *La grande Venezia. Una metropoli incompiuta tra Otto e Novecento*. Venice.

Economic Effects of Urban Cultural Policy in the Interwar Period in France and Germany

Thomas Höpel

The two decades following the First World War saw the intensification and revision of urban cultural policy due to political and economic developments. Existing research on cultural policy has primarily emphasised the increasing public regulation of the cultural field, which more and more supplanted private initiatives.[1] However, as I aim to show in this paper, economic factors also played an important role in this intensified urban cultural policy, even in the interwar period.[2] The cities had to take the economic side into account in order to allow for an increased public cultural policy during the difficult period following the First World War. At the same time, classical areas of urban culture had to account for the expansion of a commercialised popular and mass culture.[3] Furthermore, the cities sought to keep up in an escalating interurban competition. Culture became incorporated into an intensified urban image politics.[4] In the past few years there have been studies on city-marketing and image politics in the first half of the twentieth century (Guckes 2005: 84f; Mai 2004), but as yet there has been no thorough and systematic treatment of the role of urban cultural policy and local cultural industries in this intensified image policy. The specific post-WWI historical constellation led to developments very often described as characteristic of the period since the 1980s: the

---

1 This pertains especially to the period after 1945, with precursors in the 1930s. See Cummings and Katz 1987; Ellmeier and Rasky 1997; Beyme 1998.
2 Economic factors were discussed in connection with public cultural policy above all for the period since the 1980s. See for Great Britain: Bennett 1995. Gerhard Schulze argued that the cultural policy of the 1980s is characterised by the economic motive (*Ökonomiemotiv*, Schulze 1992).
3 For the distinction between popular and mass culture see Kammen 1999: 26.
4 For the increased city marketing in Leipzig since the 1920s see Mai 2004.

festivalisation of the urban culture[5], the economisation of culture, and heightened image politics. I will try to show the specificity of these developments of the interwar period and to reconstruct the continuities and ruptures. The central question of this article is how the urban cultural policy in France and Germany was used during the interwar period to support and promote the local economy, the cultural networks, and the image of the city.

This article is based on case studies of four cities. In both Germany and France I have examined an old traditional metropolis (Leipzig and Lyon) and a younger industrial city that grew in the course of the industrialisation in the nineteenth century (Chemnitz and Saint-Etienne).

The paper starts with a short description of the four cities studied and their economic and cultural infrastructure at the beginning of the interwar period. I will then discuss the characteristics of the urban cultural policy of these four cities during the interwar period. In the main section of this paper, I will focus explicitly on the economic effects of urban cultural policy and on image politics as a part of the intensified interurban competition.

A Tale of Four Cities

I have chosen two types of cities for this study: the old and traditional metropolis on the one hand, and the younger industrial city on the other. This will allow us to recognise the characteristics of urban cultural policies as well as the relations between culture and economy in the German and French cities. I have decided not to include national capitals in my comparison, since they generally tried to represent the nation and thus do not exemplify the practice of cultural policy and the possibilities of cultural economies in the majority of cities in the two nations. Lyon and Leipzig represent two cities that had already emerged as important centres of trade before industrialisation[6]: Lyon played an important role as a centre of

---

5   See Häußermann and Siebel 1987, especially the chapter *Kulturpolitik oder das Ende der Stadtkultur*, 199–215; Häußermann and Siebel 1993; Göschel 1998.

6   For the economic development of Lyon see Léon 1967: 31–62; Latreille 1975; Bayard and Cayez 1990; for Leipzig see Zwahr et al. 1999; Stadtgeschichtliches Museum Leipzig (ed.) (1990). *Neues Leipzigisches Geschichts-Buch*, Leipzig.

banking and trade in the sixteenth century, while Leipzig was famous for its fair and became the centre of the German booktrade at the end of the eighteenth century. The two cities were forerunners of industrialisation in Germany and France in the first half of the nineteenth century – for example, the entrepreneurs of Lyon and Leipzig were responsible for the first long-distance trains in France and Germany. At the beginning of the interwar period, Leipzig and Lyon were important centres of trade, industry, and culture. The most important industries in Leipzig were textiles, the book trade and machine construction; in Lyon the automobile and chemical industries and silk manufacturing. In addition, the two cities held fairs of international importance. Lyon established its fair more recently in 1916, copying the renowned Leipzig fair and trying to take over the west European trade fair commerce from Leipzig that had been cut off by the First World War (Latreille 1975: 405; Labasse and Marty 1960: 78). In 1918, Leipzig had 600,000 inhabitants and Lyon 450,000. Both cities had a sound cultural infrastructure: a university (Leipzig's dated from the beginning of the sixteenth century; Lyon's from the end of the nineteenth century (Louat 1970; Minot 1991: 44–52), two metropolitan theatres (built at the end of the eighteenth and in the nineteenth century), an arts museum and several museums of history and sciences, an old scientific library and younger popular libraries, a concert hall, a conservatory, and an arts school. Leipzig housed a renowned orchestra founded at the end of the eighteenth century, whereas in Lyon a high quality musical culture developed at the beginning of the twentieth century with the founding of the society of *grand concerts*. The Lyon concert hall was built in 1908 after the example of the renowned hall in Leipzig (Ferraton 1984: 103).

Chemnitz and Saint-Etienne are examples of younger industrial cities that grew in the course of industrialisation.[7] In the nineteenth century they developed important industries: in Chemnitz the textile industry, machine construction, and electrical engineering, in Saint-Etienne mining, textiles, arms, and metallurgy. The number of inhabitants increased sharply during the nineteenth century: Saint-Etienne became the seventh-largest town in France in 1911, whereas Chemnitz remained at fourteenth place in Germany. At the beginning of the interwar period 165,000 inhabitants lived in Saint-Etienne and 292,000 in Chemnitz. Both towns developed a cultural infrastructure in the second half of the nineteenth century. At the turn of

---

7   For Saint-Etienne see Cohen 1998; Fournial 1976; for Chemnitz see Karl-Marx-Stadt 1988.

the century, an academy of technology emerged from the trade schools created in the middle of the nineteenth century in Chemnitz. In Saint-Etienne an important mining school was founded. At the beginning of the interwar period, Chemnitz boasted two urban theatres, an arts museum and a historical museum, a metropolitan orchestra, a scientific library and a popular library. Saint-Etienne had a metropolitan theatre, an arts museum and two technical museums, a conservatory, an arts school, a scientific library, and eleven popular libraries.

All in all, the cities chosen occupied a comparable position in the system of German and French municipalities, such that they can serve as a representative picture of developments in the larger cities of France and Germany.

Cultural Policy in French and German Cities during the Interwar Period[8]

In the two decades after the First World War, a paradigm shift occurred in the field of cultural policy: democratisation, the rise of a commercial popular and mass culture, the introduction of an eight-hour working day, and the labour movement's demands for participation and a separate working culture were responsible for this change. These developments were a particular concern for cities because of their cultural infrastructure and the rising influence of the workers' parties, and for German cities especially, where the Social Democrats were politically marginalised by the three-class franchise system until 1918. Following the November Revolution, Social Democrats in Leipzig and Chemnitz dominated the council meetings. In the two French cities as well, the socialists were able to increase their influence in the city council after 1918.

At the end of the First World War, intensive discussion about culture took place in the four cities along with a great number of cultural initiatives, which led to a new urban cultural policy. Furthermore, in German cities, a strong impetus came from the workers' and soldiers' councils created during the revolution, which also concerned themselves with cultural

---

8   For a more detailed description of the urban cultural policy in Germany and France in the four cities see Höpel 2007a; Höpel 2007b.

activities. However, the long-term orientation of the new cultural policy was set by a coalition composed of republican liberals on the one hand, and, on the other, of Social Democrats in Germany as well as socialists and communists in France. They supported a participative, integrative, and active cultural policy based on a pluralistic and democratic definition of culture. For them, the idea of education by means of democratic arts and culture was central.

In these discussions about culture and the aims of cultural policy, two main objectives of the cities' cultural policy became evident: first, the democratisation of culture, and second, the consolidation of the cultural image regionally, nationally, and internationally.

These objectives were supported by efforts to refine the popular and mass cultural media, by the promotion of a pluralistic artistic production, and by the modernisation of the cities' cultural institutes.

Although these objectives were to be found in all four cities, they were emphasised differently, depending on the influence of the various protagonists in the different cities. The liberal republicans who dominated Lyon engaged the arts to serve the city's reputation as the French cultural metropolis, second to Paris. In Saint-Etienne, cultural policy was used for the democratisation of culture by a coalition of more leftist liberal republicans and left socialists and communists. In Leipzig and Chemnitz, we see efforts to recruit the arts in the service of the city's reputation as well as in the education and cultivation of the lower urban classes.

These objectives were realised in expanding the city's intervention in cultural matters. The cities used more metropolitan budget resources for culture. They opened the traditional fields of metropolitan arts policy socially and expanded their intervention to new fields.

In the traditional fields of urban arts policy, Leipzig and Chemnitz supported new spectator organisations that opened up access to theatre and music for blue- and white-collar workers.[9] The cities intensified the net-

---

9   In Leipzig the workers' education institute (*Arbeiterbildungsinstitut*) had already been created before the First World War, but after 1918 it received essential support from the city of Leipzig for the first time. In 1921, the Association of German Theatres (*Verein deutsche Bühne*) was created in Leipzig. It was a Christian-nationalist organisation directed at white-collar workers and affiliated with the German-wide *Bühnenvolksbund*. In Chemnitz, a Popular Theatre Association (*Chemnitzer Volksbühne e.V.*) was created in 1920, which became affiliated with the German-wide *Verband Deutscher Volksbühnenvereine* in 1921. In 1922, more conservative nationalist groups created the organisation *Bühnen-*

work of public libraries and promoted access to metropolitan museums by reducing or abolishing the entrance fees and by organising popular lectures and guided tours.

In Saint-Etienne, the city council reduced the entrance fees for the metropolitan theatre, created a metropolitan orchestra, and organised concerts for workers in coordination with the workers' unions. It expanded the public libraries from eleven to twenty five and extended the opening hours of the metropolitan museums. The efforts to open up the traditional institutions of culture in Lyon were on a much smaller scale. Here, the city council supported cultural activities for school children, which led to school-performances in the theatres and intensified use of the metropolitan museums for school-children. The city was dominated by liberal radical socialists, who sought cultivation and democratic education mainly through an intensified educational policy. In addition, they supported popular activities for the workers by giving small subsidies to the popular theatre, to popular concerts, or to exhibitions of workers' art. In Lyon, the lion's share of urban culture spending was directed to the high cultural institutions for the middle and upper classes: the metropolitan opera, the art museum, and the scientific library. In this way, Lyon continued the arts policy of the pre-war years.

Beside the traditional areas of urban intervention in culture and arts, the cities expanded their activities to new fields, namely, cinema and adult education. All of the cities made efforts to create a cultivated cinema. Leipzig and Chemnitz used film for educational purposes in schools and supported initiatives for a sophisticated cultural cinema (*Kulturkino*) directed at adults. In Leipzig and Chemnitz such initiatives came mainly from the cultural organisation of the workers. Lyon and Saint-Etienne created offices for educational cinema directed mainly at school-children. However, the French cities did not support initiatives for a cultivated cinema for adults, as this contradicted the liberal conception of French arts policy advocated principally by the liberal radical socialists.

After 1918 as well we find strong initiatives for adult education in Leipzig and Chemnitz, for example with the creation of adult education centres. In the 1920s Leipzig developed a whole infrastructure of adult education with new instruments that gained a certain notoriety on a national and international scale (Höpel 2007a). In Lyon and Saint-Etienne, the cities did

---

volksbund as a counter-organisation directed principally at white-collar workers (Höpel 2007b: 148–149, 174–179).

not support such efforts in adult education in the interwar period.[10] These developments in the four cities are very much characteristic of the general situation in French and German cities between the wars.

The intensified discussion about culture and the expanded intervention by municipalities in cultural matters led to an institutionalisation of urban cultural policy in German cities. Cultural policy was now seen as a central task of city government. The field of cultural policy was marked by a consolidation of cultural responsibilities in the metropolitan administration,[11] culminating in the creation of offices of culture (*Kulturämter*) by the National Socialists after 1933.[12] This concentration was perceptible even in the city budget. The development was accompanied by the professionalisation of the metropolitan administration of cultural matters and by the public appropriation of several cultural institutes during the interwar period. In Chemnitz two museums and the metropolitan theatre were publicly appropriated, and in Leipzig the Gewandhaus-orchestra, the museum of natural sciences, the conservatory and the centre for adult education. The Leipzig metropolitan theatres had already been publicly appropriated before the First World War. In this regard Leipzig was a forerunner of a development that took place in most German cities in the interwar period.[13]

In Lyon and Saint-Etienne, we do not find such a distinctive institutionalisation, due to a lower degree of professionalisation in metropolitan administration as well as an ideologically inspired rejection of massive public intervention in the area of culture. In the two French cities the theatre did not function as a public enterprise as it did in Leipzig and Chemnitz, but was rented to one or (as in the case of Lyon) two directors who bore the primary share of the risks of each season. Nevertheless, the two cities subsidised the theatres more and more during the interwar period.

---

10 In the two French cities the workers' unions created workers' education centres without metropolitan support after the First World War. These institutions died in the wake of the break-up of the French workers' movement at the beginning of the 1920s. In the 1930s a second impetus came from the workers' unions. Again, however, the cities did not sustain these initiatives.

11 The creation of new administrative instruments could also be seen in other German towns in the 1920s: for Lübeck see Fligge 1997; for Frankfurt am Main see Hansert 1992: 132–133.

12 *Kulturämter* were also created after 1933 in Munich, Breslau and Plauen. For Munich see Hanko 1981.

13 For the metropolitan appropriation of the city theatres see Dussel 1998.

In the two French cities the public cultural infrastructure was also extended and a professionalisation took place in several areas of cultural policy. This was true especially of the art museums and public libraries. Even in Lyon, the stronghold of liberal arts policy, the public intervention in culture was extended such that the public cultural institutions could hardly continue to work in the traditional manner. Thus at the end of the interwar period, Lyon sought to nationalise the metropolitan opera to allow it to continue to pursue its aspirations for a national and even international reputation.

Cultural policy was therefore accepted as a legitimate field of metropolitan intervention. Although in Germany the public appropriation of arts institutions by the city government had already begun before 1918, it took on a new quality after 1918. From this point on, the cities recognised their responsibility for a broad social access to culture and for the cultivation of the city residents. The heightened public regulation in the cultural field and the beginnings of the institutionalisation of urban and national cultural policy in Germany proves that the project of the *Kulturstaat* was not just lip-service of the Weimar constitution, but was made reality through the metropolitan cultural policy. Confronted with the same cultural development and with the examples set by cities in other European countries, the French cities could not stand by passively. Thus, we find the first steps towards an active cultural policy in French cities as well, even if the institutionalisation and professionalisation were not as pronounced as in German cities.

Cultural Policy and the Culturalization of the Economy

The development of an intensified public cultural policy in cities after 1918 was not just characterised by a growing public regulation of the cultural field, as primarily emphasised by existing research on public cultural policy. This urban cultural policy also took the economic factors of culture into account. One reason for this was the difficult economic situation the cities faced after 1918 due to an increased inflation caused by the First World War. This was aggravated in Germany by the reform of state finances that

Matthias Erzberger initiated in 1919.[14] Furthermore, culture played more and more of a role in the competition between cities and was seen as a point of attraction for local visitors and businesses. Metropolitan cultural policy was thus not just interested in democratising access to culture as a means of integration into urban society; it also aimed at the consolidation of the city's economy and thus its reputation.

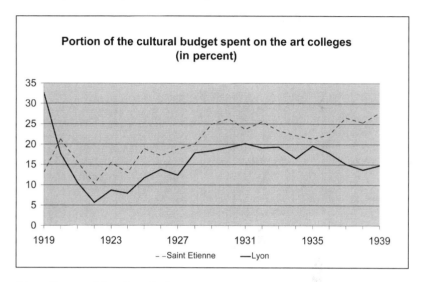

Fig. 1: Portion of the cultural budget spent on the art colleges

(Source: Own Diagram)

One selection of measures concerned the culturalization of the economy. Metropolitan art colleges in particular were used for this objective. In Lyon as well as in Saint-Etienne the art colleges were originally created as city institutions in the wake of the French Revolution of 1789 (Dablin 1897; Chaudonneret 1994), although the French federal state supported the two colleges financially from the first decades of the Third Republic onwards. Nevertheless, the two cities had to come up with the bulk of the funding. In Lyon, 10 to 20 percent of the cultural spending went to the *École des*

---

14 For the consequences the reform had on the relationship between cities and state see Rebentisch 1977: 107.

Beaux-Arts. In Saint-Etienne it was even higher: 15 to 25 percent in the twenties and 25 percent in the thirties (Fig. 1).[15] The two art colleges were originally created to stimulate the local economy, but the Lyon art college gained a reputation in the nineteenth century by producing some important artists, known collectively as the »École lyonnaise«. In Lyon the *École de Beaux-Arts* was founded in 1805, extending and supplanting the drawing school (*École de dessin*) created for the reconsolidation of the Lyon silk-industry in 1797. It was established in a secularised Benedictine monastery, where the new arts museum had already been installed in 1804. The juxtaposition of the two institutions accorded well with the idea of the museum as a place for scientific and artistic studies as well as a place for a collection of the national heritage and for entertainment (Georgel 1994: 71; Desvallées 1996). In 1876, the Lyon arts college was given the status of an *École Nationale des Beaux-Arts.* Thus the state now participated in the costs of the school, but at the same time acquired the right to have a say in administrative questions and especially in the hiring of professors. In 1906, an *École régionale d'architecture* was incorporated into the Lyon art college, which offered the same education and degree as the *École nationale supérieure* de Paris (Rosenthal 1926: 119). The *École des Beaux-Arts* of Lyon offered a course of higher education in painting and sculpture. However, the *École des Beaux-Arts* also sought to reinforce education in the applied arts for the local industries, especially the silk industry. In the interwar period, Lyon's industry demanded qualified staff more and more: draughtsmen, technical directors, *chefs d'atelier* (Rosenthal 1926: 118). Flower painting, cloth decoration, and drawing were therefore taught alongside architecture, art history, painting, sculpture, and arts and crafts.[16] The students were familiarised with different arts and crafts and initiated in modern tastes. The education in cloth decoration was completed with visits to the weaving mills, cloth-printing workshops, and to the big fashion designers in Paris (Rosenthal 1926: 118). The union of silk manufacturers and the chamber of commerce financially supported the best students of the *École des Beaux-Arts.* The Lyon École des Beaux-Arts got a new building in 1933, located in the silk district of Lyon, Croix Rousse.[17] Beside the direct education in applied arts for the local industries, different draw-

---

15 For the cultural spending of Lyon and Saint-Etienne in the interwar-period I analysed the *Comptes d'Administration* of Lyon and Saint-Etienne from 1919 to 1939.

16 *Documents: Ville de Lyon 1926.* Lyon 1927.

17 Ville de Lyon (1952). L'œuvre municipale depuis 1905. Lyon, 30.

ing schools existed, attached to the art college of Lyon, where school-
children could gain a basic education in practical arts and, starting in the
1920s, workers and apprentices of the arts and crafts received education in
the evenings. This was to serve to train the working staff of the arts and
crafts and steer the children to the local industries at an early age (Rosenthal 1926: 119).

The development of the art college in Saint-Etienne took a similar path.
The college began as an *École de dessin* (drawing school) created in 1804 to
stimulate the local economy. In 1884, the metropolitan drawing school
became *École régionale des arts industriels* due to the engagement of the state.
Consequently, the school's educational programme was expanded and
improved, developing its scientific education, improving the artistic education, and systematically building up the technical aspects. It was renamed
École des Beaux-Arts in 1922. The *École des Beaux*-Arts also provided basic
education to primary school pupils, and workers and apprentices were
educated on weekends. This primarily affected people working in local
industries, especially the arms factory and the ribbon industry. The *École des
Beaux-Arts* was also meant to serve the local industry. Beside the founda-
tional courses on drawing, modelling, and visual architecture, special
courses on geometry, art history, anatomy, style and perspective, and a
range of applied courses were connected directly to important local arts
and crafts. Engraving and inlaying work were important for the arms industry, ribbon decoration for the textile industry. As in Lyon, the *École des
Beaux-Arts* was also intended to qualify the people already working in the
local industries.[18] The chamber of commerce supported the art college
financially and also, together with the *Chambre syndicale des Tissus*, gave
grants to students. After their education at the *École des Beaux-Arts* the best
students were able to continue their studies at the *Écoles des Beaux-Arts* in
Paris or Lyon or at the Ecole of Decoratif Arts in Paris (Dablin 1897: 19).

Of the two German cities studied, only Leipzig had an art college,
which was established in the second half of the eighteenth century by the
state of Saxony and was thus financed almost exclusively by the state. The
art college was created to stimulate local industry (Kapr 1985: 3). In the
first half of the nineteenth century, it concentrated its activity on the education of painters. After the German Empire arose, craftwork education
was expanded in Germany. Education at the Leipzig art college concen-

---

18 »Conseil Municipal, session of November 19, 1926«. *Bulletin municipal de la Ville de Saint-
Etienne 1926*, 152–153.

trated more and more on letterpress printing, due also to the urging of the German Book Industry Association (*Deutscher Buchgewerbeverein*) founded in 1884. In 1890 a new building for the art college was built at the initiative of the German Book Industry Association, the city, and state of Saxony (Kapr 1985: 4). In 1900, the art college changed its name to »Academy for Graphic Arts and Letterpress Printing«. For the first time typography, bookbinding, and book design were taught on an equal footing with painting and drawing at an arts college. The modernisation was a reaction to the arts reform movement at the turn of the century, inspired by the British arts and crafts movement (Pevsner 1986: 257–267).

The following figures demonstrate the importance of the book industry for Leipzig: in 1907/08 the book-business employed 10,000 employees and the Leipzig publishing houses handled 18 percent of the German book production. Nearly 800 book industry businesses operated in Leipzig before the Second World War (Baier 1981: 79). As of the 1840s the industrialised and expanding book industry developed in a separate district of the city, the graphic district (*Graphisches Viertel*), which is east of the city centre. In this district publishing houses, printing and book businesses, bookdepots, and specific educational institutions for the book industry settled and expanded. These growing book businesses also left their mark architecturally (Knopf and Titel 2001: 85–87). The close collaboration of all branches of the book industry supported this development.

In the interwar period, the academy developed into a unique school that recruited pupils from all parts of Germany, Europe, and overseas. Walter Tiemann, the director of the academy – together with the letterpress printer Carl Ernst Poeschel and Anton Kippenberg, the head of the Insel-Verlag – developed the aesthetic conception of Leipzig book art: a book should be set in a typeface appropriate to the content, and should be carefully printed, lastingly bound, and beautiful but unobtrusive (Kapr 1985: 3–8; Debes 1981: 35–36). Even if the academy was a state institution, it was of great importance to the »book city«, Leipzig. The academy worked together with the publishing houses. The great international exhibitions of book art and the book industry of 1914 and 1927 were organised by the book industry in cooperation with the academy. The professors of the academy also worked as artistic advisors for the great Leipzig bookbinders (for example for E.A. Enders, H. Sperling, Hübel & Denk) and printing houses (Brandstetter, Spamer, and others). After the International Book Art Exhibiton of 1927 Tiemann published the yearbook »Book Art«

in 1932 and 1935 along with numerous international papers. The yearbook was produced entirely in the workshops of the academy. Moreover, following the International Book Art Exhibition the selection of the »50 most beautiful books«, organised by the *Deutsche Bücherei*, was established after the example of the United States. The professors of the academy were responsible for the aesthetic criteria for the selection. The publishing houses and the polygraphic industry of Leipzig recruited a large number of the academy graduates. Workers in the book industry had the opportunity to study at the academy's evening school (Kapr 1985: 8). The city recognised the importance of the academy for the Leipzig book industry and for Leipzig's image as a book-town and supported the academy with several thousands marks per year.

We can also see that cultural policy in the French cities took the effects on the local business very much into consideration. The French cities used a large share of the cultural funding to maintain art colleges that were also intended for the education and qualification of workers in local industries. The art colleges in French cities also had close connections to the local industries. A network existed between the metropolitan governments, the art colleges, and members and organisations of the local businesses. In Germany, on the other hand, art colleges were only to be found in important cities like Leipzig and very often were state institutions. However, as the Leipzig example shows, they were also important for the local economy and were intended to stimulate local and regional enterprise. The Leipzig Academy for Graphic Arts and Letterpress Printing was tightly bound to the city's book industry. The book city Leipzig gained a lot by the existence of the academy, through its stimulation of the local enterprise and through the academy's initiatives, which attracted attention in Germany as well as abroad. For this reason the city of Leipzig supported the academy and its relations to the local book industry. However, since it was a state institution, the city of Leipzig was not forced to dedicate a large share of the cultural budget to the academy. The art colleges in France and the Leipzig academy helped stabilise the images of the different cities propagated by the municipalities: Lyon's image as the centre of the French silk industry, the arms and ribbon fabrication in Saint-Etienne, and the image of Leipzig as a book town. In supporting the art colleges, the urban cultural policy sought to strengthen these images as well as local economic growth.

Cultural Policy, Image Politics, and the Economising of Culture

Beside their direct support of specific economic branches in backing art colleges, cities also used the existent cultural institutions to create a certain image of themselves. The cultural life played an essential role in shaping their image and also in the increasing competition for the businesses and visitors from outside the city. This was especially important for Lyon and Leipzig, and not so important or central for Chemnitz and particularly for Saint-Etienne. But even in these industrial cities a great number of urban cultural activities were aimed at this goal. The cultural and scientific life became an essential part of their identity.

The two cities Lyon and Leipzig sought to strengthen their image as a cultural metropolis by a combination of high cultural productions and mass cultural instruments. The creation and development of regional radio stations in Lyon and Leipzig is a good example of this. Both of these cities successfully supported the creation of regional radio stations in the first half of the twenties. These stations were meant to reach a broader audience outside of these cities, demonstrating their economic and cultural importance. The cities collaborated with the radio stations in different ways. The radio station in Leipzig and its financial possibilities allowed the lasting institutionalisation of a second first-class orchestra alongside the *Gewandhaus* orchestra. This was an objective the city had pursued for ages. In the major Leipzig newspaper *Leipziger Neueste Nachrichten* the city councillor for theatre, music, museums, and libraries argued publicly against the critiques from local personalities, who saw high culture endangered by the massmedium of radio.[19] During the global depression a tighter collaboration between city government and radio set in. Some prestigious cultural institutions, which had previously rejected a collaboration with the radio, associated themselves with the new medium and were integrated in the radioprogram, allowing them greater earnings. At the same time, this contributed to the cultural reputation of Leipzig as a city of music in demonstrating the high quality of its musical institutions.

The Thomaner chorus was very open to the possibilities of the new mass media. The hyperinflation had damaged the Thomaner chorus' en-

---

19 *Leipziger Neueste Nachrichten*, February 21, 1925.

dowment, and in the twenties they had already sought new forms of financing. The chorus had stepped up its concert tours in the twenties (Wörner, 2003: 20, 167) and also made its first records in 1927.[20] These measures contributed both to the financing of the chorus and to its reputation beyond the local borders.

When in December 1930 the general director of the radio station approached the leader of the chorus, Karl Straube, with the proposition of broadcasting all of the Bach cantatas, Straube and the city of Leipzig agreed. The broadcasts were a great success for the Leipzig chorus. Following in the footsteps of Leipzig radio other German radio stations as well as Austrian, Dutch, Finnish, and Czech radio started broadcasting the Thomaner chorus renditions of the Bach cantatas in 1931.[21]

In the thirties, the Leipzig radio station broadcast concerts not only by the Thomaner chorus, but also by the Leipzig *Gewandhaus* orchestra. The Gewandhaus management had previously been opposed to such broadcasts, fearing for the reputation of their orchestra. The Leipzig mayor, Carl Goerdeler, encouraged negotiations between the radio and the *Gewandhaus* management, which led to a contract in July 1931 and to regular broadcasts of *Gewandhaus* orchestra concerts.[22] In this way, Leipzig's radio station got a reputation as a music station. When the National Socialists tried to consolidate the radio infrastructure in Germany after 1933, Leipzig's radio station was primarily to play music.

In Lyon, two radio stations were created in the twenties: one public station in 1925, and one private station in 1924. The private radio station was widely supported by the local economy as a means of publicity; more than the centrally controlled public station, it could emphasise local aims. Consequently, the mayor supported the station as well. His support became especially important after the French government decided on December 28, 1926, that the existence of private radio stations had to be allowed by the government.[23] As the public radio station was seen as a branch of the Paris radio station, which thus could not answer to the regional needs, the local economy firmly supported the private radio station. The private sta-

20 Contract between the Thomaner chorus and the Polyphonwerke Aktiengesellschaft, Berlin, February 9, 1927, Stadtarchiv Leipzig, Schulamt, 2/101/4/3/15 f, 2, 22–24.
21 *Leipziger Neueste Nachrichten*, May 10, June 5, 1931.
22 Contract between the Gewandhaus-Konzertdirektion and the Mitteldeutsche Radio AG, Bayreuth July 31, 1931, Stadtarchiv Leipzig, Kap, 32, Nr. 1, supplement 2, 142–148.
23 *Décret portant Réglementation des postes privés radioélectriques et des stations émettrices de radiodiffusion*, December 28, 1926, AML, 0944 WP 003 4.

tion intended explicitly to advertise for the region of Lyon in France and abroad. The president of the Lyon chamber of commerce, Louis Pradel, asked the Minister of commerce and industry in 1927 for an operating licence for the radio station.[24] This licence was given by a decree on July 7, 1928. Subsequently, the private radio station sought to increase its transmission area.[25] The mayor of Lyon, Herriot, came out in support of this following a chorus of demand, for example by the chambers of commerce of Lyon and Vienne and the *Syndicat d'initiative* of Lyon.

At the same time, the city council and the mayor of Lyon also sought to expand the public radio station, which had long been neglected by the central administration in Paris.[26] Both radio stations existed side by side in the thirties.

Starting in 1937, the Lyon radio station broadcast local operas, which had been a matter of controversial discussion in the 1930s' city council. The town council accepted broadcasting, because of the additional earnings that radio would generate for the opera as well as the good effects of publicity. In 1938, a radio symphony orchestra was created in Lyon (Mongereau 2000: 248), which supported the local musical infrastructure. We find the same developments in Lyon as in Leipzig, although slightly staggered.

Lyon's mayor, Édouard Herriot, firmly supported local radio stations, and actively concerned himself with television as well. He arranged the first television broadcast of the local opera in May of 1939. The leaders of Lyon and Leipzig recognised the possibilities and importance of the new media early on and integrated them in their cultural policy to serve the cultural reputation of the cities. Radio and television were seen as signs of modernity and in both Leipzig and Lyon were meant to underscore the cities' status of metropolis. In the early twenties the radio was half public and half private. In Germany, at the beginning, the *Reichspost* owned the broadcasting institution, whereas the programme was put together by a broadcast company created by private capital. The Leipzig fair company (*Messegesellschaft*) held a share of the capital and tried to use the radio to advertise for the fair. Private enterprises were also involved in the Lyon radio station.

---

24 Louis Pradel to the Ministre du commerce et de l'industrie, Lyon December 16, 1927, AML, 0944 WP 003 4.
25 President of the administrative board of Radio-Lyon-Émissions to President of the Council of Ministers, Lyon. February 23, 1929, l, AML, 0944 WP 003 4.
26 Herriot to the president of the Council of Ministers, Lyon, February 1931.

The cities recognised the importance of the radio as a symbol of cultural modernity, as a way to promote the local economy and culture, and also as means to improve the cultural infrastructure and the cultural milieu. It diversified the urban music scene and attracted high quality artists who could find different opportunities for their work. These possibilities were recognised very early on in Leipzig and thus the coordinated action of the mayor, the local cultural institutions, and local entrepreneurs brought the second German radio station after the Berlin station to Leipzig, and not to Dresden as was originally planned. This was not seen positively in Dresden and the town sought to get a radio station of its own in the 1920s.[27]

The radio is only one example of Leipzig's efforts to create a diversified cultural milieu. In the 1920ies Leipzig sought in general to establish a wide range of different cultural institutions; and as in the case of the radio-station, it had to fight against the cultural ambitions of Dresden, which also sought to get the most important institutions. So in the interwar period a competition broke out between the two cities concerning the institutionalisation of a state conservatory. Leipzig feared that the creation of such an institution in Dresden would deeply harm Leipzig's important conservatory, created as the first German conservatory in 1843,[28] which would in turn harm the attractiveness of Leipzig for musicians and its image as a music town.

Leipzig and Lyon also used the opportunities presented by the fair in bringing a lot of non-locals and even foreigners to the city. All of the metropolitan cultural institutions were emphasised, particularly during the fair. A cultural programme was drawn up comprising all the important and prestigious institutions (opera, theatre, orchestra). The mayors and the city parliaments took a great interest in the programme of the different institutions and discussed it regularly during the sessions of the city parliament.

In general, the city leadership hoped that the reputation of being a cultural centre would attract guests from other regions and states. A wide range of initiatives set in between the World Wars. Lyon organised large publicity campaigns for special exhibitions in the recently modernised art museum in the second half of the thirties (Höpel 2007b: 318f). The municipality of Leipzig supported the newly hired director of the opera, Gustav Brecher, whose opera premières attracted an audience far beyond the

---

27 *Sächsische Zeitung*, May 5, 1925; Stadtarchiv Leipzig, Verkehrsamt, 13.8 Mirag, Bl. 14.
28 For the history of the Leipzig conservatory and his importance for the musical culture see Grotjahn 2005.

region. Leipzig's efforts to develop its public libraries during the interwar period were only related to its image as a publishing town. Thus, the city parliament as well as the mayor supported the efforts of Leipzig's public library director, Walter Hofmann. In Leipzig, Hofmann created a new system of four public libraries, a school for librarians for public libraries, an institute for the study of reader science (*Institut für Leser- und Schrifttumskunde*) and the *Zentralstelle für volkstümliches Büchereiwesen*, which served as an instrument to represent the public librarians as well as a regional and national advisory centre for public libraries (Höpel 2007a: 650ff.). He was also supported by the local book industry associations and created a special centre for acquiring books for public libraries. Hofmann succeeded in creating institutions that served as role models for other German as well as foreign towns.

The improved publicity for high cultural institutions coincided with the heightened efforts in city marketing in the twenties. Popular culture was used for marketing purposes as well. In 1926, Leipzig created an office for city marketing (named *Verkehrs- und Wirtschaftsamt*), which worked out a clear publicity strategy presenting Leipzig as a cultural and economic centre, a city of music, books, and fair (Mai 2004). The *Verkehrsamt* organised and co-organised cultural events that enhanced this image, such as the international book art exhibition in 1927. The office also organised events that mixed popular and high cultural activities. The most important of these events was the Leipziger Woche in 1928, which staged theatre performances, art and book-art exhibitions, an illumination of the city, a market, and other popular amusements.

In Lyon, we find similar developments. In 1920, Lyon was given the status of a tourist city, allowing it to levy a special tax from non-locals. The sum collected had to be used for local development, and thus was put to use modernising the cultural infrastructure (the arts museum, the opera). In Lyon, the city did not create an office for city marketing, but the group *comité des fêtes de Lyon* served a similar function starting in 1933. The mayor and several important members of the town council were members of the honorary committee.[29] This committee organised the *fête de Lyon*, a week of different festivities that usually took place during the Lyon fair. These festivals included illuminations of the city by night, opera performances, and popular activities such as carnival processions, fireworks, cycle races,

29 AML 0193 WP 007.

and masked balls. In 1937, the committee also organised a week of festivities during the international exposition in Paris to profit from the expected visitors. The programme comprised guided tours of the museums, operas, classical and popular concerts, illuminations, athletic competitions, dancing, and an exhibition of the famous local painter Puvis de Chavannes. At the beginning, the work of the committee was financed principally by local commerce. The city's financial participation continually increased: from 2 percent in 1933 to 22 percent in 1936. By 1938, 84 percent of the committee's income was provided by the city.

The two smaller cities Saint-Etienne and Chemnitz also sought to attract a large regional audience by various means. However, their policy was not nearly as systematically structured or constantly pursued as in the larger cities. Saint-Etienne tried to strengthen the city's reputation and to promote the local economy by organising a musical event called Festival Massenet in 1924, to which 89 musical societies from the South of France were invited. Alongside this music festival, the event also featured competitive sports and a parade. During the festival, the city also celebrated the conclusion of urban development projects started after the First World War, including electric street lighting, an athletic stadium and the first council houses. The city expected a large number of non-local visitors to promote local commerce.[30] The music festival had a popular cultural character. There were lots of concerts given by small bands and wind orchestras.[31] The festival did not become a regular institution in the interwar period; but at the end of the 1980s, the idea of the Festival Massenet was revived in the wake of a new high cultural momentum in Saint-Etienne.[32]

Chemnitz, on the other hand, sought to attract non-local visitors and regional, even national attention with a high cultural infrastructure. The city appropriated the two theatres and modernised them after 1918. The ensemble of actors was increased and hired year-round, making it possible to engage better actors than before and to increase the artistic quality of the theatres. The local orchestra had already been publicly appropriated before the First World War. After 1918, the city increased the number of

---

30 Concerning the intention of the town with the Festival Massenet see the mayor's speech in the city council on the April 13, 1924, AMSE 3 R 12.

31 »Le festival Massenet«. *La Loire*, June 10, 1924.

32 The first Festival Massenet took place in 1989, but it was dominated by high cultural music, especially opera, reflecting the new claim of Saint-Etienne to be a cultural metropolis; which they also demonstrated by creating a high quality orchestra, a new museum of modern art, and a new museum of mining in the 1980s.

musicians and the quality of the program. This allowed them to attract first-class conductors and composers in the twenties. The Chemnitz theatres modelled themselves on the theatres of Leipzig and Dresden and competed with them, as the debates of the metropolitan parliament in the interwar period show. The concentration of high cultural theatre in Chemnitz was meant to serve the city's reputation and also support the cultivation and education of blue- and white-collar workers. These efforts were reflected in the cultural budget of Chemnitz: 80 percent of the cultural budget was spent on the theatre and the orchestra in the interwar period. That means that of the four cities studied, Chemnitz spent the largest part of the cultural budget for the theatre (Fig. 2).

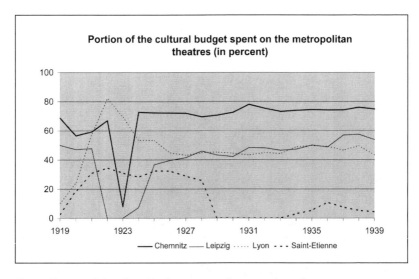

Fig. 2: Portion of the cultural budget spent on the metropolitan theatres

(Source: Own diagram)

Conclusion

The interurban competition increased in the face of the difficult economic situation following the First World War. The cities sought to reinforce their image to attract both visitors and businesses, which led to an intensification of their image politics. The creation of tourist agencies underscores this development, even if the forms they took differed between the French and German cities. Leipzig created a metropolitan marketing office, whereas in Lyon a private association acted with the support of the city leaders. Culture played an important place in city marketing: the image of the city as a modern and attractive centre was to be reinforced by cultural creativity and economic innovation in the cultural field. Big cities such as Lyon and Leipzig systematically used culture to strengthen the cities' economy and reputation. Similar developments took place in other larger French and German cities.[33] But even in the smaller cities of Chemnitz and Saint Etienne, image politics were taken in account. In Germany, which lacked a unique metropolis such as that in France, the interurban competition was even more striking. As we have seen, Leipzig engaged in an intense competition with the Saxon capital of Dresden, whether it concerned the location of the regional radio station or the state music conservatory. The rivalry was also reflected in the field of metropolitan theatres. Leipzig, and also Chemnitz, protested firmly against the state subventions for the Dresden theatres, which used this privileged status and the ensuing higher income to engage the best artists of the other Saxon theatres (Höpel 2007b: 137f., 173).

Urban cultural policy also sought to support local industries in running or sustaining art colleges. Although art colleges already played a role before the First World War, they expanded and concentrated their activity during the period studied here. In the case of Leipzig, we can see a further specialisation in book art. The French Ecoles des Beaux-Arts intensified the basic artistic education activities and included new fields like architecture in the subjects taught. Art colleges had a more important role in the metropolitan cultural policy in French cities than in German ones, but the example of Leipzig shows that the state-financed art college also played a very important role for the local publishing industry as well. Moreover, the urban cultural policy in Leipzig sustained the image of an innovative book city in supporting and backing Walter Hofmann's system of popular libraries.

---

33 Philippe Poirrier has shown this in his study about Dijon (Poirrier 1990; Poirrier 1995). In Germany the competition via cultural institutions between Leipzig and Dresden is very clear. It has also been shown for other German cities. For the case of Hannover see Wortmann 1995: 10–17.

Urban cultural policy in Germany as well as in France firmly recruited the arts into the service of the city's reputation and the local economy in the interwar period. The cultural policy reinforced the urban image policy in concentrating on different elements: first, it sought to present a creative and innovative urban high culture. Second, the urban cultural policy encouraged the high cultural institutions to cooperate with the new commercialised mass media and use them to add to the value the city's image. Finally, it supported local key industries in running and sustaining art colleges and their different activities.

With these different measures, the cities sought to widen the range of cultural institutions, hoping to strengthen the cultural infrastructure and to stimulate creativity in certain cultural fields in the 1920s; thus the cities supported new media such as radio. The second effect, bringing in more money for cultural activities, was also welcomed in a period where the financial situation of the cities was anything but easy. These measures pertained to a specific situation of economic crisis, which the intensified cultural policy was also intended to ameliorate. The propagation of urban culture and symbols was meant, in the end, to stimulate the local economy by giving direct support to local industries and by increasing the reputation of the city, thus attracting non-local visitors and businesses.

Bibliography

Baier, Hans (1981). »Verlagswesen und Buchhandel«. In *500 Jahre Buchstadt Leipzig.* 79–88, Leipzig.

Bayard, Françoise and Pierre Cayez (eds.) (1990). *Histoire de Lyon.* Le Coteau.

Bennett, Oliver (1995). »Cultural Policy in the United Kingdom: Collapsing Rationales and the End of a Tradition«. *European Journal of Cultural Policy,* 1, 2, 1995, 199–216.

Beyme, Klaus von (1998). *Kulturpolitik und nationale Identität.* Opladen.

Cohen, William B. (1998). *Urban Government and the Rise of the French City.* London.

Chaudonneret, Marie-Claude (1994). »Le salon des Fleurs du musée des Beaux-Arts de Lyon«. In Chantal Georgel (ed.). *La jeunesse des musées. Les musées en France au XIX siècle,* 71–76. Paris.

Cummings, Milton C. and Richard S. Katz (eds.) (1987). *The Patron State.* New York/Oxford.

Dablin J. (1897). »École régionale des Arts industriels«. In Association française pour l'avancement des Sciences (ed.). *Saint-Etienne,* Vol. 3. Saint-Etienne 13–29.

Debes, Dietmar (1981). »500 Jahre Buchdruck und Buchproduktion in Leipzig«. In *500 Jahre Buchstadt Leipzig*, 25–37. Leipzig.

Desvallées, André (1996). »Konvergenzen und Divergenzen am Ursprung der französischen Museen«. In Gottfried Fliedl (ed.). *Die Erfindung des Museums. Anfänge der bürgerlichen Museumsidee in der Französischen Revolution*, 65–130. Wien.

Dussel, Konrad (1998). »Theater in der Krise. Der Topos und die ökonomische Realität in der Weimarer Republik«. In Lothar Ehrlich and Jürgen John (eds.). *Weimar 1930. Politik und Kultur im Vorfeld der NS-Diktatur*, 211–223 Köln/Weimar/Wien.

Ellmeier, Andrea and Béla Rasky (1997). *Kulturpolitik in Europa – Europäische Kulturpolitik*. Wien.

Ferraton, Yves (1984). *Cinquante ans de vie musicale à Lyon. Les Witkowski et l'Orchestre Philharmonique de Lyon 1903–1953*. Trévoux.

Fligge, Jörg (1997). »Stadt und Bibliothek. Literaturversorgung als kommunale Aufgabe im Kaiserreich und in der Weimarer Republik: Das Bibliothekswesen der Freien und Hansestadt Lübeck in den Jahren 1870 bis zum Beginn des Nationalsozialismus«. In Jörg Fligge and Alois Klotzbücher (eds.). *Stadt und Bibliothek: Literaturversorgung als kommunale Aufgabe im Kaiserreich und in der Weimarer Republik*. Wiesbaden 61–178.

Fournial, Etienne (ed.) (1976). *Saint-Etienne. Histoire de la ville et de ses habitants*. Roanne.

Georgel, Chantal (1994). »Le musée, lieu d'enseignement, d'instruction et d'édification«. In Chantal Georgel (ed.). *La jeunesse des musées. Les musées en France au XIX siècle*. Paris 59–64.

Göschel, Albrecht (1998). »Kultur in der Stadt – Kulturpolitik in der Stadt«. In Albrecht Göschel and Volker Kirchberg (eds.). *Kultur in der Stadt. Stadtsoziologische Analysen zur Kultur*, 229–253, Opladen.

Grotjahn, Rebecca (2005). »Die höhere Ausbildung in der Musik«. Gründungsidee und Gründungsgeschichte des Leipziger Konservatoriums«. In Michael Fend, and Michel Noiray (eds.). *Musical Education in Europe (1770–1914)*. Berlin. Vol. 2, 301–330.

Guckes, Jochen (2005). »Stadtbilder und Stadtrepräsentationen im 20. Jahrhundert«. *Informationen zur modernen Stadtgeschichte*, 1, 2005, 75–86.

Hanko, Helmut M. (1981). »Kommunalpolitik in der ›Hauptstadt der Bewegung‹ 1933–1935. Zwischen ›revolutionärer‹ Umgestaltung und Verwaltungskontinuität«. In Martin Broszat, Elke Fröhlich and Anton Grossmann (eds.). *Bayern in der NS-Zeit III. Herrschaft und Gesellschaft im Konflikt*, 329–441. München/Wien.

Hansert, Andreas (1992). *Bürgerkultur und Kulturpolitik in Frankfurt am Main*.

Häußermann, Hartmut and Walter Siebel (1987). *Neue Urbanität*. Frankfurt am Main.

— (1993). »Die Politik der Festivalisierung und die Festivalisierung der Politik. Große Ereignisse in der Stadtpolitik«. In Hartmut Häußermann and Walter

Siebel (eds.). *Festivalisierung der Stadtpolitik. Stadtentwicklung durch große Projekte*, 7–31. Opladen.

Höpel, Thomas (2007a). »Städtische Kulturpolitik in Deutschland und Frankreich 1918–1940«. *Historische Zeitschrift*, 284, 3, 623–658.

— (2007b). *Von der Kunst- zur Kulturpolitik. Städtische Kulturpolitik in Deutschland und Frankreich 1918–1939*. Stuttgart.

Kammen, Michael (1999). *American culture, American tastes: social change in the twentieth century*. New York.

Kapr, Albert (1985). »Die Buchgestaltung an unserer Hochschule – ihre Geschichte und Bedeutung für die deutsche Buchkunst«. In Hochschule für Grafik und Buchkunst Leipzig (ed.). *Abteilung Buchgestaltung*, 3–8. Leipzig.

Karl-Marx-Stadt. Geschichte der Stadt in Wort und Bild. Berlin 1988.

Knopf, Sabine and Volker Titel (2001). *Der Leipziger Gutenbergweg. Geschichte und Topographie einer Buchstadt*. Beucha.

Labasse, Jean and André G. Marty (1960). »La foire internationale de Lyon: Evolutions et perspectives«. *Cahiers d'Histoire*, 5, 1, 77–99.

Latreille, André (1975). *Histoire de Lyon et du Lyonnais*. Toulouse.

Léon, Pierre (1967). »La région lyonnaise dans l'histoire économique et sociale de la France. Une esquisse (XVIe–XXe siècles)«. *Revue historique*, 481, 1967, 31–62.

Louat, André (1970). *L'universitaire à Lyon de 1870 à 1914*. Lyon (mémoire de maîtrise).

Mai, Andreas (2004). »Stadt als Produkt. Werbepolitik für Leipzig, 1893–1933«. In Thomas Höpel and Steffen Sammler (eds.). *Kulturpolitik und Stadtkultur in Leipzig und Lyon vom 18. zum 20. Jahrhundert*, 309–333. Leipzig.

Minot, Jacques (1991). *Histoire des universités françaises*. Paris.

Mongereau, Noël (2000). *Lyon du XXe au XXIe siècle*. Lyon.

Neues Leipzigisches Geschicht-Buch (1990). Leipzig.

Pevsner, Nikolaus (1986). *Die Geschichte der Kunstakademien*. Munich.

Poirrier, Philippe (1990). »Une politique culturelle de front populaire? La municipalité Jardillier à Dijon 1935–1940«. *Histoire Moderne et contemporaine*, 1990, 355–369.

— (1995). *Municipalité et culture au XXème siècle*. Dijon (Thèse d'Histoire).

Rebentisch, Dieter (1977). »Kommunalpolitik, Konjunktur und Arbeitsmarkt in der Endphase der Weimarer Republik«. In Rudolf Morsey (ed.), *Verwaltungsgeschichte*, 107–157. Berlin.

Rosenthal, Leon (1926). »Enseignement des beaux-arts«. In *Lyon 1906–1926*, 118–120. Lyon.

Schulze, Gerhard (1992). *Die Erlebnisgesellschaft. Kultursoziologie der Gegenwart*. Frankfurt am Main.

Wörner, Corinna (2003). *Der Thomanerchor im Spannungsfeld zwischen Kirche und Politik 1933–1945*. Hildesheim (Diplomarbeit).

Wortmann, Brigitta (1995). »Vom königlichen Hoftheater zum ›Städtischen Opern- und Schauspielhaus‹. Die Übernahme-Verhandlungen im Spiegel der Protokolle der städtischen Gremien«. In Dörte Schmidt and Brigitta Weber (eds.). *Keine Experimentierkunst. Musikleben an Städtischen Theatern der Weimarer Republik*, 10–17. Stuttgart.

Zwahr, Hartmut, Thomas Topfstedt and Günter Bentele (eds.) (1999). *Leipzigs Messen 1497–1997*. Köln/Weimar/Wien.

The Attractions of Place: The Making of Urban Tourism, 1860–1914

Jill Steward

Nineteenth-century cities were showcases for the industriousness, culture and success of their inhabitants. The new boulevards and monuments, theatres, museums and art galleries required audiences that extended beyond the confines of the cities themselves and, to that extent, their success was dependent upon the kind of publicity they attracted in the national and provincial media and the numbers who came to see and admire. Tourism also benefited the cultural economies of cities, both directly and indirectly. Some of the questions raised by the growth of contemporary urban tourism (Richards 1994: 347) apply to its nineteenth century predecessor: for example, how and why did a market develop? Was expansion a consequence of the extension of tourist practices beyond the social elites to other sectors of society, or was it a consequence of increased activity by those already participating? And, to what extent was an engagement with particular aspects of urban culture the outcome of cultural shifts and changing interests among particular social groups? And, finally did these strategies adopted by particular cities succeed in encouraging and attracting visitors? These are all questions that a systematic survey of the subject needs to address, although the focus of this particular essay is, firstly, on the factors supporting the growth of urban tourism from 1860–1910, and secondly, on the relationship between tourism, the urban economy and the media and cultural industries which helped to make cities appear as attractive places.

Urban tourism as such was not a new phenomenon although in the past it was often ancillary to other concerns.[1] Pilgrims who visited Rome,

---

1   Tourism has been defined as the »relationships and phenomena arising out of the journeys and temporary stays of people travelling primarily for leisure or recreational purposes« (cited Towner 1996: 4). Urban tourism consists of a range of practices distinguished primarily by the milieu in which they take place (Gilbert and Clark 1997: 344; Law

Santiago and Jerusalem in the late-Middle Ages certainly practiced a form
of tourism since they took guidebooks with them, looked at the sights and
brought back souvenirs. However, the growth of urban tourism as a phenomenon in its own right has received relatively little attention from historians and even its contemporary manifestations attracted serious study only
in the 1980s with the growth of interest in the »power of urban culture« to
counter the effects of urban decline (Richards 1994: 366). But, if the number of urban guidebooks published in the second half of the century is any
indication, tourists of various kinds were present in many European cities
suggesting that they were making an increasingly important contribution to
their economies as they responded to the growing attractiveness of many
cities and urban cultures offered new and exciting forms of entertainment.
To some extent the growth of urban tourism was partly a by-product of
the general expansion of tourism, as the middle classes became more prosperous and adopted lifestyles incorporating leisure, consumption and
travel, encouraged by the advent of the railways and steamships and improvements in reproductive and communications technologies which
transformed the mobility of people, goods and information (Sheller and
Urry 2006). Metropolitan cities such as London, Paris, Vienna and Berlin
became hubs for the production and diffusion of the knowledge and information that was instrumental in the creation of markets for all kinds of
goods and services, including tourism. These developments changed peo-
ples' perceptions of space and place and made the world seem increasingly
accessible (Schivelbusch 1986), informing conceptions of locality, region
and nation and influencing the way in which particular cities were perceived. This trend was most evident in the tourism associated with the
giant international exhibitions characteristic of the second half of the century and the expanded »cosmopolitan sensibility« to which they contributed (Alloway 1969: 38), but it also operated at local and regional levels as
mobility between urban areas increased and cities initiated strategies to
improve their public image and promote their own particular economic
and political agendas.

The growth of tourism not only made a contribution to many urban
economies, but also benefited their cultural industries directly and indi-

1993: 14). Until recently, most studies of tourism history have focused on the cultural
practices of the elite classes (Towner 1994) and forms of health and recreational tourism
associated with the middle classes, including their influence on the development of spa
and seaside towns (Walton 2002).

rectly. At the same time urban-based media industries were instrumental in the promotion of tourism and in the selling of place. Factors supporting these trends include: firstly, the promotion of travel by press encouraged the middle classes to engage in tourism and thereby, created work for people engaged in the tourist industry, but also in areas of cultural production geared to tourists. Secondly, the media responded to urban developments and initiatives in ways that supported tourism by publicising the attractions of particular places and making their distinctive features known to the wider world, a process assisted by the development of modern systems of transport and communication and the increasing democratisation of the press. Thirdly, the growing interconnectedness of places created by the new mobility of information meant that news, advertising and images of place produced and published in one city could generate economic opportunities for tourist centres and tourist-related industries elsewhere, just as tourist souvenirs bought in one place were increasingly produced somewhere else. Finally, some cities were clearly more visible and attractive to tourists than others, so that a particular issue to be explored in this essay is that of why some cities were more successful than others in promoting a positive image and the extent to which this made them more effective as ›people-attractors‹.

The Development of Urban Tourism

In the early modern period the stereotypical urban tourist was the young male aristocrat from northern Europe who participated in the educational and cultural rituals of the Grand Tour to Italy, including the acquisition of artistic treasures, many of which subsequently became tourist attractions for later generations as courtly and aristocratic collections were gradually opened to the public. From 1770s onwards the educated middle-classes also began to tour abroad, their itineraries displaying the influence of the new aesthetic ideologies disseminated by an expanding print culture (Towner 1985). As the taste for sublime and picturesque natural scenery and romantic monuments gradually spread, it stimulated domestic tourism across the continent (Kaschuba 1993), a practice that, in Britain, included visiting country house collections. In the course of the next century growing concerns about the un-healthiness of cities and the growth of recreational tourism encouraged movement away from the towns towards the country and seaside (Walton and Walvin 1983), institutionalised on the continent in the practices of the *Sommerfrische* and *villégietura* as the wealthy escaped the city heat in their country villas. Growing numbers of middle-class French, German and British tourists began to tour Italy benefiting from better roads, the advent of railways, steamships and improved postal communications facilitating the adoption of »circular notes«, an eighteenth century invention which lessened the financial problems associated with foreign travel (Brooker 1994: 40–71).

In the first part of the century, apart from London and Paris, few cities outside Italy entertained tourists as such although many provincial cities were important as social, retail and entertainment centres (Borsay 1989; Corfield 1994; 137; Stobart 1999). As the urban middle classes became more mobile, they began to visit towns and cities further away for business and commercial purposes, or for reasons to do with education, health or family, though such visits often included outings and sightseeing. Social and political developments encouraged the opening up of semi-private museums and galleries to a wider audience. In Britain the doctrine of »rational recreation« encouraged educational and cultural visits to the kind of institutions formerly associated with court and capital cities, such as the artistic and scientific collections, museums and libraries which now played a part in modern city life. Visits of this kind also helped to lay the foundations of civic cultures in which the promotion of knowledge and culture and the dissemination of »civilising« values to a wider audience was regarded an important municipal function (Bailey 1978; Seed 1988; Meller 2001). In Germany the pursuit of *Bildungskultur* functioned in a similar way (Lorente 1998).

Growing traffic between cities encouraged the making of comparisons (Hietala 1987: 387), as in the case of the relationship between London and Paris, for example (Hancock 1999 68–71). This tendency was accentuated as programmes of redevelopment and beautification were undertaken by modernising municipal authorities seeking to deal with the problems attendant on the rapid growth and expanding functions of their cities as they developed into regional and national cultural centres (Waagenar 1994; Meller 2001). These developments initiated a new era in cultural politics as the urban elites, particularly in relatively new industrial and commercial centres, became increasingly self-conscious about the way in which their cities were perceived by the outside world. Some evolved strategies for improving their reputations vis-à-vis their neighbours and rivals. Often, awareness of initiatives elsewhere encouraged entrepreneurial activity and competitive demonstrations of civic pride such as the funding of museums and art galleries by local benefactors and the acquisition of collections to put in them (Penny 1998; Lorente 1998). Developments of this kind also stimulated the associational and cultural life of places such as Hamburg, in ways that made them attractive to people with cultural interests and occupation.

Cities with a significant tourist presence quickly realised that this could be good for business since visitors provided customers for trade fairs, department stores, restaurants and cafes as well as pleasure gardens, concerts, music halls, pleasure boats and other forms of entertainment. Moreover, tourists formed an admiring audience for expensive developments such as the new art galleries, theatres, shopping malls, museums and exhibition halls, parks, boulevards and electric street lighting and were invaluable for promoting the reputation of a place. However, the extent to which tourism directly impacted on the economy of particular cities depended on their popularity with visitors. Figures for comparison before 1919 are often unreliable or lacking although census and overnight-stay figures are indicative where available. Within large urban conurbations, or cities with numerous satellite towns, day excursions were also increasingly important In the course of the century Paris overtook London as the most visited city and was clearly outstanding as the one most visited by foreigners, attracting c. 40,000 British visitors in 1856, a number rising to 60,000 in 1867 (Hancock 1999: 77). By 1896 the city was estimated to have c. 903,000 visitors (as against 717,000 for Berlin, 358,000 for Vienna and 153,000 for Budapest).

As one of the most important cultural centres in Europe, Paris was the model of a successful tourist honey-pot and the industry played a major role in the city's cultural economy (Green 1990), but even in cities with far fewer visitors, the cultural industries benefited from their presence. It is hard to say just how many people were employed in occupations in, or related to the cultural industries at any one time, if only because of the limitations of available sources and problems of definition (Lorente and Targett 2000: 66–67), but the numbers in major centres of cultural production were clearly significant, judging from the increasing output and sales of books (Weedon, 2003), paintings, photographs and printed materials. Industrial cities, such as Düsseldorf and Manchester, constituted a market for the output of the local cultural industries that sprang up to cater for the demands of newly affluent middle classes for goods such as paintings and photographs (Seed 1988: 64–65).[2] Studies of the art communities of English provincial cities suggest that expanding centres with thriving cultural institutions tended to become attractive to artists as their reputations as cultural centres became established. (Lorente 2000: 72–73) and although they could not compete with major artistic and literary marketplaces such as Paris, Berlin, Munich and London, they were still performed some of the same function in that they provided cultural venues and publicity, both of which were important to networks of artists and writers living elsewhere who remained dependent upon the cultural institutions of city life in order to make a living. How much of this business was directly related to tourism it is impossible to say but, clearly, the cultural economies of places with well-established tourist industries such as Florence with relatively small populations (c. 19, 200 in 1896) and less diverse functions were dependent on visitors in a way that the cultural industries of expanding industrial towns such as or Lyons (438,000 in 1896) or Manchester (c. 703, 479 in 1896) were not. In Florence for example, the Alinari brothers based their photographic business around the demand for souvenir photographs of Italian art and architecture (Berger 1978). The publicity and sales associated with exhibitions were particularly important to artists. The 1869 exhibition in Munich for example, attracted tens of thousands of visitors and more than 154,260 marks worth of sales (Lenman 1997: 109) while the Venice biennale of 1912 attracted 41,742 visitors and generated 869 sales (Alloway 1969: 193).

---

2 Paris was a magnet for cultural producers: there were c. 3,300 professional painters in 1863 and by 1863, c. 8,200 males in artistic occupations, their output estimated at around 20,000 works (White C/H 1965: n 4). By contrast, in Munich which was also a major magnet for artists, in 1886 there were 854 fine artists, excluding students (Lenman 1997: 109), a number which by 1895 had risen to 1180 as against the 1159 working in Berlin, a city which was four times larger) and 13 percent of the German total (Makela 1990: 15; Lenman 1997: 109; Gee 200: 151). Photography was an increasingly important industry. Paris in 1848 had a total of 207 studios of which 74 employed numbers between two and ten, a total of 566. By 1868 there were 365 *artistes photographes* and studios. In 1860, the industry generated a total volume of sales at c. 6, 547, 410 francs, nineteen times that of 1848 compared with a rise in the total of all Parisian industries, which increased during the period by a factor of less than three, from 1,463,628,350 to 3,369,092,949 francs (McCaulay 1994: 50, 55). Photography was also thriving in Germany where the industry employed 4,574 people in 1875 rising to 6,364 in 1882, 11,851 in 1895 and 19,407 in 1907, including finishing jobs in factories (Lenman 1997b 247).

On a wider front, the general growth of tourism was beneficial to the media and cultural industries (Steward 2001) since it generated work across occupational networks extending from artists, illustrators, engravers and photographers to journalists and brochure writers (Green 1990; Steward 2005). The transport industry required all sorts of printed materials from posters to timetables. In Trieste for example, the privately run company of Austrian Lloyd, which combined extensive railway, shipping and publishing interests founded a studio of artists and writers who produced handbooks and advertising to publicise its routes. Professional writers routinely supplemented their income from writing about their travels. Tourists bought postcard images of iconic city sites, prestigious new buildings and places of entertainment and sent them to their friends creating new opportunities for enterprising commercial photographers who also provided images for retailers elsewhere. Valentine's of Dundee employed 1000 people in 1897 (Lenman 2005: 652), G.W. Wilson of Aberdeen was the largest producer of views in Britain, Lévy et Cie and Neurdin of Paris were major industrial concerns supplying topographical, architectural and ethnographical views to the international postcard trade (Ripert and Frère 1983; Durie 1990; Godden 1996: 92–106) as did the London publishing company of Raphael Tuck which published art cards of cities all over the world. The highest quality cards were printed in Leipzig, a major centre of the trade, which benefited hugely from the growth of tourism demonstrating that the growing interconnectedness of communication and commercial networks meant that the benefits of tourist growth were not confined to the places actually visited by tourists. The *Times* (1898) noted that the numbers of picture postcards »posted from the Berlin-Trade and Industrial Exhibition were over a million, and from the Hamburg Horticultural Exhibition 327,000. This new trade not only affects the Post Office, but also the paper industry and those concerned in illustrating, as well as various branches of the stationers' trade« (July 12, 4 F).

Selling Travel, Selling Places

Not all cities were equally well known or popular with tourists however, so what made some more visible and attractive than others? What kinds of information were available to potential tourists about the attractions of particular places and what were the factors most likely give a city a positive tourist image?

First of all it is necessary to say something about the growth of tourist travel, a development actively fostered by the transport companies and the travel agents responsible for the institutionalisation and »social organisation« of tourist traffic (Urry 1995: 142–145). A new kind of business phenomenon, the agents were responsible not only for rationalising travel, but also the systematic selling of place. By the last quarter of the century their offices symbolised modernity as much as did street lighting and omnibuses. The systematic organisation, packaging and promotion of tourist destinations as commodities added a new dimension to the service industries and to the »world of goods« available for purchase by the wealthier classes for whom choice of recreational activities and travel destinations were included among the ways in which they signified their social and cultural identities (Steward 2005). The success of this kind of business was dependent on the spread of modern commercial practices across the continent and proximity to the communication hubs of metropolitan cities where news and information about the world was received, processed and redirected with a density and a speed that was wholly new (Conboy 2004: 124–127; Hahn 2006). One of the world's best-known agents, the firm of Thomas Cook occupied premises in London in Ludgate Circus, sandwiched between the business-quarter of the city and »Newspaperland«, as Fleet Street and its environs were known. London represented an ideal location for the headquarters of a company with global aspirations since it provided easy access to the areas where the majority of the wealthier British »travelling classes« resided and the kind of facilities necessary for dispatching travellers round the world. The elder Cook understood the value of publicity and his house magazine the *Excursionist and Tourist Gazette* (later the *International Tourist Advertiser*) carried articles about the firm's activities and the places included in his tours, a practice also adopted by other agents. By 1867 the *Excursionist* was selling 58 000 copies: ten years later it was read in London clubs by an up-market clientele and in the 1890s foreign editions were also published in Paris, Hamburg, Vienna, New Delhi and New York achieving a global circulation of 120,000 (Brendon 1991: 236. n.21).

As this indicates, the growth of the printing, publishing and media industries was a key factor in making places visible and attractive to potential visitors and it was largely due to their efforts that information about particular places was disseminated beyond the immediate vicinity. From the middle of the eighteenth century the printing and publishing industries supplied the general public with a stream of printed images, books, newspapers and journals that opened it up to the wider world in ways that were instrumental to the mobilisation of travellers. Equally important was the experience of place offered by well-established forms of visual entertainment such as dioramas, panoramas and stereoscopes. At the end of the century the images of modern forms of transport, trains, steamers, electric trams, hot-air balloons, motorcar and airplanes that circulated among an increasingly popular audience, thanks to the use of new reproductive technologies, came to symbolise and shape ways in which the world was perceived and experienced (Friedberg 1993; Schwartz, 1998; Dalbello 2002; Strain 2003). The news events films and travelogues of early cinematography enabled people to experience for themselves forms of motion and ways of seeing places very different from those associated with the static images of the illustrated weeklies.

»People-Attractors«: Attractiveness as a Relative Concept

In the course of the century the relative attractiveness of particular cities as tourist centres changed as transport networks developed, communications improved and cities were redeveloped. Census and overnight stay figures available for some cities give some indication, but as yet there is little comparative work available for the construction of the hierarchical tables beloved of contemporary tourism planners. Exhibition numbers are frequently cited but they fail to distinguish between categories of visitors: local people for example, often went several times to a popular exhibition. It is however, possible to make assumptions on which kind of cities might be expected to attract visitors. Studies of contemporary tourism use models of various kinds in order to identify the elements in place images most likely to have tourist appeal (Selwyn 1996; Kearns and Philo 1993; Gold and Ward 1994). Such models do not map neatly onto the tourist flows of the past, but they do possess heuristic value and offer a way of thinking about the kind of images places might project to potential visitors, why people might choose to go there and constitute a basis for explaining and predicting why some might be seen as more attractive than others. One such a model for example, refers to the sum of what any particular city offers potential visitors as the »total tourist product« (Van der Berg et al. 1995: 15, 190), a concept that covers the principal assets of a place (the primary product), such as its natural resources such as scenic environs and historic and cultural attractions, and any additional reasons why people might want to go there (the complementary product) such as accessibility, place image and special events. Together, these suggest reasons why a place might be seen as particularly attractive and enjoy an advantage over its rivals. Projected back into the long nineteenth century, this model constitutes a useful heuristic tool for analysing the relative attractiveness of different types of city over a specific period of time, the kind of image they might be expected to project and reasons why some might be more successful than others as »people-attractors«.

Applying these criteria, a number of different categories emerge, none of which are exclusive. The first focuses on features with the most obvious tourist appeal, such as historic cores of cities such as Amsterdam, Nuremburg or Canterbury. Picturesque medieval cities were of particular interest to nineteenth-century romantics and followers of John Ruskin, one of the reasons why Florence became incorporated into the British middle-class tour and Venetian tourism gained a new lease of life (Davis and Marvin 2004). Also in this category are cities with outstanding or aesthetically significant monuments such as Rouen or Dresden; religious shrines or relics as in Cracow or Lyons; outstanding artistic collections of the kind found in Vienna, Munich and Düsseldorf, or natural resources such as the beautiful surroundings and hinterlands of Lyons and Glasgow, the good air of Montpellier, or the hot-springs of Budapest. A second category includes important commercial and industrial centres such as Birmingham, Manchester, Lille and Lyons and a number of the major port cities such as Hamburg, Liverpool and Marseilles, all of which would attract a considerable amount of business traffic. These cities often lacked historic cores and monuments and were often, initially at least, without monuments or architectural distinction. They were also most likely to be subjected to extensive programmes of civic improvements and to possess new and lively cultural institutions. In the third category are national and regional capitals distinguished by their cultural, political, courtly, symbolic and religious functions. Of these some such as London and Paris were also imperial capitals. The acquisition of capital city status gave cities such as Berlin, Brussels, Budapest and Rome new importance and more visitors while the rise of nationalism gave others such as Barcelona and Prague and other cities on the periphery of the old Habsburg monarchy greater significance because of their new symbolic function. Former capitals such as Florence, Munich and Pressburg/Pozsony lost ground. Regional and national capitals were usually at the hub of transportation systems and benefited from the diplomatic, political and commercial functions they performed. A final category includes cities with outstanding cultural, entertainment or retail facilities, something for which Rouen was noted, or attractions of a kind not usually noted in tourist guides, except in coded ways, and particularly associated with port cities such as Hamburg and metropolitan capitals such as Berlin, Paris and Vienna, all of which had thriving forms of nightlife and where prostitution was an industry in its own right (Koshar 2000: 44–45).

High scoring cities such as Paris, London and Vienna, were national and imperial capitals and performed a number of economic and symbolic functions; they possessed many historic and aesthetic features and had a thriving artistic and cultural life. Others, such as Birmingham, Hamburg and Manchester, scored poorly initially, because of relatively late development and industrial and commercial origins so they were lacking in the kind of historical features of particular interest to tourists. However, cities of this kind attracted businessmen and people from within the region who took advantage of the leisure infrastructure and retail facilities (Stobart 2000), a process that could be expected to intensify in the next century, particularly when the city centres were remodelled. The existence of a thriving and cultured middle class often generated lively cultural institutions. Hamburg, for example, had active and enterprising private patrons of art and a thriving community of amateur photographers. Development affected some cities adversely. Dusseldorf for example, formerly a magnet for artists and tourists by virtue of its artistic reputation, in 1895 still had the third largest art community in Germany of c 335 fine artists, but its relative decline as a cultural centre by 1911 earned it the description of ›a steel town with a few resident picture makers‹ (Lenman 1999: 46). Capitals, such as London, Paris and Vienna attracted visitors on diplomatic and administrative business because of their function, as did Brussels, Berlin, Budapest and Rome after their change of status. The effects of nation building also had implications for many regional capitals such as Munich and Turin as they lost ground in the face of new nationalist agendas. Conversely nationalist feeling was also supportive of tourism in cities such as Prague, which functioned as a cultural capital for the Czechs, and in Cracow where, in the early twentieth century pilgrimage and tourism supported the growth of Polish nationalism (Crowley 1999: 102–107).

An additional feature was accessibility, even more important in the nineteenth century than it is today. Not surprisingly it was an organising principle of many of the guidebooks available to travellers (Rauch 2001: 58). Baedeker guides, for example, were organised around the international railway networks so that Bucharest, appears in the 1911 Baedeker for Austria-Hungary, but not Sofia, which was not at that point accessible via the main route through the Balkans. Accessibility was often closely associated with the economic function of a place. The port cities of Liverpool, Hamburg, Trieste and Marseilles, for example, were easily accessible because of their role as human entrepôts and points of entry and exit to and from the continent. Also scoring well on accessibility were cities at junctions on major transport routes, such as Lyons, or functioning as gateways to popular tourist areas, such as Basle and Salzburg. Cities of this kind would be expected to benefit from the general expansion of travel and tourism, especially if they were easily accessible from large conurbations. Brussels for example, was easily reached from southeast England and was a staging post for Britons travelling to Germany, particularly to the Rhineland, Switzerland and Italy. Lyons, at the confluence of two major rivers, was an important stop for northern *hivernant*s travelling to Marseilles and the Riviera.

For potential travellers, guidebooks were indispensable sources of information about what places had to offer. Unlike more personal kinds of material they were produced and published as commercial products for a particular kind of customer and the reputation of the brand and their market success was reliant on the accuracy, currency and helpfulness of the information they contained. To that extent, particularly if reprinted and updated, they represent attempts by authors and publishers to identify and list the principal features of a place in the light of the kind of information they considered relevant to the needs of travellers. Over the century the appearance of different kinds of guidebook indicates the growing democratisation of travel and emergence of a more diversified tourist market.[3] Lists

---

3   The handbooks used for this essay include *The Queen Newspaper Book of Travel*, (Hornby 1905, 1909, 1912), souvenir handbooks for Hamburg/American Line, and the North German Lloyd published for transatlantic visitors, many of them businessmen. Works published by Karl Baedeker and John Murray were serious affairs with a great deal of detail.

of key features generally conform to the model utilised above in that they invariably refer to significant historic features, new and old architectural monuments and artistic collections. Also noted are »natural« features such as promenades and parks and scenic environs. Other features mentioned are theatres, new civic buildings, monuments and cultural institutions such as modern town halls, galleries and museums all of which regularly appear on suggested itineraries. Sections on accommodation list hotels and boarding houses, restaurants and cafes, places of entertainment and shops. A brief inspection of entries for particular cities taken from a selection of handbooks published during the period 1860–1914 provides a rough basis for a comparison of their respective ratings and how these changed over time. Lyons for example, clearly rises in the estimation of editors for, whereas Bradshaw (1854) describes the place as an industrial city noted for silk production and known to the British as the »Manchester of France« with »narrow and badly paved streets« that were impossible in bad weather (70), by the 1880s civic improvements had changed the place to such an extent that it was highly regarded for its modern hotels with electric lighting, ancient and modern buildings, riverside quays, museums and collections, theatres and casino. Significantly the city was also a major pilgrimage centre, with 1.5 million visitors a year to the shrine of Notre-Dame-de-Fourvières (Hart 1901: 764–765).

The earliest images of place were the woodblock stereotypes used in printed travel books which were used and reused in a number of different contexts. Such texts were limited to an elite audience, but they anticipated the way in which more complex place-images subsequently functioned within a culture of travel, mediating between actual places and the way they were experienced. In the course of the nineteenth century the role of the place-images became increasingly important as more places acquired the kind of features that might attract tourists since, unless people were aware of what it had to offer, a place might remain invisible and unvisited. Moreover, as the »supply« of potential destinations increased, cities hoping for visitors were faced with growing competition and potential tourists with choice, circumstances in which a positive and distinctive place image was helpful. But what made for a positive image?

Cities in which this question was addressed were those most likely to have developed an infrastructure supportive of tourists. One indication of the extent to which visitors were welcomed was the presence of a tourist association. In the 1880s information offices began to open in cities with a

high volume of tourist traffic such as Hamburg, Stuttgart, Lyons and
Dresden. The latter was reported by the *Queen* »*Newspaper*« *Book of Travel*
(1905), as »the most popular of German cities with English speaking people« since it »lays itself out to provide hospitality to strangers on a large
scale, and is, of all cities in Germany, perhaps, the best provided with hotels and pensions, schools and instructive institutions of every kind
(Hornby, 138–139).« Tourist offices also produced publicity, publishing
posters and guidebooks. In some places they represented a response to
fears of economic decline of the kind afflicting the towns of the Tirol or
the Massif centrale (Rauch 2001: 42–43). In France the first *syndicat
d'initiative* appeared in the spa town of Cauterets (1884), followed by many
others usually set up by local businessmen or hoteliers such the one in Lille
(1901) which took a very active role in the city's post-war redevelopment
(Labiausse 2003). In Austria, the first tourist office opened in Graz (1881)
and in Vienna a municipal subvention for the purpose was given in 1884
which was subsequently supplemented by public and private contributions:
collaboration with the local trade organisations included sponsored exhibition displays (Steward 2001: 114–115). As these examples indicate, initiatives of this kind were often undertaken by interested parties in order to
boost trade.

The most important arena for the circulation and promotion of place-
images was undoubtedly that of the press. Modern communications made
it possible for information and publicity emanating from one city to reach
people in cities elsewhere (Brown 1985) and to impact on the economies
of towns and cities hundreds of miles away. The *Times* and the *Illustrated
London News* were available in most major continental cities while the up-
market *Queen Newspaper* ran a service for answering readers' travel enquiries
(Steward 2005). In Britain, provincial centres of middle-class associational
and cultural life such as the Literary and Philosophical Societies subscribed
to lifestyle publications such as the *Strand*.[4] The appearance of illustrated
newspapers modelled on the *Illustrated London News,* such as *L'Illustration*
(1843) offered readers visual information about places elsewhere (Charle,

---

4   By 1909 the Strand was producing 400,000 copies per month and had printed 30,000
     illustrations (Jackson, 2001: 99). In Germany, the Berliner Illustrirte Zeitung had a
     subscription circulation of 23,000 in 1894 rising to 58,000 in 1898 and 1135,000 in 1901.
     In 1874 the city received over 6,65 million copies of papers per year published where
     and sent through the post (the main medium of distribution at the time) (Vizetelly 1879,
     Vol. 2, 393).

2004: 69), as did other general interest publications such as the *Leipziger Illustrierte Zeitung, Westermanns Monatschafte, Le Monde Illustré* and *Gartenlaube*, carrying articles about art, culture and travel aimed at cultivated, if diverse, middle-class readerships. These topics also suited people working in the media and cultural industries, the professional and amateur writers, journalists, artists and photographers, who were able to capitalise on their specialist cultural knowledge and personal travels in the interests of making a living in a competitive world. This was particularly the case with the specialist art press such as *Die Kunst für Alle* (Munich), the *Art Journal* and *Studio* (London) which kept readers informed about European developments, publicising and reviewing exhibitions, fostering artistic careers and providing an income for critics (Gee 2002). While these developments represented responses to social and cultural changes they also encouraged the formation of those lifestyles through which different cultural communities expressed their socially coded tastes and preferences (Steward 2005), including a taste for urban tourism.

A study of magazines such as the upmarket *Westermanns Monatshefte* and the *Illustrated London News* gives a strong sense of the kind of places and features regarded as interesting to readers. *Westermanns*, published in Brunswick, in particular was a good example of a magazine supportive of urban tourism to a cultured German readership, disseminating information about important events and exhibitions and contributing to the formation of positive images of place. A ›family‹ journal, *Westermanns* (founded 1856) was particularly known for its innovative combination of illustrations and text. The ratio of images to text rose from 5.2 percent in 1856 to 12 percent in 1885 and in 1914 to 28.3 percent (Lachenicht 2005). It also gives an insight into what Rudy Koshar (1998) describes as the ›deep shift in the optic identity‹ of the German nation, which revived interest in historic urban landscapes, a trend also evident in Britain although the travel coverage in the 1880s also covered relatively modern cities. By the 1890s the art critic Ludwig Pietsch was contributing articles on cities, as did the artist Eduard Zetzche who used his own drawings as illustrations. »Picturesque« scenes were depicted by line drawings and »artistic« watercolour drawings while articles on art and modern architecture used photographs using the halftone process developed in the 1880s, showing to the emerging market for photographic illustrations in the illustrated press.

Westermanns' coverage of European cities falls into clear categories: historic and picturesque cities and cultural centres; cities with historic centres that were evolving into modern cities, and finally, the thriving metropolitan cities such as Berlin, Paris and Hamburg. In the early twentieth century there was increased focus on architecture, art and culture with the advent of the Secession movements, particularly in Germany. In Britain, the equivalent journals were more focused on sport than culture, but the increasingly cosmopolitan nature of upper-class lifestyles was appealed to with series such as the »Cafes of Europe« in the *Strand Magazine,* implying the casual familiarity of author and readership with the places concerned. Implicit in many of these articles is an interest in the outcome of the many programmes of urban development and civic improvement that were transforming so many European cities. Intercity rivalry and the desire to show off were important incentives for the development of strategies to attract visitors. The civic monument and lively cultural institutions that were enriching modern urban life were objects of interest beyond the immediate locality and were attractive to curious visitors. However, although these developments might feed local pride, they did not always lead to a more positive tourist image. While American tourists were directed to Nuremberg as the »quaintest town in Germany« and were assured that its historic core was protected from intrusive new buildings (Hart 1901: 403), the dame could not be said of Hamburg, Germany's major port city which lacked public moments and demolished its its gothic cathedral in 1802. In 1897 one guidebook found it difficult to recommend anything for visitors to see but the Bourse since there were no promenades, no parks or resorts (Evans 1987: 37). Similarly Birmingham, a world class manufacturing centre, was described by one author as possessing »little of interest« apart from »a few public edifices« and visits to »manufactories« (Hart 1901: 881) though another felt that it was a city that »one regrets to leave« (Reichmann and Cantor 1896). *Queen* omitted it altogether from its annual compendium. And yet, by 1911 Birmingham could claim to be the Britain's »second city« with a population of 840,000 and was enjoying new public buildings, parks, art exhibitions and a new university, in short, all features appropriate to a dynamic modern city. There were however, no historic buildings, although they city possessed a collection of Shakespeariana.

By contrast, Amsterdam enjoyed a very different image, not because of modern improvements which were highly controversial, but because of its historic core (Waagenar 2000). The case of Brussels was also interesting. John Murray (1859) wrote of the splendour of individual buildings in Belgian cities but concluded: »it is difficult to traverse, in the present day, the deserted and inanimate streets of the great Belgian cities without feeling a sense of melancholy at the aspect they exhibit« (96–97). By 1889 all this had changed. The appearance of a new channel steamer caused the *Illustrated London News* (1889) to devote two pages of illustrations to the city and its adjacent towns, praising the former for its commerce, wealth and pleasure and for its transformation into a »first class modern city« with cafes, shopping, souvenir lace and excursions, but which nevertheless still possessed »superb remains of former times« (*ILN* Feb 2: 144–145). It was not so much the relatively new status of Brussels as a capital city which elicited approval although this was the reason for impressive new public buildings (Fig 1), as its high class educational and cultural institutions and general atmosphere as »one of the brightest and most cheerful near-to-England capitals, and the least expensive« (Hornsby 1905). In the second half of the century many other cities were in still in the throes of redevelopment and building sites were important, if temporary, features of the urban landscape as old buildings and quarters were demolished to make way for the new monumental structures considered more appropriate to the image of a successful modern city. In large conurbations some of the tourists viewing these sights were often day-trippers from the suburbs or residents who wanted to inspect the changes for themselves (Fritzsche 1996: 66–72; Gyáni 2004: 68–70). At the same time, the fate of older buildings and historically significant but run down areas was often a highly contentious matter and issues of restoration and conservation were widely discussed in the press (Waagenar 1994; Meller 2001).

Fig. 1: International exhibition Brussels. Published by the »Maison à la innovation«. Postcard (1897), souvenir for the International Brussels Exhibition 1897 showing the Maison du Roi and the Palais de Justice.

(Source: Author's collection.)

Finally, a very important strategy for attracting press attention and bringing in the crowds were special events. Examining the history of these events, although it is evident that the number of people visiting cities was gradually increasing, a powerful stimulus on urban tourism was the increase in the number and types of special events. Many of these were put on by particular interest groups or were related to the growth of civic associations associated with trade and middle-class life. Art exhibitions, trade fairs and exhibitions, music festivals and agricultural exhibitions, pageants and air shows were all events that enlivened urban life in the second half of the century and provided copy for the media. In regional and national capitals, rituals and spectacles associated with their symbolic functions were designed to impress the general public and encouraged the perception of urban spaces as arenas for staging productions that anticipated the events management of our own day. Exhibitions have been identified as one of the most distinctive and innovatory cultural forms offered by the nineteenth century and constituted an important element in the new spectacular culture shaping city life. Originating in the eighteenth century with the activities of the London Society of Arts and a series of national exhibition put on Paris, exhibitions were initially conceived of as showcases for trade and industry and arts and crafts and were staged everywhere in Europe except the Balkans (Luckhurst 1951: 80). The idea of the trade exhibition was initially less successful in Britain than in continental Europe although the first display put on by the Mechanics Institute in Manchester in 1837– 1838 attracted around 50,000 people, rising to over 100,000 for subsequent ones (Seed 1988). The Art Treasures exhibition (1857) attracted almost a million and a half visitors, including trainloads of workers and some foreigners, demonstrating the way that a successful event could raise the cultural profile of a city and attract favourable publicity in the national press (61–72). The real landmark in urban tourism however, was the huge popular success of the 1851 Exhibition in London as large numbers of people from across the social spectrum visited the capital for the first time and stayed away from home to enjoy sightseeing and urban entertainments (Barton 2005: 65–68). For this reason the event has often been taken as the starting point of modern mass urban tourism although its rationale was primarily educative and commercial and it was far less attractive to foreigners than the Paris exhibition four years later (Luckhurst 1951: 220–221). Events of this size highlighted a key requirement for large-scale urban tourism, the existence of a well-developed and extensive infrastructure capable of mobilising, accommodating and dealing with large numbers of people, including foreigners.

The most successful exhibitions were the huge international ones held in Paris, part of the ›self-celebratory‹ display that supported the city's self-image against that of its London rival (Hancock 1999: 69). But there were many lesser events staged elsewhere in the hope of attracting visitors and improving the image of a place. As their novelty wore off, popular entertainments were used to draw in the crowds (Greenhalgh 1988: 41). International agricultural, horticultural and art exhibitions appealed to different sections of the public and attracted domestic and foreign visitors and were used as a means of attracting business (Fig 2). Hamburg, for example staged an agricultural show in 1889, which attracted 30,000–70,000 visitors daily (LT July 13: 7 c D). While the staging of international exhibitions was driven by the desire to attract trade and showcase the host city, this was often combined with identity politics (Greenhalgh 1989; Rowe 1995; West 1995; Driver and Gilbert 1999; Geppert 2002): the first exhibition of this was held in Brussels in 1830 (the year in which the Belgians achieved independence from the Dutch) and covered all the states of the Netherlands. The Berlin exhibition of 1844 included all the German states: it attracted over 3000 exhibitors and was clearly intended to promote and showcase German national identity (1844) (Luckhurst 1951: 81; Greenhalgh 1988: 9). In Plovdiv in Bulgaria (1892) an industrial and agricultural exhibition established the city's status as a major regional centre, while the 1891 exhibition in Prague developed into a statement about the city's status as the centre of Czech culture and nationalist aspirations and the 1896 Millennial Exhibition in Budapest performed a similar function for the Magyars. The Franco-British exhibition in London and the 1901 Glasgow exhibition were both supportive of imperialism (Greenhalgh 1988; Mackenzie 1999). Dynastic events such as coronations and jubilees were part of the spectacular life of capital cities. In Vienna, for example (Unowski, 2006), local rituals associated with Corpus Christi were replaced by a formal procession along the Ringstrasse led by the Emperor which combined dynastic promotion with tourist spectacle, an example of the way that redevelopment of modern capital cities such as Rome (Atkinson et al. 1999: 49) provided a stage for the performance of invented traditions associated with »imagined communities«, requiring the cooperation of the press to maximise their effect (Hobsbawm and Ranger 1984; Anderson 1991).

While the success of an event depended on effective mechanisms for the circulation and diffusion of information and publicity, this also carried the risk of adverse publicity, as was the case with the 1872 trade exhibition in Lyons (LT July 10: 10, C. D), and the 1873 International Exhibition in Vienna when the inadequacy of the arrangements was pilloried in the London press (Steward 1998: 125). Fear of invidious comparisons was also a factor in the decision to demote the status of the proposed trade exhibition in Berlin (1896) from international to national, the Kaiser noting »There is nothing in Berlin that can captivate the foreigner, except a few museums, castles and soldiers« (Rowe 1995: 221). In the case of Glasgow the exhibitions of 1888 and 1901 created very positive media coverage at home and abroad, reinforcing the city's sense of superiority over Edinburgh (Mackenzie 1999; Fraser 2000) and supporting its claim to be the empire's second city against strong competition from Liverpool.

Fig. 2: Postcard (1904). Art and Horticultural exhibition (with Pain's fireworks). Düsseldorf. Printed in Leipzig by Louis Glaser. Postcard (1897). General Horticultural Exhibition, Hamburg. Published in Frankfurt am Main by Kunst Anstalt Rosenblatt.

(*Source: Author's collection.*)

Liverpool was a particularly interesting case. As a world-class port city with a strong civic consciousness, an impressive new centre and many cultural institutions, the city's public image failed to match its own self-perceptions. In the last decades of the century Liverpool was anxious to distance itself morally and socially from the slave trade on which the city's fortunes were founded and in order to present an image of civic grandeur to outdo that of its nearby rival, Manchester, and commensurate with its world status as a centre of commerce, the city engaged in a re-branding exercise, redeveloping the centre and founding educational and cultural institutions

(Belchem 2006). As part of the process of moving away from its past, the city put on an international exhibition of Navigation, Commerce and Industry in 1886 attracted favourable coverage in the London press (Belchem 2000: 3–5). A few years later however, *Queen*, clearly influenced by publicity given to the city's social problems in the national press, commented on its high death rate and noted that »its education and other intellectual advantages are enormous, but meant rather for those who reside and must reside there than to attract strangers« (Hornby 1905: 19). This was disappointing and in 1907 the city mounted an Historical Exhibition of Liverpool Antiquities and a pageant to celebrate the 700th anniversary of its borough status and evolution »from a humble fishing hamlet to the mightiest seaport of the world« (Belchem 2000: 2). In Britain pageants were a popular means of »constructing memory« (Ryan, 2007: 64), but in ways more easily achieved in historic cities such as St Albans and Oxford than multiethnic Liverpool (Belchem 2000: 22). As tourist attractions, pageants were related to events such as the Easter celebrations in Rome or Carnival in Venice in that they took place within a compressed time-space frame and made »visible the social life« of urban landscapes, possibly rich in »historic and architectural significance, but lacking in animation« (Picard and Robinson 2006: 1). For this reason events such as the London pageant (1911), which focused on the city's imperial status (Ryan 1999), were highly popular with visitors.

Success encouraged emulation. The adoption of music by the middle classes (Weber 1975) helped to make music festivals popular as regional events. Choral festivals were popular in Britain, Germany and Austria. In Britain, the Three Choirs Festival associated with the cathedral cities of the west Midlands from 1715, flourished, as did fundraising events in many industrial cities such as Birmingham. On the continent commemorative festivals became linked to evolving regional and national agendas. Salzburg, for example, put on a Mozart festival in 1877, which made the composer into a symbol of the city's distinctiveness (Hoffmann 2002: 47–55). One participant Mary Cowden Clarke, remarked on the »gastronomic pleasures which are now taken to be a necessary concomitant to enterprises designed to accommodate touristic interest« (cited NMD 1980: 508). Elsewhere in Germany a widespread culture of festival activity was associated with the growth of civic associations, which in southern Germany became linked to the *großdeutsch* movement. Nuremberg, for example, held a *großdeutsch* singing festival in 1861 (Hiebl 2007: 112–113). Growing interest in attracting tourists encouraged cities with a musical and cultural heritage, such as

Munich and Vienna, to capitalise on their assets (Steward 1999) by staging various kinds of cultural festivals. Popular events for a different kind of customer included beer festivals such as Munich's *Oktoberfest* which was rooted in the city's working class beer culture (Carpenter 2006) while congresses of various kinds arising out of confessional concerns or the associational activities characteristic of the period, such as collecting, anticipated the way that many contemporary cities have developed their tourist profile. At the beginning of the next century motor and air shows celebrating modern transport technology also became popular. The first French international motor show (1898) was held in the Paris with London only following suit in 1910. Air shows at Vienna and Brescia near Milan (1909) created great excitement while one at Rheims (1909) attracted half a million spectators.

In conclusion: while it is impossible to calculate exactly what contribution urban tourism made to the cultural economy of any particular city, it is possible to indicate which cities were most likely to have benefited economically in some way or another from particular kinds of visitors and where these might have impacted directly on particular sectors of the cultural industries. However, as this essay has tried to demonstrate, because of the growing interconnectedness of cities and the structure and operation of the media and cultural industries, the growth of tourism in one city could also impact on the cultural economies of cities elsewhere. The provincial and national press provided the oxygen of advertising and publicity for new developments in city life, stimulated the making of comparisons and encouraged people to go and see for themselves. Publicity made known civic achievements and turned them into tourist attractions; it stimulated competition between cities, encouraging awareness of the benefits of tourism to cultural economies and generating new forms of cultural politics, including the creation of special events likely to attract tourists and business. The democratisation of the press combined with the pressures of competition for visitors encouraged the staging of events aimed at a more popular market. The most successful cities seem to be those with a large industrial hinterland or which were close to large conurbations, which were able to use the success of particular events to publicise their distinctiveness and possession of attractive features, or which were able to link their images with some kind of wider theme such as imperialism, as in the case of Glasgow or to national or regional aspirations, as in the case of Berlin and Liverpool. Then, as now, the way that places were written about in the press and the constant search for new ways of attracting tourists indicate that, in an increasingly competitive marketplace, tourists were perceived to be motivated by search for novelty and distinctiveness and that they were regarded as a valuable source of income for cultural industries and urban economies.

Bibliography

Illustrated London News (ILN), 1860–1914.
The Strand Magazine, 1891–1927, Vols. 1–73.
Westermanns Monatshefte (WM), 1861–1914.
The Times, 1860–1914.

Alloway, Lawence (1969). *The Venice Biennale: 1895–1968, from Salon to Goldfish Bowl.* London.
Atkinson, Dennis, Denis Cotgrove and Anna Notaro (1999). »Empire in Modern Rome: Shaping and Remembering an Imperial City«. In David Gilbert and Felix Driver (eds.). *Imperial Cities: Landscape, Display and Identity*, 40–63, Manchester.
Bailey, Peter (1978). *Victorian England: Rational Recreation and the Contest for Control: 1830–1865.* London.
Barton, Susan (2005). *Working-Class Organisations and Popular Tourism 1840–1970.* Manchester.
Belchelm, John (2000). *Merseypride: Essays in Liverpool Exceptionalism.* Liverpool.
— (2006). »Introduction: Celebrating Liverpool«. In *Liverpool 800, Culture, character and History*, 9–57. Liverpool.
Borsay, Peter (1989). *The English Urban Renaissance, Culture and Society Culture and Society in the Provincial Town 1660–1770.* Oxford.
Bradshaw, George (1854). *Bradshaw's Illustrated Traveller's Handbook in France, Adapted to all the Railway Routes with a Short Itinerary of Corsica and a Guide to Paris.* London.
Brendon, Piers (1991). *150 Years of Popular Tourism.* London.
Brooker, John (1994). *Traveller's Money.* Stroud.
Brown, Lucy (1985). *Victorian News and Newspapers.* Oxford.
Charle, Christophe, (2004). *Le siècle de la press (1830–1930).* Paris.
Conboy, Martin (2004). *Journalism: a Critical History.* London.
Crowley, David (1999). »Castles, cabarets and Cartoons: Claims on Polishness in Kraków around 1905«. In Malcolm Gee, Tim Kirk and Jill (eds.). *The City in Central Europe: Culture and Society from 1800 to the Present*, 101–117. Aldershot.

Dalbello, Marija. (2002).»Franz Joseph's time machine, images of modernity in an era of mechanical photo-reproduction». In Ezra Greenspan, Jonathan Rose (eds.). *Book History*, Vol. 5, 67–104.

Didier, Jean-Didier (1993). *L'idiot de voyage*. Paris.

Durie,. Alistair J. (1992).»Tourism and commercial photography in Victorian Scotland: the rise and fall of G.W. Wilson & Co., 1853–1908«. *Northern Scotland*, 12, 89–104.

Fraser, W. Hamish (2000).»Competing with the capital: the case of Glasgow versus Edinburgh«. In Lars Nilssen (ed.). *Capital Cities: Images and realities in the historical development of European capital cities*, 27–46. Stockholm.

Fritzsche, Peter (1996). *Reading Berlin 1900*. Cambridge. Mass.

Gee, Malcolm (2002).»The ›Cultured City‹ the Art Press in the Berlin and Paris in the Early Twentieth Century«. In Malcolm Gee and Tim Kirk (eds.). *Printed Matters: Printing, Publishing and Urban Culture in Europe in the Early Modern Period*, 150–173. Aldershot.

Geppert, Alexander C. (2002).»True Copies – Time and Space Travels at the British Imperial exhibitions, 1880–1930«. In Hartmut Berghoff, Barbara, Korte, Ralf Schneider and Christopher Harvie (eds.). *The Making of Modern tourism: The Cultural History of the British Experience, 1600–2000*, 223–249. Basingstoke/New York.

Gilbert, David and Clark Mark (1997).»An exploratory examination of urban tourism impact, with reference to residents' attitudes in the cities of Canterbury and Guildford«. *Cities*, 4, 6, 343–352.

Godden, Geoffrey (1996). *Collecting Picture Postcards*. Guildford.

Gold, John and Stephan V. Ward (eds.) (1994). *Place Promotion: the Use of Advertising and Marketing to Sell Towns and Regions*. Chichester.

Green, Nicholas (1990). *The Spectacle of Nature: Landscape and Nature in Bourgeois France*. Manchester.

Greenhalgh, P. (1988). *Ephemeral Vistas: the Expositions universelles, Great Exhibitions and World's Fairs*, 1851–1939. Manchester.

Gyáni, Gábor (2004). *Identity and the Urban Experience: Fin-de-Siècle Budapest*. Colorado/New Jersey.

Hacock, Claire (1999).»Capitale du plaisir: the Remaking of Imperial Paris«. In David Gilbert and Felix Driver (eds.). *Imperial Cities: Landscape, Display and Identity*, 64–67. Manchester.

Hahn, Hazel (2006).»Boulevard Culture and Advertising as Spectacle in Nineteenth-Century Paris«. In Alexander Cowan and Jill Steward (eds.). *The City and the Senses: Urban Culture since 1900*, 156–178. Aldershot.

Hall, Thomas (1997). *Planning Europe's Capital Cities: Aspects of Nineteenth-Century Urban Development*. London.

Hart, S. Milton (1901). *Guide through Germany, Austria-Hungary, Switzerland, Italy, France, Belgium, Holland and England, Souvenir of the Hamburg-American Line to Hamburg-American Line*. Berlin.

Hiebl, Ewart (2007). »German, Austrian or ›Salzburger‹? National identities in Salzburg c. 1830–702«. In Laurence Cole (ed.). *Different Paths to the Nation: Regional and national Identities in Central Europe and Italy, 1830–70*, 100–121. Basingstoke.

Hietala, Marjatta (1987). *Services and Urbanisation at the Turn of the Century: the Diffusion of Innovations.* Helsinki.

Hobsbawm, Eric and Terence Ranger (1984). *The Invention of Tradition.* Cambridge.

Hoffmann, Robert (2002). *Mythos Salzburg.* Salzburg/München.

Hornsby, Marcus (ed.) (1905/1909/1912). *The »Queen« Newspaper Book of Travel.* London.

Jackson, Kate (2001). *George Newnes and the New Journalism in Britain, 1880–1910: Culture and Profit.* Aldershot.

Kaschuba, Wolfgang (1993). »German *Bürgerlichkeit* after 1800: Culture as Symbolic Practice«. In J. Kocka and A. Mitchell (eds.). *Bourgeois Society in Nineteenth-Century Europe*, 392–422. Oxford.

Kearns, Gerry and Chris Philo (eds.) (1993). *Selling the City: the City as Cultural Capital, Past and Present.* Oxford.

Kocka, Jürgen and Adrian Mitchell (eds.) (1993). *Bourgeois Society in Nineteenth-Century Europe.* Oxford.

Kooy, Pim and Piet Pellenbarg (eds.). *Regional Capitals: Past, Present, Prospects, Assen,* 129–148. Groningen.

Koshar, Rudy (1998). »What ought to be seen«. Tourists guidebooks and national identities in Modern Germany and Europe«. *Journal of Contemporary History*, 33, 323–340.

— (2000). *German Travel Cultures.* Oxford/New York.

Labiausse, K. (2003). »Un sydicat d'initiative Durant l'entre-deux guerres: les Amis de Lille«. *Revue du Nord [France]*, 85, 349, 117–138.

Lachenicht, Susanne (2006). »Die neue Visualität der Zeitschrift im frühen 20. Jahrhundert und die *culture de masse*«. In Clemens Zimmermann and Manfred Schmeling (eds.). *Die Zeitschrift – Medium der Moderne/La Presse magazine – un Media de l'epoque moderne: Deutschland und Frankreich im Vergleich*, 63–84. Bielefeld.

Lasansky, D. Medina and Brian McLaren (eds.). *Architecture and Tourism: Perception, Performance and Place.* Oxford/New York.

Law, Christopher (1993). *Urbant Tourism: Attracting Visitors to Large Cities.* London.

Lenman, Robin (1997). *Artists and Society in Germany 1850–1914.* Manchester.

— (1999). »Networks and Boundaries; German Art Centres and their Satellites, 1815–1914«. In Malcolm Gee, Tim Kirk and Jill Steward (eds.). *The City in Central Europe; Culture and Society from 1800 to the Present.* Aldershot.

— (ed.) (2005). *The Oxford companion to the Photograph.* Oxford.

Lorente, Jesús Pedro (1998). *Cathedrals of Urban Modernity: The First Museums of Contemporary Art, 1800–1930.* Aldershot.

— and Clare Targett (2000). »Comparative Growth and Urban distribution of the population of victorian Artists in Victorian London«. In Peter Borsay, Gunther

Hirschfelder and Ruth E. Mohrmnan (eds.). *New Directions in Urban History; Aspects of European Art, Health, Tourism and Leisure since the Enlightenment.* 65–86, Münster.

Luckhurst, Kenneth (1951). *The Story of Exhibitions.* London and New York.

Mackenzie, John (1999). »The Second City of the Empire: Glasgow – imperial municipality«. In Felix Driver and David Gilbert (eds.). *Imperial Cities: Landscape, Display and Identity.* Manchester.

Makela, Marian (1990). *The Munich Secession: art and Artist in Turn-of-the-Century Munich.* Princeton, New Jersey.

McCauley, Elizabeth (1994). ›The Business of Photography‹. *Industrial Madness: Commercial Photography in Paris, 1848–1871.* London/New Haven.

Meller, Helen (2001). *European Cities: 1890–1930s: History, Culture and the Built Environment.* Chichester/New York.

Murray, John (1859). *A Handbook for Travellers on the Continent, Being a Guide to Holland, Belgium, Prussia, Northern Germany and the Rhine form Holland to Switzerland.* London.

Nilssen, Lars (ed.). *Capital Cities: Images and realities in the historical development of European capital cities.* Stockholm.

North, Gottfried (1991). »Eine Revolution im Reiseverkehr. Die Schnellpost«. In Hermann Bausinger, Klaus Beyrer and Gottfried Korff (eds.). *Reisekultur: Von der Pilgerfahrt zum modernen Tourismus,* 291–297. München.

Pemble, John (1987). The Mediterranean Passion. Oxford.

Penny, Glen (1998). »Municipal displays. Civic self-promotion and the development of German ethnographic museums: 1870–1914«. *Social Anthropology,* 6, 2, 157–166.

Picard, David and Mike Robinson (2006). *Festivals, Tourism and Social Change: Remaking Worlds.* Cleveland.

Reichman, J. and Cantor (1896). *Guide through Central Europe and Italy (with the compliments of the North-German Lloyd Bremen).* Berlin.

Richard, Greg (1994). »Developments in European Cultural Tourism«. In Anthony V. Seaton (ed.), *Tourism: the State of the Art,* 366–376. Chichester.

Ripert, Aline and Claude Frère (1983). *La Carte postale: son historie, sa function sociale.* Paris.

Rowe, Dorothy (1995). »Georg Simmel and the Berlin Trade Exhibition of 1896«. *Urban History,* 22, 2, 216–228.

Ryan, Deborah (1999). »Staging the Imperial City: the Pageant of London, 1911«. In Felix Driver and David Gilbert (eds.). *Imperial Cities: Landscape, Display and Identity,* 117–135. Manchester.

— (2007). »Pageantitis‹: Frank Lascelles' 1907 Oxford Historical Pageant, visual spectacle and popular memory«. *Visual Culture in Britain,* 8, 2, 263–282.

Sadie, Stanley (ed.) (1980). *The New Grove Dictionary of Music and Musicians (NGD) 6.* London.

Schwarz, Vanessa (1998). *Spectacular Realities: Early Mass Culture in fin-de-siècle Paris.* California.

Seed, J. (1988). »Commerce and the Liberal Arts, the Political Economy of Art in Manchester, 1777–1860«. In Janet Wolff and John Seed (eds.). *The Culture of Capital: Art, Power and the Nineteenth-Century Middle Class*, 45–81. Manchester.

Selwyn, Tom (ed.) (1996). *The Tourist Image.* Chichester.

Sheller, Mimi and John Urry (2006). *Mobile Technologies of the City.* Oxford/New York.

Steward, Jill (1999). »Gruss aus Wien«: urban tourism in Austro-Hungary before the First World War«. In Malcolm Gee, Tim Kirk and Jill Steward (eds.). *The City in Central Europe: Culture and Society from 1800 to the Present*, 123–144. Aldershot.

— (2001). »Tourism in Late-Imperial Austria: the Development of Tourist Cultures and their Associated Images of Place«. In Shelley Baranowski and Ellen Furlough (eds.). *Tourism, Consumer Culture, and Identity in Modern Europe and North America*, 108–134. Ann Arbor.

— (2004). »Performing Abroad: British Tourists in Italy and their Practices, 1840–1914«. In D. Medina Lasansky and Brian McLaren (eds.). *Architecture and Tourism: Perception, Performance and Place*, 53–74. Oxford/New York.

— (2005). »How and where to go?«: the role of travel journalism in Britain and the evolution of foreign tourism, 1840–1914«. In John. K. Walton (ed.), *Histories of Tourism: Representation, Identity, Conflict*, 39–54. Cleveland.

Stobart, Jon (2000). »In Search of a Leisure Hierarchy: English Spa Towns and their Place in the Eighteenth Century Urban System«. In Peter Borsay, Gunther Hirschfelder and Ruth E. Mohrmnan (eds.). *New Directions in Urban History; Aspects of European Art, Health, Tourism and Leisure since the Enlightenment*, 19–40. Münster.

Strain, Ellen (2003). *Public Places, Private Journeys: Ethnography, Entertainment and the Tourist Gaze.* New Brunswick.

Towner, John (1985). »The Grand Tour: a Key Phase in the History of Tourism«. *Annals of Tourism Research*, 12, 3, 297–333.

— (1994). »Tourism History: Past, Present and Future«. In A.V. Seaton (ed.). *Tourism: the State of the Art*, 721–728. Chichester.

— (1996). *An Historical Geography of Recreation and Tourism in the Western World: 1540–1940.* Chichester.

Unowski, Daniel (2004). »Staging Habsburg Patriotism; Dynastic Loyalty and the 1898 Jubilee«. In Pieter Judson and Marsha Rosenblitt (eds.). *Constructing nationalities in East Central Europe*, 141–156. Oxford.

Urry, John (1995). *Consuming Places.* London/New York.

Van der Berg, Leo, Jan van der Borg and Jan Van der Meer (1995). *Urban Tourism: Performance and strategies in eight European Cities.* Aldershot.

Vandermotten, C. (ed.) (1994). *Planification et strategies de developpement dans les capitales européenes.* Brussels.

Vizetelly, Henry (1879). *Berlin Under the New Empire, its Institutions, Inhabitants, Industry, Monuments, Museums, Social Life, Manners, and Amusements. 2 Vols.* London.

Waagenar, Michael (1994). »Monumental Centre, Picturesque Environs, Contrasting Landscapes and Divergent Land Use in Six European Capitals, 1850–1914«. In C. Vandermotten (ed.). *Planification et strategies de developpement dans les capitales européenes,* Brussels.

— (2000). »Capital without Capital: Amsterdam's Quest for a Convincing Urban Image, 1870–1940«. In Lars Nilssen (ed.). *Capital Cities: Images and Realities in the Historical Development of European Capital Cities,* 27–46. Stockholm.

Walton, John (2002). »British Tourism Between Industrialisation and Globalisation – an Overview«. In Hartmut Berghoff, Barbara Korte, Ralf Schneider and Christopher Harvie (eds.). *The Making of Modern Tourism: the Cultural History of British Experience,* 1600–2000, 109–132. Basingstoke.

— and James Walvin (eds.) (1989). *Leisure in Britain,* 1780–1939. Manchester.

Weber, William (1975). *Music and the Middle Class: the Social Structure of Concert Life in London.* Paris/Wien/London.

Weedon, Alexis (2003). *Victorian Publishing: the Economics of Book Production for a Mass Market 1836–1916.* Aldershot.

West. Shearer (1995). »National desires and regional realities in the Venice Biennale, 1895–1914«. *Art History,* 18, 3, 404–434.

Zevi, Phillipo (ed.) (1978). *Alinari: Photographers of Florence 1852–1920.* Edinburgh/London.

Urban Creativity and Popular Music in Europe since the 1970s: Representation, Materiality, and Branding

Giacomo Bottà

Introduction

The term popular music refers to music that is »made commercially, in a particular kind of legal (copyright) and economic (market) system; music made using an ever-changing technology of sound storage; music significantly experienced as mass mediated; music primarily made for social and bodily pleasure; music which is formally hybrid« (Frith 2004). Nonetheless, popular music increasingly addresses questions of identity and representation, and seems to reinforce urbanity in the global flow of people, goods, and information.

Normally, discussions about music and place are set in the field of popular music studies only. Previous publications have emphasized so-called *local* music scenes and *local* music styles, without analysing the impact of actual urban phenomena (gentrification, segregation) and of the socio-spatial environment on music creativity. Additionally, the adopted terminology is often ambiguous, using space and place as synonymous or overlapping national and local scales (Whiteley et al. 2004). On the other hand, urban studies have too often referred to cultural regeneration or cultural districts without considering the specificities of different forms of cultural expression (Zukin 1996).

This article considers popular music and discusses issues of urban creativity by adopting a third approach which seeks to bring together debates from popular music and urban studies, as shown, for example, by the work of Brown, O'Connor and Cohen (2000), Kloosterman (2005), or Cohen (2007). From the point of view of this method, this article adopts an innovative division into three dimensions, representation, materiality and branding, broadening the significance of popular music in the urban environment.

Three European cities will be investigated in the course of this article: Manchester, Berlin and Helsinki. The three cities have been chosen because of their similarities. They all share an industrial past, and industrial heritage (partly reconverted) is still a major element of their urban landscape. They developed (urbanized) in the eighteenth (Manchester) and nineteenth century (Berlin and Helsinki), thanks to industrialisation. They have been labelled »artificial« cities because of their lack of cultural layers going back to the Middle Ages or Antiquity, unlike the historically significant European centres of London, Rome, Vienna, or Paris. Additionally, all three cities are, to some extent, peripheral. In England, Manchester has always been regarded as a city »of the North«, antithetical on many levels to London (Shields 1991: 207–245). In the Nordic/Scandinavian region, Helsinki could be considered minor, as the centrality has traditionally been assigned to Stockholm. In Germany, Berlin has had a peculiar role, especially between 1945 and 1990, because economic development largely took place in cities located in the west of the country, including Cologne, Hamburg, Frankfurt am Main and Munich.

The three cities are also deeply dissimilar. Their size varies from 3,400,000 inhabitants in Berlin to 570,000 in Helsinki and 450,000 in Manchester (excluding each metropolitan area). They belong to three distinct regions of Europe. Two of them are capitals.

Nonetheless, popular music scenes, styles, and movements shaped the image and the built environment of all three cities, although at different times, in different circumstances, and with different outcomes. Some of these scenes acquired international recognition, contributing to the circulation of certain images and forging the reputation of these cities on a global level. All three urban centres are, at present, discovering their present or past popular music connections, and using them in various ways as an incentive for the city's image and economy (for a historical account on each city see: Richie 1998; Bell and Hietala 2002; Haslam 2000).

Popular Music and the Creative City

The production, circulation, and consumption of popular culture, and popular music in particular, has always found its place in cities (Chambers 1986). Recently this location has emerged as decisive because of the spread of transnational economies, where cities work as »nodes« in the global flow of people, goods and information. The growing significance of popular music for cities could be connected to the convergence of the cultural and the economic realm (Scott 2001). On one hand, the economy of cities has been dealing more and more with symbols provided by the cultural field. On the other, urban culture has been increasingly produced and used as a commodity. Cultural industries have played a decisive role in this reorganisation of powers and values inside cities (O'Connor and Wynne 1996; Hesmondhalgh 2002). In fact, these kinds of industries benefit greatly from the intense social interactions and synergies present in cities as creative milieus (Camagni 1991). Cultural industries influence the way people perceive their own environment (urban environment in particular). On the other hand, the way people live in the city inspires the production of cultural industries (consumer creativity). Cultural industries are today on the forefront of the urban economy because, despite de-industrialisation, they have remained in cities and could not exist elsewhere. This narrative about the reorganisation of the interests, powers, and agents active in European cities has been adopted by politicians and entrepreneurs of the »creative city«.

»Creativity« has been particularly appealing as an instrument to provide cities with a new direction. In particular, Charles Landry's work (2000) has stirred a keen interest on the revitalisation of city centres, districts, and even entire cities, making innovative use of cultural heritage. Landry also emphasises the need for both »hard« and »soft« infrastructures for the existence of creative milieus in cities. Richard Florida (2002) has contributed to this debate with the concept of a »creative class«, which re-shapes contemporary urban societies according to the professional choices of citizens and newcomers. The »creative class« members are individuals choosing their working/living environment according to amenities (nightlife, local music scene, gay scene, bohemian districts). Florida has also developed a definition of the creative city that includes three major features: tolerance, technology, and talent.

Despite these contributions, it remains unclear how a city can increase »talent« or »creativity« and what we should understand by these terms. Lately, citizens, tourists, and city officials have targeted popular music as one of the main symbols of urban creativity. It has been clear for some time that popular music represents an important ingredient in the *folklore* of the creative class. Its presence is traceable in tourist material and, through city reports, in the media. Popular music heritage has created new places of pilgrimage. Such is the case with the reconstructed Cavern club in Liverpool, where the Beatles started their career. Also in bids (e.g. European Capital of Culture) the origin of famous bands or a particular local scene are used to define the vibrancy of a place and the dynamism of its urban culture. More and more regeneration or preservation projects (e.g. Battersea power station in London, featured in the 1969 *Animals* LP by the Pink Floyd) and even flagship projects (like the U2 Tower on the Dublin docklands) are also connected, on a variety of levels, to music. Large and small cities have also adopted dedicated policies to boost local scenes and increase their visibility (e.g. through rehearsal spaces, training schemes, municipal offices, urban festivals).

Surely these branding strategies and policies have had an important role in the economic and cultural reorganisation of some cities. It is still yet to be demonstrated if any of these have been able to affect the music scene and its rate of creativity, which finds expression, according to this article, in two main dimensions:

Popular music is able to autonomously reshape place-images and representations through *textscapes, soundscapes* and *landscapes.*

Popular music is able to autonomously affect the built material environment, for example through regeneration.

Representation, Materiality, and Branding through Music

According to this article, a place can be represented in popular music in three distinct ways; first, as a *textscape,* it can appear in the lyrics and titles of songs. There are a great number of songs whose title is the name of a city; other references could be more hidden, connected to local architecture or to some spots, areas, streets, or buildings. Secondly, the *soundscape* consists of the way a place shapes a band's distinctive sound, for example in the use of typical local styles, city sounds and noises, and in the use of local dialect or accent. Thirdly, the *landscape* includes the place connections in a band's visual material (e.g. CD covers, posters, stage design, clothes, photo shootings, videos). All three dimensions often appear together and their media circulation deeply influences the listeners' perception of place. Places mentioned in songs, or used in CD covers acquire a mythical status; they attract fans and tourists and often determine the reputation of a city or a district as a whole.

Music in itself may seem ethereal, but its production, circulation, and consumption rely on material factors (recording studios, concert halls, distribution retails, record shops, music scenes, bars, financial resources) located in cities. This spatial distribution of popular music can be experienced as central to the regeneration of the post-industrial landscape. In this article, we will identify different examples which concern the regeneration of individual buildings and their role as catalysts for creativity in the cities considered.

Popular music has always been associated with certain cities: traditional jazz with New Orleans, »urban« blues with Chicago, country with Nashville, the Motown sound with Detroit, hip-hop with New York, and grunge with Seattle. This branding of a city in connection to a certain music style can be long lasting (as in the case of New Orleans and jazz) or volatile (as in the case of Seattle and grunge). It could originate from a programmatic marketing strategy or media construction (as in the case of Britpop and London) or it could be deeply tied to the cultural history of a place (as in the case of tango and Buenos Aires). Today's branding strategies are more subtle and imply great effort by local governments, city marketing agencies, and tourist offices. Popular music acquired relevance as a branding instrument because of its attractiveness for tourists and because of its power in the re-imagining and regeneration of cities.

Manchester, 1976–1997

Representation

In Manchester, between 1976 and 1997, the cultural sensibility of a few enthusiastic musicians, photographers, independent producers, and entrepreneurs became an instrument to re-imagine the city, its built landscape, and its culture. This article examines the work of new wave and post-punk bands such as Buzzcocks, Joy Division, The Smiths, The Fall, and the following *madchester* scene, which spread out of the interaction between the local *indie* bands and US-imported house music.

The time period is based on two events, which symbolically started and ended this era. In 1976, the infamous London punk band The Sex Pistols played twice at the Lesser Free Trade Hall on June 4 and on July 20. Fewer than 40 people attended the first gig. Many more attended the second, just six weeks later. It was already evident that many initiators and fans of the developing music scene were in the audience. Among the spectators of the two gigs, we can list two members of Buzzcocks (who organized the first gig), Morrissey, the singer of The Smiths, members of Joy Division, the NME journalist and author Rob Morley, the sound technician and producer Martin Hannett, and Factory Records founder and entrepreneur Tony Wilson (Nolan 2006). The presence of such a notable contingent of listeners could confirm the existence of a creative milieu based on higher interaction, which is a basic element for understanding local creativity and innovation (Landry 2000). The individuals listed above, involved in various roles, as members of the local popular music scene, were proud, independent, self-determining, aware of the cultural distance from London, and of their own industrial and working-class heritage (Milestone 1996). They all considered it crucial to stay in Manchester and develop a scene there, rather than move to London to look for media visibility, record deals with multinationals, and easy success.

The Haçienda FAC 51, a club owned by a local team, including Tony Wilson and New Order (the band that featured the three remaining members of Joy Division) closed in 1997, ending, in a way, the creative parable of this scene. In the same year, the national political context changed drastically, with the election of Tony Blair as prime minister. The people involved in the scene shifted their interest to the national level (which turned local popular music scenes into the all-encompassing »Britpop«), and, additionally, the internationalisation of their success made them less committed to the local sphere.

The Manchester scene made significant use of landscapes; nearly all of these bands, from Buzzcocks to Joy Division and The Smiths were photographed, especially at the beginning of their career, outside, in open spaces, posing in front of factories. Chimneys, cobblestone streets, and red brick buildings have been part of the Manchester imagery since the descriptions of Friedrich Engels and the novels of Charles Dickens (Shields 1991; Moretti 1998). The bands adopted these architectural elements as symbolic »authenticity seals« for their local belonging and for their being »for real«. Additionally, two other considerations could be made. First, showing the empty and decaying temples of capitalism can be linked to the gloom expressed by these bands. They exemplify the emptiness of capitalist society and of industrialism, which can be best understood when money stops coming in, unemployment grows, and whole districts are left in physical and social decay. Second, it could be read as an ironic overtone. In 1985, The Smiths posed in front of the Salford Lads Club (youth leisure club) for a shot by Stephen Wright, which appeared in the gatefold of the band's *The Queen is Dead* LP (1986). The club was opened at the beginning of the twentieth century, to keep the local Salford youth »off the streets« and educate them to become »good citizens«, as was usual for many other philanthropic initiatives of the time (Lindner 2004). The Smiths posing in front of the club, located at the end of the real Coronation Street, opens up a series of questions concerning identity, as the band was increasingly the focus of media attention for its overt subversion of working class values, while seeming celebrating, at first sight, idleness, criminality, and social indifference.

The references to the unmistakable built environment are diversely present in the textscape of these bands. The Smiths refer to iron bridges, disused railway lines, and cemetery gates. Additionally the city's districts are more or less openly referred to, in particular those most rundown and disfavoured at the time, like Whalley Range, Cheetham Hill, and Ancoats. The band Joy Division relies less on the direct nomination or representation of the built environment and concentrates much more on its subjective psychological effects. In their lyrics, the built environment is evoked because of its monotony and desolation, structuring a sinister textscape, which only through circulation as LP, cassette and CD, goes back to being identified by the listeners with Manchester.

The soundscape of Manchester is built upon the local music tradition, local sounds and noises, and the vernacular. »Local music tradition« refers here to the influence of early North American rock 'n' roll and soul music (which in the UK is epitomized in *northern* soul), widely played in local fairs, workers' clubs, and local pubs, the places of the working class. The use of certain sound effects (harmonica, synthetic drums) has often been associated with industrial noises (trains, alarms, heavy industry machinery). Additionally, the bands' singers often accentuated the Mancunian accent, both in performances and interviews.

Manchester as a place is present in each of the three levels of representation considered here. The city's local music scene was able to deconstruct previous media representation and was able to develop, through individual sensibilities, a different image of the city. Through circulation, this image reached millions of people who were able to make it their own, reshape it, and keep it viable (the single *Blue Monday* by New Order is still the most sold 12-inch of all time, with a sale of about one million copies in the UK alone).

Materiality

The Haçienda FAC 51 (each product of the Factory catalogue was given an increasing number, the club being number 51) opened in May 1982 on the corner between Albion Street and Whitworth Street West in a run-down area, close to the almost abandoned city centre. Architect Ben Kelly redesigned the former yacht showroom, retaining many of the original features of the building, such as the big iron doors, the inner columns, and the red brick façade. Its financial existence was based on the co-ownership of Factory Records, Rob Gretton, and New Order, at the time most successful band on the label.

The success of New Order guaranteed the economic survival of the club and influenced the style of the music it played. Because of the band's fascination with New York and the American dance and electronic music scene, The Haçienda became the first club in Europe to play house music. The DJs Graeme Park and Mike Pickering started playing house at the Friday *Nude* night in 1986. New local bands, such as Happy Mondays, began mixing local pop music tradition with this new exciting dance music. The Haçienda gave birth to the first European house music scene, which later developed into the practice of raves. This scene became infamous as *acid* house, because of the involvement of a new synthetic drug: ecstasy. The music press coined the term *madchester* (Manchester and madness) to designate the local scene (Haslam 2000).

1989 saw the first ecstasy-related death in the UK, as a girl collapsed on the club's dance floor. Drug dealers began haunting the area, slowly bringing the club to a financial crisis. The club's customers were in fact more interested in the drugs sold by the pushers than in the drinks offered by the bar, which were, of course, the most important source of income from nightlife activity. At the same time, violent incidents (rival gang fights involving shootings) damaged the reputation of the whole area.

The Haçienda closed in 1991, under pressure from the Grater Manchester Police. Three months later it reopened, however Factory records went bankrupt in 1992 and The Haçienda had to close definitively in 1997. A private company, Crosby Homes, bought and demolished it. Between 2002 and 2004, an office and apartment complex was built on the site. Of course, the project retained the name of the club, in accordance to the entrepreneurial strategies, which employ cultural elements as a way to market themselves.

Parallel to the Haçienda, and on a different scale, the »Northern Quarter« also represents an important aspect of the relationship between popular music and the built environment in Manchester. The name was conceived to designate what it used to be, a »leftover« of the unitary city centre plan. Located between Piccadilly Gateway, Ancoats, and Shudehill, the Northern Quarter had been a major shopping area since the nineteenth century, especially Oldham Street and Smithfield Market. It was later devastated by the 1960s developments, which culminated with the construction of the Arndale centre (the largest indoor shopping mall in Europe at the time of its construction in the 1970s). The area was rapidly abandoned in the 1970s, left to its fate by speculators.

The availability of cheap buildings with affordable rents, together with the *Enterprise Allowance Scheme* (a start-up project for self-employed entrepreneurs) encouraged many musicians and music entrepreneurs to move to the area. Record shops, recording studios, rehearsal rooms, and small alternative shops began to appear in the district, together with flats (Brown et al. 2000). Factory records also opened a bar (The Dry Bar) and a shop (The Area) in the Northern Quarter. The Afflecks Palace opened its premises in a five-storey building, selling street fashion and design connected to the various styles of popular music scenes (punk, dance etc.) in about 50 independent stalls.

The entrepreneurs, workers, and inhabitants of the area joined the Northern Quarter Association (NQA), which tried to put forward the needs and agenda of a »creative district« in the municipality. From the 1990s on, the Northern Quarter, just like the Haçienda, faced problems in connection to the rise of gang violence and the consumption of illicit substances, which the municipality was not ready to control, due to its »hands off« approach to the district.

Parallel to the Northern Quarter, the Gay Village (along Channel Street) and China Town developed, extending further the notion of »cultural districts« through tolerance, diversity, and ethnicity. Today they are all formally recognized by the municipality as neighbourhoods.

Popular music had a strong impact on the material and institutional level turning what used to be a »leftover« of the city plan (Brown et al. 2000) into a key district in Manchester's contemporary tourist appeal.

Branding

It could be stated that Manchester's musical heritage, in terms of popular music, is great and its symbolic value is continuously confirmed by new bands and new musical styles paying tribute to the scene (e.g. the so-called *nu-rave*, which is deeply indebted to *madchester*). The era has also been commemorated in films such as *24-hour party people* (directed by Michael Winterbottom, 2002) about the career of Tony Wilson and *Control* (by Dutch director Anton Corbijn, 2007) about the life of Ian Curtis (singer of Joy Division).

At the time of its greatest global visibility in the 1990s, the city adopted some minor measures to market itself through popular music, like featuring pictures of The Haçienda and of dancing crowds in tourist brochures and quoting music events in bids. These bids concerned mainly sporting events (e.g. the Olympics, the Commonwealth Games). Sport was considered safer, as it did not address problems of licensing, opening hours, and public control as music was doing.

Now, after more than 30 years since the Sex Pistols gigs in the Lesser Free Trade Hall (now a city hotel), the strategies adopted by Manchester in attracting tourists include popular music, mainly in the form of cultural heritage. In particular, the campaign *Manchester Music Speaks* (www.visitmanchester.com/podcasts), launched on the internet by the Greater Manchester Tourist Board and sponsored by the budget airline jet2, seems particularly relevant for our analysis.

The campaign is based on *podcasts*, a sort of »downloadable radio show«, of about 10 minutes each, where »old stars« of the local music legacy are able to describe contemporary Manchester, the appeal of its contemporary hangouts, and underline the liveliness of the contemporary local music scene. Additionally, there are references to »back in the days«, to the period taken into consideration here (1976–1997) and to the speakers' favourite places. In the first podcast, Mike Joyce, former drummer of The Smiths, visits the Dry Bar in the Northern Quarter and the Salford Lads Club. Whereas, at the Dry Bar he interviews a member of Keith, a contemporary band, at the club he interviews the club's manager and tells about the picture of The Smiths in front of it. Inside the club, he visits the »Smiths room«, where fans leave pictures and memorabilia, just like in a place of religious pilgrimage. Other examples of available podcasts include those by Peter Hook (bass player in Joy Division and New Order) and by the music journalist John Robb.

The campaign addresses popular music directly, through the testimonies of musicians who made the city famous in the past and continue to live there today. The podcasts' hosts observe the changes in Manchester, both at the representational and at the material level, and underline the supposed continuities in the creative dimension of the city. Clearly the aim of this campaign is to attract young tourists to the city, infiltrating the same media popular music is using nowadays: digital downloading, i-pods and other mp3 players. The fact that a budget airline sponsors the initiative, and that the website is available in English, Spanish, and Italian, seems to confirm the intent to sell Manchester as a »city break« destination. This tourist practice consists of visiting a European city for a weekend. Increasingly, young adults have become eager to discover other cities' nightlife, and popular music has become a clear ingredient of this experience.

Berlin, 1990–2002

Representation

Popular music and Berlin have a complex relationship, based on the political history of the city and its tradition of alternative scenes and political activism.

The *Große Untergangshow – Festival genialer Dilletanten* (sic) took place on September 4, 1981 in the Tempodrom, Berlin. The bands that hit the stage were all connected to the post-punk scene and collectively defined themselves as *Geniale Dillettanten* (ingenious amateurs). Some internationally well-known artists like Dr. Motte (initiator of the Love Parade in 1989), Westbam (internationally acclaimed techno DJ and writer), Blixa Bargeld (singer in Einstürzende Neubauten and solo artist), and Gudrun Gut (Monika Enterprises) were members of these bands and participated in the festival. Apart from shaping the subcultural life of West Berlin in the 1980s, they have all had a determining role in reorganising it since 1989.

Various kinds of artists, ranging from poets to visual artists, from filmmakers to musicians, gathered under the label *Geniale Dilletanten*. They were deeply influenced by British punk (including the bands previously mentioned in reference to Manchester) and active in a continuous and rebellious re-arranging of the aims, methods, and ethos of art and of the »artist's way of life«. The attitude of these bands, the use of the German language, the exhibited lack of traditional technical skills (in playing and singing), and the adoption of nicknames later developed commercially into the *Neue Deutsche Welle*, the German new wave, with internationally acclaimed acts like Nena, Ideal and Trio and also into German punk (e.g. Die Ärtze, Die Toten Hosen).

Concentrating on the period after the reunification (1989–1990), it is useful to note how the image of the city was quickly rebuilt on a fictional »world city« narrative. This narrative saw Berlin as a city-to-be of services, businesses, and florid global economy exchanges, symbolized by the postmodern architecture of Potsdamer Platz, where multinational companies like Daimler Benz and Sony decided to locate their headquarters. The Friedrichstrasse, formerly divided by the Wall at the infamous Checkpoint Charlie, was redesigned as a shopping and business street with huge media centres (Mosse-Zentrum), shopping malls (Galeries Lafayette) and expensive office spaces, many of which are still vacant.

At the same time, the grassroots tradition, based on a combination of popular culture and political elements, continued to address issues related to the city and its image, often de-structuring or distorting the official narrative or continuing to use images and sounds of the recent past.

In relation to popular music, it is possible to affirm that the use of Berlin as a landscape has been widespread since the 1970s. The wall (its west side) represented not only a place to be inscribed and sprayed, but also something perfectly recognizable, as symbol of the Cold War, but most significantly of a certain urban angst, which still survives today. It is present, for example, on the cover of U2's *Achtung Baby* CD (1991). On the other hand, during the 1990s, the architecture of East Berlin, the *Fernsehturm* (TV tower) in particular, also became iconographic in record company logos and record covers (for example in the logo of bpitch control, a record label).

The wall also brings together the textscape of bands of the 1970s, ranging from David Bowie (*Heroes*) to Sex Pistols (*Holidays in the Sun*) and Lou Reed (*Berlin*). On a local level, bands such as Ton Steine Scherben were involved in the textual representation of city elements, followed by the praxis of squatting buildings for collective cultural use, especially in relation to Kreuzberg (*Rauch-Haus-Song* is dedicated to the former Betanien hospital illegal squatting). Other bands, especially the ones bound to the Neue Deutsche Welle movement tried to create a positive image of the city. The band Ideal wrote *Ich steh' auf Berlin* (I like Berlin), offering a positive and exciting image of the city and its multiculturalism.

The soundscape of Berlin has always been deeply bound on one hand to the industrial sound, to the extreme use of urban noises and on the other to cabaret and the Brecht/Weill tradition of on-stage performance. The West Berlin based Einstürzende Neubauten (imploding buildings) were one of the first bands to implement the noises of pneumatic hammers and other construction (and destruction) tools into their music. This tendency went on to develop into techno and other forms of electronic music.

It is self-evident that, after 1989, such a rich tradition of popular music representation of the city could not be erased by adopting an inauthentic narrative about a vague, new, economy-related »world city«. *Einstürzende Neubauten*, for example, directly referred to Potsdamer Platz in *Die Befindlichkeit des Landes* (from the album *Silence is sexy*, 2000). The song portrays the square as a future ruin, as nothing but another layer of the city, to be covered by nature. Berlin is continuously haunted by its destroyed, hidden, or empty spaces (see Ladd 1997). The bunkers that the song refers to are the ones where Hitler hid until his suicide and are in close physical proximity to Potsdamer Platz. Although the song directly addresses some new issues related to the reunified city, its gloomy tone maintains some of the features typical of the previously mentioned West Berlin tradition of urban angst.

Materiality

The peculiar economic and political situation of West Berlin also determined its creative concentration and the formation of a creative milieu. The city, administratively an autonomous *Land* of the GFR, was surrounded by the GDR and enclosed by a wall since 1961. The only way to keep the city viable was through high subsidies, which interested companies and institutions. Additionally, the fact that Berlin residents were not required to attend the national service convinced many male leftist radicals, outsiders, and pacifists to move there from all over West Germany. Another reason for immigrating to the city was the price of accommodation, which was rather low, especially in the districts in the direct proximity of the wall (Kreuzberg, Neukölln) and in large working class areas (Moabit, Schöneberg). The practice of squatting was also widespread among students and artists, and was connected to the huge availability of abandoned or partly ruined buildings.

The 1990s could have meant the end of this scene for various reasons: the fall of the Wall ended the special status awarded to the *Inselstadt* West Berlin. Furthermore, its built environment had become denser at the end of the 1980s (thanks to immigration) and it had grown difficult to find new physical spaces of expression for new musical styles and new scenes. The contribution from East Berlin, both in terms of people and the built environment, and the flow of national and international people became essential (Krüger 1998). One good example of this coming together could be the *spoken word* scene, which has been very active since the beginning of the 1990s. In this case, we cannot talk about popular music, but of popular literature, imitating in many aspects the strategies adopted by popular music. At the same time, musical experimentation grew in connection to electronic and dance music (which had already shaped the soundscape of West Berlin since the 1970s and which, in the 1990s, gave birth to techno).

The regeneration of East Berlin and of Prenzlauer Berg in particular, was based on one hand on the fast emigration of many of its original dwellers and on the availability of cheap flats, which were in the beginning simply squatted (Levine 2004; Bottà 2006). The district also featured long-abandoned buildings (former factories, warehouses, but also deserted restaurants, cafés, and theatres) that could be transformed more or less legally into clubs, restaurants, pubs, design shops, record shops, second hand clothes shops and bars. At the same time, the so-called *deathstrip*, running along the Wall, offered a void central area, with abandoned warehouses and open fields. The techno music scene, which requires big empty spaces for the organisation of raves, immediately targeted that spot. Of course, private corporate entrepreneurs also began focusing on the area, eager to profit from the increase in real estate price. This coexistence of different interests could be exemplified by the case of Tresor (Hegemann 2005). Dimitri Hegemann, previously involved in the West Berlin techno scene, and Johnnie Stieler from East Berlin set their eyes on the building on the former death strip in the Leipziger Strasse, in the basement of the Wertheim Department Store, and opened the club in 1991. Tresor quickly became one of the world centres of techno and house music, together with The Haçienda FAC 51 in Manchester. Tresor was just a few hundred meters away from Potsdamer Platz, whose futuristic reconstruction in the hands of a few multinationals began approximately at the same time as the club opened. In a few years,»the biggest construction site in Europe« became a threat to the existence of the club. In fact, the high real estate value of the building attracted investors, who succeeded in 2005 in closing it down. It is interesting to note that the club existed between 1991 and 2005 thanks to the status of *Zwischennutzung*, temporary/in-between use. This kind of contract, awarded in the case of unused former East German buildings with unclear or state ownership, has been fundamental to the development of the music scene in Berlin since 1990 and for the partial regeneration of most of the built environment used for popular music in districts like Prenzlauer Berg, Friedrichshain and Mitte.

In this article, we suggest 2002 as the hypothetical end of an era. That year, Universal Music Germany decided to move from Hamburg to Berlin. MTV followed in 2004 and located its European headquarter in the German capital. Both are in direct the proximity, along the Spree, between Friedrichshain and Kreuzberg, of an area that is increasingly referred to as a cluster. In fact, other record labels, e.g., Motor, Four Music and V2, moved in the same area, together with music magazine offices (Spex) and new clubs. In a certain way, the former dissemination of scenes around the city and lack of a real clustering, seems to be ending, bringing a more corporate and organized *milieu*, whose role has yet to be examined.

Branding

Since 1990, Berlin has tried in different ways to overcome the bulk of its history, which in just one century, encompasses five very different eras: the Empire, the Weimar Republic, Nazism, socialism in the East and the Federal Republic in the West, and the reunified *Berlin Republik*. According to the way the new Berlin has been branded, the city should have grown to become a world city, a knot in the global economic net, and a city of services. The disastrous economic situation that the reunified city inherited became an enormous obstacle to the adoption of such strategies, which were eager to attract capital from national and multinational companies. Today it is still possible to spot vast renovated office buildings waiting for renters or buyers.

The more evident connections to popular music in Berlin's marketing strategies have been the importance assigned to Tacheles (a huge squatted cultural centre, where gigs and club nights also take place) and to the Love Parade (annual gathering and parade of techno music fans). It seems that a coherent strategy in connection to popular music has not been adopted by the German capital. The reasons for this might be found in the independent stance that popular music scenes have always taken in the city.

In fact, branding campaigns targeting youth tourists, like *Bock auf Berlin* (see: www.bock-auf-berlin.de), also rely only partially on popular music, preferring to concentrate on the variety of cultural offerings.

To capture the city in its bohemian flair, the idea of Berlin as »poor but sexy« has stepped forward, as underlined by Färber (2007). A contemporary trend is connected to the promotion of design and fashion, whose distribution around the city has been affecting the areas of Prenzlauer Berg and Friedrichshain. Projects like *Berliner Klamotten* and *Berlinomat*, which gather a great number of small and independent designers in *ad hoc* department stores, suggest that style, street wear and appearance are eager to brand the contemporary German capital, in spite of music.

Helsinki: 2000–Present Time

Representation

Helsinki has been, since the 1990s, a model of technological and informational innovation, based, for example, on the achievements of Nokia (see: Bell and Hietala 2002). Lately, this success has also brought forward the need for a cultural image of the city. The city officials took this to heart and were able to found a whole range of new and creative activities in a few years. Events like the Night of the Arts (since 1989) and the European City of Culture 2000, the Total and later the Global Balalaika Show (1993–2003) have shaped a new understanding of culture in the city (see: Cantell 1999). At the same time, Helsinki-based designers (Artek, Iittala, Marimekko), rock bands (HIM, Sunrise Avenue) and film directors (Aki and Mika Kaurismäki), have contributed enormously to the popularity of the Finnish capital in the global market.

The shift in the city perception could also be analyzed in the way the city was represented in popular music, on the three identified levels of urban representation: textscape, landscape and soundscape.

An example of a poignant Helsinki textscape could be the song *Helsinki* (from *Vapaaherran elämää*, 1996) by the band Ultra Bra, who gained huge national popularity in the 1990s, before splitting up in 2001. The song refers directly to two significant streets: Bulevardi and Mannerheimintie. It additionally describes Helsinki on two temporal levels: the city of the 1990s, stating its huge development, and the city of the author's childhood, described along the lines of time, memory, and melancholy. It is very interesting also to realize that the »modernisation« of Helsinki occurs, in the song, in reference to elements of mass culture: the European clothes stores and the licensing laws. Fashion and nightlife (signified by alcohol consumption) are deeply connected to the experience of popular music and to the way people perceive them as engines of urban creativity.

The jazz band Five Corners Quintet uses the Helsinki landscape in a very convincing way. To begin with, the Viiskulma (five corners), inspiring their name, is a real place and has always retained a certain meaning for the Helsinki citizens. It is a node in the district of Punavuori, where several streets depart; three record shops are located in the node and many other clubs and bars are a short distance from it. The place has a cinematic aura, which could inspire comparisons with similar corners in Manhattan or Montmartre, the New York and Paris districts where, in the 1950s, a particular kind of jazz music was born. The band, which ichnographically and stylistically refers to that era and those places, used a black and white photograph of the Viiskulma on the centre fold of its first album *Chasin' the Jazz gone by* (2005). Nevertheless, on the back cover they distance themselves ironically from its evocations, by stating that:

»looking at the photo on the centrefold of this record, you'd be forgiven to think [sic] that Five Corners in Helsinki is comprised of Flatiron buildings, like tiny versions of the famous one at Broadway and 5th Avenue in New York. That is not the case. The camera betrays the eye and turns the shabby classicist buildings into cinemascope variety. It is after all a long way from Five Corners to Manhattan, in more ways than one etc.«.

The birth of the music video and the spread of its popularity through dedicated TV channels (MTV, The Voice.) also supported the use of urbanity as landscape, often using creatively unusual settings. For example, the single *Freestyler* by the hip-hop act Bomfunk MC's, achieved enormous success in 2000 because of its video set in the Helsinki Metro (the *Hakaniemi* station in particular). The video portrayed Helsinki as a city of the future, where the latest technologies, street fashion, and post-modern urban settings are the rule. The often-despised metro would never be the same again.

The soundscape of Helsinki is a much more difficult issue to relate to. A »Helsinki sound« is partly traceable in the use of *stadislangi* (local dialect partly influenced by Swedish and Russian) or in the use of music styles which are conventionally linked to urbanity (as in the case of hip-hop and electronic music).

Materiality

Turning to the regeneration level, in Helsinki, the two biggest live music venues, Kaapelitehdas (cable factory) and Nosturi (crane) remain faithful, in name and design, to their previous function as places of the shipyard industry.

Kaapelitehdas is Finland's largest centre for arts, culture and creativity and covers over 50000 square meters. As reported by Verwijnen and Lethovuori (1999), in 1989, a community of artists occupied it, as Nokia Oy began to lease premises it no longer needed. The management of the building and the ownership of the land were transferred to the City of Helsinki. A community of artists gathered rather spontaneously and decided to voice out their discontent, because the planning of the Ruoholahti residential area wanted to empty and completely regenerate the factory. The *Pro Kaapeli* association succeeded in offering an alternative plan, which secured the area and its artistic purposes. Nowadays there are about 100 artists and 70 bands working and rehearsing at the Cable Factory, among other institutions, schools, and clubs. Its biggest hall, the Marine Cable Hall is widely used for live concerts and festivals of rock and electronic music. The history of Nosturi is quite different. The venue perpetuates the experience of Lepakko. In 1979, Lepakko, a former hostel for homeless alcoholics, became the first squat in Finland, although the squatting was negotiated with the city through the association Elmu. It is the cradle of the punk movement in the country and the premise of the first commercial radio (Radio City), which started broadcasting in 1985. Lepakko offered rehearsal spaces and a stage for the first Finnish independent bands like Shadowplay and Kingston Wall. When the place was forcefully closed in 1999 (due to the fact that, this time, Nokia bought the area) some of the people involved had the chance to open Nosturi in a shipyard hall in Punavuori, a central area. Nosturi works mainly as a concert hall, but also contains rehearsal spaces for bands.

Both events are quite recent and have not yet attained any mythical status in the Helsinki music mythology and in popular culture representation as Lepakko, for example, succeeded in doing.

A third example could be the rock club Tavastia, whose building is bound to student unions and to the centenarian creative self-organisation of Helsinki university life. Tavastia has been widely represented as a landscape (in hundreds of bands' pictures) and textscape (one example is *Tavastia Rock* by Jussi and the Boys) and today is still the best known club in the country. This is confirmed, for example, in the mythical status the place has, in the film *Pitkä kuuma kesä* (Perttu Leppä, 1999). The film, set in the 1980s, portrays the efforts of a band from Joensuu to get the chance to play there.

In Helsinki, it is not possible to talk about the influence of popular music on whole districts for various reasons: first of all, a first wave of gentrification, which involved the district of Kallio was abruptly stopped by the recession (*lama*), which afflicted the nation in the 1990s (Tani 2001, p. 152). Second, Helsinki's city planning department has been using so-called *social mixing* for years. Social mixing implies the division of buildings into flats, which are sold on the free market, next to others which are rented by the city. This procedure is able to make the city a fairer place, but at the same time, seems to be an obstacle to developing concentrations of particular scenes.

Branding

The main problem with Helsinki has always been the neutrality of its image, which was able to attract middle-aged tourists looking for tranquillity, good services, and a human dimension. These were more or less confined to the main peninsula, which constitutes Helsinki's »city-centre«. In 2000, the events related to the European Capital of Culture revealed some of the hidden symbolic capital of the city (Cantell 1999; Bell and Hietala 2002); this was followed by the international recognition of Finnish music acts, especially in the »odd« fields of Heavy Metal and Gothic Rock (HIM, Lordi, Apocalyptica, Nightwish etc.).

The *Nordic Oddity* campaign was first launched in 2003 and aimed principally at attracting young members of the creative class to visit the city. »Nordic« refers to the geographic location of Finland, but at the same time it also has a cultural connotation, being more neutral than »Scandinavian« in defining the North of Europe. »Oddity« could be interpreted more widely: the use of the word with a spatial connotation – in this case »Nordic« – recalls immediately, in the mind of a pop music fan, *Space Oddity*, the first single of British pop star David Bowie, released in 1969. The connection to the pop song is, of course, the first obvious element and is clearly addressed to an audience of tourists, defined as urban, young, and interested in popular culture. Additionally, »oddities« (in the plural form) also refer to »something worth collecting«. The Nordic Oddity flyers in fact contain a list of 24 experiences, which can be collected, by a tourist as individual *Erlebnisse*.

It seems important to note the success of the term »oddity«. It has been used in reference not only to Helsinki, but to Finland as a whole, for example after the 2006 Eurovision victory of the band Lordi, which could be fittingly addressed as »odd«. In addition, the Kaurismäki brothers' filmography has been frequently addressed around the world as »odd« for the laconic attitude of its protagonists and for the surreal dimensions of settings and plots. The coincidence of the birth of oddity branding and the international response to some successful expressions of Finnish culture was definitely not an accident.

In 2005, the campaign was re-launched and the three brochures were redesigned: Bohemian Nordic Oddity, Smooth Nordic Oddity, and Groovy Nordic Oddity. In the brochures, there are 20 direct references to popular music (clubs, festivals, bars with particular kinds of music, gig venues, record shops, karaoke bars, bands etc.) and a small number of indirect ones (second hand shops, »street style« boutiques etc.). Also visually, each brochure contains one or more pictures of musicians, record buyers or gig crowds. Helsinki is represented as a vital »rock city«, with an underground scene, more or less obscure hang-outs (bars, gig venues, discos and, amazingly, three »heavy-metal karaoke bars«) devoted to a huge variety of music styles (jazz, electronic music, garage-rock, heavy metal etc.).

Conclusion

Popular music has a significant impact on cities. These effects can be best grasped in connection to a city's representation, materiality, and branding.

Not all three noted dimensions make the same contribution to the cultural economy of a city. For example, the case of Manchester shows that the decaying industrial environment became a fundamental element in the poetics of successful bands such as The Smiths or Joy Division. While the local government was trying to cleanse the city of its industrial connotations and embrace a post-industrial dream of services, European cafés, and sport events, the local music scenes affirmed how embedded the industrial culture was in the city texture and image.

The image conveyed by local music scenes is often dissimilar to the one the municipality is trying to give and its effects seem to be more durable. This is due to the chances, provided by popular music, to adopt places on the textual, visual, and aural levels and by the significance allotted to them by circulation.

In the case of Berlin it seems that the odd material organisation of the city (at least since 1961, with the construction of the Wall) had a favourable impact on the spread of a multitude of autonomous and self-sufficient scenes and to their vehement and belligerent radicalism.

On the other hand, the case of Tresor shows that non-intervention at the municipal level can bring with it negative effects: the club closed in connection to the increase of real estate value attracting other private investors. This non-intervention originated partly from the difficulty the local government had in recognizing the cultural and economic importance of popular music, partly because of the diffidence of some music scenes in the involvement of city officials.

The connection between urban branding and the city can be best grasped in reference to Helsinki. The use of contemporary popular music challenges the tourists' fear of getting into trouble by entering non-tourist districts. This sort of branding overcomes traditional divisions between a »culturally loaded city-centre« and the »not culturally loaded« (and therefore uninteresting) surroundings. The city's cultural territory is extended well beyond the usual borders, both in a symbolic and geographic dimension.

Making popular music a significant element in the city marketing strategy and branding Helsinki as a rock-city seems to imply that the former is seen as a winning economic asset. In fact, the development of a local music scene and its international recognition is rather new, starting in the 1990s and achieving the first significant results in 2000 (with world chart-topping singles like *Freestyler* by Bomfunk MC's and *Sandstorm* by Darude). This success was also made possible through the creation of a national agency for music export, Musex, in 2002.

From the temporal point of view, it is possible to recognize that popular music played a significant role in Manchester in the 1980s, in Berlin in the 1990s and in Helsinki in the 2000s. This can be understood as connected to cycles of cultural economy. Investments in the built environment for cultural purposes (in this case for music) are linked to transformations in the representational and material dimension of the cities considered.

In Manchester, the sudden end of industry and manufacturing, and the consequent crisis in employment brought popular music to the forefront. In Berlin, the reunification of the city awoke the creative potential of its eastern part, in connection to the already developed western tradition of independent creativity. The rise of popular music export gave Helsinki the confidence to rely on its music potential, alongside the IT and communication boom, which was already boosting the economy, thanks to Nokia.

In addition, the national and international success of individual artists and the recognition of their origins in a particular local scene determine an increase in the circulation of certain images, which remain viable over time. This is why, Manchester is still today, trying to brand itself as the city of Joy Division and The Smiths and Berlin is still known as a city of techno and industrial music, whereas, Helsinki is trying to sell itself as a city where music is part of its contemporary appeal.

Bibliography

Bell, Marjatta and Marjatta Hietala (2002). *Helsinki. The Innovative City.* Helsinki.

Bottà, Giacomo (2006). »Interculturalism and new Russians in Berlin«. *Comparative Literature and Culture: A WWWeb Journal,* 8, 2, http://clcwebjournal.lib. purdue.edu/clcweb06-2/botta06.html.

Brown, Adam, Justin O'Connor and Sara Cohen (2000). »*Local Music Policies within a Global Music Industry: Cultural Quarters in Manchester and Sheffield*«. *Geoforum,* 31, 437–451.

Camagni, Roberto (1991). *Innovation Networks: Spatial Perspectives.* London/New York.

Cantell, Timo (1999). *Helsinki and a Vision of Place.* Helsinki.

Chambers, Ian (1986). *Popular Culture. The Metropolitan Experience.* London/New York.

Cohen, Sara (2007). *Decline, Renewal and the City in Popular Music Culture: beyond the Beatles.* Aldershot.

Färber, Alexa (2007). *Flourishing Cultural Production in Economic Wasteland: three Ways of Making Sense of Cultural Economy in Berlin at the Beginning of the 21 century.* Paper presented at *Culture, Economy and the City,* international conference, February 22–24, in Saarbrücken, Germany. Compare also her article in this volume.

Florida, Richard (2002). *The Rise of the Creative Class.* New York.

Frith, Simon 2004. »Popular Music«. In Simon Frith (ed.). *Critical Concepts in Media and Cultural Studies Vol. 1,* 9–21. New York.

Haslam, Dave (2000). *Manchester, England. The Story of the Pop Cult City.* London.

Hegemann, Dimitri (2005). »Techno nach dem Mauerfall. Die Geschichte des Tresors«. In Albert Scharenberg and Ingo Bader (eds.). *Der Sound der Stadt. Musikindustrie und Subkultur in Berlin.* Münster.

Hesmondhalgh, David (2002). *The Cultural Industries.* London/Thousand Oaks/New Delhi.

Kloosterman, Robert (2005). »*Come Together: An Introduction to Music and the City*«. *Built Environment,* 31, 3, 181–191.

Krüger, Thomas (1998). *Die bewegte Stadt. Berlin am Ende der Neunziger.* Berlin.

Ladd, Brian (1997). *The Ghosts of Berlin.* Chicago.

Landry, Charles (2000). *The Creative City. A Toolkit for Urban Innovators.* London.

Levine, Myron A. (2004). »Government Policy, the Local State and Gentrification: the Case of Prenzlauer Berg (Berlin), Germany«. *Journal of Urban Affairs,* 26, 1, 89–108.

Lindner, Rolf (2004). *Walks on the Wild Side. Eine Geschichte der Stadtforschung.* Frankfurt am Main/New York

Milestone, Katie (1996). »Regional Variations: Northernness and New Urban Economies of Hedonism«. In Justin O'Connor and Derek Wynne (eds.). *From the Margins to the Centre. Cultural production and Consumption in the Post-Industrial City.* Hants.

308 GIACOMO BOTTÀ

Moretti, Franco (1998). *Atlas of the European Novel 1800–1900*. London/New York.

Nolan, David (2006). *I swear I was there. The Gig that Changed the World*. Shropshire.

O'Connor, Justin and Derek Wynne (eds.). (1996). *From the Margins to the Centre. Cultural production and Consumption in the Post-Industrial City*. Hants.

Richie, Alexandra (1998). *Faust's Metropolis. A History of Berlin*. London

Scott, Alain J. (2001). »Capitalism, Cities, and the Production of Symbolic Forms«. *Royal Geographical Society*, 26, 11–23.

Shields, Rob (1991). *Places on the Margin*. London/New York.

Tani, Sirpa (2001). »Bad Reputation – Bad Reality? The Intertwining and Contested Images of a Place«. *Fennia. International Journal of Geography*, 179, 2, 143–157.

Verwijnen, Jan and Panu Lehtovuori (1999). *Creative Cities. Cultural Industries, Urban Development and the Information Society*. Jyväskylä.

Whiteley, Sheila, Anthony Bennett and Stan Hawkins (2004). *Music, Space and Place. Popular Music and Cultural Identity*. Hants/Burlington.

Zukin, Sharon (1996). *The Cultures of the Cities*. London.

4   Scientific Creative Milieus
in the Twentieth Century

Science Cities, Creativity, and Urban Economic Effects

Martina Heßler

Introduction: Creative Cities

»Creative cities are spaces you want to be in, places to be seen. Their workshops, restaurants, and bars are both the ›most superficial manifestations of a creative environment‹ and the signpost of a dynamic and vibrant lifestyle. […] Broadly, ›creative city‹ is about how local urban spaces can be re-imagined, rejuvenated and re-purposed within a competitive global framework.« (Tay 2005: 220)

Cities have been re-discovered in a global world of information technologies. While some scholars talk of the ›death of cities‹, cities are at the same time enthusiastically believed to be more important than ever before. They are thought to be a dynamo of economic growth and prosperity. Policy makers, urban planners, as well as scholars from different disciplines praise and celebrate the city as the most promising place in the future of a global economy (Florida 2002, 2005; Landry 2000). What is it then about the city *per se* that thrills policy makers, economists and urban planners?

It is the creative milieus and creative industries in the cities which are regarded as the decisive elements for economic growth: artists, designers, film makers, clubs, restaurants and nightlife; in short the ›creative class‹ and its lifestyle. Currently, there is a heated debate about the potential of a creative class as a driving force for economic growth. The ›creative city‹ has become synonymous with economic success, with the re-vitalisation of the city and the improvement of a city's image.

That, of course, has to be seen in the context of structural economic change, which is described as both the decline of industrial societies and, at the same time, the rise of a symbolic economy: a ›new economy‹ in which service, entertainment as well as signs and symbols are decisive economic factors. Cultural industries or creative industries are the producers of these symbolic goods and services (Lash and Urry 1993).

However, the use of the term ›creative industries‹ remains blurred. Thus – to mention only one aspect – it is not exactly clear what counts as creative industries and what does not (Hartely 2005/introduction of this volume). The promises made in the context of the rise of creative industries often reveal less about the actual economic situation than about the political goals of the creative class itself, which is for ever seeking to convince policy makers that they themselves represent the future and thus need more support from the state.

Moreover, as John Howkins observed, the fuzzy term ›creative industries‹ generally excludes science (Howkins 2005). According to the common use of the term, science is not creative; it is at best innovative, which is considered something different. Of course we know that this is not true. Scientists have to be creative, and innovation does not only mean the development of new products or new processes as neo-classical economic theory puts it, but also the creation of new ideas, new theories, and new concepts. High-tech-clusters, scientific creative milieus or technopoles are the counterpart to the *cultural* creative city. Technopolis, Sophie-Antipolis, Biopolis, Fusionopolis or Multi-Function-Polis are some of the terms for recently founded or transformed places of scientific research. They all designate places with a high number of scientific institutes, universities, and high-tech industries such as biotechnology, nanotechnology, or information technology.

From the perspective of economic history as well as from the perspective of urban history, it is necessary to integrate theses places into the debate about creative industries and creative cities for at least two important reasons:

– First, like the cultural industries they indicate *economic* changes. Scientific creative milieus are not so much a sign of the symbolic economy, but of the *knowledge economy* in which the city is also regarded as the most promising place for the generation of economic growth.[1] What I would like to stress is that the rise of the term creative industries hints at more than the symbolic economy. The knowledge economy is at least as important for the emergence of creative cities and creative industries and, thus, should also come under close scrutiny.

---

1   See also Gert-Jan Hospers' article in this volume.

– Second, as we can see from the occurrence of the word *polis* in their names, places such as Sophie-Antipolis, Biopolis etc., refer to the city. Accordingly, the city is also discussed as a creative place in the context of scientific research. However, most of these places are not located in the city itself, but rather on the periphery of cities. Thus, while we can observe a difference between cultural industries and scientific industries in terms of geography, both believe in the concept of the creative city as a driving force for growth and a guarantee of prosperity. I will come back later in my article to the question of which role the city plays in the context of ›scientific creative milieus‹. Suffice it to say at this point that the concept of the creative city as it is applied in science and technology is going to change the structure of cities.

Of course ›scientific creative milieus‹ or ›innovative milieus‹ have already been a topic of research. Scholars in regional economics, geography, sociology as well as a few historians have worked on the topic.[2] They have written the history of single places such as the Soviet Akademogorodok (Josephson 1997) and of French *technopoles* (Wakeman 2003). They have made international comparisons of technopoles (Castells and Hall 1994; Smilor et al. 1988) and investigated the conditions under which an ›innovative milieu‹ may evolve. Moreover, they have analyzed how these milieus work, have traced their networks and, finally, they have examined their relationship to the city.[3]

However, what is absent in all this – doubtless outstanding – work is a historical perspective. While it is often said that the idea of a creative city is relatively recent, it is in fact clear that it is much older. The city as the genuine place of arts *and* science, of innovation and creativity, is a concept that attracted the attention of thinkers such as Socrates, the Moslem philosopher Ibn Khaldūn as well as that of the utopians Thomas More, Tommaso Campanella and Francis Bacon (Basalla 1984). The central role of cities in the generation of knowledge has been a matter of course for centuries. Universities came into existence simultaneously with the generally growing importance of cities from the twelfth century onwards. Whereas, cities have served as transfer points of knowledge since the six-

2   For more detailed information see the following research overview: Heßler 2002.
3   See in particular the work of the European research group GREMI, Roberto Camagni's and Martina Fromhold-Eisebit's publications. For more details see Heßler 2002.

teenth century, the foundation of academies took place in the cities of the seventeenth century. Furthmore, since the end of the eighteenth century, coffee houses have also played a crucial role in the intellectual life of Europe. Likewise, associations and clubs influenced the production of knowledge and led to the emergence of local ways of thinking in the nineteenth century, as was the case with *Wittgenstein's Vienna* as Toulmin and Janik have shown. (Toumin and Janik 1972). However, the idea that scientific research has to be pursued within the city is not the only concept in the course of history. Over time, the belief in the concept of the creative city has had its ups and downs,[4] as we shall see in this article.

If we focus on science cities, techno cities or technopoles, we can broadly distinguish two historical phases. From the twelfth to the nineteenth century, cities had already existed before they became known as ›science cities‹. The existence of a ›hard‹ and ›soft infrastructure‹ of science (Landry 2000) such as universities, laboratories, libraries, scientific societies, coffee houses and salons played an important role in their transformation into science cities. Contrary to these evolving cities, in the twentieth century, in particular in its second half, ›science cities‹ were created from scratch as a result of political, economic and scientific will. This can be observed almost all over the world, or at least in western and eastern Europe, in the United States as well as in Asia (Castells and Hall 1994). The newly founded science cities are a completely different phenomenon than the old science cities which grew naturally, like Berlin, Manchester, Vienna or Philadelphia. The list of these newly founded science cities is quite long: Los Alamos in the USA (Abbot 1988), Akademgorod in the USSR (Josephson 1997), France's Sophie-Antipolis (Wakeman 2003), Spain's Cartuja near Seville (Castells and Hall 1994), Japan's Tsukubu (Castells and Hall 1994; Smilor et al. 1988) as well as Adlershof in Berlin (Kunst 1998) – to name but a few.

These new science cities of the twentieth century, can be divided again into two categories. For the sake of a better understanding of their purposes and their functions I would suggest using the term ›science cities‹ not for all of them, but rather only for a particular type. I propose a distinction between two types of scientific-technological research localities: first, ›science cities‹ and second ›technopoles‹ or ›creative milieus‹.[5]

---

4   Compare for example the American campus (Turner 1984).
5   For the often confused terminology, see the suggestions by Castells and Hall 1994 as well as Heßler 2002.

Science cities, mostly founded in the 1950s and 1960s, are characterized by various aspects, not all of them of interest here. In the scope of this article their relationship to the city is of primary interest. It is important to know that these science cities were heavily oriented towards basic research and pure science. As Castells and Hall put it, they were »considered a positive aim in (their) own right, in the hope that better scientific research will progressively percolate through the entire economy and the whole social fabric« (Castells and Hall 1994: 39). Most, though not all of them, were planned and built as whole cities with housing areas, shopping facilities and scientific institutes. Thus in their planning these newly built cities referred to a tradition which conceived science as remote from the distraction of everyday life. It referred to a monastic tradition of isolation and seclusion (Castells and Hall 1994: 39). These science cities were mostly located in the countryside and in rural regions.

Since the 1970s, science cities of this type have no longer been established. Instead, places have been created which integrate science and industry or science and technology. They are strictly application-oriented and seek to create an urban atmosphere for the pursuit of scientific-technological research. They follow the idea of the creative city and are often called ›technopoles‹. What is striking is that many of them do not have housing areas and, thus, are not built as whole cities. This is an international tendency, as Castells and Hall in particular have underlined (Castells and Hall as well as Smilor et al.).

Thus, the evidence suggests that the concept of the creative city was re-discovered or re-invented in the 1970s, while a couple of decades before nobody had paid any attention to the idea of the city as the genuine place of science. Instead, the concept of secluded science was dominant in the western world, at least in the 1950s and 1960s.

My aim in this article is to explain the re-invention of the concept since the 1970s by focusing on the specific historical situation in which it occurred. I will, therefore, examine the second half of the twentieth century. We will see that while in the 1950s and 60s science and the city were not connected at all, in the 1970s the city was re-discovered as the only appropriate setting for scientific research. It should be noted, however, that the creative city was a very specific historical type insofar as most of them are not supposed to be real cities. I will focus on two closely interwoven factors to explain this re-invention of the creative city referring to science and technology: namely the economisation of science in the context of a changed technology policy as well as the importance of knowledge as an economic resource.[6]

In addition, I would like to reflect on the idea that the creative city leads to economic growth and prosperity. While this idea has recently become a myth, I would like to investigate the actual economic consequences of the siting of scientific institutes for the *local* space. That is, of course, no easy task, and it requires further statistical research. I would, nevertheless, like to point to some problems which may emerge for the locality. I will not comment on the economic effects for the region or the nation within a global economy.

The Case Study: The City of Munich

My case study will be the city of Munich or to be more precise the town of Garching, which is well-known as one of Munich's innovative milieus. Today, Munich is regarded as a prosperous high-tech city and has become known in some circles as ›Municon Valley‹, suggesting its position as one of the most successful high-tech regions in Germany. The name ›Municon Valley‹ was coined by a journalist in the 1980s (Castells and Hall 1994: 173) and has been repeated enthusiastically by the city itself. However, a glance at Munich's history makes it clear that in the past Munich was anything but a promising candidate for such a distinction.

Whereas in the early nineteenth century Munich was variously described as a city of the bourgeoisie, a state capital and a royal capital, in the course of the nineteenth century its image changed. Munich then came to be regarded as an ›art city‹ with lively artistic communities and a university (Zimmermann 2000). After the Second World War, Munich developed into an industrial town. In the 1950s it was the third biggest German industrial town. However, some contemporaries were still surprised at Munich's ›agrarian character‹, although Munich had started to replace Berlin in

---

6   In order to fully explain the re-invention of the concept of the »creative city« it is also necessary to focus on urban history, since changes in urban planning and changing concepts about how the city should be organized played an crucial role for the re-discovery of the »creative city« in the 1970s. In this article it is not possible to consider both strands of history – economic history/history of science and technology in addition to urban history. See for both Heßler 2007.

terms of the electrical industry at this time. The name Municon Valley is a reference to Munich's dominant position in the German – and European – electronics industry. Munich has only evolved into an economic boom-town since the 1980s. Castells and Hall describe Munich as an »upstart city« (Castells and Hall 1994: 173). Since then, high-tech industries, and that means science-based industries, have been concentrated in Munich.

Existing literature offers various explanations for Munich's radical transformation in the second half of the twentieth century (Castells and Hall 1994; Deutinger 1999, 2001; Sternberg 1995, 1998), frequently under-lining the importance of Siemens's move to Munich after the Second World War. Moreover, the absence of old industries is said to have enabled Munich to have a stake in new technologies more easily than old industrial regions; Bavaria's technology policy, the high number of scientific insti-tutes, the existence of three universities and the influence of the arma-ments industry as well as the attractive landscape and Munich's image as a cultural city have all been cited as explanations of the city's transformation into a high-tech city.

It is not my aim to add other explanations for Munich's transformation into a high-tech city. Rather, as I mentioned, I will focus on the relation-ship of science, economy, and the city in the second half of the twentieth century. In doing so, I will focus especially on the re-discovery of the con-cept of creative cities.

Topography of Science in Munich – Suburbanisation of Science

While creative industries are always thought to be located in the heart of cities, thereby re-vitalizing the inner city and guaranteeing a vibrant life, that is not the case with scientific creative milieus in the second half of the twentieth century. If we look at the topography of science and high-tech industry in Munich, we have to state that in the course of the second half of the twentieth century various centres or clusters evolved for different sciences and technologies, all located on the outskirts of Munich: for ex-ample nuclear physics in Garching, microelectronics in Neuperlach – where Siemens built a so-called science city in the 1970s in order to have a stake in information technology – and biotechnology in Martinsried. This move to the periphery corresponds to a general trend in Europe after the Second World War, the suburbanisation of science, which constituted a break in European traditions. Up until the twentieth century academies, universities and scientific institutes had usually been located within the city (see Burke 2002: 69ff, Jessen 2003: 1–6, Nägelke 2003). A university on the outskirts of a city was thus an exception. The few cases in Germany, such as Berlin Dahlem, where universities and an agglomeration of science institutes were located outside the inner city at the end of the nineteenth century, met with resistance (Nägelke 2003: 19). However, in the 1960s these reservations no longer applied, and a process of suburbanisation started. There are various reasons for this, which shall not be analysed further here.[7] The decisive argument here is that we can talk of a suburbanisation of science.[8] We shall come back to this point later.

The Re-Discovery of the Creative City in the 1970s

Separated Spheres: Science and the City in the 1950s and 1960s

Thus, Munich's sites of knowledge turned their back on the city. I will now take the relationship of scientific creative milieus and the city under closer consideration, which is more complex than it may seem to be, when we state that a process of suburbanisation of science took place. I will thus focus on the example of one of the mentioned scientific milieus in Munich: Garching. Unlike the other sites of knowledge, which have only been established since the 1970s and onward, Garching is one of the oldest ›science cities‹ within or around Munich and thus makes it possible to analyze changes in the relationship of science and the city since the 1950s.

---

7 Not surprisingly, one main reason for the suburbanisation was the lack of space within cities and the real estate costs were much lower on the outskirts than in the centre of cities. Peripheral locations moreover ensured that problems like unclean air, noise and earth tremors from subway trains etc. did not limit the scientific technological work. Other scientific institutions were spread all over the city of Munich, which began to be perceived as a problem for scientific research. Universities and scientific institutes aimed at the concentration of institutes and thus needed a vast amount of space, which was not available in the city anymore. The aim was to concentrate several departments in one place in order to ensure the spatial proximity of employees to enable their interaction.
8 The newly emerged sites of knowledge are still connected with the city of Munich in different respects (administration, commuting scientists and so on). However, they develop as autonomous units at the edge of the city of Munich. Thus it would be worthwhile considering whether we can still talk of suburbanisation or whether Munich is instead developing into a polycentric city.

Garching is located 15 kilometers to the north east of Munich. Unlike many science cities or technopoles that emerged after the Second World War, it is not the result of a master plan. It is a town which has been transformed from a small Bavarian village into a so-called ›science city‹ and later, over the last 40-50 years, into a ›creative milieu‹. Before the settlement of science institutions, life was very unhurried and tranquil right up until the Second World War. Up to that point, it was impossible to distinguish Garching from other Bavarian villages. People made their living mainly from agriculture and the inhabitants all knew each other. One contemporary described Garching as a village that was characterized by cows on the street, small cottages, and dung heaps (Stieglitz 1909). However, the second half of the twentieth century brought some dramatic changes for Garching. It evolved into a »centre of science and technology of international significance«.[9] The village expanded: the number of inhabitants, workplaces and buildings grew enormously. The starting point of this process was the first German nuclear research reactor, which was built in 1957 and which is called ›Atom-Ei‹ – Atomic Egg – on account of its shape. More and more of the Munich Universities' research institutes and departments have gradually settled around the ›Atom-Ei‹. Included among these are research organisations such as a number of different Max Planck Institutes (MPI of Astrophysics, MPI of Plasma Physics, MPI of Extraterrestrial Physics) and very recently companies like General Electric, which decided to locate its German research institute in Garching. The development of Garching has still not come to an end though. In 1990, the former village of Garching was officially declared a town. Following that in 1997, Garching was named a university town, because the number of students and employees in Garching had reached the level of a small college.[10]

Garching was notable for its exceptionally enthusiastic attitude towards the siting of scientific institutes. The community's attitude towards the building of both a nuclear reactor and of further scientific institutions was a very positive and supportive one, especially during the first decades after the Second World War (Deutinger 1999). People hoped that the village would be transformed into a modern town. The farming village saw an

---

9 Gemeinde Garching b. Munich (1990). *Sitzungsvorlage (Dokumentation) zum Antrag auf Stadterhebung.* 22. Referred to hereafter as: Local Archive of Garching.
10 Local Archive of Garching, *Protokolle der Stadtratssitzung, 21.11.1997.* Referred to hereafter as SRS – and for the period before being designated as a town: GRS (*Gemeinderatssitzung*).

opportunity to enter the ›modern era‹ by participating in scientific and technological progress. And, finally, it expected economic growth and prosperity. The local priest even called nuclear energy a »gift from God«.[11]

The decisive point here is that scientific institutes turned their back on the city and were located at the edge of a small village which hoped to enter the modern age. Thus, scientific institutes and universities did not just move out of the city of Munich: Garching's research area lies even at a certain distance from the town of Garching. It was created *ex nihilo* a few kilometers from Garching. No streets existed, no infrastructure, no buildings, no public transport; nor did the village offer a stimulating atmosphere.

Focusing on the spatial organisation of the research area and the underlying concept of an appropriate space for pursuing scientific research – which was rather a monastic concept at the time – makes it clear that the idea of the city as a place for scientific research and for creativity did not play any role.

First, the research area consisted of a scattering of institutes sited near one another, not physically connected, and with plenty of green spaces in between. This follows the model of the dispersed city, such as was determined by the discourse of urban planners at the time. This was a model which aimed to give order to the city, countering its chaos: it could be described as an anti-urban model of urban planning.

Fig. 1: Garching's research area in the 1960s.

(Source: Broshure Max-Planck-Institut für Plasmaphysik, Cover, July 1974)

---

11   40 Jahre »Atom-Ei« Garching (1997): 47.

Second, the research area was a separate, mono-functional site, where only scientific institutes were placed. Contrary to many other science cities founded at that time, no houses, no apartments, no cafés, no restaurants and no shops were built on the research area here, since scientists were supposed to pursue their research undisturbed and undisrupted by daily affairs and political/economic constraints. Until recently, work time and leisure time were distinctly separated. This spatial separation of the research area from the town and thus from everyday life corresponds to a concept which clearly lays preference on the isolation of scientists. The planners intended to ensure a certain distance from the day-to-day conflicts and short-term interests of society. Scientists were enabled to pursue their research detached from mundane material concerns. Castells and Hall claim that this refers to an ideal that follows the tradition of middle-age monasteries: »To build a community of researchers and scholars, isolated from the rest of the society – or at least from its vibrant centers – is an old, well-entrenched idea; in western societies, it goes back to the medieval tradition of monasteries as islands of culture and civilisation in the midst of an ocean of barbarism« (Castells and Hall 1994: 39). In the first two decades after the Second World War, the city did not play a role as a setting for pursuing science – neither the city of Munich nor the village of Garching. Neither the administration of the Technical University nor the Max Planck Institutes nor urban planners nor Bavarian politicians regarded the city as an appropriate setting for scientific research. Garching's research area was perceived as an independent unit at the edge of the small village – independent of Garching as well as of everyday life and questions of the technical application and commercialisation of pure science.

This spatial separation corresponded to the image of scientists in the 1950s, to the idea of an autonomous science, which pursued research far away from society and from any distraction; it was the model of a cloistered seclusion, the idea of doing research in an ivory tower. Rejecting the city symbolized the role of science in the German society of the 1950s and the early 1960s – its autonomy, which was said not to be determined by politics, economy, and society.

Making the Creative City an Economic Tool

At the end of the1960s and 1970s, when technology policy changed and society demanded concrete solutions to various political, economic and environmental problems, change came too, to Garching's research area. The first phenomenon was the establishment of the »Garching Instrumente Gesellschaft zur industriellen Nutzung von Forschungsergebnissen«, an institution of technology transfer, which was founded by the Max Planck Society. The institute's main task was, first, to review scientific and technological developments of the Max Planck Institutes from the perspective of possible industrial applications, and second, to start market assessment in order to find companies that might be interested in some of the research results. The institution and its tasks clearly reflect a mode of technology policy which did not believe in the so-called ›linear model‹ anymore. This model claimed a strict separation of pure research and applied science; it promised that basic research automatically leads to innovation and economic prosperity.

The 1970s were a decade of change, as many scholars have recently stressed. In respect to science and technology policy Dominique Pestre talked of the end of an era, which can be observed in the middle of the 1970s. He discovered a »new regime of knowledge production«, which I would like to summarize very broadly with the terms privatisation and economisation of science.

The historical background of this change is well-known. I just would like to call some aspects to mind: the economic recession in the 1960s, the oil crisis in the 1970s, and the heated debate about a ›technological gap‹ whereby Europe was perceived to be falling behind the United States, which determined technology policy in West Germany (Trischler 1999; Szöllosi-Janse 1999). In this context it became clear that pure science did not automatically lead to useful applications and technical innovations (Szöllösi-Janze 1999: 43ff., compare also Felt et al. 1995: 216).

Moreover, the growth of universities was accompanied by a decrease in financial support, which led to a crisis of legitimisation of universities. Universities and institutions had to legitimise themselves more and more economically (Schmoch et al. 2000). As Peter Weingart has noted, there was a great debate in the 1960s and 70s about the relationship between basic science or technology and applied science. (Weingart 2001) It was the period of ›technology transfer‹ – and the above mentioned Garching Instrumente Gesellschaft was a further indication of this change.

This was also the time when places such as Sophia-Antipolis, Biopolis and other high-tech cities were built. These places represent efforts to create ›innovative milieus‹ in order to guarantee economic growth in a changed world. The model of creativity and of the generation of knowledge was completely different to that of the 1950s and 1960s, when researchers were isolated from the world. Instead, the city came back in and the creative city was re-invented. Now, policy makers, technology policy and urban planners tried to create an urban mode of knowledge production on the periphery of cities. These developments can be observed very clearly in Garching. But what exactly does it mean that the city came back in?

Various changes can be observed when politicians as well as science administrators re-discovered the city as an appropriate setting for pursuing scientific research, and in particular, for creating scientific-technological innovations.

First, the idea that science should be clearly separated from the city or the town disappeared. In the 1970s, Garching's local politicians and inhabitants began to perceive the *separation of the research area from the town* as a problem. The criticism was made that science as well as scientists themselves had become an alien element.[12] Now, the research area itself was described using such terms as ›isolation‹ and ›ghetto‹.[13] Instead efforts were made to re-connect science and the town of Garching. Thus, in 1978, for example, Garching's politicians made real efforts to reduce the separation between Garching town and the science area in order to »overcome the bad functionalism«.[14] The aim was »to connect the alien element, the university, more closely to the center of Garching«[15.] These efforts culminated in a »plan to construct a walking route between Garching and the research centre«.[16] Similar to that idea is the recently discussed plan to build a bridge connecting the research area with Garching town where various shops, sports facilities, meeting spaces and so on are to be located.

Second, an attempt was made to transform the mono-functional character of the research area and the ivory tower model into a lively, vibrant and urban space, since complaints about lifelessness could be heard more and more. In the 1970s some satirical terms for Garching, such as Akademgorodok[17] or Novigarchinsk (Wengenroth 1993: 297) arose, indicating

12 »Der Landkreis München«. *Münchner Merkur* Supplement, July 6/7, 1963.
13 *Süddeutsche Zeitung*, November 22/23, 1975: 17.
14 *Stadtanzeiger*, August 17, 1982, 6. »Garching: Eine Gemeinde sucht ihr Gesicht.«
15 Local Archive of Garching, Anlage 3 zum Protokoll der GRS, May 19, 1978.
16 Local Archive of Garching, GRS. May 13, 1977.
17 *Süddeutsche Zeitung*, November 22/23, 1975: 17.

changing concepts of scientific research. These terms, which allude to huge planned Soviet cities, must be read as critical metaphors for lifelessness, artificiality and isolation. They implicitly indicated a new importance attached to urbanity, which was absent in the research area. The revival of urbanity can be found in efforts to change the face and atmosphere of the research area. This implied an orientation towards urban features as were typical of the European city in the nineteenth century and which include compactness, density, proximity, blurring of function, etc. The administration of the TU as well as the Bavarian state government decreed that facilities for shopping and sports as well as housing areas should be built.[18] These plans have been re-made especially since the 1990s. Local and state politicians as well as the TU administration have planned to build book shops, copy-shops, pubs, restaurants, shops, apartments, medical services, kindergartens, apartments etc.[19] TU administrators claimed that the city must be regarded as a motivating, provocative, diverse, and stimulating environment, while the »splendid isolation« of scientists runs the risk of removing science from society.[20] The concept of the isolation of scientists has been transformed into an ideal of integrating science into society accompanied by a revitalisation of urban features. This highlights the new importance of cities for scientific research, as demonstrated by the effort to create an urban environment.

Finally, the research area's orientation towards basic science was criticized. Thus, in the 1980s, a memorandum of the Technological University bemoaned the ›isolation‹ of Garching's scientists.[21] *Integrating science and technology* appeared on the agenda. Attempts were made to bring together basic and applied research at one location. In 1980, the TU heavily criticized the spatial separation of engineering science from basic research. It was stated that this was extremely dysfunctional.[22] »The status quo is extraordinarily unsatisfactory, because the necessary scientific exchange between basic research (in Garching) and technical departments (in Munich) is very difficult«.[23] Applied science and application-oriented institutes such as the Walter Schottky Institute or the Bavarian Centre for Applied

---

18 Denkschrift: 2.
19 Archive of TU-Bauamt (1996). *Garching 5000.*
20 Lehrstuhl für Planen und Bauen (2001): 18.
21 Denkschrift: 13.
22 Denkschrift: 11.
23 Denkschrift: 12.

Energy Research have been founded in Garching since the 1980s. Recently, the departments of computer science and mathematics have also moved there, in immediate proximity to the departments of physics, chemistry and engineering in order to create a »centre for mathematical-scientific research and software technology«. At the end of the 1990s, the chancellor of the TU claimed that a ›founding culture‹ should evolve in Garching.[24] The TU and the town of Garching recently built a Technology and Founder's Centre in order to encourage the establishment of new businesses.[25] In addition, General Electric has decided to locate a company in Garching. The research area of Garching has, without a doubt, begun to change its face by integrating application-oriented institutes.

In this process, the awareness of the importance of *spatial proximity* and *communication spaces* has dramatically increased. Communication spaces were created in the 1980s with new architectural forms. The architecture of the MPI for Astrophysics (1979) as well as that of the neighbouring European Southern Observatory building (1981) is a very communicative one and is supposed to encourage lively, spontaneous communication between scientists. The open cafeteria, which is found there, serves also as a reading room for recent publications. Researchers can meet there and discuss scientific problems, and they can take the opportunity to make spontaneous use of the small conference rooms to hold debates.[26] As stylized as the notion of scientists holding spontaneous discussions may be, it is clear that awareness of the synergetic effects of face-to-face communication, of informal and spontaneous contacts, has increased since the late 1970s and 1980s.

A high priority has been the architectural support of communication, particularly since the 1990s. Architectural and social density, interaction, informal communication and integration are the objectives of policy makers, urban planners and the administrators of universities and scientific institutions, in short: it was the concept of the creative city. The inner structure of buildings was supposed to enhance chance encounters, in particular between different disciplines. This was meant to enhance ›scientific performance‹ which actually meant economic performance. As the architect of one building stated »the main objective was to get science out

---

24   Archive of TU-Bauamt (1998). *Akten Garching 5000.*
25   *Stadt Garching bei München – Informationsbroschüre*, 1998: 42.
26   *Süddeutsche Zeitung*, May 6, 1981.

of its ivory tower and to promote communication«.[27] Moreover public places were planned, where scientists and entrepreneurs can meet; buildings integrated niches with coffee tables and chairs in order to offer space for spontaneous and informal discussions.

We cannot fail to recognise that the efforts to redesign the research area are indebted to the idea of the city as the place of innovation, of creativity and generation of knowledge. It is the concept of a creative city which I mentioned at the beginning of this article. The concept of the creative city has thus evolved into a tool for enhancing economic success.

Fig. 2: The »Piazza« in Martinsried

(Source: Photography by the author)

If we take a brief look at another example in Munich's periphery, namely Martinsried, a place where biotechnology is very strong, we can observe the same development. The architecture and the urban planning for this research areas also aim at an »infrastructure of chance encounter«; urban

27 Interview with the architect, printed in *Süddeutsche Zeitung*, May 14, 1997: 41.

structures such as a cafe, a restaurant, a shop, and an ›Italian-style piazza‹ have been built. As one of the directors of the founding centre there stated: »We thought of a small town with Italian flair: the outdoor facilities of the IZB (i.e. the founding centre) shows the realized idea of a piazza with fountain. It serves as a communication space for basic researchers from the Max Planck Institutes, the university as well as entrepreneurs«.[28]

However, the picture of the piazza makes it clear that the plan to develop an urban space for science and technology in suburbia is paradoxical. Scientific institutions moved out of the city and are located at the edge of small villages – after a certain time it is noticed that something has been lost, something that could be of importance to science, namely urban culture. Since the suburbanisation of science the urban atmosphere in the ›real‹ city has not been available. Thus »the city« was imitated in the city's periphery. The city or the urban culture was on stage now. While the real city as a place of contradictions, conflicts, plurality, multi-layeredness and confusion loses importance as a setting for the pursuit of scientific research, the *concept* of the city is held by urban planners, science policy, universities as well as industries to be the only appropriate space for science. The model is an ideal of the European city, which is reproduced on the outskirts of a city. However, the crucial point is that the concept is just a *metaphor* which leaves out all ›disturbing‹ features of the city – and thus it has paradoxically also disturbed the concept of a creative city.

Everybody who visits these places knows they do not look like cities. They are not really »spaces you want to be in, places to be seen. Their workshops, restaurants, and bars are both the ›most superficial manifestations of a creative environment‹ and the signpost of a dynamic and vibrant lifestyle«. Many of the planned infrastructures have still not been built. Martinsried appears like a post-modern, artificial place, built in the fields some distance from the village.

Referring to scientific creative milieus, it needs to be pointed out that the concept of the creative city is reduced to a *metaphor*, which shows more similarities to shopping malls than to real cities. That means that in the context of a changed technology policy, in the context of the economisation of science, a stylized model of the European city is re-invented as a tool for enhancing economic growth. It is expected that certain features of the city such as concentration, compactness, density, heterogeneity (which

28 Innovations- und Gründerzentrum (2002): 11.

here means the confrontation of scientist and entrepreneurs or of different disciplines), the creation of space for meeting accidentally, for informal as well as formal communication will enhance creativity and ultimately economic prosperity. However, one thing is clear: the ›creative industries‹ on the outskirts of cities will not contribute to the hoped-for revitalisation of cities.

Economic Effects of the Settlement of Science?

So, if creative scientific milieus do not revitalize the city but instead have the opposite effect, what about the economic effect on the places that host the scientific institutions? Does the city, the town or the village benefit from the siting of scientific creative milieus?

As I have already mentioned, the farming village of Garching hoped for economic growth and prosperity resulting from science and technology in the research area. Today, we might wonder why Garching's inhabitants expected that institutions such as the MPI for Plasma Physics or the MPI for Astrophysics, which moved to Garching in the 1960s, should lead to economic prosperity at all. However, the following considerations determined the discourse in the village in the late 1950s and 1960s.[29]

– First, a growth of population was expected. Local politicians hoped that scientists with money to spend as well as students would move to Garching and do their shopping there, live there with their families and spend their free time in the village. However, that did not happen. Scientists and students avoided even visiting Garching, let alone living there.
– Second the siting of the first nuclear research reactor has to be seen in the context of enthusiastic debates about nuclear energy, which promised prosperity, wealth, energy in plentiful supply as well as economic growth. What was overlooked in Garching was that the nuclear reactor was a very small research tool which did not attract any interest from industry at all. Contrary to expectations, no industry was established there.

---

29 For the following see Heßler (2007).

- Third, in the 1950s and 1960s society believed in the above mentioned ›linear model‹ which promised that basic research automatically leads to innovation and economic success. Garching as a space of basic research seemed to be very promising in this respect. However, as have I shown above, it became clear in the 1970s that the prophecies simply were not fulfilled. Moreover, if these effects can be observed at all, they are not such as to bring benefits automatically to the locality.

Garching itself has placed great emphasis on the benefits which resulted from the development of the research area. The ›Atom-Ei‹ was stylised as a ›magnet‹. According to the narrative presented by the community of Garching and emphatically endorsed by the TU München, the dynamic development of Garching was attributable to the locating of the research institute; the first research reactor in the Federal Republic was regarded – still in 1990 – as a significant stimulus for growth and a catalyst of development.[30] Locally, public discourse stressed the economic impulses »for Garching, which profits from this new research boom, it is above all important that the community should be given impulses for development and that jobs are created«[31], as the mayor Mr Karl said in the mid 1970s. The community chronicles stated: »In less than ten years the once forgotten village of Garching became an attractive industrial area. The explanation is simple: the ›Atom-Ei‹ had a magnetic effect.«[32] Similarly in a TU brochure issued on the 40th anniversary of the ›Atom-Ei‹ the president of the TU wrote: »Just as the research reactor is a source of neutrons, the ›Atom-Ei‹ at Garching has given this region – and not only this region – positive impulses for science, the economy and above all for the people who work here.«[33]

And indeed at the beginning it did look as though the hopeful expectations would be met. Non-scientific personnel for the reactor were recruited from the community; 140 people worked there, among them typists, doormen, etc.[34] It was furthermore claimed that there were knock-on benefits for agriculture, gastronomy, etc. These claims, however, were never substantiated empirically.

---

30 See Antrag auf Stadterhebung: 2.
31 *Süddeutsche Zeitung*, December 5, 1975.
32 *Chronik*, 1964: 117.
33 40 Jahre »Atom-Ei«, Vorwort.
34 See *Münchner Merkur*, August 6, 1963.

Stephan Deutinger has already pointed out that the industrial and the scientific development of Garching grew from two entirely different roots and that no connection between them existed. »A causal connection with natural science research at the site was a chimaera.« (Deutinger 1999: 237)

In fact, the settlement of the scientific research site resulted in enormous costs for Garching. Far from the economic growth and the revenue expected from science and technology, the research area meant extraordinary financial burdens for the community. Since German communities receive revenue from corporate tax (which is the main source of capital for German communities) and since no industry actually settled in the research area, Garching did not get any revenue from the research area. On the other hand, it was obliged to pay for the infrastructure such as streets, sewerage, etc. The community of Garching complained about this on more than one occasion. Petitions were signed and open letters were addressed to the federal government. However, the community received only modest assistance. Some concrete support was received from the scientific institutes. The Institute of Plasmaphysics wrote to the Federal Ministry of Research, requesting financial support so that facilities and infrastructure in the village could be improved in accordance with the research centre's needs. The request was signed by professors from the MPG, the Bavarian Academy of Science and the TH.[35] The Max Planck Institute also, for instance, contributed to the cost of improving the sewerage system and in 1960 a contract was signed with the MPG on the defrayment of future costs.[36] Assistance of this kind remained rare, however. From the mid 1960s the costs in fact became genuinely hard for the community to bear. Garching's appeals for help to various official bodies largely came to nothing: »All the responsible authorities employed well-proven delaying tactics«, claimed the village council, which therefore decided to go public with its grievances at a press conference.[37] Far from being a magnet, the ›Atom-Ei‹ proved to be a lasting burden for the community, which consequently endeavoured to initiate the establishment of industrial enterprises in order to raise revenue through corporate tax. Attracting industry to the area thus appears to be a *compensation* for the science establishments there.

A brochure published on the tenth anniversary of the reactor contains the following statements:

35 See GRS, 17 January 1967.
36 See GRS, March 18, 1960; Appendix in GRS, September 9, 1960.
37 See GRS, September 16, 1966.

»Since the research institutes yielded no revenue for the community and while considerable funds were required for construction of the school building, the sewerage system etc., it was decided to seek relief through the siting of industrial enterprises here. These enterprises will provide revenue in the form of corporate tax, which will secure the financial basis of the community in the future.«[38]

Despite these enormous burdens Garching did not question its support for scientific institutes for a very long time. In 1990 the nuclear reactor was still described as a crucial stimulus for the generation of new jobs.[39] However, this rhetoric of legitimisation came to be less and less accepted in the course of time. During the last two decades the acceptance among Garching's inhabitants has been eroded. When planning a new nuclear research reactor, Bavarian politicians as well as the administration of the Technical University again promised economic growth and job creation in Garching, before realizing that the inhabitants remembered hearing that promise before – and that it had not come true, despite the rhetoric of the chronicles. The inhabitants turned the argument around, claiming the siting of a new research reactor would not bring any tangible benefits. Ultimately, after long and heavy conflicts the second nuclear reactor *was* built; the research area is still growing.

Conclusion

Since the 1970s and in particular since the 1990s, politicians, the administrations of universities and research institutes, urban planners as well as entrepreneurs have tried to transform Garching's former monastic research area – in which creativity, new ideas, innovation and scientific progress were supposed to result from isolation and cloistered seclusion – into a creative city where an urban culture with shops, restaurants, meeting spaces such as piazzas could evolve and guarantee creativity and economic prosperity. Changes in technology policy, which forced scientific institutes and universities to produce useful knowledge and scientific-technological innovations instead of pursuing basic research, were important for the reinvention of the concept of the creative city. In short, the economisation of science, as well as – the closely connected – growing importance of

38 Festschrift zur Festwoche.
39 Antrag auf Stadterhebung: 2.

knowledge for economy constitutes the historical background for the re-discovery of the concept of the creative city. It is believed that the integra-tion of science and industry, the face-to-face communication of researchers from different institutes as well as their confrontation are important stimuli for creativity. The city with its public places, its concentration and density, and its heterogeneity thus seemed to offer the infrastructure for this mode of knowledge production. However, the case of Garching clearly demon-strates that the concept of the scientific creative city does not really refer to the city, since it focuses only on certain features of cities, while many as-pects, in particular any disturbances and social problems, are left out. The scientific creative city is supposed to be a ›pure‹ place for academics, an imitated urban environment which refers only to some ›good‹ aspects of urbanity. Hence, the city is staged or represented on the outskirts of the city. It will, therefore, not contribute to the rejuvenation, revival or revital-izing of cities.

Nevertheless, belief in the creative city remains strong. All over the world, policy makers and urban planners aim to build creative cities. Schol-ars and researchers, especially from urban planning and regional economy, still tinker with recipes to create the next creative city. They thus re-write and reproduce a concept which has experienced its ups and downs during history and has been stylized into a myth from time to time – as it has been recently. However, as we know from history: it is difficult to create a new city from scratch, and almost impossible to create urban culture. This is especially true of such stylized and reduced concepts as the scientific crea-tive city proves to be.

Whether Garching will indeed change from an isolated research area on the outskirts of the city of Munich into a creative city and finally bring prosperity to the town is still open to question.

Bibliography

Abbott, Carl (1998). »Building the Atomic Cities. Richland, Los Alamos, and the American Planning Language«. In Bruce Hevly and John M. Findlay (eds.). *The Atomic West*, 90–115. Washington/Seattle/London.

Basalla, George (1984). »Science and the City before the Nineteenth Century«. In Everett Mendelsohn (ed.). *Transformation and Tradition in the Sciences: Essays in Es-says in honor of I. Bernhard Cohen.* Cambridge et al.

Burke, Peter (2002). *Papier und Marktgeschrei. Die Geburt der Wissensgesellschaft.* Berlin.

Denkschrift zur Verlagerung der Technischen Universität München von München nach Garching. Beschluss der ständigen Kommission für Hochschulplanung der TUM vom 19.3.1980 auf der Grundlage des Senatsbeschlusses vom 23.1.1980. Hrsg. im Auftrag des Präsidenten von der Bauabteilung 4 – Liegenschaften – der zentralen Verwaltung der TU München, März 1980.

Deutinger, Stephan (1999). »›Garching: Deutschland modernstes Dorf‹. Die Modernisierung Bayerns seit 1945 unter dem Mikroskop«. In Katharina Weigand and Guido Treffler (eds.). *Neue Ansätze zur Erforschung der neueren bayerischen Geschichte*, 223–247. Neuried.

— (2001). *Vom Agrarland zum High-Tech-Staat. Zur Geschichte des Forschungsstandorts Bayern 1945–1980.* München/Wien.

Felt, Ulrike, Helga Nowotny and Klaus Taschwer (1995). *Wissenschaftsforschung. Eine Einführung.* Frankfurt am Main/New York.

Florida, Richard (2002). *The Rise of the Creative Class.* New York.

— (2005). *Cities and the Creative Class.* New York/London.

Hartley, John (2005). »Creative Industries«. In John Hartley (ed.). *Creative Industries*, 1–40. Malden/Oxford/Carlton.

Heßler, Martina (2002). »Stadt als innovatives Milieu – Ein transdisziplinärer Forschungsansatz«. *Neue Politische Literatur*, 47, 2, 193–223.

— (2007). *Die kreative Stadt. Zur Neuerfindung eines Topos.* Bielefeld.

Howkins, John (2005). »The Mayor's Commission on the Creative Industries«. In John Hartley (ed.). *Creative Industries*, 117–125. Oxford.

Innovations- und Gründerzentrum Biotechnologie IZB (ed.). *Das Tor zur Biotechnologie – Festschrift.* Martinsried 2002.

Kunst, Friedemann (1998). »Leitbilder für Berliner Stadträume – der ›innovative Nordosten‹ und die ›Wissenschaftsstadt Adlershof«. In Heidede Becker, Johann Jessen and Robert Sander (eds.). *Ohne Leitbild? – Städtebau in Deutschland und Europa*, 205–214. Stuttgart/Zürich.

Jessen, Johann (2003). »Editorial«. *Die Alte Stadt*, 30, 1–6.

Josephson, Paul R. (1997). *New Atlantis Revisted.* Princeton/New Jersey.

Landry, Charles (2000). *The Creative City. A Toolkit for Urban Innovators.* London.

Lash, Scott and John Ury (1993). *Economies of Signs and Space.* London.

Lehrstuhl für Planen und Bauen im ländlichen Raum, TU München (ed.) (2001). Perspektive TUM Workshop. *Der Student als Nomade.* München.

Nägelke, Hans-Dieter (2003). »Einheitswunsch und Spezialisierungszwang: Stadt und Universität im 19. Jahrhundert«. *Die Alte Stadt*, 30, 7–19.

Schmoch, Ulrich, Georg Licht and Michael Reinhard (2000). *Wissens- und Technologietransfer in Deutschland.* Stuttgart.

Smilor, Raymond W., George Kozmetsky and David V. Gibson (eds.) (1988). *Creating the Technopolis: Linking Technology Commercialisation and Economic Development.* Cambridge, Mass.

Stadtverwaltung Garching b. München (ed.) (1990). *Stadt Garching. Stadtführer.* Garching.

Sternberg, Rolf (1995). »Wie entstehen High-Tech-Regionen? Theoretische Erklä-rungen und empirische Befunde aus fünf Industriestaaten«. *Geographische Zeit-schrift*, 83, 48–63.

— (1998). *Technologiepolitik und High-Tech Regionen – ein internationaler Vergleich*. 2nd edition. Münster.

Stieglitz, Hans (1909). *Der Lehrer auf der Heimatscholle*. München/Berlin.

Szöllösi-Janze, Margit (1999). »Forschung im Spannungsfeld von Wissenschaft und Markt«. In Gerhard A. Ritter, Margit Szöllösi-Janze and Helmuth Trischler (eds.). *Antworten auf die amerikanische Herausforderung. Forschung in der Bundesrepu-blik und der DDR in den »langen« siebziger Jahren*, 43–49. Frankfurt am Main/New York.

Tay, Jinna (2002). »Creative Cities«. In John Hartley (ed.). *Creative Industries*, 220–232. Oxford.

Toulmin, Allan and Steven Janik (1972). *Wittgenstein's Vienna*. London.

Trischler, Helmuth (1999). »Die ›amerikanische Herausforderung‹ in den ›langen‹ siebziger Jahren: Konzeptionelle Überlegungen«. In Gerhard A. Ritter, Margit Szöllösi-Janze and Helmuth Trischler (eds.). *Antworten auf die amerikanische Her-ausforderung. Forschung in der Bundesrepublik und der DDR in den »langen« siebziger Jahren*, 11–18. Frankfurt am Main/New York.

— (2001). »Das bundesdeutsche Innovationssystem in den ›langen 70er Jahren‹: Antworten auf die ›amerikanische Herausforderung‹«. In Johannes Abele, Ger-hard Barkleit and Thomas Hänseroth (ed.). *Innovationskulturen und Fortschrittser-wartungen im geteilten Deutschland*, 47–70. Köln.

Turner, Paul Venable (1984). *Campus. An American Planning Tradition*. Cam-bridge/London.

Wakeman, Rosemary (2003). »Planning the New Atlantis: Science and the planning of Technopolis, 1955–1985«. *Osiris*, 18, 255–270.

Weingart, Peter (2001). *Die Stunde der Wahrheit? Zum Verhältnis der Wissenschaft zu Politik, Wirtschaft und Medien in der Wissensgesellschaft*. Weilerswist.

Wengenroth, Ulrich (1993). »Die Technische Hochschule nach dem Zweiten Weltkrieg. Auf dem Weg zu High-Tech and Massenbetrieb«. In Ulrich Wen-genroth (ed.). *Die Technische Universität München*, 261–298. München.

Zimmermann, Clemens (2000). *Die Zeit der Metropolen. Urbanisierung und Großstadt-entwicklung*. 2nd edition. Frankfurt am Main.

40 Jahre »Atom-Ei« Garching (1997). Edited by the TU München, 1997.

Festschrift zur Festwoche anläßlich des 10jährigen Bestehens des Atomreaktors Garching bei München, Garching 1967.

Sources from the Local Archive of the town of Garching and the TU Bauamt; Süddeutsche Zeitung, Münchner Merkur.

Helsinki – Examples of Urban Creativity and Innovativeness

Marjatta Hietala

In this day and age, cities compete innovatively and creatively with each other. The latter, creativity, has evolved into a hot topic in recent city discussions, because public authorities aim to promote more of it in their towns. They want to increase the interaction between culture and commerce in today's mixed economy of leisure, culture and creativity. The underlying presumption is that new innovations will be born from the union between the parallelism of the traditional cultural institutions and popular culture and the latest technology and its appliances. According to the present view, creativity is an essential and autonomous component of human life.

Creativity can be seen as an anti-utilitarian act and stands in opposition to the concept of innovation, which, on the contrary, is registered in the utilitarian system of behaviour. The creative effort produces positive values. It functions as a factor of self realisation; it is rich in intrinsic enjoyment and in self-fulfilment. Furthermore, creativity is a non-cumulative good. It is rupture, whereas »normal« is conceived within the frame of a given scientific paradigm.[1] When we examine cities we often speak of creative environments and innovative environments, which are very closely connected. Innovativeness of a society is embedded in a city's traditions that include institutions, buildings and support services, such as transport and communication, all belonging to the so called »hard infrastructure.« The so-called »soft infrastructure« consists of various kinds of social networks in the forms of informal groups, clubs and common interest networks (Landry 2000: 87–90).

Lately historians, sociologists and economists, such as Peter Hall, Manuel Castells, and Sverker Sörlin, have analysed cities as creative and innovative centres. Manuel Castells has emphasized new knowledge-

---

1   Walter Santagata's definition of creativity is based on S. Howarths article, »Economic modelling in Creative Behaviour« (Santanaga 2005).

intensive environments where creative synergies arise (Castells 1996; 1997; 1998; Bell and Hietala 2002: 341–373). Both Castells and Swedish researchers, Sörlin and Gunnar Törnquist, use the term »the social fabric« when emphasizing countless contacts, meetings and social events, as well as cultural and communicative infrastructure (Sörlin 2002: 377–388; Sörlin 1996: 31–41). Mobility is among the factors which are typical for innovative communities, milieus and environments. According to Peter Hall, innovative environments, cities and places provide opportunities for unexpected meetings between people and different areas of activity. He has emphasized in his analysis on the city as an innovative milieu that there are two different models of innovation: the freewheeling laissez-faire one, which could be described as the American model, and the state-guided centralized one, which was previously the German model and is currently the Japanese model. Hall also notes that these models seemed to be able to perform equally effectively on the basis of quite different systems, international organisation and access to capital. He predicts that the organized Japanese model might be the »winner« in the long run. The most important element in the Japanese model is the social and organisational process that has brought technologies successfully to market (Hall 1998: 496f.).

Traditionally the cultural industries have not found much of a place in mainstream economics, where they have generally been considered to be of peripheral importance. In more recent years, though, some economists and socialists have come to see the cultural or creative industries as either already or potentially central to contemporary economic life (Hesmond-halgh 2005).

During the last ten or fifteen years the creation or nourishment of cultural clusters has been taken as a new alternative source for urban cultural development. In many cities, public authorities have given culture and creativity new roles in economically and culturally revitalising post industrial cities. The aim may be to mix different cultural activities from production to presentation and consumption of theatre and the visual arts as well as pop music and new media and to give them space to act. Sometimes the cultural clusters began their existence in the minds of cultural managers and sometimes the projects came to life on the drawing board of urban planners (Mommaas 2004).

In the following I will analyse the case study of Helsinki in order to show different phases of its cultural milieus, both in terms of culture and science and technology. I will describe how cultural milieus have changed over time and ask which factors had played decisive roles in the development of Helsinki from a small shipping town at the beginning of nineteenth century to a major player in the world in the twentieth century as far as information and telecommunication are concerned. Helsinki became the capital of Finland in 1812 when Sweden lost Finland to the Russian Empire. Finland received the status of an autonomous state in the Russian Empire which opened good markets for Finnish products such as textiles or shoes as well as labour markets for Finns. Helsinki became not only a centre of administration and higher education when the university had moved from Turku to Helsinki in 1827, but also the hub of the nation's cultural life and a major industrial centre.

I would now like to explore the importance of the cultural sector for city growth and economy through chronological, partly overlapping periods. The first period began in the 1880s and continued up to the 1950s. The rapid growth that started in the 1880s is typical for this period and was connected not only to industrialisation, but also to the strong desire of the public authorities to raise Helsinki abreast with European metropolises. During this period creative milieus and co-operations between writers, artists, musicians and architects were strongly oriented on nationalistic ideologies.

The second period began at the end of the 1940s when Finland survived the Second World War and maintained its independence. After the bombings, Helsinki was rebuilt and the latest technologies were introduced. It was at this time that Helsinki invested in the 1952 Olympic Games, and the Sibelius Weeks, which grew in the 1960s into the Helsinki Festival, started in 1951. This period also saw the birth of Helsinki as a music city (see also Bottás' article in this volume). Furthermore, during the 1950s, Finland also gained international acclaim in design.

The third period is closely connected to the wide spread utilisation of IT technology in Finland and the rise of Nokia. The predecessor of Nokia was Suomen Kaapelitehdas (The Finnish Cable Factory), established in 1912. In addition, joining the European Union in 1994 helped to further internationalize Helsinki. And although former school buildings were already being converted into cultural centres (City of Helsinki Urban Facts 2004: 105) since the 1980s, in the 1990s Helsinki started to systematically invest in creative milieus both in the heart of the city and in the suburbs.

The Golden Age of Finnish Art

The end of the nineteenth century and the beginning of twentieth century is sometimes called the Golden Age of Finnish Art (Bell and Hietala 2002: 144–157; Hietala 2002). As is typical for this period, the cultural production in Finland at this time was exclusively a nationalistic one. Artists sought their inspiration from Finnish folklore and from Finnish mythology, for example, from the Kalevala. Artists, writers and composers included nationalistic components in their art forms. Art Nouveau was given highly individual national flavours. Typical were its folk art themes and the use of the native granite especially in public and corporate buildings. Finnish National Romanticism was an urban style, which permeated not only applied arts, but also architecture. It received its element of nature from Art Nouveau, rendered in the stylized Finnish way. According to some researchers, symbolism with a national orientation heavily influenced Finnish art (Ringbom 2000: 221f.).

William Morris' idea of a building's total environment and its interior being designed up to the finest detail started a similar movement in Finland in the 1890s. Among others, painters Akseli Gallen-Kallela and Louis Sparre started to design for the Friends of the Finnish Handicraft, becoming pioneers of Finnish industrial design. Gallen-Kallela's house in Ruovesi, north of Tampere and Eliel Saarinen's, Armas Lindgren's and Hermann Gesellius's common *ateljee* and homes in Hvitträsk near Helsinki, are celebrated examples of a total milieu with harmonious architecture and interior design. When Finnish artists Eliel Saarinen, Herman Gesellius and Armas Lindgren won the competition for designing the pavillon for the World's Fair in Paris 1900 they wanted to use it as a forum for presenting Finland as a nation in its own right to the widest possible international public. Altogether thirty Finnish artists were represented in the Paris World Fair (Bell and Hietala 2002: 153–257).

In Helsinki a number of groups were to carry out significant innovative actions in strengthening their own national identity. The most important and oldest of these bodies was the University, while the early 1890s also saw increasing activity by Helsingin Suomalainen klubi (the Finnish Club of Helsinki), a society of younger academics and university students and Nuori Suomi (Young Finland), a group of Finnish artists, writers and journalists whose endeavours resulted not only in the music of Sibelius, but also in the Golden Age of Finnish Art. The growth of Pan-Slavic Russian nationalism as well as the russification policy by the Russian tsar[2] and the strong patriotic concern led almost all members of the Finnish artistic community to return to Finland. In the early 1890s the spa in Kaivopuisto became a base for the young cultural elite, people who had studied abroad but had not yet established any permanent home in Helsinki. It became an unofficial forum for discussions and co-operations between artists, writers and musicians (Konttinen 2001: 9–14). Moreover, the restaurant Kämp in the centre of Helsinki became an unofficial meeting place for artists and musicians such as Jean Sibelius and Robert Kajanus, painter Akseli Gallen-Kallela and poet Eino Leino who spent their evenings, and sometimes days, in the restaurant.

Creative environments can be found not only in the middle of Helsinki in the Ateneum, a center for fine art and crafts school as well as an art museum, but also in the neighbourhoods, e.g. in Tuusula, in the area surrounding the lake, where Jean Sibelius and some artists and writers had their homes and ateljees.[3] The original plans of the future temple of the arts in Helsinki were similar to the Crystal Palace in London, a joint base for arts and industries accommodating fine art and crafts schools, museums and libraries as well as shops and even meeting places for the workers' associations (Maunula 1989: 185). This idea was manifested in the opening of the Ateneum in 1887 on the Railway Square as a base for institutes training in fine arts and industrial arts alike as well as for a museum for both aspects of the visual arts. At the same time, other cultural centres like the Finnish National Theatre and libraries were being built even in so-called »blue collar« areas of the city. Libraries, which in Helsinki and throughout Finland have remained free of charge, became important meeting places for different age groups.

In order to develop the city's municipal services as they had done with culture, the civic authorities, certainly like their colleagues in the Nordic cities were willing to finance fact-finding tours and visits to municipal conferences and exhibitions abroad. What distinguished Helsinki in this respect was the very systematic approach the city adopted in order to

---

2   The Post Manifesto of 1890 linking the previously independent Finnish postal system to that of the rest of the empire as well as other signs of systematic unification were evident both in the appointment of civil servants and in demands to increase the use of the Russian language in administration and at schools (Bell and Hietala 2002: 150–151).

3   Besides Jean Sibelius, the painters Pekka Halonen and Eero Järnefelt, the writer Juhani Aho with his wife Venny Soldan-Brofeldt had houses on the Tuusula lake (Konttinen 2001: 83, 113, 117–118).

maximize the efficiency of this search for relevant know-how, especially in the field of infrastructure. Travels by city officials and elected representatives were based on a careful preliminary study of statistical data and other material from other capitals before selecting the most promising destinations. During the trip they spent a great deal of time making personal observations and thorough comparisons before finally submitting an extensive report on their travels. This meant that the authorities adopted innovations quickly when required, but that they also behaved cautiously and selectively, especially in case of technical solutions for their problems and challenges (Bell and Hietala 2002: 106–109; Hietala 1992: 229–238). Municipal authorities and city officials wanted to develop Helsinki in the same direction as other larger capitals such as London, Paris, Berlin, Vienna or Stockholm. Moreover, different sectors of the public administration had their own »model cities«.

Typical for this period, the nationalistic attitude of the Finnish cultural milieus went hand in hand with the mobility of innovative milieus and rapid adoption of know-how and its dissemination to the people. Gallen-Kallela for example illustrated publications that were intended for the wider public. »National« was seen as a task for intellectuals and educated people. Articles on hygiene and the latest technological innovations were written for general readers by doctors and engineers. The motive behind the idea of »national enlightenment« was the strong nationalistic identity. A free flow of information sped up Helsinki's growth during the nineteenth century and at the beginning of twentieth century, knowledge and new innovations transferred quite freely over national borders as well as between municipal authorities all over Europe and North America.

The financial support by the city of Helsinki and by the state, was decisive with regards to acquiring the latest know-how. Experts from different fields were given funding to travel to conferences and exhibitions and to visit municipal centres. Starting in the 1920s a special fund was reserved in Helsinki's annual budget to be allocated to city officials who wanted to travel abroad in order to learn about the latest developments in their fields.

This period also coincides with Nokia's birth and early history (made possible by the second industrial revolution) and is seen to have begun during the late nineteenth century and to have accelerated in the beginning of the twentieth century. Nokia's history is rooted in the rubber industry and in milling wood pulp – the production of which was a part of the technical revolution in the paper industry. Consumption and use of paper and rubber goods spread fast and new industrial plants were built. Electricity and telephones became more common, thus creating the need for producing cables. At this time the management of Nokia was very international. In 1922, Nokia became a major shareholder in Oy Suomen Kaapelitehdas Ab (The Finnish Cable Factory), a company which had been using rubber from Gummitehdas for insulating its cables for electricity and telephone lines (Hoffman 1997: 290).

Rebuilding Helsinki, Design and Music

As mentioned above, the second period began in the late 1940s and continued up to the 1990s. During the 1950s Finland gained international acclaim in design. Much of this limelight was due to Helsinki, the site of the main training institutions as well as the major establishments of Finnish design in general and the ceramics and textile design in particular. Moreover, from the 1950s on we can also speak of Helsinki as a music city.

From the 1951 Milano Triennale, when Finnish Designers won no less than six Grand Prix, seven gold medals and eight silver medals, until the end of the 1960s Finland was considered internationally as one of the major players in the field of design. The foundation of this reputation gained in 1951 was further strengthened during the 1954 and 1957 Triennales, then considered the most prestigious design exhibitions in the world. Their success at these events even inspired some to calculate that Finnish artists were awarded 25 percent of the Grand Prix and that between 1951 and 1964 they were given on average about one fifth of the total number of awards. Names of such Helsinki based designers as Tapio Wirkkala, Timo Sarpaneva and Kai Franck became known not only among their compatriots and their foreign professional colleagues, but also among wider international audiences interested in design. In the 1960s they were followed by the fame gained by Marimekko textiles and by such young furniture designers as Antti Nurmesniemi and Eero Aarnio (Bell and Hietala 2002: 259–261).

A new period in the cultural life of Helsinki began in the spring of 1950, when the sport and hiking board of Helsinki City came up with an idea to organise a summertime art festival. The city government set up a committee to plan the festival.[4] The consultative committee reached the conclusion that Finnish music was the area of fine art which was world-famous and an object of interest particularly in the English-speaking world. The music festivals in Salzburg and Edinburgh as well as the Grieg music festival in Norway were models for the organisation of the Sibelius Weeks. National traditions and national myth were thus parts of an early politics of festivalisation in order to also attract an international audience. Similarly, the Swedes were also arranging theatre performances at Drottningholm castle and in the yard of Stockholm city hall. These Nordic cultural events also defined the schedule to the extent that the date of the Sibelius Weeks was determined to be June 13–19, 1951. The first Sibelius Weeks consisted of eight concerts, given by the Helsinki City Orchestra, Finnish Radio Orchestra, and Sibelius String Quartet. The programme included all of Sibelius' symphonies. Later in the 1950s, the Sibelius Weeks was extended to consist of twelve concerts. A measure of the international significance of the Sibelius Weeks is the number of international visitors arriving in Helsinki. The extensive radio broadcasting of the festival was an important means to distribute the content of the festival. In 1956, 30 foreign radio stations broadcasted the Sibelius Festival's programme and an estimated 250 million people listened in.[5]

In 1964, the organisers in Helsinki realised that the Sibelius Festival did not arouse sufficient interest among foreign tourists. There was also pressure to change it from the political left.[6] The numbers in the audience had been a disappointment. The organisers, therefore, wanted to extend the programme range to include more than just concerts i.e., the concerts were to be accompanied by other fields of art.[7] The organising committee paid attention to the festival's name, date, programme, and organisation. Their suggestion was that the festival be moved to autumn, and that the name be changed to Helsinki Festival. The valuable music traditions of the Sibelius Weeks were to be developed so that the festival would turn into an important overall survey of the entire Finnish art life, mainly performing arts, employing both Finnish and international artists. The Helsinki Festival's

4   The committee included representatives from the music board, the national radio, the Union of Finnish Composers, Finnish Musicians' Union, Finnish Tourist Society, Workers' Travel Union, and the Helsinki Society.
5   Sibelius Festival, Helsingin Sanomat May 26, 1957.
6   »Sibelius Festival Replaced by Helsinki Festival Committee – Report Delivered Yesterday«. Kansan Uutiset, June 3, 1964.
7   »Sibeliusveckan skall ersättas av festspel«. Hufvudstadsbladet, June 3, 1964.

organisers were pleased that the festival was being made more appealing to the masses. Today, the Helsinki Festival which takes place in August and September is the largest festival in Helsinki and a major part of it concentrates on locally produced music. The programme embraces classical music, jazz, rock and ethnic music. Usually the Helsinki Festival draws in around 300,000 visitors annually, around 250,000 of whom attend the free events.

Starting in the 1970s, music education, i.e., music schools or institutes for children and adolescents became a focus. In 2004 there were 14 of them with 5114 students. The Sibelius Academy which is the third largest classical music university in Europe offers subjects such as musical performance, musical pedagogies, church music, jazz and folk music. Several internationally acclaimed conductors belong to the Academy's alumni and some 1500 students are engaged yearly in its various master programs (City of Helsinki Urban Facts 1999: 10). There are three full-size Symphony orchestras in the metropolitan area of Helsinki, one professional chamber orchestra, the *Avanti!* chamber orchestra, the National Opera and a number of other ensembles, which together attracted a total of 433,166 concert goers in 2002. In addition, there is a conservatory for classical music and a pop-jazz conservatory. The Finnish Amateur Musician's Association alone has 50 choirs and over 2000 members in Helsinki. It is more difficult to know the exact number of rock bands and musicians in Helsinki, but there are 70 practice rooms for rent, each of which are being used by three or four bands (Cantell 2004).

Statistics do not usually cover the kind of commercial musical events that are on offer in Helsinki every weekend. However, according to a case study on musical events, during one weekend in April 2004 a total of 132 musical events were advertised in the Helsinki papers as taking place at various venues in the metropolitan area. Since 2002, Scandinavia's largest electronic music festival, the *Koneisto*, has been held in Helsinki at the Cable Factory, a large old industrial complex originally used by Nokia that was converted in the early 1990s into premises for artists and small firms working in the cultural economy sector. The old factory contains a large concert hall and several smaller venues and stages (Keskinen 2004).

Thus, the festivalisation of culture began in a celebration of nationalistic music events, using nationalistic composers such as Sibelius. Meanwhile, however, the cultural production has become much more diversified. It encompasses high culture as well as popular music and mirrors international music styles. In comparison to the previous phase, the cultural production in Finland during this period was not as reduced to nationalistic production.

IT-technology, Nokia and Examples of Cultural Consumption

During the last twenty years Helsinki, like many other European cities, has experienced a rapid transformation from an industrial city to a more or less service city as the service sector has increased tremendously. The end of the 1990s saw a brisk growth of Nokia's sales which went on to become the biggest and the most profitable Finnish company. Nokia became involved in electronics through its Helsinki-based cable arm, the Cable Factory (Suomen Kaapelitehdas), which had established an electronics department in 1960. This was auspicious timing as semiconductor technology was just making its way from the laboratories to industry. By the early 1960s the electronics department had become the sole import agent and support organisation in Finland for a number of well-known western computer manufacturers, such as the British Elliott, the French Bull (later Bull-General Electric), the German Siemens and the American Honeywell (Häikiö 2002: 54-56). The critical decision in Nokia's history was made in the 1970s, when Nokia entered into the production of digital telephone exchanges, the markets for which were remarkably larger than those for transmission equipment. The newly introduced integrated telephone network, made possible by digital technology, allowed opportunities, but also created pressure to expand into digital exchanges. Research in this field had already begun at the beginning of the 1970s and had led to the acquisition of a technology license from a leading European provider of digital exchange technology, France's CIT-ALCATEL, in 1976.

However, Nokia first became a world-class corporation in the 1990s. It was part of the so-called >third industrial revolution< in which digital telecommunications emerged as the primary engine of global economics (Häikiö 2002: 49; Bell and Hietala 2002: 344). Nokia's and Finland's success can be attributed to the phenomenon of an exponential increase of users when a new technology has made a breakthrough. This exponential growth occurred with two generations of cellular phones. However, in Nokia's operational environment four greater trends highlighted the late

1980s:»The most important was technological development, and particularly digitalisation, which now prevailed in electronics. Secondly, deregulation opened competition in the previously protected national markets. Thirdly, national borders opened as the European Economic Community evolved into the European Union and obstacles to free trade were gradually removed« (Häikiö 2002: 73). Additionally, in conjunction with these trends the economy badly overheated, especially in Finland where it qualified as a ›casino economy‹ at the end of 1980s. This resulted in pressure to make acquisitions and expand internationally. The eventual success of Finnish IT was the result of a quarter-century of technology policy. In the early 1990s, the Finnish government decided to raise research and development investments including in particular the establishment of the Science and Technology Policy Council and the Finnish Funding Agency for Technology (TEKES).

When looking at Nokia, which in fact started the Finnish technological revolution, we cannot overlook the unofficial groups of university students at the Helsinki University of Technology. Castells and Himanen call them hackers. They developed Erwise, the first web browser with a graphical user interface running on major Unix operating systems, two years before the introduction of Netscape. The development of the Finnish national network also depended on the efforts of young computer enthusiasts who, beginning in 1985, helped connect it to international networks. They also helped to develop it from being a mere tool for calculating capacity, used mainly by the academic community which had employed the FUNET network in Finland, into a social communication medium for the general public. According to Castells and Himanen, this process displayed innovativeness equal to that demonstrated by Nokia when they turned the mobile phone into an everyday tool.

The most famous Finnish software programme of all, the Linux operating system, was developed by Linus Torvalds in 1991 at the University of Helsinki, when he was 22 years old. The main concept was to make Linux as open-source operating system. Thousands of programmers have participated in the development of Linux. The most important innovation about Linux was social, openness, i.e. the full open-source model emulated the scientific model: it started with an individual who had a problem and published his or her first solution. Others who were interested in the same problem joined in solving it (Castells and Himanen 2002: 66–72; Bell and Hietala 2002: 354–357).

The rapid development of electronic media is based on the new technology and on a more liberal legislation. A working group appointed by the Ministry of Education has defined the arts and culture industry as a new umbrella concept for arts and culture and public media. In 2002 the aggregate turnover of cultural sector businesses in Helsinki amounted to 4.8 billion, which is 9.2 percent of the aggregate turnover in all industries in the city. When looking at jobs in the arts and cultural sector we find that these cover 8.5 percent of all jobs. The corresponding figure for the entire metropolitan area in late 2001 was 7 percent.

Background Factors for Innovativeness and Creativity in Helsinki

Cultural Policy and Public Authorities

The role of public authorities in Finland and in Helsinki has been crucial in advancing the latest developments in all sectors, including the cultural sector. The general rule in Finnish cultural policy is that municipalities carry responsibilities for public cultural services, whereas the state is in charge of supporting professional artists and art.

The Finnish and Helsinki system is very close to the German or Japanese state-guided centralized model. The state has had the long-term tradition of providing support especially for developing the latest technology. Since the 1990s, the Finnish Funding Agency for Technology and Innovations has funded innovative research and development projects in companies, universities and research institutes. Funding given by the state to high-level research in the universities in Helsinki and directly to R&D in Nokia has had an important role also in Nokia's success story.

During the earlier years Helsinki invested in the follow-up of the latest innovations by distributing money for its municipal officials and for experts of various fields. The policy of municipal authorities in Helsinki has helped to develop services especially on the cultural sector. Since 1984, Helsinki has hired out old schools or other buildings owned by the city in the eastern, western and north-eastern parts and given them to artists or built new municipal cultural centres. This is based on the concept of local democracy, according to which cultural services should be close by and accessible to local residents (Niemi 2004). For the Annantalo Arts Centre, the idea was to create a favourable atmosphere and conditions for children and adolescents in Helsinki to practice, experience and see arts and culture. The latest innovation in this field is the Artist House in Vuosaari, which was built by the Foundation for Helsinki's 450th anniversary. The house provides homes for 52 artists with their families as well as a creative milieu where people can meet each other and where common projects are planned and carried out (Susiluoto 2004). In principle, this is something researchers Castells, Sörlin, and Törnquist have expected from innovative environments.

The city of Helsinki provides considerable support for art institutions and artists. The City of Helsinki's Cultural and Library Committee is the country's second biggest provider of funds for arts and culture. The majority of allocations in 2003 granted for arts and culture went for professional theatres, for music, festivals and museums as well as various organisations for education.

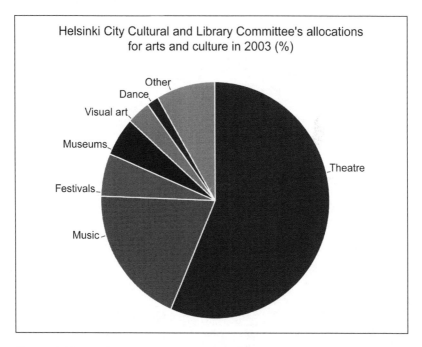

Helsinki City Cultural and Library Committee's allocations for arts and culture in 2003 (%)

Fig. 1: Helsinki City Cultural and Library Committee's Allocations forArts and Culture in 2003

(Source: City of Helsinki Cultural Office)

Education

A high level of education has contributed to the success of Helsinki and more for Finland in general (Dahlman et al. 2006; Hietala 2006). According to the censuses, in 1920, 94 percent of Helsinki people over the age of 15 were able to read and write. The number of literate women in Helsinki increased faster than that of men. Literate women outnumbered literate men for the first time in the census from 1900 (City of Helsinki Urban Facts 2000: 122–124). In Helsinki the strong emphasis on education, which is typical of Finns, was demonstrated by the establishment of secondary schools, which included the pioneering girls' and co-educational schools. These Helsinki schools also reflected the strong position of women in Finnish society[8] while also strengthening the reputation of schooling as one of the most important means of promoting upward social mobility. In addition, transferring innovations was facilitated by the weak barriers between social classes.

With regards to cultural education, the main point that needs to be emphasized is the concept of *free education* (i.e. without any fee) on all levels. That means that studying is also free of charge in three universities in Helsinki which specialize in arts and culture (the Sibelius Academy; the University of Arts and Design and the Theatre Academy of Finland). These three universities had a total enrolment of 3800 students in 2002. Competition for entry is hard; only six percent of applicants to these universities were accepted (Äikäs 2004).

Since 1999, Finnish law has stated that the basic education in arts and culture should above all give children the opportunity to develop their skills in self expression in a structured manner.

Quick Adaptation of the Latest Technology

It is often claimed that the Finns have a special skill for quickly adopting innovations, which is typical for small countries who are latecomers in terms of technology. The Finns were quick to adopt new technologies in the fields of gas, electricity and home appliances as well as GSM telephones and the internet in the 1990s. Similarly, Finland was one of the first

---

8   Manifested in the granting of universal suffrage in 1906, earlier than in any other European country.

countries in Europe to make use of electricity. Following the Paris Electrical Exhibition of August 1881, Edison lighting was installed in London, Paris and Strasbourg in January 1882, but by March it had also reached Tampere in Finland – two years before Berlin. In 1884 Helsinki obtained electric lighting only some six months later than Berlin and also quickly developed a dense telephone network. During the 1970s and 1980s the creativity and activity in adopting internet and software programming found at the University of Helsinki and at the University of Technology, showed exceptional innovativeness and enthusiasm from young students – for example, from Linus Torvalds, among others.

Democratic Traditions

During the autonomous period (1809–1917) and due to the reform of municipal administration in the 1860s, Helsinki also gained a more democratically elected city council. Helsinki was able to take advantage of technological innovations when endeavouring to develop the city to standards that were commonplace in such major European cities as Berlin, Paris and London – the reference group of most Helsinki decision-makers (Hietala 1987: 188–226; Bell and Hietala 2002: 93). This strategy seems typical of small countries and even a major country such as Japan has adopted a similar policy in following up the latest innovations.

To apply the terms used by Landry one can conclude that although Helsinki sometimes lacked a »hard infrastructure« for innovations, the city has always been teeming with the elements of a »soft infrastructure« (Landry 2000: 87–90). The renaissance of Finnish music from the 1960s onwards, for example, has had much to do with the simultaneous development of both hard and soft infrastructures throughout the whole country as well as the presence of a few pioneering music enthusiasts.

It is interesting to note how many of the significant innovations in Helsinki during the past two hundred years were the work of people who in their youth had encountered the challenge of foreign cultures whether by studying, working or inter-railing. Thus, emulation and national competition was one of the driving forces for high mobility as well as for the efforts to enhance Finnish innovativeness.

Conclusion

In this article I have analyzed three periods of the growth of the cultural sector in Helsinki. The role of public authorities in Helsinki has always been crucial in advancing the latest developments. During the first period from the end of nineteenth century to the First World War, strong nationalistic ideology was a common factor for Finnish artists, musicians, engineers and school teachers as well as for other experts of various fields. It was typical for Finland during this period that cultural production was exclusively a nationalistic production, contrary to cultural economies in other cities such as described by Simon Gunn for Manchester, where nationalistic considerations or aims did not play a role at all. Finns travelled widely, but returned back to Helsinki in order to build the city of their own and to contribute to Finnish culture. They formed official and unofficial groups and were strongly motivated to build a nation. During that time the main cultural institutions like theatres and libraries as well as schools were built. Strong national identity has been seen paradoxically as one of the major factors in explaining the international success of the Finnish modern IT society (Castells and Himanen 2002: 166–169). Thus, the combination of Finnish nationalism and international influences has to be mentioned if we aim to describe the cultural milieus of that time.

During the second period the role of public authorities was even stronger. They attempted to rebuild Helsinki and to market it for foreigners via the Olympic Games in 1952, the Sibelius Weeks and later the Helsinki Festivals. Their aim was to mark Helsinki on the maps of world. The 1950s was the decade of Finnish Design. Support by the state for export of Finnish Design was remarkable and designers like Tapio Wirkkala, Timo Sarpaneva and Kai Franck won medals at the Milano Triennale several times in the 1950s. The Sibelius Festival started a new epoch in Helsinki, followed by the Helsinki Festivals, which broadened the audience and programme of the event. Again, national traditions were crucial. Here, they were used in a politics of festivalisation in the hope that they would attract both national as well as international travellers.

During the third period, from the 1990s onwards, which we call the Finnish technological revolution, new forms of dissemination of culture were born. This is reflected in expenditures on consumption of culture and leisure and in different cultural sectors. Books, periodicals and newspapers received competition from equipments for reception, recording and reproduction of sounds and pictures. Remarkable activity and creativity was to be found not only in Nokia, but also among several unofficial groups of young students including Linus Torvalds one of the pioneers, who showed their skills in adapting the internet and in programming software. Cultural events spread to different cultural centres around the metropolitan area and with the support of the city of Helsinki, the range of culture received new forms and channels.

Summarizing the key factors behind Helsinki's success, investments in the cultural sector, e.g., music, art and libraries as well as the investment in education in all sectors played a crucial role in the success story of Helsinki. Furthermore, we cannot forget the strong position of women. Like their male counterparts women were eligible for scholarships for studying abroad and day care arrangements were setup to enable them to work. Also among the most important aspects was the following up of the latest know-how in service sectors, in technology and in the rationalisation of work. Other key factors included the promotion of mobility on all levels, which meant that not only executives, but also staff were given the opportunity to travel abroad.

Bibliography

Äikäs, Timo (2004). »Arts and Culture Education«. In City of Helsinki Urban Facts (ed.). *Arts and Culture in Helsinki, Vol. 2004:15*, 94–103. Helsinki.

Bell, Marjatta and Marjatta Hietala (2002). *Helsinki: The Innovative City. Historical Perspectives.* Helsinki.

Cantell, Timo (2004). »Helsinki as a Music City«. In City of Helsinki Urban Facts (ed.). *Arts and Culture in Helsinki, Vol. 2004:15*, 30–33. Helsinki.

Castells, Manuel (1996-98). *The Information Age. Economy, Society and Culture, Vol. 1-3. The Rise of the Network Society, The Power of Identity, End of Millenium.* Malden (Mass.).

Castells, Manuel and Pekka Himanen (2002). *The Information Society and the Welfare State. The Finnish Model.* Oxford.

City of Helsinki Urban Facts (ed.) (1999). *Arts and Culture in Helsinki, Vol. 1999:15.* Helsinki.

City of Helsinki Urban Facts (ed.) (2000). *Arts and Culture in Helsinki, Vol. 2000:15.* Helsinki.

City of Helsinki Urban Facts (ed.) (2004). *Arts and Culture in Helsinki, Vol. 2004:15.* Helsinki.

Dahlman, Carl J., Jorma Routti and Pekka Ylä-Anttila (2006). *Finland as a Knowledge Economy. Elements of Success and Lessons Learned.* New York.

— (2002). *The Rise of the Creative Class.* New York.

— (2005). *Cities and the Creative Class.* New York.

Häikiö, Martti (2002). *Nokia. The Inside Story.* Helsinki.

Hall, Peter (1998). *Cities in Civilisation. Culture, Innovation and Urban Order.* New York.

Hesmondhalgh, David and Andy C. Pratt (2005). »Cultural Industries and Cultural Policy«. *International Journal of Cultural Policy*, 11, 1, 1–13.

Hietala, Marjatta (1987). *Services and Urbanisation at the Turn of the Century. The Diffusion of Innovations.* Helsinki.

— (1992). *Innovaatioiden ja kansainvälistymisen vuosikymmenet. Tietoa, taitoa, asiantuntemusta: Helsinki eurooppalaisessa kehityksessä 1875–1917 I–III.* Helsinki.

— (2002). »Key Factors behind the innovativeness of Helsinki«. In *ESF Exploratory Workshop Berlin. December 12–14, 2002,* http://de.scientificcommons.org/17690970/.

— (2006). »*The Finnish Education System and its Role in Knowledge based, Innovation-driven Economy*«. http://info.worldbank.org/etools/docs/library/.

Hoffman, Kai (1997). *›Elinkeinot‹. Helsingin historia vuodesta 1945. 1. Väestö, kaupunkisuunnittelu ja asuminen.* Helsinki.

Keskinen, Vesa (2004). »Musical Events in Helsinki During a Spring Weekend in 2004«. In City of Helsinki Urban Facts (ed.). *Arts and Culture in Helsinki, Vol. 2004:15,* 34–37. Helsinki.

Konttinen, Riitta (2001). *Sammon takojat. Nuoren Suomen taiteilijat ja suomalaisuuden kuvat.* Helsinki.

Landry, Charles (2000). *The Creative City. A Toolkit for Urban Innovators.* London.

Maunula, Leena (1989). *Taideteollisuuden järjestäytymisen aika 1870–1910. Ars – Suomen taide 4.* Helsinki.

Mommaas, Hans (2004). »Cultural Clusters and Post-industrial City: Towards the Remapping of Urban Cultural Policy«. *Urban Studies*, 41, 3, 507–532.

Niemi, Irmeli (2004). »Neighbourhoods and cultural centres«. In City of Helsinki Urban Facts (ed.). *Arts and Culture in Helsinki, Vol. 2004:15,* 10–11. Helsinki.

Ringbom, Sixten (2000). *Symbolism, Synthetism and the Kalevala. Art in Finland. From the Middle Ages to the Present Day.* Helsinki.

Santagata, Walter (2005). »Creativity, fashion, and market behaviour. Cultural Industries and the Production of Culture«. In Dominic Power and Allen J. Scott (eds.). *Cultural Industries and the Production of Culture,* 75–90. London.

Sörlin, Sverker (1996). »Science and National Mobilisation in Sweden«. In Märtha Norrback and Kristiina Ranki (eds.). *University and Nation. The University and the Making of the Nation in Northern Europe in the 19th and 20th Centuries,* 31–41. Helsinki.

— (2002). *Cultivating the Places of Knowledge.* Stockholm.

Susiluoto, Saila (2004). »The Artist House in Vuosaari«. In City of Helsinki Urban Facts (ed.). *Arts and Culture in Helsinki, Vol. 2004:15,* 19. Helsinki.

What is the City but the People?
Creative Cities beyond the Hype

Gert-Jan Hospers

Introduction: The Hype of Creative Cities

If anything, the twenty-first century's economy is a knowledge economy. In the highly developed area of Western Europe knowledge has become a determining competitive factor, not only in the commercial world but also in regions and cities. Greater investments will have to be made in the knowledge economy if we wish to maintain present levels of European welfare (Cooke 2002). Development of knowledge, in fact, underlies new products, services and processes (innovations) that end up constituting the engine of economic progress. To express it in the words of the well-known economist Schumpeter: knowledge-intensive activities set off a process of ›creative destruction‹ whereby the existing disappears and something new is born (Schumpeter 1943). New knowledge can lead to a wide range of innovations, varying from breakthroughs in information technology, life sciences and nanotechnology (radical innovation) to small changes in everyday objects (incremental innovation).

However, where knowledge and innovation are concerned it does not necessarily have to be about new technologies; innovation is possible as well in the field of organisation, marketing and logistics, as for example the McDonald's fast food chain has demonstrated. Throughout the centuries knowledge and innovation have, of course, always played an important part in economic life – here we only need think of the steam engine that heralded the Industrial Revolution. But in contrast to earlier times, innovations follow one another much more quickly today (Cooke 2002; Rutten 2003). It is, for instance, estimated that between 1966 and 1990 there were as many innovations as between 1900 and 1966. And in a country such as the United States in 1999 more than half the economic growth came from activities that had scarcely, if at all, existed ten years previously. No company, region or city can hold itself aloof any longer from this ›knowledge race‹ and its economic consequences. In turn, policy makers struggle with the question how their locality can become a ›winner‹.

This article analyses in particular what the knowledge economy means for cities in the European Union. Fuelled by the work of urban guru Richard Florida cities are increasingly seen as the most suitable locations where knowledge, creativity and innovation flourish (Florida 2002; 2005). Especially in Europe this has led to the popularity of the concept of creative cities. In fact, the creative city is developing into a hype (Landry 2006). Mayors and aldermen of many cities, big and small, look for recipes how to implement the appealing message of the knowledge economy in their local context. In this paper, which is particularly written from such a policy perspective, we suggest that Europe's knowledge economy indeed asks for creative cities and supporting policies – but that there is much more to explore than Florida's hype. We rather see creative cities as phenomena of all ages and define them as competitive urban areas that are able to combine both concentration, diversity, instability as well as a positive image. After having discussed these elements we deal with the policy question what city authorities can do to create and reinforce them. Then the focus is on the experience of local authorities in two European areas – to wit Copenhagen/Malmö (Øresund) and Manchester – with targeted policy initiatives in the field of the knowledge economy. Finally we round off the article with brief conclusions and policy recommendations.

Cities in the European Knowledge Economy

The rise of the knowledge economy in Europe is closely linked to a structural trend in the world order familiar to all of us as ›globalisation‹. Globalisation is a far-reaching form of internationalisation that has slowly but surely led to a worldwide integration of spatially spread activities since the 1980s (Dicken 2003). The movement towards the European Union, the fall of the Berlin Wall, and with it the collapse of Communism, have led to an increasing belief in the advantages of free trade and the market mechanism. Indicators for the globalisation trend are the gradual disappearance of borders, the rise in exports and imports, an increase in foreign investments and the lively mobility of labour and capital. On the one hand the countries of Western Europe benefit from this development because companies have found new markets and investment opportunities abroad. On the other hand globalisation gives rise to new players competing against the West-European economy. The rise of areas where labour costs are far lower, such as Eastern Europe, South-East Asia and Latin America, has not only sharpened up international competition but has also changed its character radically (Krugman and Obstfeld 2003). It is no longer sufficient for highly developed countries such as Germany, Denmark and France to compete on the basis of cost; instead they have to draw their competitive advantage from knowledge-intensive and high-quality innovations. It is not only countries, large companies and employees – the ›knowledge workers‹ in Drucker's words – that are having trouble keeping their feet (Drucker 1999). The same applies to cities: they too have to ask themselves how they can compete in an intelligent manner in the globalised knowledge-based economy.

The consequences of the worldwide knowledge economy for cities are not immediately obvious. Some authors are pessimistic and see the growing increase in integration as a threat to the continuing existence of the traditional city. They point to the major effect of what are known as ›space-shrinking technologies‹, which have made the knowledge society and the global community possible (Dicken 2003). These are technologies that make the world smaller, as it were, such as transport technology (ever-faster planes and efficient logistic solutions) and information and communications technology (for instance e-mail, internet and i-mode). These technological developments are said to have done away with the role played by distance and proximity, and thus the requirement that knowledge workers should be positioned at a particular physical place. In the view of the pessimists the place where you happen to be is no longer of importance: all the world citizen needs is a good cable connection that puts the entire world within easy reach. The consequence of this ›death of distance‹ is said to be that the city of streets, squares, stations, shops and restaurants will be replaced by a ›city of bits‹, a virtual city with a street pattern consisting of digital ›information highways‹ (Mitchell 1995). Other writers are less pessimistic and see globalisation as an exceptional opportunity for cities. In order to develop new knowledge and the innovations it leads to, they believe that face-to-face contacts between people at a certain place remain of

GERT-JAN HOSPERS

crucial importance. New ideas and innovative solutions, in fact, come into being by intensive communication and exchange of knowledge with others. The proximity of people is a condition here, as the Silicon Valley success story demonstrates: it makes more sense for knowledge workers to pop into a colleague's office than to work via e-mail on a new project with an unknown person on the other side of the world (Saxenian 1994). In addition, people still have the need for physical contact with others not only in their work but also in their free time. And it is precisely the city, with its vibrance and range of pubs, cinemas and shopping centres that offers all the space required for this. How can we explain otherwise the fact that it is precisely innovative cities such as Stockholm, Barcelona, Munich, Toulouse, Dublin en Louvain that have blossomed in the world of the knowledge economy? The optimists then reply by saying that knowledge development, globalisation and vital cities do not need to be mutually exclusive. On the contrary: for the cities the knowledge economy means ›localisation‹ – the increasing importance of the local level and thus the city – rather than globalisation (Cooke and Morgan 1998). We can propose equally valid arguments for the views both of pessimists and of optimists. By way of compromise, let us agree that there is an apparent contradiction between cities and globalisation. In other words, we may be dealing here with a ›global-local paradox‹: it is precisely in a world that is becoming increasingly integrated that cities must lean more and more heavily on their specific local characteristics. These unique characteristics, indeed, determine that in which a city excels and in which it can distinguish itself in the competition with other cities in the knowledge economy.

The European knowledge economy and the related global-local paradox mean that cities, more than in the past, compete for the favours of inhabitants, companies and visitors. Here every city derives benefits by drawing in and binding to itself knowledge workers and knowledge-intensive activities. This is something from which a city can derive competitive advantage. And the battle for knowledge is being hard fought in Europe, a process caused partly by the advancing process of European integration: every city that wishes to have something of a high profile has its own university or institute of higher education, high-quality shops, a music centre or a renowned theatre. This similarity in the form of cities, demonstrated especially in a comparable range of facilities, knowledge institutions and cultural provisions, is seen in Europe particularly in the region known – because of its shape – as the ›Blue Banana‹ (Delamaide

WHAT IS THE CITY BUT THE PEOPLE? 357

1994). In this homogenous and prosperous region between Manchester and Milan the cities have come more and more to resemble one another over time. European convergence of this nature has major consequences. In fact it means that small details, such as the city's image, can be decisive in decisions taken by companies or individuals looking for a place to settle or to visit. In order to maintain and increase their attractiveness to knowledge workers and other target groups cities must reflect on what sort of profile they should have. For this a clear competitiveness strategy is required. If someone is free to choose, in the end it is the most attractive city that will win. The local parties involved in this process have to deal with a wide variety of questions. Which target groups should they focus on? What sorts of activities (culture, economy and/or leisure) should be employed in the strategy? How do they want their city to be known to the outside world? Providing answers to such questions requires a great deal of creativity on the part of city authorities, the local population and business community. Cities can hope to distinguish themselves from others only by finding creative solutions and in this way hope to beat the competition. In other words, the hefty inter-city competition for knowledge and innovation requires that they become so-called ›creative cities‹.

The Concept of Creative Cities

Though the world-wide knowledge economy may lead to a ›global village‹, we have just seen that this does not necessarily mean that the city is on its last legs. And what is more, paradoxically enough vital and innovative cities have the future in their hands. But cities – especially in Europe – will certainly have to defend and strengthen their competitiveness in order to ensure that they are not wiped off the map by their rivals. Clever and original strategies on a local scale are required for this. Cities that succeed in developing such strategies have the opportunity to grow to become competitive, creative cities. But what, in fact, are creative cities – and how can we recognise them? It should be stated from the outset that it is no simple task to indicate precisely what a creative city is (Simmie 2001; Hemel 2002; Landry 2006). This can be seen, for instance, in the book ›Cities in Civilisation‹ (1998) written by the famous English professor Sir Peter Hall (Hall 1998; Florida 2002). He shows that the creative city is a phenomenon that belongs to every era, but that no single city is always creative. In the course of history various types of creative cities existed: technological-innovative, cultural-intellectual, cultural-technological and technological-organisational cities. We will deal with them briefly in order to find out what the cities in the current European knowledge economy might be able to learn from their earlier colleagues.

Technological-innovative cities. For a start, we can find examples of technological-innovative cities in the past. Such places functioned as birthplaces for new technological developments or sometimes even for real technological revolutions. Generally only a few innovative entrepreneurs – ›new men‹, as Schumpeter calls them – were capable of causing the city to bloom by creating an atmosphere of collaboration, specialisation and innovation (Schumpeter 1912). A classic example of this type of technological-innovative city was Detroit, where Henry Ford and his Model T laid the foundations of the American automobile industry around 1900. Other examples are nineteenth-century Manchester (textiles), Glasgow (shipbuilding), the cities of the Ruhr (coal and steel) and Berlin (electricity). Technological-innovative cities of more recent date are to be found particularly in America's Silicon Valley (San Francisco and Palo Alto) and Cambridge, both of them Meccas of the information technology. Currently such ›technopoles‹ are the target to be aimed at for many European areas: simply the names such as Dommel Valley (Eindhoven), Silicon Glen (Scotland), Silicon Saxony (Dresden) show how much people hope to imitate the technological success of Silicon Valley.

Cultural-intellectual cities. Creativity in cultural-intellectual cities is of a totally different order from that found in technological-innovative cities. History shows that in ›soft‹ cities of this type culture (e.g. the figurative and performing arts) and science bloomed in a period of tension between the established conservative order and a small group of innovation-minded radicals. It is precisely that generation gap that produced creative reactions on the part of artists, philosophers and intellectuals. In its turn this ›creative revolution‹ again acted on outsiders as a magnet, outsiders who saw the cities as places where they could give free rein to their talents. By way of illustration we could call to mind the Athens of classical antiquity – the cradle of democracy – and Florence during the Renaissance. But also in seventeenth-century London (theatre) and Paris (painting), Vienna (science and art) and Berlin (theatre) in the early twentieth century are examples of cultural-intellectual cities. With a little goodwill we could also regard lively university cities such as Dublin, Heidelberg, Toulouse, Amsterdam and Louvain as contemporary European representatives of the cultural-intellectual city.

Cultural-technological cities. The third type of creative city is represented by the cultural-technological cities. In essence this type of city is a merger of the major characteristics of the two already referred to. In cultural-technological cities, in fact, technology and culture go hand in hand. In the past this has resulted in so-called ›cultural industries‹, such as the film industry in Hollywood (1920) and its Indian variant (Bollywood) in Bombay, the music branch in Memphis and the fashion (haute couture) industry in Paris and Milan. Examples of this sort of city in the 1990s are Manchester (New Wave music) and Leipzig after the fall of the Berlin Wall (multimedia). Moreover, we encounter cultural-technological elements in Amsterdam, not only during the city's Golden Age but also today (Amsterdam Osdorp) and in Rotterdam, a city chosen as European Capital of Culture in 2001 partly because of its architecture and film festival. Hall (1998) expects a great deal from this type in the twenty-first century. He particularly sees a golden future for places that combine internet and multimedia in an intelligent manner with culture, for instance in the form of virtual museum visits.

Technological-organisational cities. The last category is that of the technological-organisational cities. Such cities are creative to the extent that local actors have found original solutions to problems stemming from large-scale urban life. Here we can think of the supply of water for the population, the need for infrastructure, transport and housing. Examples of cities that shine in this type of ›urban innovation‹ are Rome under Caesar (aquaducts), nineteenth-century London and Paris (underground rail system), New York around 1900 (skyscrapers), post-war Stockholm (durable housing) and London in the 1980s (the re-structuring of the Docklands). Currently some European cities have shown that they have technological-organisational creativity at their disposal: here we are thinking of Tilburg (running the city as a company) and Rotterdam (revitalisation of the docks area with the Kop van Zuid). In contrast to the other types of creative city, in the technological-organisational cities it is mainly the government that goes to work in a creative fashion in collaboration with the local business community. In such cases we then speak of public-private collaboration.

Conditions for a Creative City

If history from the time of the ancient Greeks up to the present makes one thing clear, it is that *the* creative city does not exist. At first sight the Athens of Pericles, Manchester during the Industrial Revolution, film city Hollywood and the Rotterdam of the 1990s have little in common. But on closer inspection these cities can be seen to agree on one point: they were without exception breeding places of creativity, whether on the technological, cultural, intellectual or organisational level. It is impossible to predict where and when a creative city of this sort will come into existence. That is related to the essence of creativity: the capacity to think up original solutions to day-to-day problems and challenges. The creative mind sees what others see but thinks and does something different. The result is that existing ideas not previously linked together lead to an innovation. In the words of Schumpeter: creativity leads to *neue Kombinationen* (new combinations, Schumpeter 1912). An illustration of how creativity works is the invention of the bra (Jacobs 1969; Desrochers 2001). Mrs. Ida Rosenthal, a seamstress in a small shop in New York, did not like the way the dresses she made hung on her customers. In an attempt to improve the dresses' fit, she made improvements to underclothing. The result of that was the first brassiere. The customers liked the tailor-made bra with each dress they bought and soon came to the shop to ask for bras as such. Gradually, Mrs. Rosenthal dropped dress making, opened a workroom and devoted herself entirely to producing and selling bras. This example shows that creativity is not only human work but is surrounded by coincidence and unexpected circumstances. So it is an illusion to think that one can force creativity or ›construct‹ a knowledge-intensive city. And yet there are a few factors that can increase the chances of urban creativity developing and that thus can contribute to an urban knowledge economy. In general terms these factors are (1) concentration (2) diversity and (3) instability. The three elements are elaborated below.

Concentration. Urban creativity is first stimulated by the presence of a substantial number of people at a certain location. Concentration leads to the critical mass required for sufficient human interaction and communication. In the end, indeed, creativity, knowledge development and innovation are human work: not a city in itself but only its population can be innovative. The actual number of inhabitants in a city is, incidentally, a limited rule of thumb for defining concentration (Jacobs 1961; Landry 2000). Although in a city housing large number of people the chances of creative ideas emerging are greater, a large population is definitely not a requirement for creativity. A knowledge city *par excellence*, the Athens of classical times, contained at its peak something like 200,000 people, including slaves. And indeed, that is more people than live in a standard provincial town, but it is hardly represents the character of metropolis with which creative cities are often associated. Concentration is not so much a matter of the number of people but rather of the density of interaction. A dense concentration of people at a certain location favours frequent meetings and happenstance contact between individuals and thus makes new ideas and innovations more likely. As far as this is concerned we have no cause for complaint in Western Europe. The Netherlands, for example, is small and densely populated, so that it seems as if each Dutchman can meet the rest of the country.

Diversity. Diversity is the second factor that encourages urban creativity. Here we are talking about diversity in the widest meaning of the word: not just variation between the citizens, their knowledge and skills and the activities they pursue, but also variation in the image the city projects as far as buildings are concerned. Nobody has been as enthusiastic as the American publicist Jane Jacobs in propagating the notion of diversity as the fertile soil for creativity of cities (Jacobs 1961; 1969). In her eyes a city with a diverse population (families, entrepreneurs, artists, migrants, old people, students) can benefit from an equally varied set of skills and demands. In a city of this nature there is every possible opportunity for the inhabitants to meet one another on the street, swap knowledge, pick up new ideas and bring about innovations. The built-up environment can give an extra helping hand here: in a street with ›function mixing‹ – that is, a mix of buildings with differing functions (old buildings, new dwellings, offices, shops, churches, pubs and restaurants) – there is always something happening, day and night, and the chance of accidental encounters and Schumpeterian ›new combinations‹ the greater. In this way a city can, says Jacobs, develop into a real breeding place for entrepreneurship, creativity and innovation. In short: diversity leads to dynamism and thus to a flourishing city life.

Instability. Concentration and diversity of people at a certain location are not, however, sufficient to allow us to speak of a creative city. Some cities possess these essential ingredients and yet they are not creative. If we dip back into the past we notice that it is precisely in a period of crisis, confrontation and chaos that cities show the greatest creativity. Amsterdam around 1600, nineteenth-century Vienna, London and Paris as also Berlin between the two World Wars – they were all far from stable. Some see ›instability‹ as an extra condition for urban creativity. To clarify this vague and unpredictable factor – often referred to as ›bifurcation‹ – we can think in metaphorical terms of a river running off a mountain: if the river's fall is steep, the direction of flow is clearly defined (stable); but when the fall levels out and the river's situation becomes unstable – with the river ›hesitating‹, as it were, as to which direction to take (Buttimer 1983). It then takes very little to determine the further progress of the river. Like a river, a city can also find itself in a vulnerable situation and invite creativity. Small, chance events such as the meeting between a few creative and enterprising persons can then be of major influence on the way the city is to develop in the near future.

An example is Vienna during the *fin de siècle*. To be honest, Vienna today does not make a particularly strong impression of creativity on the unsuspecting tourist. A century ago things were different: the Austrian capital was *the* intellectual and artistic focus of Europe – in other words, the centre of the then knowledge economy (Francis 1985). In a relatively brief period (1890–1930) countless learned people and artists with a reputation, such as Wittgenstein (philosophy), Freud (psychology), Hertz (physics), Schumpeter (economics), Loos (architecture), Klimt (painting) and Kraus (political ideology) were present in the city. In the Vienna of the time we find all three conditions for creativity. The city was coloured by over-population, a rich public life and tight networks. All the academic institutes were within walking distance of one another, something that fostered communication and interaction between intellectuals working in a wide variety of disciplines. In addition the city was in a state of permanent political instability: the crumbling of the Austro-Hungarian Empire and the First World War were widely opposed by the population and provoked lively discussions and every type of creative expression (philosophical treatises, writings, works of art). But perhaps the most important background to Vienna's creativity around and after 1900 was the ›café factor‹: the countless *Kaffeehäuser* in the city, open from early in the morning till late at night, served as *the* meeting place of creative minds. In these cafés many *neue Kombinationen* were born over a cup of Wiener mélange.

The Role of Spatial Cognition

Above we saw that a creative city with opportunities in the knowledge economy is, whatever else, a densely populated and diverse city with sufficient opportunity for the happenstance to occur. A reasonably large number of cities in Europe match this profile. And yet not every city has an equal chance of growing into a creative knowledge city. Even if a particular location possesses the basic ingredients for creativity, in the end the place is creative only if recognised as such. This has everything to do with what psychologists call ›perception‹. Because people – whether they be citizens, entrepreneurs or tourists – do not know everything when they take decisions, they use whatever knowledge they may happen to possess. That knowledge is always selective and is formed out of experiences from the past and by outside sources, by information gleaned from the media, for instance. Using this perception, people construct for themselves an image of reality. The view we have of the world is therefore always coloured. And the image we have of a particular human settlement is also formed in this way. In this context geographers speak of ›spatial cognition‹: the knowledge people have of spatial unities such as regions and cities (Pred 1967; Gold and Ward 1994). That image is of major importance for the choices people make when deciding on where to work, live or spend their free time. Such decisions are not made on the basis of the objective characteristics of an area but on subjective grounds such as the perception people have of the area. The image summoned up in people by a particular region – in brief, its ›image‹ – has, in other words, a great deal of influence on the choice of a place to settle down.

Positive image. That which applies to areas in general also applies to cities in particular: unconsciously we all have a more or less well defined image of certain cities, whether based on correct information or prejudices. Research shows that a city's image is influenced in a positive manner by the extent to which the city is known, or ›unknown, unloved‹ and ›known, loved‹ (Anholt 2007). It would also seem that Einstein's famous statement (»It is easier to split an atom than a prejudice«) applies to the image forming of cities in the knowledge economy. This explains why metropolises such as New York and London – but also smaller cities, such as in the Dutch Randstad – are often seen by outsiders as more creative and innovative than they really are. At the same time, cities that are relatively unknown to the wider public, such as places in the German Ruhr Area and in

364   GERT-JAN HOSPERS

the Dutch regions of Twente and Zealand, have a traditional image, though all the ingredients necessary for creativity are present there. Here the past history of such regions often plays a decisive role. Which means that they have been burdened for years with a rural, traditional and dull – even negative – image. In promoting such urban areas as a knowledge regions, they will always lose out to cities in the Randstad that are already seen as ›cool‹. Thus, creative cities such as London, Paris, Berlin and Amsterdam can rest for years on the laurels gained in their creative past. Here we see a clear example of the ›Matthew effect‹, a phenomenon named after the old biblical principle: »For whosoever hath, to him shall be given [...] but whosoever hath not, from him shall be taken away even that he hath« (Matthew 13:12).

Most cities in Europe realise that apparently minor details such as the city's image can be decisive for (knowledge-intensive) companies who may wish to settle in the city and for people looking for a place to live or spend their holidays. A bad image perceived by one or more of these target groups can drive them away and mean a loss of income for the city. More and more cities are therefore finding it insufficient merely to invest in the provision of urban facilities: they make efforts to communicate their attractiveness and creativity inside and outside the city. This strategy of positive image-forming is known as ›city marketing‹ or ›branding‹. Currently it is a popular instrument which, it is hoped, will contribute to making the city known and to improving its reputation. Cities make extensive use of a headline-grabbing slogans and promotion campaigns to put themselves on the map. Though the effect of this city marketing is difficult to measure, it would seem that some cities really have succeeded in developing a ›strong brand‹ (Anholt 2007). There are examples of this throughout Europe, such as Hull, Birmingham, Glasgow, Dublin, Munich, Lille and Sevilla.

It is remarkable how little trouble cities throughout Europe take to distinguish themselves from their rivals (Hospers 2006a). For instance the Dutch cities of Delft, Enschede and Eindhoven have all adopted the profile of technology and knowledge cities – therefore qualifying themselves as ›creative cities‹ of the technological-innovative type – without placing any emphasis on their own uniqueness. The result of this herd behaviour can be easily guessed at: vague slogans imparting little information, such as ›Eindhoven: Leading in Technology‹ and ›Knowledge City‹ (Delft and Enschede). By giving themselves this sort of profile, none of the three cities make it clear how they differ from one another nor do they give any idea of what they have to offer to the knowledge worker looking for a place to work and live. In this way the three university cities undermine their own competitiveness: in fact, real competitive edge can be gained from building on and emphasising the local conditions – in other words, a strategy of ›trend through tradition‹.

That it is still possible to get a reputation as a relatively unknown city, shows the example of ›city marketing‹ in the Dutch city of Almere (Bulthuis and Patmos 1999). The ›geographical market research‹ commissioned by the city of Almere in the mid-1990s showed that the average Dutch citizen had little idea of what Almere was like. People usually came no further than descriptions such as ›dull new town‹ and ›city in the polder‹. The city authorities then decided that a large-scale marketing campaign was needed to tackle the image problem. The aim was particularly that of attracting new commercial activity to the city, since as far as population was concerned Almere had already reached the position of fastest growing city in the country. In order to establish the city's image as a centre of business activity the city council, aided by substantial financial support from the local business community, set up the *Stichting Stadspromotie Almere* (Foundation for the Promotion of the City of Almere). Under the slogan ›It's Really Possible in Almere‹ the organisation launched a promotion campaign which, apart from adverts placed in the national press, had an advertising spot on TV showing Almere inhabitants singing an urban anthem. Since then the foundation has pulled in large-scale events and projects within the city limits such as Holland Sand Sculpture and a branch of the World Trade Centre. The effectiveness of Almere's branding strategy weapon in the urban competition struggle can be seen from the problems that surrounding local councils such as Lelystad and Dronten are having in their efforts to put their own cities on the map. Almere was ahead of them and its strong brand image will help it to benefit for years to come from its ›first mover advantage‹.

The Role of Local Economic Policy

If anything has become clear from the above, it is that there is no recipe for cities in the European knowledge economy. There are various types of creative city, and even cities of the same type, such as technological-innovative and cultural-intellectual cities, show enormous differences. The Detroit of Henry Ford is, at first sight, difficult to compare with today's Palo Alto, and fourteenth-century Florence would appear to have little in common with the Dublin of today. Despite their differences, however, all creative cities possess a number of basic ingredients: a high concentration of people, a dose of happenstance and luck and – definitely not unimportant – a positive image familiar to the outside world. Local authority policy as an essential condition for urban creativity does not appear in this list because policymakers have played scarcely any part in the history of the birth of creative cities. It was only when a city had grown and problems were occurring, for instance in transport and housing, that the city authorities sometimes proposed creative solutions on the technological-organisational level. London and Paris, Stockholm and Rotterdam, for example, can thank the local authorities for their underground train systems and original housing projects respectively. At present, our cities are facing totally different problems, such as how to cope with maintaining their momentum on a global level in the inter-city knowledge race. In principle it ought to be possible for the authorities to come up with creative solutions in this case – even if the question of urban competitiveness is rather less tangible than the more fundamental problems that cities are used to wrestling with.

When making the city more attractive in the knowledge economy the local authorities can invest in the creativity of their own population. But a word of warning: creative cities cannot be constructed from the ground up. The roots of creativity, in fact, always lie in the existing, historically developed urban environment. In their enthusiasm, local authorities sometimes tend to forget this. Inspired by success stories such as Silicon Valley they hope to be able to make of their city a technopolis of similar stature. Terms such as Silicon Saxony (Dresden), Silicon Kashba (Istanbul) and Food Valley (Wageningen) speak volumes in this regard. That sort of copycat behaviour is, however, far from creative (Hospers 2006a). The local authority would do better to proceed from the city's specific characteristics, using them as a basis in the search for urban creativity (›localisation‹). This is not the same thing as blue print planning: local authorities will have to be content with measures designed to create conditions whereby they do no more than increase the chances of creative powers coming into existence. To start with, the authorities can contribute to increasing the critical mass of their city by seeking collaboration with a neighbouring city in the fields of infrastructural, educational and cultural facilities (inter-urban networking). It is also possible to increase the diversity of the city with targeted policies, for instance by mixing residential and working locations (function mixing) and removing obstacles to migrant entrepreneurs (ethnic entrepreneurship). Finally the city government can consider holding a major event or organising a new project, for instance a competition for the population or for the business community with the winner submitting the most creative proposal. Although this type of measure does not lead directly to urban creativity, it does increase the chances of it appearing.

In addition to creating conditions, the local authority can fulfil a useful role in promoting the city with a targeted ›branding strategy‹ (Van Ham 2001; Anholt 2007). A particular place may fulfil all the conditions for creativity but it is a creative city only when perceived as such by the outside world. Because the ›unknown, unloved‹ principle also applies to cities, local authorities would do well to invest in making the name of their city known and improving its reputation. It is of major importance that the authorities put out a realistic image of the city when branding it – in other words, project an image derived from and matching up with the specific context of the city in question. A small, sleepy, rural town that presents itself to the outside world as a cool technopolis tests credibility and is only treated as an object of derision. City marketing, it should also be said, is not a matter for the local authorities on their own. Work on a positive urban image requires collaboration on the part of the entire city, particularly entrepreneurs, of whom it can be expected that they have wide-ranging experience of marketing products to the people. Moreover local authorities and the business community have a common interest, namely that the city should remain attractive in the inter-city competition. One conurbation where a result-targeted and broadly supported branding strategy has borne fruit is the German Ruhr Area (Hospers 2004). In this ›Rust Belt‹ of coal and steel local parties have invested heavily in the integration of new technologies and trends into the existing local economic structure. Young, technologically high-value companies (›technostarters‹) are housed in former factories and warehouses. And the industrial heritage is being recycled as exhibition halls, concert halls or restaurants. These symbols underpin the Ruhr Area brand as a place where trend and tradition are not mutually exclusive but get along fine together. With campaigns such as ›The Ruhr Area: a Strong Piece of Germany‹ and ›The Ruhr Area is Hard to Beat‹ the local authorities and entrepreneurs have succeeded in dragging the traditional industrial area into the era of the modern knowledge economy.

Creative Cities: Two Case Study Examples

There are various interesting examples of cities where urban management has contributed to the rise of a local knowledge economy. Different authorities have had varying degrees of success in – for example – transplanting the success of the Silicon Valley towns to their own city. Sometimes it has succeeded, but the beckoning future of this Californian ›hot spot‹ has also led regularly to disappointments. The doom-laden example in this context is Akademgorodok in Russia (Castells and Hall 1994). This ›city of science‹ built in Siberia and based on the Silicon Valley model was, from its earliest beginnings in the 1950s, anything but knowledge-intensive and has been languishing for decades. The lesson to be learnt from ›great planning disasters‹ of this sort is that a local knowledge economy cannot be produced *ex nihilo*. Knowledge-intensive activity must always have a basis in the existing local economic structure or at least be able to find some sort of link-up there. In addition, clear vision, collaboration, an eye for practical details and good marketing are indispensable ingredients for the successful development of knowledge cities. At least, those are the most important lessons that we can draw from successful examples of local knowledge policy. By way of illustration, below we examine experience with ›creative city‹-policy in two European urban areas. Successively we deal with strategies applied in the Scandinavian Øresund (Copenhagen/Malmö) and the English city of Manchester. These cases do not only illustrate the factors leading to local economic success: they also make clear that urban policies to support the development of a local knowledge economy can have several faces.

Øresund: The Human Capital

The Øresund is a cross-border (Euregional) ›twin city‹, linking Copenhagen (Denmark) and Malmö (Sweden) together via a large bridge, the Øresund Link. Historically, the Øresund was the core of the Danish Kingdom, but since the peace of Roskilde (1660) that followed after the Swedish-Danish war, the Swedish part came under Swedish rule. Despite incidental negotations to foster Danish-Swedish contacts, it was only in the 1990s that more and more policy makers in the Øresund realised that increased cross-border cooperation could be beneficial for the region as a whole. Obviously, one of the aims was to create the critical mass needed for more urban creativity (Landry 2000). Although the Øresund with more than three million inhabitants is a region rather than a city as regards surface area, it can be regarded as a single urban knowledge area. It is the most densely populated agglomeration in Scandinavia.

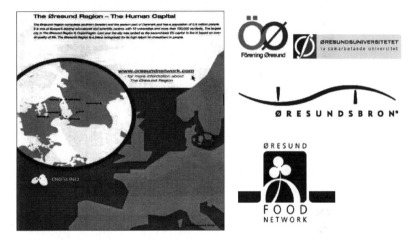

Fig. 1: Policy makers in the Øresund pay a lot of attention to place branding. Here we see a few logos used in the Øresund branding strategy.

(Source: Øresund Network)

Since the 1990s the location grew from a relatively traditional industrial area to become a true ›creative hub‹. The Øresund excels in ›health‹, i.e. all activities to do with health care (e.g. medical technology and life sciences). Next to London and Paris, the Øresund has already gained recognition as one of the top three ›hot spots‹ in Europe in this youthful branch of the knowledge economy (Hospers 2006b). Collaboration in medical matters has been practised on both sides of the border since the late 1980s, collaboration that was sealed in 1997 by the establishment of the Medicon Valley Academy, a joint venture between local medical technology companies, universities and hospitals. The project received extensive support from the EU because of its innovative character. Employment in the health sector in the Øresund has shown vigorous growth in the last few years, especially as regards technically high-flying jobs. This is partly because the conurbation has shown itself able to draw in an increasing number of knowledge-intensive foreign companies, particularly from the United States.

What is the background to the excellent economic achievements of the Øresund? In the few studies carried out to explain the development of the region, at least two success factors are identified: effective collaboration between local parties and a clear branding strategy (OECD 2003). Indeed, there are few places in Europe where government, education and commerce have operated so effectively in a united manner as in the Øresund. The Øresund Committee, with representatives from all the social parties, opted for the theme ›man and his needs‹ as regional spearhead. Under this banner the committee has invested in local economic diversity, in particular in a variety of facilities related to human needs, such as health (medical technology), contact with others (the Øresund Bridge) and recreation (varied supply of culture). The local parties realised that the presence of these elements was insufficient to place the region properly on the map – the Øresund did not have a real image yet. So they also worked on making the name of the Øresund familiar in Europe through a targeted branding strategy (Øresundsbro Konsortiet 2007), partly by creating a web page and producing marketing brochures. For this branding a special organisation has been called into existence, the Øresund Network. The network owns the rights of the trademark of the Øresund area comprising a graphic profile, logotype (the typical Scandinavian ›Ø‹) and a number of messages that can be used in the marketing of the area. Meanwhile, many Danish and Swedish companies and public organisations have become member of the Øresund Identity Network. Thus, they have free access to the regional logotype that can be used for their own marketing efforts. Moreover, the media the region has been actively promoted as ›The Human Capital‹ – note the double meaning – where it is good to live, work and take recreation. And even though it may be difficult to measure the effect of the branding strategy, one gets the impression that this localised approach to the Øresund has not left its creators empty-handed (Hospers 2006b). After almost 350 years the Øresund is slowly but surely re-uniting itself.

Manchester: Original and Modern

Manchester, an agglomeration of about three million people in the North-West of England, can be proud of its glorious past: it was the cradle of the Industrial Revolution. In the eighteenth century it was the textiles capital of the world and as such the city can be called an example of a >classic industrial metroplis< (Zimmermann 2000). However, the first industrial city, in which half of the workforce used to work in manufacturing, was also the first place that has experienced massive de-industrialisation. Since the 1960s onwards factories closed, workers were fired and the city entered into a heavy economic crisis. Due to a lack of sectoral diversity it was hard to find local Schumpeterian >new combinations< of trend and tradition that could help to rejuvenate the Mancunian economy. With the establishment of the Central Manchester Development Corporation in 1986 however a new strategic tool was employed in an attempt to restructure the economy, namely public-private partnership (PPP). Thanks to this cooperative strategy in which the private and public sector join forces major redevelopment projects in the city could be realised relatively rapidly. Examples of such succesful PPP-projects were the Central Station, the first phase of Metrolink, the creation of Manchester's inward investment agency MIDAS and the opening of the Urbis-museum. Ironically, the explosion of an IRA-bomb in 1996, which devastated the Vicorian city centre, paved the way for the local authorities to rebuild Manchester's heart as well and to develop a new image of the city from scratch (Peck and Ward 2002). Over the years, the economy of Manchester has improved. Less than one-fifth of the city's workers are employed in factories now; most of them work in service occupations, although these are often relatively low-paid retail, personal-service and clerical jobs. However, business in Manchester is doing well: it is the fastest growing municipality outside London (Manchester City Council 2007). In the 1990s the City Council also established Marketing Manchester to promote the >new< Manchester. The branding campaign this body developed around the slogan >We're up and going< was heavily critized, mainly by a group calling itself >The McEnroe Group< (after the famous tennisplayer McEnroe who used to say »You cannot be serious«). One of the dissenters was the Mancunian designer Peter Saville, who ultimately took up the challenge to try better: the Manchester City Council appointed him in 2004 as Manchester's city brander.

Fig. 2: Manchester brands itself also in the city centre itself. Here we see banners that should reflect the ›original and modern‹ image of Manchester

(Source: Photography by Albert Square)

Recently, Peter Saville – officially entitled ›Manchester's Creative Director‹ – has launched a new branding campaign for Manchester with ›original modern‹ as the organising concept (Manchester City Council 2007). This concept, which is meant to be more than a marketing slogan, draws on the industrial tradition of the city, but simultaneously tries to make clear that Manchester has shifted from an *industrial* city to an industrial *city*. According to Saville in an interview with researcher O'Connor (2006): »Manchester is a city concerned with the now. It knows it has a history, but it's not historically minded. Originality and modernity are values characteristic of Manchester, values which the city has epitomised. Original and modern thinking built it. My vision for the brand was the pursuit of the original and modern in this century« (Saville, cited in O'Connor 2006). The relevant city authories have greeted the new branding strategy of Manchester with open arms. For example, Manchester Knowledge Capital, a public-private partnership aimed at the promotion of the local knowledge economy, now makes use of the branding concept to stimulate creativity and innovation in Mancunian neighbourhoods. In its policy the platform puts emphasis on ›real world science‹ rather than ›rocket science‹: for a local knowledge economy to develop, it is important that many people are involved rather than a small group of scientists. To stir up enthusiasm among the public Manchester Knowledge Capital has started the Innovation Investment Fund that supports each Mancunian citizen with a realistic and feasible innovative idea. In this way, Manchester's authorities hope to attain the critical mass needed for the whole city to become creative.

Conclusion: Giving Coincidence a Hand

In the European knowledge economy cities still hold the future. History teaches us that cities are the places *par excellence* where knowledge, creativity and innovation reach full maturity. But not every city has unquestionably good prospects in the knowledge economy. In the end the cities that will win the inter-city knowledge race are the ›creative cities‹. These are cities that possess not only sufficient concentration, diversity and instability, but also project a matching image based on innovation and modernity. For the rest, the success of cities in the knowledge economy remains a question of human effort and happenstance. This somewhat fatalistic conclusion does not mean that cities can simply rely on fate and afford to adopt a passive attitude. On the contrary: certainly in the current inter-city competitive race it will be precisely its creative powers that a city will need to bring into play. But the unpredictability surrounding creativity and innovation means that a tailor-made, unambiguous creative competitive strategy for cities in the knowledge economy is simply not available. The only thing the authorities can do, in collaboration with local parties, is to increase the chances of creativity coming into being. In principle this is possible if certain conditions are created and investments are made to make the city's name known to outsiders. But success here is not assured. Local authorities wishing to give their city a place in the European knowledge economy will have to be content with the fact that they can only give chance a helping hand. Perhaps the famous chemist Louis Pasteur, an unrivalled ›knowledge worker‹, best expressed what a realistic urban knowledge strategy should be. When he was asked how he arrived at his creative discoveries and innovations, he said: »Chance favours only the prepared mind« (cited in Florida 2002). Similarly, the English writer and free spirit William Shakespeare was right when he asserted »What is the city but the people?« (Shakespeare, cited in

Halliday 1964). Both statements suggest what ultimately makes up a creative city: a fertile ground for happenchance and human creativity. If policymakers take this notion into account, cities indeed may have a large role to play in the European knowledge economy.

Bibliography

Ajuntament de Barcelona (2000). *City of Barcelona*. Barcelona.

Andersson, Åke. (1985). »Creativity and regional development«. *Papers of the Regional Science Association*, 56, 5–20.

Anholt, Simon (2007). *Competitive Identity: The New Brand Management of Nations, Cities and Regions*. New York.

Bulthuis, J. H. And J. H. A. Padmos (1999). *Regionale Beeldvorming* (in Dutch). Amsterdam.

Buttimer, Anne (1983). *Creativity and Context*. Lund.

Castells, Manuel and Peter Hall (1994). *Technopoles of the World: The Making of Twenty-First Industrial Complexes*. London.

Cooke, Philip and K. Morgan (1998). *The Associational Economy: Firms, Regions and Innovation*. Oxford.

Cooke, Philip (2002). *Knowledge Economies: Clusters, Learning and Cooperative Advantage*. London.

Delamaide, Darrell (1994). *The New Superregions of Europe*. New York.

Desrochers, Pierre (2001). »Local diversity, human creativity, and technological innovation«. *Growth and Change*, 32, 369–394.

Dicken, Peter (2003). *Global Shift: Reshaping the Global Economic Map in the 21st Century*, 4th edition. London.

Drucker, Peter (1999). *Management Challenges for the 21st Century*. New York.

Florida, Richard (2002). *The Rise of the Creative Class and how it's Transforming Work, Leisure, Community and Everyday Life*. New York.

— (2005). *Cities and the Creative Class*. New York.

Francis, Mark (ed.) (1985). *The Viennese Enlightenment*. London.

Gold, John R. and S. V. Ward (1994). *Place Promotion: The Use of Publicity and Marketing to Sell Towns and Regions*. Chichester.

Hall, Peter (1998). *Cities in Civilisation*. London.

Halliday, F. E. (1964). *A Shakespeare Companion 1564–1964*. Baltimore.

Hemel, Zef (2002). *Creative Cities!* The Hague.

Hospers, Gert-Jan (2004). »Restructuring Europe's Rustbelt: the case of the German Ruhrgebiet«. *Intereconomics: Review of European Economic Policy*, 39, 147–156.

— (2006a). »Silicon Somewhere? Assessing the usefulness of best practices in regional policy«. *Policy Studies*, 27, 1–15.

— (2006b). »Borders, bridges and branding: the transformation of the Øresund Region into an imagined space«. *European Planning Studies*, 14, 1023–1041.

Jacobs, Jane (1961). *The Death and Life of Great American Cities*. New York.

— (1969). *The Economy of Cities*. New York.

Krugman, Paul and M. Obstfeld (2003). *International Economics: Theory and Policy*, 6th edition. Boston.

Landry, Charles (2000). *The Creative City: A Toolkit for Uban Innovators*. London.

— (2006). *The Art of City Making*. London.

Manchester City Council (2007). *Manchester Edition*. Manchester.

Mitchell, William. J. (1995). *City of Bits: Space, Place and the infobahn*. Cambridge, Mass.

O'Connor, Justin (2006). »Creative cities: the role of creative industries in regeneration«. *Power Point Presentation, University of Leeds*, Leeds.

Øresundsbro Konsortiet (2007). *Facts Worth Knowing about the Øresund*. Copenhagen

Peck, Jamie and K. Ward (2002). *City of Revolution: Restructuring Manchester*. Manchester.

Pred, Allan R. (1967). *Behaviour and Location: Foundations for a Geographic and Dynamic Location Theory: Part 1*. Lund.

Revilla Diez, Javier, M. Fisher, F. Snickars and A. Varga (2001). *Metropolitan Systems of Innovation: Theory and Evidence from Three Metropolitan Regions in Europe*. Berlin.

Rutten, Roel (2003). *Knowledge and Innovation in Regional Industry: An Entrepreneurial Coalition*. London.

Saxenian, AnnLee (1994). *Regional Advantage: Culture and Competition in Silicon Valley and Route 128*. Cambridge, Mass.

Schumpeter, Joseph. A. (1912). *Die Theorie der Wirtschaftlichen Entwicklung*. Leipzig.

— (1943). *Capitalism, Socialism and Democracy*. London.

Simmie, J. (ed.) (2001). *Innovative Cities*. London.

Zimmermann, Clemens (2000). *Die Zeit der Metropolen: Urbanisierung und Großstadtentwicklung*. 2nd edition. Frankfurt am Main.

5   Creative Milieus in the Late
     Twentieth and the Twentyfirst
     Century and the Question of Failure

Creative Milieus: Concepts and Failures[1]

Birgit Metzger

In the current discussion about creativity and cities, various terms and concepts are used to highlight – often in an affirmative and enthusiastic way – the interdependence of creativity, culture, urban space, an urban way of life, and economic success. Such terms, as for example »creative city«, »creative industries«, »cultural industries«, »creative class«, and »creative milieu« are situated in a debate which is concerned with the emergence of creative dynamics, and how they are influenced by spatial proximity. The increasing interest in this topic should be seen in the context of the current, more general debates concerning globalisation and its implications, as well as a dramatic structural change in the economy and the society of industrialised countries since the 1970s. One principal issue in the debate about globalisation is the relevance of space and place in an increasingly politically and economically interwoven, as well as medially connected world (Beck 1998; Robertson 1998). Concerning the debate on structural change, it is often taken for granted that creativity and knowledge are more important than ever before in the post-modern world, especially in terms of economics. Consequently, this change is interpreted as being the development of a »knowledge society« or the development of an »economy of signs« (Lash and Urry 1994; Stehr 1994:171 f, 2001; Hartley 2005). One effect of these discussions was that *space* and *place*, as well as *creativity* and *knowledge* were re-introduced as central themes into scientific research, and were subsequently challenged as categories in different disciplines (Löw 2001; Osterhammel and Peterson 2003; Burke 2001; Vogel 2004: 639–644).

---

1 This article is a shorter version of my diploma thesis that I wrote between January and September 2006 at the Department of History at Saarland University, Saarbrücken. The title of the thesis is: *Kreative Milieus in der Stadt, Geschichte und Gegenwart. Chinatown an der Saar?* Furthermore, this article extends the idea of not so successful creative milieus.

In the context of the mentioned debates, the concepts of *creative milieus,* and/or of *creative environments,* have gained a certain degree of popularity among researchers. In historical and social research, »creative milieu« is generally used as a descriptive term referring to phenomena which are assumed to be creative in one way or another. However, when researchers are talking or writing about creative milieus they often refer to slightly different things. Some researchers talk about the arts in a broad way of meaning; others talk about cultural industries, others about science, knowledge, or technology. Also what is described as a *milieu* differs: some describe groups of people as creative milieus, others address places in which creativity can be found, others whole cities, and again others ascribe a more or less mysterious atmosphere to creativity. Altogether the use of the term is often vague and imprecise. In this field of historical and social research, theoretical and conceptual reflection is a desideratum (Ash 2000; Heßler 2002: 194–195; Matthiesen 2004).

However, in other disciplines there are more elaborate concepts regarding creative milieus. If we focus on the interrelations of culture, creativity, the role of space and place, the significance of the city and the economy, the most interesting concepts can be found in geography and economics. One concept that should be regarded in more detail was developed by the *Groupe de Recherche sur les Milieux Innovateurs* (GREMI), an international research group. This concept accounts for the emergence of creativity by appeal to synergies arising from dense communication and cooperation networks in spatial proximity. Both, GREMI's concept and the concept of (neo-)*bohemia,* which focuses on cultural milieus in cities, will be discussed furthermore in part 2.

The principal objective of this text is to contribute to a more precise terminology, and to a better systematisation of the concept of *creative milieus* in historical and social research. Therefore, the following analysis will firstly take a closer look at the concepts of creativity, milieu, and the city. I will argue that, if used in its original meaning, the concept *creative milieu* is well-suited to describe the interrelations between creative dynamics, urbanity, space, and place. Secondly, this essay will discuss two concepts that seem to be suited in a combined perspective to analyse more systematically cultural creative milieus in the city including their economic impact. Thirdly, I will employ the previously mentioned analytical instruments in a concrete case: the *Nauwieser Viertel* in the southwest German town of Saarbrücken. As we will see, the example of the *Nauwieser Viertel* can be interpreted as being a moderately successful creative milieu. This example will be used to test the concept of creative milieus more broadly, and in turn, it raises the question of success and/or failure of a milieu. This question is more or less neglected by publications in this field of research. It is often taken for granted, that the city is a preferred or even the best place for the rise and flow of creative dynamics. Moreover, social and geographical contributions claim that creativity comprises economic development (for example Florida 2004: Xiii; Hartley 2005: 2 Scott 2000: X). Consequently, research mainly focuses on success-stories of *creative milieus*. The tendency to write only a history of success has often been criticised by historians. For example, research on the history of technology has shown that we must also examine failures if we want to be able to understand the complex conditions of success (compare König 1984; Fremdling 1983; Mathieu 2004). Through an analysis of the *Nauwieser Viertel,* this essay may assist to challenge the myth of creative milieus and cultural economies.

Creativity, Milieu, and the City

In the following paragraphs, I will illustrate that in the areas of dense communication and cooperation, as well as diversity and heterogeneity, the concepts of creativity, milieu, and urbanity overlap.

Creativity

Generally, the term »creativity« signifies the ability to think and act in an inventive and constructive way. Creativity occurs in multiple places and fields of human activity, for instance in scientific research, politics, techniques, as well as culture including art and social life. In the narrower sense of »creativity«, the term applies solely to the field of artistic activity (for a summary about creativity research see Funke 2000, detailed Sternberg 1999).

Fundamentally, creativity is understood as an individual ability. Historically, it was for a long time considered to be an exceptional ability of cer-

tain individuals, of so-called geniuses (Schmidt 1985).[2] Not before the
1950s, creativity was understood as describing a more common, everyday
phenomenon and was systematically examined. In more recent research,
the idea that creativity is not merely a result of individual abilities, but also
a product of the creative individual's interaction with his or her social,
cultural and physical environment has gained increasing attention (Csikszentmihalyi 1999). The influence of the environment in relation to the
creative process is also a focal point in this text.

Recent research divides creativity into different phases. First, the examination of the environment in which a problem is perceived; second, the
emergence of an idea; third the elaboration of the idea, and fourth its realisation. During each phase the environment has a specific influence on the
process. The social, cultural, and physical environment constitute the starting point of each creative process – there is always a point of reference to
what previously exists. The environment also provides the concrete conditions in which creativity may take place. The potential for inventions and
for new experiences depends on how much »free space« a society allows
for new ideas. This is especially important since it is broadly accepted that
divergent thinking, an independent mind, flexibility, and nonconformity
are conducive to creativity (Jung 1993; Funke 2000: 289–291). Psychological research and historical examples show that both encouragement and
challenging tasks are beneficial for creativity (Brix and Janik 1993a). Furthermore, the environment provides the resources and capabilities which
are necessary to implement an invention. Implementation is a critical factor
and should not be overlooked. While »invention« may refer to nothing but
an original idea, the term »innovation« implies that the idea is at least partly
implemented or socially accepted (Csikszentmihalyi 1999: 314; Funke 2000:
288–289). Ultimately what may or may not be considered creative depends
on the social environment.

The relevance of communication for the development of creativity is
another point discussed in recent research. An important mode of creativity is the new combination of already established elements, or the transfer
of ideas and knowledge from one context to another. So, one could argue
that communication in-between individuals that have access to different
fields of knowledge, or different cultural (sub)-systems, is favourable to
creativity. Historical examples show that innovations and inventions occur

---

2   This should also be understood with respect to the philosophical understanding of
     aesthetics as a method of acquiring knowledge.

frequently in places where a crossover of different traditions and cultures is possible (Funke 2000: 292; Csikszentmihalyi 1999: 318–319; Brix and Janik 1993b). In this context, an interesting question is whether the appropriation of ideas already known elsewhere could be characterised as a creative act. In the narrower sense of creativity it could not, for creativity is understood as the invention of something completely original. However, examples show that the adoption of a phenomenon in another local or cultural context may constitute a creative process; for instance in the history of colonisation, and more recently with respect to the development of popular culture. In the majority of cases, a phenomenon is not just repeated, but also converted and modified to a respective context (see for examples Schulte 2006).

So, one hypothesis would be that cultural diversity can stimulate and enhance creativity.

Milieu

In the present, the concept *milieu* is usually used to refer to social groups. However, the etymology of the concept refers to many different dimensions (very sound and detailed Spitzer 1942). The word »milieu«, which means middle, medium and environment, was adopted from the French language. Its original significance – which can be traced back to the ancient Greeks – included a spatial meaning referring to space, the sky, air and atmosphere. It was not until the eighteenth and nineteenth century, when the concept of a *milieu* was utilized by the emerging faculty of social studies,[3] that the spatial connotations of the term »milieu« gradually disappeared while its reference to social groups became dominant. Currently, it is debated to what extent in the post-modern world, the affiliation of a person with a milieu depends on his or her subjective choice (Schulze 1993), and to what extent it depends on social and economic structures nonetheless (Bourdieu 1982, for current research on milieu see Georg 2002; Keim 1997; Matthiesen 1998).

For the objective of this text, the following issues are of special interest: First, the term »milieu« refers to the social, as well as to the physical environment, and has an explicit spatial meaning. Second, in one sense, »mi-

---

3   Influential for the modern understanding of »milieu« were the writings of: Montesquieu, Balzac, Comte, Taine, Durkheim (Spitzer 1942).

lieu« applies to social groups which are integrated by certain common beliefs about the world, common social practices and collectively shared knowledge. Usually these social groups are characterised by shared interaction and communication networks. Third, it is likely that belonging to a milieu partially depends on social structures, but also on individual choices (Keim 1997: 387–399).

The City

Some points conducive to creativity that I mentioned before seem to coincide with the characteristics of the modern city. Heterogeneity, diversity and a dense net of communication and interaction are well-known attributes of the modern city (classic: Simmel 1995, a current discussion about cities and their characteristics: Läpple 2004; Johanek and Post 2004), as well as favourable elements for creativity. Another characteristic of the city that could be favourable to creativity is its function as a centre. In cities, the concentration of institutions such as universities, libraries, marketplaces, government buildings and religious orders contributes to a compilation, as well as an exchange of knowledge and ideas. Furthermore, cities are considered to be more liberal and more open minded than rural areas; the concept of the city has always had a progressive connotation (Lindner 2000; Häußermann and Siebel 1987: 238–250; Göschel and Kirchberg 1998; Heit 2004: 12). Anonymous, diversified, unstructured, confusing, and less socially controlled, the city can be assumed to provide more leeway than rural areas for experiments, as well as it encourages favourable environments for new ideas to be conceived and adopted. It also should be noted, that political and social problems which are characteristic of a certain historical period tend to cumulate in cities. This can be seen to pose a challenge, which is again favourable to creativity.

All things considered, the term »creative milieu« can be used (a) to designate an environment which is favourable to the emergence of creativity and (b) to describe creative groups of people which share common practices and beliefs. A concept of creative milieus should include the notion of creativity as a communicative process, and should take into account that people's social, cultural and physical environment are integrative parts of the creative process. Even if we just go by the meaning of the term »creative milieu«, the city seems to be a favourable place for creativity.

In addition to these general statements, we should also consider that creativity occurs in various fields of human activity, and therefore there could be different types of milieus. The following paragraphs will firstly discuss a more general concept of creative milieus; correspondingly a concept of cultural creative milieus will then be specified.

A Concept of Creative Milieus

Concepts of creative milieus can be found in different disciplines and fields of research belonging to different traditions of thinking. For example, in the history of art, the French philosopher and art historian, *Hyppolite Adolphe Taine,* developed an influential although deterministic concept of artistic milieus (Taine 1882: 227–237; for a discussion see Hall 1998: 15–16; Spitzer 1942: 177). In the sociology of knowledge, *Ludwik Fleck's* concept of *thought collectives* (*Denkkollektive*) could be interpreted as an approach to creative milieus, insofar as it deals with the genesis of new ideas and knowledge through communicative and social processes (Fleck 1980).

However, these concepts do not adequately address what is of interest here: the role of the environment as social or historic context, or as space and place, the significance of the city and the economy. The interdependences of space, communication, and creativity have been picked up as a central theme by economists and geographers since the 1970s. At this time, particular innovative dynamics and economic efforts were observed in some regions, for example *Third Italy*[4] or Silicon Valley. Against the background of the aforementioned debates about globalisation, the importance of place and space, and the supposed new importance of creativity, these regions attracted the interest of researchers. Different concepts and theories about creativity, communication, the environment, and economic success resulted, as for example the concepts of *industrial districts, flexible*

---

4   A region in Italy located east of Lombardy and in the regions of Veneto and Toscana, which was characterised by a group of small enterprises especially within the textile sector. It was called »Third Italy« because the productions system differed clearly from the older industrial systems of Lombardy and Piemont on the one hand and the agrarian South on the other (Klaus 2006: 29).

specialisation, regional networking, learning regions, and *creative milieus* (for an overview regarding the different concepts see Storper 1997, 2004). A shared feature of these concepts is the reference to the spatial clustering of companies and the resulting synergies.

Within this context of mainly economy- and policy-orientated research, the theoretical approach developed by the *Groupe de Recherche sur les Milieux Innovateurs* (GREMI) seems especially interesting for our purpose. This concept differs from other economic and geographic conceptions insofar as it exhibits an advantageous focus on cultural and social elements. Furthermore, it seems to constitute the most elaborated and well-tried analytic tool for researching creative milieus as of now (for an overview see Crevoisier 2000, 2001).

According to GREMI, creative milieus are sets or complex networks »of mainly informal social relationships within a limited geographical area, often determining a specific external ›image‹ and a specific internal ›representation‹ and a sense of belonging, which enhance the local innovative capability through synergetic and collective learning processes« (Camagni 1991: 3). It is the frequent communication and interaction between agents that are integrated in a similar way as a social milieu in spatial proximity, which is considered favourable to creative dynamics. The underlying assumption is that face-to-face communication, informal contacts and a kind of a shared common ground are crucial for the transfer of knowledge and synergies. The other critical idea is that spatial proximity and the specific characteristics of a place influence the constitution of a milieu and are favourable for communication networks and informal contacts. The local presents a common point of reference which is essential for mutual understanding and thus for communication and knowledge transfer (especially tacit knowledge transfer).[5]

There are some key points that make the GREMI-conception worth further consideration. First, this approach corresponds to the requirements developed in the first chapter: Creativity is considered as a communicative process; the environment is included as an integral part of the creative process. Space is not seen as a mere container, but as an entity that is socially and historically constituted and thus influences the milieu. The appropriated place of a milieu also constitutes a lasting structure in time,

---

5 Underlying this theory is the assumption that knowledge is context-specific, i.e. sense and understanding are always dependent upon a specific context (Gertler 2003: 75–99, Freundt 2003: 20).

which provides a sort of continuity in the development of the milieu (Crevoisier 2000: 7, 2001: 255).

Most important for our objective is, that this approach seems to be suited to historicisation, although this was not GREMI's concern. The milieu itself is seen as a historical phenomenon that changes through time and is a product of human actions. The categories of principal agents and the relationships between them including cooperation and competition, trust-building, integrative and identity-building structures can be applied to earlier periods in history. In contrast to traditional economic theories, the agents of the milieu are not assumed to be completely rational (Fromhold-Eisebith 1999). However, GREMI's concept does not address the fact that a milieu is always situated in a broader historical context. From a historian's perspective, a stronger emphasis ought to be placed on this aspect.

Furthermore, in its combined perspective of economic and cultural dimensions, the GREMI concept provides the possibility to introduce the more or less neglected economic aspects into the historical debate on creative milieus. However, GREMI's approach of measuring success only in terms of technological innovation and economic development seems too narrow for a broader analysis of creative milieus. The issue of how to define the success of a creative milieu should be developed more thoroughly. Overall, the concept seems to provide useful analytical categories for the examination of contemporary and historic creative milieus. Although the concept was elaborated to fit the interests of economists, the terms seem to be general enough to be applied to other types of creative milieus.

Having built upon GREMI's research, we now are able to focus on creative milieus in the cultural economy, as well as the significance of cities. The second part of this chapter will address the concept of *bohemia*, which seems to provide a useful additional means of understanding for certain type of urban cultural creative milieu.

The term »bohemia« does not refer to an elaborated concept but to a certain lifestyle often embraced by artists and intellectuals, as well as several spatial practices in the city.

Beginning in the fifteenth century, the term »bohemian« was used to denote gypsies, which were assumed to have come from Bohemia. Subsequently, the term referred to a messy vagrant, as well as an unconventional and adventurous lifestyle. Later in the eighteenth and nineteenth century, the concept of a »bohemian« gained favour and popularity. Idealised and romanticised, the term became associated with liberty, nature, enjoyment of life and independence from social constraints (Kreuzer 1968: 1–24). During the early nineteenth century, when the *Quartier Latin* in Paris became a popular district for young, not yet established artists and students, the concept of bohemia took on an urban connotation. This low-rent quarter attracted the socially and economically marginalised, as well as students and young artists who improvised their existence. Pennilessness, antibourgeois attitudes, an unconventional lifestyle, an association with the *avantgarde*, as well as an openness to experiment characterised the emergence of an urban bohemia (Lloyd 2006: 50–54).

Essentially, the concept of urban *bohemia* emerged from Paris – after it was popularised by a number of literary descriptions (Kreuzer 1968: 1–24, 42–139) – to later become a model for a certain type of an urban, (sub-) cultural neighbourhood. Combining a lifestyle and the place of an urban quarter which offers material and social free space, bohemian quarter can be found in cities throughout Europe and North America (for examples see Lloyd 2006: 54–65). It is characteristic for these neighbourhoods that they provide cheap rooms and a certain social and cultural openness in the beginning. As a result, socially underprivileged people are attracted to such districts, as well as students, young artists, and other people who begin to use the quarter as »laboratory« for their creativity. Bars, cafes, and clubs serve as places where the creative agents meet and communicate. Usually, both a unique identity and an image of the place subsequently become actualized. Typical elements of such an image are alternativeness (or even wickedness), tolerance, and an ethos of experimentation and creativity (Klaus 2006: 76–78).

Currently, it seems that this model of an urban quarter also has special significance in the cultural and symbolic economy. Recent publications stress that there are some cities and some quarters in cities that are particularly important for the production of new signs, cultural codes, and cultural products. These quarters often have all the characteristics of an urban bohemia. These seem to be the places where the images, symbols, and cultural products are produced which are economically valued in the cultural and the symbolic economy. Music stores, book stores and other related cultural products typify a street-level economy. People working in the domain of the creative services are attracted to these quarters because they offer a certain urban quality of life and a creative atmosphere (Helbrecht 2001; Klaus 2006: 75–76; Lloyd 2006: 65–70). However, often when gentrification follows and the place becomes economically valorised, usually the young, not yet established creative people leave (Klaus 2006: 61–63; Lloyd 2006: 99–115).

The idea is now to combine GREMI's abstract and more general approach with the concept of an urban bohemia. As a result, this combination could provide an analytical instrument for the analysis of urban creative milieus in the cultural economy.

Both concepts can be employed to focus on the creative agents and their activities, as well as the relevance of spatial proximity and a concrete place. The GREMI-concept is useful because it helps us to understand creativity as a communicative process. It provides well-suited categories to analyse the relevance and the interrelations of communication, informal encounters, synergies, and spatial proximity for creative processes. It also conceptualises the advantages of the creative agents' integration, who share common values and a common identity, and who interact frequently among each other. The concept of bohemia does not deal with these questions on a theoretical level, but it provides a concrete idea of common values, and a common identity which seem to be relevant for an understanding of (sub-)cultural creative milieus.

Furthermore, the concept of bohemia includes the idea of urbanity, which the GREMI-concept clearly does not. Diversity and openness are integral parts of urban bohemia as well as of the concept of the city. As mentioned above, these are also elements that are favourable to creativity. Equally important, material »free space« and social nonconformity are constituents for urban bohemia and central for the realisation of creativity.

Concerning creativity GREMI focuses on economic and technological innovations, whereas *bohemia* deals mainly with artistic and intellectual creativity. Focusing on the cultural economy, artistic and intellectual creativity may be more relevant for us, but in general, there is no need to restrict the understanding of creativity. I propose instead to consider a broad understanding of creativity including technological innovation, artistic and intellectual creativity, as well as science.

As mentioned above, economic success is one important element of the GREMI-concept, but it does not pertain to the concept of bohemia. While economic success is not an essential aspect of creativity in general, it is nevertheless a crucial point to investigate if we are interested in the cultural economy. In this sense, it would be interesting to analyse the interrelations of the anti-market or anti-capitalist mentality, which is typical for bohemia, and the economic valorisation in the cultural economy.

As a whole, I propose to understand cultural creative milieus as a concept referring to informal groups of agents within a limited area in the city and in a specific historic context. Several common cultural and social practices, as well as common beliefs, integrate the agents into a collective body. Creativity results from synergies and learning processes within this group. The urban territory is an integral part of the milieu; it provides the material basis for the milieu's activities, and it also influences the outcome of both a specific image, and a sense of identity. Needless to say, economic impacts may result from creative activities.

Thus, four elements are integral parts of the concept: (1) an integrated group of the creative agents, (2) the territory of a milieu in the city providing the material basis, (3) time and a historic context, (4) creativity which occurs in a milieu and the question of its economic impact.

The following paragraphs will now illustrate and test the discussed concepts in the concrete case of the *Nauwieser Viertel* in Saarbrücken.

Chinatown upon Saar? The Nauwieser Viertel in Saarbrücken as an Example

The *Nauwieser Viertel*, also known as *Chinesenviertel*, is a small downtown neighbourhood in Saarbrücken located between *Großherzog-Friedrich Straße* in the South, *Richard-Wagner-* (or *Brauerstraße*) in the North, *Dudweilerstraße* in the West and *Egon-Reinert-Straße* in the East. Neither Saarbrücken nor the *Nauwieser Viertel* is very famous for its creativity. There are no innovations or cultural products in which Saarbrücken, or the quarter is renowned for. Also there is no special urban attractiveness usually resulting from a creative milieu. However, there are signs indicating that the quarter could be a (sub-)cultural creative milieu. If there is any place in Saarbrücken where urban, alternative, and experimental life takes place, it is the the *Nauwieser Viertel*, or the *Mainzer Straße*. The *Nauwieser* neighbourhood has some of the infrastructure of a »cool«, bohemian quarter: bars, cafes, eccentric shops, and cultural products, social projects, creative services, graffiti and flyers on the walls characterise the quarter. Furthermore, it is im-

---

6   There is no single explanation but several legends that illustrate why the Nauwieser Viertel is also known as Chinesenviertel (Häffner 1990).

portant to note, that within the city of Saarbrücken it has an image and an identity of its own. All these elements seem to indicate the presence of a cultural creative milieu. In the following paragraphs I will examine more closely the development of this quarter and its milieu since the 1970s. The objective is to illustrate and to test the discussed concepts and categories in a concrete case. As we will see, the quarter was the place of a typical alternative, politically left orientated milieu in the 1970s and 1980s, with some characteristics of a bohemian creative milieu. In the mid of the 1980s, cultural and economic aspects became more important.

The content of the following paragraphs is a result from research I undertook for my diploma thesis in 2006. This research was based on the analysis of different published and unpublished contemporary sources, as well as 15 interviews with experts from the neighbourhood.[7] Two journals were systematically analysed between the years 1970 and 1990: the *Saarbrücker Zeitung*, the ordinary daily newspaper for Saarbrücken and the Saar region, and the *Stadtzeitung*, an alternative newspaper and itself a product from the *Nauwieser* milieu. The latter appeared monthly since 1976 and was an important medium of communication and information for the local alternative movement. Apart from critical articles about what was happening in the city, the region, and the country, this journal provided information regularly about the local alternative movement and its activities; for example, about which groups had newly formed, about what they were doing, and when and where they were meeting. Flyers, posters, booklets, and transcripts of meetings, which I found in the local archives, complemented the information about the activities in the neighbourhood. Some historical and contemporary studies provided useful information about the context of the local urban development.

Time: Historical Context and Development

At the end of the 1960s, there was only little cultural life in Saarbrücken and the *Nauwieser Viertel*. The author Gerhard Bungert, who moved to Saarbrücken at this time, described the city as »critically ill« concerning

---

7   Thirteen people interviewed were former agents in the Nauwieser milieu. In addition, two people interviewed were engaged in the municipal administration and politics at the time. The interviews were conducted between May and September 2006.

cultural life.[8] The *Nauwieser Viertel* appeared at this time in the *Saarbrücker Zeitung* as a »centre of nuisance« where prostitutes and shady characters hung around.[9] At the same time, the initial places and establishments that became centres of the alternative milieu appeared: one small independent theatre, the so called *Sog. Theater* (later: *Überzwerg*), two political bookstores (*Lehnchen Demuth* and *der buchladen*), the *Gasthaus Bingert*, an inn located on *Nauwieserstraße* that became *the* meeting point of the alternative milieu, and the youth centre on *Försterstraße* (Conrath 1995a).

It is no coincidence that all these places were alternatively and politically oriented; such as the *Bingert* and *der buchladen* were even collectively owned and organised. Indeed, the historical development of the *Nauwieser* creative milieu has to be contextualised in the new social movements that emerged since the end of the 1960s. The agents of this heterogeneous movement were politically left oriented, and protested against different traditional social norms and cultural conventions. They criticised the existing political system as democratically insufficient, and they aspired to promote the utopia of a free egalitarian grassroots democracy. Crucial themes of this movement were freedom and demobilisation, emancipation of women, decolonisation and international justice, human and civil rights, environment (especially nuclear energy), and the realisation of an alternative lifestyle (Langguth 1983: 24–35; Rucht 2001; Roth and Rucht 2002; Wolfrum 2005: 505–507). These tendencies found concrete expression in many different forms and at many places in West Germany. In Saarbrücken, and that is the point of interest here, it was the *Nauwieser Viertel* that became the regional centre of the alternative movement. An analysis of the monthly calendar of the *Stadtzeitung* and of two booklets (Schäfer et al. 1983 Redaktionsgruppe Eiszeit 1993) that list alternative projects shows that a majority of the groups and projects had their local base in this quarter.

The first alternative and sub-culture projects and activities are documented around 1970. Their number increased notably from the mid 1970s onwards. The *Stadtzeitung* mentioned about 60 projects and groups between 1976 and 1980, from which about 30 were localised in the quarter. During this time, the number of projects in the quarter remained relatively stable until 1984. From 1985 and onwards, each calendar of the *Stadtzeitung* mentioned about 100 groups and projects in the whole Saar region (between 25

8 *Stadtzeitung*, 143, 1990: 14–15.
9 *Saarbrücker Zeitung*, 137, 1971: 19.

percent and 50 percent were located in the quarter).[10] The spatial concentration of activities in the quarter is specially striking as the neighbourhood is very small: In 1979, 3,300 people lived there, where as in 1999, 3,600 people lived in the quarter (Lukascyk: 31–33). That was less than two percent of all residents of the entire city of Saarbrücken (1980: 193,554, 2000: 187, 257).

Agents: Milieu-like Integration

An affiliation to the milieu can be analysed by the criteria of residency, participation in certain projects and activities, as well as self-identification with the alternative movement and the *Nauwieser* neighbourhood. As we will see below, a certain lifestyle and habitus can also be taken as an indicator for belonging to the milieu. In the interviews conducted for this study, the presence of a person in certain places, and participation in activities in the neighbourhood was often mentioned as an indicator for his or her belonging to the milieu.

Those agents that could be identified within the scale and scope of this research[11] by the previously mentioned criteria correspond in terms of their social characteristics to what is known about the new social movements in the 1970s and 1980s. In general, the agents of this movement were young middle-class people, most of them students or university graduates. Social service professionals were particularly well represented (Roth and Rucht 2002: 298, Wolfrum 2005: 507). The results of the interviews as well as contemporary documents indicate that these characteristics probably apply to the *Nauwieser* milieu as well.

In 1984, the journalist and author Michael Mallmann described the *Nauwieser* neighbourhood as a milieu in which even the worker's organisa-

10 The considerable increase is also due to a more professional approach by the *Stadtzeitung* at the time. From 1985 on, the *Stadtzeitung* employed a salaried editor, which not only lead to more extensive and thorough investigations, but also benefited the layout and overall structure of the journal.
The organisation *Netzwerk* estimates that about 90 percent of the projects during this time originated from the neighbourhood (interview with a former agent from *Netzwerk*, June 6, 2006).
11 Within the scale and the scope of this study, it was not possible to carry out a quantitative analysis concerning the agents of the milieu, nor do the local statistics provide more detailed conclusions about them.

tion was academically educated, where taps were handled by poets, and waiters were graphic artists (Mallmann 1980). Other contemporary texts draw a similar tableau of the milieu (Bierbrauer 1987a: 12). Furthermore, there are some details about the residents of the *Nauwieser* quarter. In 1979 and in 1999, the group of residents in the neighbourhood was characterised by a strong presence of single persons, aged between 20 and 60; people with low income were overrepresented in comparison to the whole city of Saarbrücken, such as students, immigrants, and people living on social welfare or unemployment benefits (Landeshauptstadt Saarbrücken 1979: 85; Nauwieser 19 e.V. Kultur- und Werkhof 1992: 16–39; Lukascyk 2001: 31–33).[12] However, not all residents were agents of the alternative milieu and not all agents were residents. The residential addresses of the contributors of the Stadtzeitung support this claim. Also, some of the interviewed agents mentioned that they did not live all the time in the neighbourhood, but they nevertheless identified with the quarter, its milieu and spent most of their spare time in the neighbourhood.[13] On the other side, many people lived in the quarter who did not participate in activities of the neighbourhood (Landeshauptstadt Saarbrücken 1979: 89–90). Some residents even complained about the milieu.[14]

The group of agents in the *Nauwieser Viertel* corresponded to the mentioned criteria of a milieu: they were integrated by a common identity, common social practices, and dense communication. As mentioned above, a common identity was formed in the neighbourhood with the new social movements or its beliefs about the world. Common values among the agents included: political activism, an antibourgeois and anti-market mindset, as well as radical criticism concerning the existing society and the uto-

---

12 In 1979, 27 percent of the households was said to have had a monthly income of less than 1,000 DM, 27 percent was said to have had an income of 1,000 to 2,000 DM. In 1988, it was estimated that 30–35 percent of the residents had a low income, where as regarding the whole city the estimated average was 22.5 percent (Landeshauptstadt Saarbrücken 1979: 85, Nauwieser 19 e.V. Kultur- und Werkhof 1992: 16–39, Lukascyk 2001: 31–33).

13 Interviews with a former actor from *Blaue Maus* (June 22, 2006), with three former journalists from the *Stadtzeitung* (July 10, 2006 and July 20, 2006), and a member of *der buchladen* (August 1, 2006).

14 The culmination was a complaint by neighbours about the project *Nauwieser 19* during the summer 1992. Neighbours collected 80 signatures within the neighbourhood in an organised protest against a noise violation (written minutes of the *Nauwieser 19* from 1992, private archives of Nauwieser 19 e.V., folder »Nauwieser 19, Protokolle 4/92 bis 12/96«).

pia of a grassroots democracy. Moreover, the agents of the *Nauwieser Viertel* understood themselves as alternative and creative, as all interviewed former agents reported. Frequent interaction and casual meetings were a component of everyday life. Mutual interaction was mostly informal, unconstrained and deliberately breaking through certain common *bourgeois* manners (Bierbrauer 1987b). Many of the former agents reported that it was this everyday life that made the neighbourhood special. One was sure to meet like-minded people in the quarter at any time. In addition to appointed meetings in projects and groups, people met frequently on the road, in shops and cafés, and in certain special places of the milieu, like the old fire station or the youth centre among others. Interaction and communication within the quarter was intensified by the unique spatial proximity (Mallmann 1980) and constituted also a central element concerning the identity of the neighbourhood. The *Stadtzeitung* and other publications characterised the quarter as one of the last communicative neighbourhoods in town (Menard 1989: 61; Mallmann 1984: 31).[15]

Moreover, a varied set of characteristics formed a sort of alternative lifestyle. This consisted in living in flat-sharing communities, spending time regularly in some cafés and bars, cultivating certain behaviour, certain forms of communication, and particular clothing. This lifestyle distinguished the people of the milieu, visibly marked the quarter, and was a component of a common identity (Mallmann 1984: 32, Mörgen 1989: 92–96). As mentioned in several interviews, upon entering the *Nauwieser Viertel*, one had the impression of entering a different world.[16]

The integration of the milieu risked even a tendency towards isolation »like a ghetto«[17], as a *Stadtzeitung's* journalist observed. In 1988, there were complaints about the *Netzwerk's* policy to allocate financial support: projects were supported because they were advanced by known agents of the milieu, whereas utopian ideas seemed to be secondary (ibid.: 17).

While a tendency towards isolation was the deficiency of the integration, the benefit was the emergence of a local knowledge. The agents knew each other and knew whom to ask when they needed equipment, knowl-

---

15 *Stadtzeitung*, 17, 1978: 3.
16 A former actor from Blaue Maus reported that people from outside of town came even to visit the alternative quarter (interview June 22, 2006).
17 *Stadtzeitung*, 115, 1988: 16.

edge, or ideas. Thus, it was much easier to organise an event or an enterprise.[18]

Space and Place: Identity and Interaction

The reasons why the *Nauwieser Viertel* became a stage for the activities of the alternative milieu only can be reconstructed approximately in the retrospective. As is typical for the development of bohemian neighbourhoods, the houses in the quarter were in a poor condition at the beginning of the 1970s relatively speaking. Most of the houses were not renovated and many flats did not have a bathroom inside. This contributed to proportionally low rent fees, which were attractive to people with a low income (Landeshauptstadt Saarbrücken 1979: 85, 89; Nauwieser 19 e.V. Kultur- und Werkhof 1992: 38).

The location near to the city centre was probably another factor as well as the development of the market place. Up until the 1970s, the city-centre of Saarbrücken, the St. Johanner Markt, had the reputation of »small St. Pauli«, where prostitutes, some artists, and some students lived (Buchhorn 1984). After a top-to-bottom renovation gentrification took place around 1970 (Buchhorn 1984),[19] It is very likely that the *Nauwieser Viertel* became the place for those displaced from the market.[20] This was also reflected by the image of the quarter as a wicked place that continued up until the 1990s.[21]

When a few years later the *Nauwieser Viertel* was also declared an object of renovation and redevelopment, the identification of a group of people with this neighbourhood became very concrete. Suspecting gentrification as it had happened at the market, this group protested persistently against the planed redevelopment and turned the neighbourhood into an object of

---

18 Mentioned in the interviews with a former actor from *Blaue Maus* (June 22, 2006), a former actor from *Studiotheater* (June 17, 2006), a member of *der buchladen* (August 1, 2006) and a former journalist from *Lila Distel* (July 28, 2006).

19 Stadtzeitung, 7, 1977: 3–6; Stadtzeitung, 8, 1977: 3–5.

20 *Saarbrücker Zeitung*, 137, 1971: 19.

21 Up to the 1990s, people phoned the *Studiotheater* to ask whether their parked cars would be safe in the quarter while they attended the theatre (interview with a former actor from *Studiotheater* (June 17, 2006), interview with a former actor from *Blaue Maus* (June 22, 2006).

spatial struggle.[22] Beginning in spring 1978, citizen's action groups were formed, which made and distributed flyers, organised discussions with representatives of the city, and arranged various other protest actions.[23] The activities even culminated in sit-ins (Brenner and Rausch 1989).[24] For the first time the image of an »intact« and communicating neighbourhood is documented in this context. It was argued that the social structure with its heterogeneity and openness to marginalised people, »bohemia and the avant-garde« (Mallmann 1980) was threatened by the planned renovations that would attract swells and people in »disco-look« (Mallmann 1984).[25]

The redevelopment was implemented all the same, but in a moderate form. This was due partially to the protests, partially to the financial situation of the city, and partially to the engagement of some people within the municipality.[26]

The example of the old fire station (*Alte Feuerwache*), which became another object of struggle in the context of redevelopment, illustrates well the identification with the place and the relevance of free space for the activities of the milieu.

As the municipality planned to establish another playhouse for the municipal theatre at the *Landwehrplatz*, people protested against it out of a fear of gentrification and pleaded for a centre for activities of the alternative milieu.[27] After lengthy negotiations a rental agreement was determined between the municipality of Saarbrücken and the organisation *Alter Feuerdrache*[28] in November 1981. In the agreement was formulated that the old fire station should be an open centre for communication, and it should promote experimental projects.[29] No rental fee was demanded by the municipality, the groups only had to pay utility fees for water and electricity. Generally, the centre was open to all interested people and groups. Yet, the

22 *Stadtzeitung*, 11, 1978: 5–6; 13, 1978: 21; 17, 1978: 3; 29, 1979.

23 *Stadtzeitung*, 29, 1979: 4–5.

24 *Stadtzeitung*, 129, 1989: 2, 8–16; 130, 1989: 2, 10–12; 141, 1990: 13–16.

25 *Stadtzeitung*, 17, 1978: 3; 63, 1983: 6; 45, 1981: 10; 51, 1982: 10.

26 *Saarbrücker Zeitung*, 259, 1981: 17; 20, 1982: 3; *Stadtzeitung*, 54, 1982: 11, interview with a former municipal employee June 12, 2006.

27 *Stadtzeitung*, 26, 1979: 8.

28 The *Alter Feuerdrache* (old firedrake) was a federation of different alternative projects and groups that was founded on the purpose of managing the use of the building, *Alte Feuerwache* (old fire station).

29 StA Saarbrücken Presse 2004/24, folder Nr. 13.

Alter Feuerdrache pursued a strong human rights policy excluding for example racist groups.

In the 1980s, the fire station developed into an increasingly important place for the *Nauwieser* milieu. Concerts, exhibitions, cinema, parties etc. took place there, as well as it functioned as a unique venue where a number of groups could realise their projects (Mörgen 1989: 92). This open space was especially helpful for the formation of new groups and for spontaneous projects, as people were permitted easy and inexpensive access to rooms for their activities.[30] The project was so successful, that in 1988/89, some established groups in the meantime decided to move conjointly to another building in order to make room for newly emerging projects in the fire station. This project on *Nauwieserstraße* 19 still exists today. An independent cinema, a café, a bureau for regional film production, a bike-garage and some other cultural and social projects are still located there.[31]

Creativity

There were many activities and projects that took place in the quarter and which can be seen as products of an alternative sub-culture milieu. Three categories of products can be differentiated: first, socially and politically motivated activities, second, projects and activities in the domain of culture and arts, and third, a certain lifestyle.

1) Socially and politically motivated activities and projects were the immediate expression of the protest movement. Different groups engaged with themes concerning the environment, peace, feminism, human and civil rights and social aid. Some groups were protest oriented, such as the local anti-nuclear power movement or groups that formed spontaneously to protest against concrete local politics; as for example the construction of a four-lane highway in the *Meerwiesertal*[32], or the redevelopment of the *Nauwieser Viertel*. Others formed support groups, for example for homosexuals, workers, abused women or prostitutes.

2) Among the cultural products in the neighbourhood, there were different journals and magazines, independent theatres, an independent cin-

30 I found 32 different groups that used the old fire station as a place to meet between 1982 and 1990.
31 For more details see http://www.nauwieser19.de/.
32 *Stadtzeitung*, 62, 1983: 3–5.

ema, at least two projects for film production, music groups, visual arts, and literature. Magazines like the *Stadtzeitung*, the *Saarhexe* (later: *Voyeur*), and *Lila Distel*, a women's magazine, pursued the objective to form a critical and oppositional public and promoted communication within the alternative milieu.[33] The *Stadtzeitung* also regularly gave space to young authors to publish their texts.[34] Similarly, other cultural projects reclaimed a critical, enlightening role. The different theatre groups, authors, visual artists and the cinema dealt with themes ranging from professional banning (*Berufsverbot*),[35] marginalised groups,[36] sit-ins, to urban redevelopment and gender.[37] Thus, the arts were at least partially politically motivated, but there was a wide range of artistic experiments and professional art. [38] Professional artists and student artists were present as well as amateur artists.

3) The practical arranging and concrete organising of an alternative environment and lifestyle was a central concern of the new social movements. A number of collectively owned and organised enterprises emerged: cafés and inns like the *Café Jonas* (later: *Schrill*) and the *Gasthaus Bingert*, book stores like *der buchladen*, craft enterprises like the *holzbock* or the *fahrradladen*, and print shops like the *TUK* and the *Blattlaus*. Additionally, there were organisations which promoted and encouraged alternative projects by means of practical advice and financial support, for example the *Zukunftswerkstatt* and the *Netzwerk Saar.*[39] These were also the activities of the milieu that had the most economic impact, developing a very small alternative economy.

---

33 *Stadtzeitung*, 0, 1976: 8.

34 Between July 1980 and January 1983, the *Stadtzeitung* had a literary supplement titled *Einzelheiten*, later between 1986 and 1989, a literary rubric named *Stein und Feder*.

35 For example *Etwas ist faul im Staate Germany …*, play of the *Sog. Theater* in 1977, see the critic published in *Stadtzeitung*, 5, 1977: 13.

36 For example *Krüppel aus dem Sack*, play by the *Theater Überzwerg*. The play dealt with the subject of disabled people within the alternative movement (*Stadtzeitung*, 51, 1982: 24).

37 *Blaue Maus: Die Melniks*. The play was improvised by actors from *Blaue Maus* and dealt with different political and social themes (Stadtarchiv Saarbrücken Dok. 402–8). The women's theatre *S'Irene* performed different plays dealing critically with gender, for example *Allweile genn die Frau iwerzwersch*, *Komm, ich hab Lust auf dich*, or *Die Stärkere* (*Stadtzeitung*, 81, 1985: 26).

38 A former actor from *Blaue Maus* remembered: »There were so many different cultural and creative activities that it's impossible to remember them all«, (interview June 22, 2006).

39 The *Netzwerk* was an organisation that was originally founded in Berlin and then spread out to many cities in Germany (Stadtzeitung, 32, 1980: 16).

Also, a specific, above-described lifestyle including a certain design is to be mentioned here. The *Stadtzeitung* even published a series of articles about the design of the milieu. In this regard, the author Peter Bierbrauer advanced the thesis that the design was *the* constituent element of the milieu (Bierbrauer 1987a: 13, 1987b, 1987c, 1987d, 1988). He argued that the political dimension became less important since the mid 1980s, and that the design, originally a byproduct, came to the centre of the milieu. This shift in the alternative milieu towards a more fashionable consumer orientation was also observed in other cities at the time (Weinberger 1987), and can be understood as one step in the development of a cultural economy (Klaus 2006: 76–81). At the same time, a shift towards institutionalisation took place and a more professional approach within several groups and projects was observed.[40]

Altogether, it seems that a specific group of people in the neighbourhood played both an active and an experimental role in the 1970s and 1980s. The *Nauwieser Viertel* became a place of lively interaction within the alternative milieu. In addition to low rent fees, the quarter offered free space for a plurality of creative projects and activities, several of which were motivated by social and political activism. Furthermore, there was a relatively high degree of identification among people with the neighbourhood. Moreover, rudiments of a cultural economy can be observed in the 1980s.

Evaluation and Conclusion

In the theoretical part of this article, it has been shown that the concept of creative milieus deals with the relationship of dense communication and cooperation in limited spaces, at particular places, and with its implications for creative dynamics. Throughout history, cities have apparently provided favourable conditions for creativity and creative milieus.

Concerning the literature on this topic, different notions and theories about creative milieus can be found. However, as a result of my investigations and analysis, I have found that a combination of GREMI's approach and the idea of bohemia offers the best model for understanding cultural

---

40 Nauwieser 19: Protokolle 4/92 to 12/96, interview with a member of *der buchladen* (August 1, 2006) and with a member of *Netzwerk* (June 6, 2006).

creative milieus in cities as collectives, which are situated in spatial proximity at particular urban places, and through communication and interaction, generate creative and possibly economic dynamics. I have proposed to test this concept as a heuristic device to analyse creative milieus, and to systematise our understanding of them in a historical perspective.

The analysis of the *Nauwieser Viertel* in Saarbrücken was motivated by the purpose to test and to illustrate the proposed concept of creative milieus and eventually pose the question of failure.

It seems that the *Nauwieser Viertel* with its alternative milieu, which developed in the 1970s and 1980s, meets all the criteria of a creative milieu as defined in the first part of this article. There were agents that formed a milieu and communicated actively. Creative activities and synergetic dynamics resulted. The *Nauwieser Viertel* in Saarbrücken could be identified as the appropriated place of this milieu. This quarter meets the criteria of a bohemian, ›cool‹ quarter: cheap rent, an image of wickedness, and »free space« for the creative agents to interact. The alternative agents' struggle for this place clearly shows the importance that the place gained for the milieu, especially in terms of identification and interaction. The quarter was also distinctive and visibly marked by the milieu's activities and lifestyle. Graffiti and flyers on the walls characterise the neighbourhood until now as a place of sub-culture.

As a model the *Nauwieser Viertel* was not entirely original because it was influenced by other similar trends and developments. However, if we accept the idea that creativity can consist of inventive implementation, or appropriation of more general tendencies and ideas known elsewhere, the *Nauwieser Viertel* can be called a *creative* milieu.

In a retrospective view, the most important product of this milieu was its distinctive image as a place of alternativeness and urbanity in Saarbrücken (Conrath 1995a, 1995b, 1995c, 1995d; Felk 1990). Also, some alternative projects and enterprises still exist and characterise the neighbourhood, such as the *Nauwieser 19*, the youth centre, and the *Bingert* among other places. But today, even if the *Nauwieser* neighbourhood remains a place for sub-culture, there is no longer the creative vibrancy that seems to have existed in the 1970s and 1980s.

As mentioned above, the quarter has also become a location for further cultural products, enterprises and stores constituting a small street level cultural economy.[41] Yet, interestingly during the 1980s, while a shift occurred towards a more fashionable consumer orientation, and a more professional approach regarding the milieu's projects and activities, the politically motivated milieu decayed. This discontinuity observed in the *Nauwieser Viertel* is consistent with claims made by several geographical and sociological contributions. It is often argued, that it was not until the 1980s, that the phenomena of the today described cultural economy first appeared (Hartley 2005; Scott 2000: X).

However, it is also important to note that the *Nauwieser Viertel* never became a centre of the cultural economy, but rather it always remained on the fringes. Even if the alternative milieu contributed to change Saarbrücken's cultural life, as Gerhard Bungert and a former municipal employee mentioned, it did not change the city's image as a whole, nor did it make the quarter a preferred location of the cultural economy, or for other creative activities.

In the eyes of the interviewed former agents, the creativity of the milieu broke when political motivation lost its importance during the second half of the 1980s. [42] This interpretation corresponds to the emphasis that was placed upon political activism. It seems that in the case of Saarbrücken, the creative vibrancy of the alternative milieu did not continue in a developing cultural economy. Hence, the interrelations of an anti-capitalist counterculture milieu and the development of a cultural economy, which are also observed in other cases (for example Hartley 2005: 13; Klaus 2006: 110–113; Lloyd 2006: 63–70), should be analysed in more detail.

To conclude, it can be said that the *Nauwieser Viertel* can be interpreted as a case of an urban creative milieu, which includes some elements of a cultural economy, as defined in the theoretical part of this article. The given definition seems to offer useful categories and parameters in order to analyse creative milieus. However, the *Nauwieser* milieu was not very successful in terms of lasting innovations or in terms of economic development. There seem to be several additional elements which contribute to a degree of success regarding a creative milieu, as well as concerning the development of a cultural economy. The simple presence of a bohemian, alternative milieu in a city seems not to be a sufficient condition for eco-

---

41 A relative actual list can be seen at the website: www.unserviertel.de (last access: July 15, 2007).

42 Specially mentioned by a former journalist from the *Stadtzeitung* (July 20, 2006) and by an author and writer (May 16, 2006).

nomic development as claimed especially by Richard Florida (2002, 2004). In order to learn more about the conditions of success, we should continue to study more cases concerning creative milieus and the cultural economy, including cases of »failure«.

Another point can be made: the analysis of the *Nauwieser Viertel* shows clearly that creative milieus are a historical phenomenon, resulting from a specific historical situation. Without considering the broader historical context of a creative milieu, in the case of the *Nauwieser Viertel* the new social movements and the local politics at the time, it would be hard to understand what happened in the neighbourhood.

This leads to another aspect: an analysis of the *Nauwieser* milieu also provides another perspective on the history of the new social movements. Perhaps the concept of creative milieus could be useful for the analysis of other phenomena in history, as well contribute to a better understanding of dynamic developments.

Bibliography

Primary sources

Stadtarchiv Saarbrücken

Dok. 402–8
Presse 2004/24, Folder No. 13.

Archiv der Saarbrücker Zeitung

Ordner Nauwieser Viertel: Artikel aus der Saarbrücker Zeitung 1971–1995.
Conrath, Martin (1995a). »Dem Chinesenviertel geht's wie den Indianern Amerikas. Die ›Nauwies‹ zwischen Mythos und Realität«. *Saarbrücker Zeitung*, 51, March 1, 1995, L3.
Conrath, Martin (1995b). »Ein trunkener Narr stört hier niemanden. Die meisten Bewohner des Nauwieser Viertels üben sich in Gelassenheit«. *Saarbrücker Zeitung*, 55, March 6, 1995, L3.
— (1995c). »Wo sich Umstürzler und Aufmüpfige wohl fühlen«. *Saarbrücker Zeitung*, 71, March 24, 1995, L5.
— (1995d). »Brennpunkt Chinatown: Immer weniger Kinder und Alte. Ins Nauwieser Viertel paßt das multikulturelle Angebot – Viele ziehen weg, andere finden das, was sie brauchen«. *Saarbrücker Zeitung*, 86, April 11, 1995, L3.

Mallmann, Klaus-Michael (1980). »Das Nauwieser Viertel – Saarbrückens Chinatown«. *Saarbrücker Zeitung*, 5, January 7, 1980, 3.

Filmarchiv Saarländischer Rundfunk

Felk, Wolfgang (1990). »Was los im Chinesenviertel«. SWF 3 Saarland, broadcasted on October 10, 1990.

Archiv der Nauwieser 19

Nauwieser 19, Protokolle 4/92 bis 12/96

Stadtzeitung 1976–1990

Bierbrauer, Peter (1987a). »Die ›Szene‹ und ihre Wohnkultur«. *Stadtzeitung*, 108, 8/9, 1987, 12–15.
— (1987b). »Design der Szene: Freundlichkeit. Eine Cool-tour Kritik«. *Stadtzeitung*, 109, 10, 1987, 8–10.
— (1987c). »Bekleidungsformen D-SEIN oder?«. *Stadtzeitung*, 111, 12, 1987, 4–7.
— (1987d). »Der Widerspenstigen Zähmung oder doch nicht?«. *Stadtzeitung*, 111, 12, 1987, 12.
— (1988). »Was zieht sich der Szene Mensch in die Rübe? Karl Marx, Chinaliteratur und was sonst noch in den Regalen der Szene steht. Ein Bildbericht über die Bücher der Szene«. *Stadtzeitung*, 112, 1, 1988, 44–48.

Internet Sources

http://www.nauwieser19.de/ (July 15, 2007).
http://www.unserviertel.de (July 15, 2007).

References

Ash, Mitchell G. (2000). »Räume des Wissens – was und wo sind sie? Einleitung in das Thema«. In *Berichte zur Wissenschaftsgeschichte*, 23, 235–242.
Beck, Ulrich (1998). *Was ist Globalisierung? Irrtümer des Globalismus – Antworten auf Globalisierung.* 4th edition, Frankfurt am Main.
Bourdieu, Pierre (1982). *Die feinen Unterschiede. Kritik der gesellschaftlichen Unterschiede.* Frankfurt am Main.
Brenner, Joachim and Bernd Rausch (1989). *Tatort Nassauer Str. 13. Sanierung – Roter Filz im Rathaus.* Saarbrücken.

Brix, Emil and Allan Janik (1993a). »Einleitung«. In Emil Brix and Allan Janik (eds.). *Kreatives Milieu, Wien um 1900: Ergebnisse eines Forschungsgesprächs der Arbeitsgemeinschaft ›Wien um 1900‹*, 10–14. Wien.

Brix, Emil and Allan Janik (1993b). »Vorwort«, In Emil Brix and Allan Janik (eds.). *Kreatives Milieu, Wien um 1900: Ergebnisse eines Forschungsgesprächs der Arbeitsgemeinschaft ›Wien um 1900‹*, 7–9. Wien.

Buchhorn, Martin (1984). »Kopf oder Zahl oder die Rückseite des St. Johanner Marktes«. In Klaus-Michael Mallmann (ed.). *Saarbrücker Augenblicke*, 17–23. Saarbrücken.

Burke, Peter (2001). *Papier und Marktgeschrei. Die Geburt der Wissensgesellschaft*. Berlin.

Camagni, Roberto (1991). »Introduction: From the local ›milieu‹ to innovation through cooperation networks«. In Roberto Camagni (ed.). *Innovation Networks. Spatial Perspectives*, 1–9. London.

Crevoisier, Olivier and Roberto Camagni (eds.) (2000). *Les milieux urbains: innovation, systèmes de production et ancrage*. Neuchatel.

Crevoisier, Olivier (2000). »Les milieux innovateurs et la ville. Une introduction«. In Olivier Crevoisier and Roberto Camagni (eds.). *Les milieux urbains: innovation, systèmes de production et ancrage*, 7–32. Neuchatel.

— (2001). »Der Ansatz des kreativen Milieus. Bestandsaufnahme und Forschungsperspektiven am Beispiel urbaner Milieus«. *Zeitschrift für Wirtschaftsgeographie*, 45, 246–256.

Csikszentmihalyi, Michail (1999). »Implications of a Systems Perspective for the Study of Creativity«. In: Robert J. Sternberg (ed.). *Handbook of Creativity*, 313–335. Cambridge.

Fleck, Ludwik (1980). *Entstehung und Entwicklung einer wissenschaftlichen Tatsache. Einführung in die Lehre vom Denkstil und Denkkollektiv*. Frankfurt am Main.

Florida, Richard (2004). *The Rise of the Creative Class*. New York.

— (2002). »The Economic Geography of Talent«. *Annals of the Association of American Geographers*, 92, 743-755.

Fremdling, Rainer (1983). »Die Ausbreitung des Puddelverfahrens und des Kokshochofens in Belgien, Frankreich und Deutschland«. *Technikgeschichte*, 50, 197–212.

Freundt, Andreas (2003). *Entwicklungspotenziale der Kulturwirtschaft in altindustrialisierten Regionen. Chancen der Förderung von Clustern im Ruhrgebiet und im Merseyside*. Diss. Dortmund.

Fromhold-Eisebith, Martina (1999). »Das kreative Milieu« – Nur theoretisches Konzept oder Instrument der Regionalentwicklung?«. *Raumforschung und Raumordnung*, 57, 2/3, 168–175.

Funke, Joachim (2000). »*Psychologie der Kreativität*«. In Rainer Matthias Holm-Hadulla (ed.). *Kreativität*, 283–300. Heidelberg.

Georg, Werner (2002). »Milieus/Lebensstile«. In Martin Greiffenhagen and Sylvia Greiffenhagen (eds.). *Handwörterbuch zur politischen Kultur der Bundesrepublik Deutschland*, 261–264. Wiesbaden.

Gertler, Meric S. (2003). »Tacit knowledge and the economic geography of context, or the undefinable tacitness of being (there)«. *Journal of Economic Geography*, 3, 75–99.

Göschel, Albrecht and Volker Kirchberg (1998). »Einleitung. Kultur der Stadt – Kultur in der Stadt«. in: Albrecht Göschel and Volker Kirchberg (eds.). *Kultur in der Stadt. Stadtsoziologische Analysen zur Kultur*, 7–15. Opladen.

Häffner, Jürgen (1990). *Das Chinesenviertel*. Saarbrücken.

Hall, Peter (1998). *Cities in Civilisation. Civilisation. Culture, Innovation and Urban Order*. London.

Hartley, John (2005). »Creative Industries«. In John Hartley (ed.). *Creative Industries*, 1–40. Malden/Oxford.

Häußermann, Hartmut and Walter Siebel (1987). *Neue Urbanität*. Frankfurt am Main.

Helbrecht, Ilse (2001). »Postmetropolis: Die Stadt als Sphinx«. *Geographica Helvetica*, 56, 3, 2001, 214–222.

Heit, Alfred (2004). »Vielfalt der Erscheinung – Einheit des Begriffs? Die Stadtdefinition in der deutschsprachigen Stadtgeschichtsforschung seit dem 18. Jahrhundert«. In Peter Johanek and Franz-Joseph Post (eds.). *Vielerlei Städte. Der Stadtbegriff*, 1–12. Köln.

Heßler, Martina (2002). »Stadt als innovatives Milieu – Ein transdisziplinärer Forschungsansatz«. *Neue Politische Literatur*, 47, 193–223.

Johanek, Peter and Franz-Joseph Post (eds.) (2004). *Vielerlei Städte. Der Stadtbegriff*, Köln.

Jung, Joachim (1993). »*Die psychologischen Grundlagen der Kreativität*«. In Emil Brix and Allan Janik (eds.). *Kreatives Milieu – Wien um 1900. Ergebnisse eines Forschungsgesprächs der Arbeitsgemeinschaft ›Wien um 1900‹*, 26–32. Wien.

Keim, Karl-Dieter (1997). »Milieu und Moderne. Zum Gebrauch und Gehalt eines nachtraditionalen sozial-räumlichen Milieubegriffs«. *Berliner Journal für Soziologie*, 7, 3, 1997, 387–399.

Klaus, Philipp (2006). *Stadt, Kultur, Innovation. Kulturwirtschaft und kreative innovative Kleinstunternehmen in der Stadt Zürich*. Zürich.

König, Wolfgang (1984). »Retrospective Technology Assessment – Technikbewertung im Rückblick«. *Technikgeschichte*, 51, 247–262.

Kreuzer, Helmut (1968). *Die Boheme. Beiträge zu ihrer Beschreibung*. Stuttgart.

Landeshauptstadt Saarbrücken (ed.) (1979). *Saarbrücken Nauwieser Viertel. Vorbereitende Untersuchungen nach dem Städtebauförderungsgesetz, (Arbeitsberichte zur Kommunalen Planung Nr. 18)*. Saarbrücken.

Langguth, Gerd (1983). *Protestbewegung. Entwicklung, Niedergang, Renaissance. Die Neue Linke seit 1968*. Köln.

Läpple, Dieter (2004). »Thesen zur Renaissance der Stadt in der Wissensgesellschaft«. *Jahrbuch StadtRegion 2003*, 61–77. Opladen.

Lash, Scott and John Urry (1994). *Economies of Signs and Space*. London.

Lindner, Rolf (2000). »Stadtkultur«. in: Hartmut Häußermann (ed.). *Großstadt, Soziologische Stichworte*, 258–264. Opladen.

Lloyd, Richard (2006). *Neo-Bohemia. Art and Commerce in the postindustrial city*. New York.

Löw, Martina (2001). *Raumsoziologie*. Frankfurt am Main.

Lukascyk, Tanja (2001). *Entwicklungstendenzen innerstädtischer Wohngebiete, dargestellt am Beispiel Nauwieser Viertel*. Diploma Thesis (Geography), Saarbrücken.

Mallmann, Klaus-Michael (1984). Saarbrückens Chinatown – Das Nauwieser Viertel. In Klaus-Michael Mallmann (ed.). *Saarbrücker Augenblicke*. Saarbrücken.

Mathieu, Christian (2004). »Fiat experientia!« Zur Wahrnehmung von Technikfolgen und ihren Auswirkungen auf das venezianische Patentverfahren in der frühen Neuzeit«. *Zeitsprünge. Forschungen zur Frühen Neuzeit*, 8, 3/4, 2004, 376–388.

Matthiesen, Ulf (ed.) (1998). *Die Räume der Milieus. Neue Tendenzen in der sozial- und raumwissenschaftlichen Milieuforschung sowie in der Stadt- und Raumplanung*. Berlin.

— (2004). »Wissen in Stadtregionen. Forschungsresultate und Streitfragen, Orientierungswissen und Handlungsoptionen«. In Ulf Matthiesen (ed.). *Stadtregion und Wissen. Analysen und Plädoyers für eine wissensbasierte Stadtpolitik*, 11–28. Wiesbaden.

Menard, Johannes (1989). »Gemütliche Alternative und viel Kneipen-Theater. Das Nauwieser Viertel«. In Jürgen Albers (ed.). *Saarbrücken zu Fuß. 17 Stadtteilrundgänge durch Geschichte und Gegenwart*, 61–71. Saarbrücken.

Mörgen, Tilo (1989). *Professionalität und Selbstverwaltung. Eine Analyse der Stadtzeitung Saarbrücken*. Diploma Thesis (Sociology), Saarbrücken.

Nauwieser 19 e.V. Kultur- und Werkhof (ed.) (1992). *Das Nauwieserviertel. Sozialstruktur, Probleme und Maßnahmevorschläge zur Verbesserung der Wohn- und Lebensqualität*. Saarbrücken.

Osterhammel, Jürgen and Niels P. Peterson (2003). *Geschichte der Globalisierung. Dimensionen, Prozesse, Epochen*. München.

Robertson, Roland (1998). »Glokalisierung. Homogenität und Heterogenität in Raum und Zeit«. In Ulrich Beck (ed.). Perspektiven der Weltgesellschaft, 192–220. Frankfurt am Main.

Rösch, Andreas (2000). »Kreative Milieus als Faktoren der Regionalentwicklung«. *Raumforschung und Raumordnung*, 58, 2/3, 2000, 161–172.

Roth, Roland and Dieter Rucht (2002). »Neue soziale Bewegungen«. In Martin Greiffenhagen and Sylvia Greiffenhagen (eds.). *Handwörterbuch zur politischen Kultur der Bundesrepublik Deutschland*, 296–302. Wiesbaden.

Rucht, Dieter (ed.) (2001). *Protest in der Bundesrepublik Deutschland. Strukturen und Entwicklungen*. Frankfurt am Main.

Redaktionsgruppe Eiszeit (ed.) (1993). *Tischlein deck dich, Esel streck dich, Knüppel aus dem Sack! Der ultimative Führer durch die saarländische Projektelandschaft*. St. Ingbert.

Schäfer, Frank et al. (1983). *Alternative Projekte im Saarland*. Saarbrücken.

Schmidt, Jochen (1985). *Die Geschichte des Genie-Gedankens in der deutschen Literatur, Philosophie und Politik 1750–1945*. Darmstadt.

Schulte, Barbara (ed.) (2006). *Transfer lokalisiert: Konzepte, Akteure, Kontexte. Comparativ – Zeitschrift für Globalgeschichte und vergleichende Gesellschaftsforschung 16, 3/2006*.

Schulze, Gerhard (1993). *Die Erlebnisgesellschaft. Kultursoziologie der Gegenwart.* Frankfurt am Main.

Scott, Allen J. (2000). *The Cultural Economy of Cities. Essays on the Geography of Image-Producing Industries.* London.

Simmel, Georg (1995). »Die Großstadt und das Geistesleben«. In Georg Simmel. *Aufsätze und Abhandlungen 1901–1908*, edited by Rüdiger Krame, Angela Ramstedt and Otthein Ramstedt, 116–130. Frankfurt am Main.

Spitzer, Leo (1942). »Milieu and Ambiance: an Essay in Historical Semantics«. *Philosophy and Phenomenological Research*, 3, 1, 1942, 1–42 and 169–218.

Stehr, Nico (1994). *Arbeit, Eigentum und Wissen. Zur Theorie von Wissensgesellschaften.* Frankfurt am Main.

Stehr, Nico (2001). *Wissen und Wirtschaften. Die gesellschaftlichen Grundlagen der modernen Ökonomie.* Frankfurt am Main.

Sternberg, Robert J. (ed.) (1999). *Handbook of Creativity.* Cambridge.

Storper, Michael (1997). *The regional world. Territorial development in a global economy.* New York.

— (2004). *Institutions, Incentives and Communication in economic geography, Hettner-Lectures 7.* Stuttgart.

Taine, Hippolyte (1882). *Philosophie de l'art.* Paris.

Vogel, Jakob (2004). »Von der Wissenschafts- zur Wissensgeschichte. Für eine Historisierung der ›Wissensgesellschaft‹«, *Geschichte und Gesellschaft*, 30, 639–660.

Weinberger, Marie-Luise (1987). »Von der Müsli-Kultur zur Yuppie-Kultur. Über den sozialen Wandel in innerstädtischen Revieren von Ballungsgebieten«. *Die neue Gesellschaft, Frankfurter Hefte*, 34, 4, 1987, 352–358.

Wolfrum, Edgar (2005). *Die Bundesrepublik Deutschland 1949–1990.* Stuttgart.

Flourishing Cultural Production in Economic Wasteland: Three Ways of Making Sense of a Cultural Economy in Berlin at the Beginning of the Twentyfirst Century

Alexa Färber

The title of this article appears to evoke a contradiction between cultivation and wilderness as well as growth and destruction. It thus provokes a range of ambivalent structures that have been highlighted as relevant to understand the creative processes in capitalist societies, where a situation of destruction is considered the very condition for/effect of creativity in economic processes. Economist Joseph Schumpeter demonstrated this with the concept of creative destruction in the 1940s. This was then re-examined in historical research on urban development and architecture (Page 1999). Similarly but less explicitly, the more recent call for a creative class as location factor relies on the assumption that a given city is *in need of* the potential re-evaluation of its economy through the activities of such a class, its economic and symbolic capital (as the debates around Richard Florida's concept of the creative class suggest).

These authors proclaim an internal, almost natural relationship between »destruction« and »creativity«, or between »vacant city space« and »productive cultural economies«. Berlin could, at first sight, be understood as the most valuable example for the productive conjunction of an urban situation characterised within the twentieth century by disruptive historical moments and the astonishing recovery in the two post-war phases and the post-socialist times we live in today – including the cultural sphere. Destruction and a flourishing cultural production seem to have succeeded one another as if they adhered to an internal law. Nevertheless, a closer examination of the possible simultaneity of a stagnating economic situation and a parallel growing sector of cultural production in Berlin since 1989 points to different (voluntary) performative acts which try to make sense of this situation.[1]

Thus, the key to the cultural logic that I analyse in this article lies in the different performative entanglements of urban economic space, cultural production and the imagery of the city (Lindner 2003; Lindner and Musner 2005). In my research on Berlin's remodelling as a potential world city since 1989,[2] we conceptualised these performative acts that are inscribed into a city's imagery as practices of *urban imagineering* (Färber 2007). In Berlin, urban imagineering seems to resonate especially well with the cultural production sector, be it for the concrete intersection of specific actors which link the spheres of culture and economy together, or because of a shared aesthetic practice relating cultural products to the cultural logic of the late modern city (Zukin 1995).

This paper proposes to explore the specific cultural logic of urban imagineering that gives shape to the simultaneity of a stagnating economic situation and a parallel growing sector of cultural production on three levels:

1) the discursive re-evaluation and relocation of this tension through those public and private institutions such as the Senat and other administrations, as well as the Chamber of Commerce. All these actors treat the economic situation and Berlin *as a whole* and inscribe economic wasteland and cultural production into a juxtaposing rhetoric (»but«);

2) the intersections, created by public and private actors in the city that take part in explicitly shaping the relationship between the city's economic space and the sector of cultural production. Here, industrial wasteland becomes the very condition for cultural production through a causal rhetoric (»because«);

1   I would like to thank Martina Heßler and Clemens Zimmermann for sharing their insights in the historical depth of urban culture and inviting me, as a anthropologist of contemporary practices, to contribute to this book. Special thanks go to Isabel Schoppe for editing this text.

2   This paper results from research conducted in Berlin for the comparative research project »Urban culture and ethnic representation: Berlin and Moscow as emerging ›world cities‹« It was generously funded by the German Research Foundation at the Department of European Ethnology, Humboldt University, Berlin. Cordula Gdaniec conducted the research in Moscow.

3) finally, the example of entrepreneurs – in this case owners and collaborators of »department stores« – serves as example for another intermediate format, providing a space to consume cultural products. Among the stores that are relevant for the problematic of this chapter, I include those, which are closely intertwined with local processes and actors of cultural economy in that they exclusively sell products from Berlin's »creative industries«, are run by designers themselves, or are explicitly partaking in the idea of Berlin as a place of cultural production. I draw here on data from fieldwork in one department store project as well as supplementary material collected between 2003 and 2007.

Thus the terrain that I cover in this article proposes a close reading of how economic crisis and cultural production have been framed in Berlin during the first decade of the new millennium.

»Poor but ...«: Antagonism from Berlin as a *Whole*

Economic crisis and the parallel cultural attractiveness of Berlin has become a recurrent topic to a wide range of actors within the city's political field. The following statement by the Mayor of Berlin, Klaus Wowereit, re-elected in 2006 for a second four-year term, may count as the most stunning illustration of this ambivalence. During a visit to London, aimed to attract British investors to Berlin, Wowereit described Berlin as a young and »unfinished city«, with very cheap sites for sale, and concluded that Berlin was »poor but sexy« (*Tagesspiegel*, December 4, 2003).

This comment, since a popular view of the city, may represent one of the most disproportionate ways to evoke the city's economic difficulties, which are also illustrated in figures: compared to the other 15 Federal Republic *Länder*, Berlin's GDP was one of the four lowest in 2006 (1.9 percent adjusted to price – see IHK/HWK 2007: 16). In the same year, Berlin had one of the highest unemployment rates in Germany (16.1 percent). It ranked top again in 2006, with one in seven households unable to pay off debts which were at 15.2 percent, five percent above the average (2006 SCHUFA report, *Berliner Zeitung*, November 23, 2006)[3]. Also its image as

---

3   The credit check organisation, SCHUFA publishes an anual report which includes an analysis of citizens' creditworthiness in specific places. Results from these types of re-

»capital of debtors« (*tageszeitung*, November 25, 2005, junge welt December 21, 2006) did not disappear. This was also not helped by the »bank affair« which led to the change of government in 2001. In 2002, the Senat approved an »extraordinary emergency budget« (»extreme Haushaltsnotlage«) with debts totalling approx. €46 billion, followed by a request for extra funding help from the Federal Republic (Senatsverwaltung für Finanzen 2002, 1).[4]

Since 1989 and particularly the end of the 1990s, Berlin has been shaped by different performative practices (discursive, institutionally formative and daily practices of cultural production) which tried to differentiate between a cultural production and an economic wasteland. The actors involved rely on knowledge and knowledge practices that intertwine the specific character of space as urban wasteland, with cultural production, and an image of the city. Recurring actors to highlight include the Mayor, the Administration of Economics, Labour and Women's issues (ELW), the Administration for Science, Research and Culture (SRC), the Chamber of Commerce and Industry (CCI), the Berlin Marketing Company (BMC) and individual representatives from the cultural industries' sector, universities/research institutions and the media. Analysis of these actors' statements reveals that when it comes to the economic situation as a whole or its central sectors, they tend to construct an ambivalence, inscribed in a rhetoric of juxtapositions. Thus, the shortfalls of the manufacturing industry are presented as follows: »Berlin industry has changed, *but* it is very active«; »it has shrunk, *but* it competes well with its products in the global market«; »there are fewer employees in the industrial sector, *but* on average, they have more qualifications and a higher income«. (CCI press release, June 7, 2002, italics and translation I. Sch.)

Harald Wolf, Senator for the Economy, commented on the astonishing high number of enterprises created in 2004[5]: »reality and potential are miles

---

port are of great interest to investors as they indicate the purchasing power of a city's inhabitants.

4   The Constitutional Court in Karslruhe did not approve this request.The vice president of the Constitutional Court in Karlsruhe, Winfried Hassemer, slightly inverted Wowereit's image of Berlin, considering that »Berlin might appear sexy because it is not so poor« (quoted in Die Zeit, 43, 2006).

5   In 2004, around 50,000 companies were registered: 85 percent were new and 50 percent of them were based on the self-employment model (Ich-AG) in the trade (Handel) and service sectors. Between 1999 and 2002, the number of companies registered and deregistered was almost the same (Statistisches Landesamt Berlin 2005: 1).

from one another in Berlin«, which as he stated at the CCI annual press conference in 2005 »is the basic dilemma in this location« (Tagesspiegel March 24/25, 2005). This dilemma leads, as I have shown, to an antagonistic rhetoric if you take Berlin as a whole.

»Deserted – thus«: A Conditional Relationship of Space and Cultural Industries

In the previous section, I showed that torn between the mere postulation of a contradiction, the rhetoric of juxtapositions could not account for the plausibility of the obvious ambivalence. Thus, I would argue that from the perspective of the institutions involved, only the distinction of cultural economy as a measurable sector allowed for another version of this ambivalence. While economic wasteland as a whole contradicted the flourishing cultural sphere, industrial wasteland could account for an inversion of this relationship

In their introduction to the first *Creative Industries Report 2005*, the above-mentioned Senator Wolf and his colleague Thomas Flier, Senator for Culture, wrote that together, the private cultural enterprises and the publicly-funded cultural sector »contribute to the image that Berlin represents to its inhabitants and its millions of visitors – a young, creative city with a unique combination of creative industries, culture (*Hochkultur*) and history. The quality and diversity of its cultural programme and its creative industry contribute undoubtedly towards the excellent advantages of Berlin as a location.« (Kulturwirtschaft in Berlin 2005, 3, translation I. Sch.)[6]

The report, a result of the »*Berlin Initiative for Creative Industries*«, began in July 2004 and relied on two former reports on culture and economy in Berlin from 1992 and 2002.[7] It created a link between the economy portfo-

---

6   In 2005, another two Länder and one city region published a Cultural Industries report (Schleswig-Holstein, Hessen, and the city region of Aachen) whilst the first report went back to the initiative of the Land North Rhine-Westphalia in 1992. See German Comission for UNESCO (2007): 31–34.

7   The German Institute for Economic Research (DIW) conducted both studies. The CCI Berlin commissioned the latter. See DIW – Deutsches Institut für Wirtschaftsforschung (1992) and Frank et al. (2002). A major problem for comparative analysis of these reports was their different definitions of the cultural industry sectors. This incongruence

lio and the public cultural sector – the »Senat Administration for Science, Research and Culture«. More important in my view, it offered all actors involved, the opportunity to distinguish between the cultural economy and the facts and images of other economic sectors by »cutting it out«. This distinction allowed for the identification of actors, networks, mediator formats (retailers, fairs), media communication platforms, (public) galleries, museums and archives plus special events, all involved in shaping the realm of Berlin's creative industries – and from then on officially labelled as such. Once the creative industries' sector had been made visible in that way, the balance achieved meant that one could be much more optimistic. As Senator Wolf explained with respect to the design sector:

»Designers, fashion creators, photographers and architects all benefit from favourable office rents, low costs of living, synergetic networks and an enthusiastic design audience. In addition, Berlin offers a great variety of educational and career training opportunities. Last, but not least, Berlin's more than 1,300 designers make the city the designer capital of Germany. Many new companies joined over the last few years. In order to benefit from this creative atmosphere, even large enterprises, such as Volkswagen AG, have transferred their design departments to the region.« (Projekt Zukunft Berlin 2006: 1)

Furthermore, with the help of this instrument one was able to give clear figures on the productivity of this newly identified economic sector. Thus, the report showed that in 2002, more than 18,000 (mainly) small and medium-sized enterprises in the cultural industries registered a turnover of eight billion euros, eleven percent of the GDP, as much as the traditional trade (Kulturwirtschaft in Berlin 2005: 22). But even so, in Berlin more than anywhere, it was considered that the city competed, because of its urban »surplus«, as Wolf concludes in a comparative mode: »In contrast to established design metropolises, such as Paris, Milan or London, the inspiring nature of Berlin is based on an atmosphere of transformation, progress and constant change.«[8] (Projekt Zukunft Berlin 2006: 1)

---

was also considered a problem by those actors who tried to compare the situation of cultural industries between different cities, Länder and states.

8 Jesko Fezer and Axel John Wieder argue that one of the central modes of negotiating official urban development and temporary strategies of use after the fall of the Wall had been built around the topos of Berlin as locus of permanent change and »in the making«. They show how in the early 1990s »space seemed to be freely available for a brief time« while today this practice is »officially adopted in the iconography« of Berlin (Fezer and Wieder 2004: 74).

Klaus Siebenhaar, professor for cultural management in Berlin[9] and a collaborator in the »*Berlin Initiative for Creative Industries*«, underlined in his statement published in the report, that the same report gives the opportunity to »[...] see for the first time the so-called non-profit sector and the profit sector together, and not in the perspective of subsidies, but as having a joint creative value [...]«. In his view, Berlin could be seen as a »[...] model of collaboration, strategic alliances and joint initiatives [...]« between public and private sector. There are »[...] many good examples of entrepreneurship that can be clearly demonstrated.« (Kulturwirtschaft in Berlin 2005, 16, translation I. Sch.).

Another similar initiative, the temporary commission to the Senat, »A Future for Berlin« (Enquête-Kommission *Eine Zukunft für Berlin* 2004–2005), published its final report, pointing out the same principle of »entrepreneurial mood«:

»To think and act in an entrepreneurial way means basically to be in control of one's own future. Being responsible for yourself and using your own initiative and having the courage to make errors are central to entrepreneurial success.« (Schlussbericht der Enquête-Kommission 2005, 20, translation I. Sch.)

The identification of a distinctive sector of cultural industries and the promotion of an entrepreneurial mood by these initiatives and commissions, emphasised by the participation of successful *culturepreneurs*, (note: in both forums, actors from organisations such as record labels, galleries, theatres, museums and scientific commentators have been involved) relate to two semantic fields:

First, in terms of a cultural economy's distinctive field, another approach to space is evolving. If one analyses the common cultural logic that links Berlin's spatial characteristics with cultural production, the most prevalent topos is neither »destroyed« nor »devastated space«. It is the vacancy topos that evolved in the 1990s (Fezer and Wieder 2004, 80), rearticulated with the debate of the shrinking cities (Oswalt et al.) that offered a semantic structure where the ambivalence of economic stagnation and growing cultural production could be inscribed. As Berlin was seen as a shrinking city, its »empty space«, i.e. its stagnating real estate market and low purchasing power, was attractive, especially for those involved in cul-

---

9   He is also editor of the »Culture index« (*Kulturindex*) which was created with the CCI. It provides a biannual survey of non-profit and profit organisations in the culture sector, recording their development and valuation of the cultural sector etc.

tural industries. Thus techno culture was one of the first successful cultural practices after the fall of the Wall *because* the city offered empty space, industrial wasteland for temporary use (Vogt 2005). The same holds true for young designers (fashion, art etc.) who were attracted all over the world, as the storyline and the empirical data of qualitative research assumes, *because* there was enough vacant space to build cheap studios for start-ups at a low risk (Lange 2005).

Second, entrepreneurial practices – a topos to think about economic risk and cultural economy was explicitly introduced into the ambivalent economic space. *Failure* proved to be a particularly plausible figure to rationalise an economic enterprise within an all-inclusive atmosphere of economic stagnation. *Failure* might even turn into a success story. As I have shown elsewhere (Färber 2007), the specific imagery of Berlin as the city of bohemian, alternative lifestyles and weak economic power offers a cultural reference where economic weakness and failure may be considered as a resource. Those who »invest themselves« and their enterprise in the cultural economy sector in Berlin often do so as entrepreneurial bohemians who turn bohemian culture into an enterprise. They relate successfully to an imagery of Berlin as a ground for bohemian lifestyles. They would probably fail if they related to an image of powerful economic development that did not resonate with this imagery. Failure became calculable within the space-related logic of Berlin's cultural economy. Within this cultural logic of the »city of imperfection« (Klein 2005, 255) the (successful) role models which appropriate this material and imagery space of Berlin are in their essence bohemian: They are coming together in Berlin as the »world club of international losers« (Litichevsky 2003, 20), as self-labelled »universal dilettantes« (Lange 2005, 58). They live and work as urban dossers/clochard (*»urbane Penner«*, Bunz 2006) or digital bohemia, which may count as a more economically successful model (Friebe and Lobo 2006).[10] From an institutional perspective such as the Senat of City Development, they are perceived and labelled as »urban pioneers« (Overmeyer 2007).

Those actors and modes of representation that identify Berlin's »creative industry« contributed to the plausibility of a distinctively flourishing cultural economy and an overall stagnating economy. Both these actors and the media interest they aroused were the expression of a specific

10 Richard Lloyd stressed the ambivalence of »neo-bohemian« practices in the contribution to re-shaping an urban space in Chicago. See Lloyd 2006.

space-related knowledge where space is actually the resource for cultural production in Berlin. Thus the economic wasteland, which Mayor Wowereit and his political partners pointed to in a contradictory logic, is inversed in the realm of cultural production and its representation. Industrial wasteland became the very condition for knowledge practices and the production of cultural goods that turned Berlin into the most attractive place[11]. This cultural logic of space and cultural production does not juxtapose these two as poor, *but* attractive as the Mayor and the representatives of Berlin suggested. It addresses Berlin as attractive, *because of* the spatial reminders (industrial wasteland) of a poor economy and echoes the abovementioned »internal« or »natural« relationship between cultural productivity and destruction. The most specific pattern of the internal relationship between industrial wasteland and cultural production in Berlin is this reflexive inscription into the topos of economic failure.

Failure and *industrial wasteland* both count among the imagery of the city and thus are part of the cultural economy's success.[12] In Berlin the potential for failure can be a resource or even a »vision« as the book *Minusvisionen* with portraits of young entrepreneurs, whose Berlin business have failed over the last ten years, suggests (Niermann 2003). Their evaluation of the failed enterprises shows the extent to which failure has been incorporated as an integral part of a contemporary economic »spirit«.[13]

»In Spite of«: The Department Store as a Site to Experience (Successful) Failure

In its client journal, the *Berliner Sparkasse* profiled, under the headline »take 2«, a few shops that followed the »shop-in-shop principle«: »why be re-

---

11 These initiatives were included in the »UNESCO Certification as a City of Design«, received in January 2006, and the conference »International Creative Cities Conference on Collaboration for Economic Development« that took place in Berlin in September 2006 and launched the »Berlin Manifesto for a Partnership of European Cities in Creativity«.

12 Nevertheless in this incorporation of failure there relies an interesting contradiction: the vacant space is primarily marked by the failure of others (old industries), not of new economies.

13 Since the 1960s this entrepreneurial logic spreads out from the enterprise into all kinds of social realms (Boltanski and Chiapello 2003).

stricted to one idea when you can create at least two« (Berliner Akzente 1–2–3/2006, 4). In the same article, small businesses were presented, which offered two services under one roof – a barbershop plus yoga classes, a barbershop plus bar or a launderette plus bar. Even though this model of multiple economic usage of space may be found in other German cities, it may be considered as symptomatic for Berlin to use space like this. This common practice points in two directions that are relevant here. On the one hand, the relationship of space and economic practice is reconfigured into multiple usage of space, as if space were a rare resource. On the other hand, this multiple usage could be a sign for transferring the likely risk of entrepreneurial failure into a partial spatio-economic engagement in urban wasteland. In the perspective of this paper I understand this kind of partial conjunction of space and economic practice that incorporates failure as a risk – or risk-management – and an alternative form of urban imagineering.

I chose to explore this partial spatio-economic enterprise by taking the department store as an example, because it demonstrates this multilayered and dense usage of space. Focussing on stores that sell designer products created in Berlin and labelled as such, the sample offers insight into one of the most dynamic and emblematic sectors of Berlin's cultural economy. They are part of the 6,700 mini-enterprises and collectives in fashion, design and art, registered in 2005 and their annual turnover is €1.5 billion.[14] As their modern counterparts are seen as major urban representations of modern capitalism those stores that are at stake here may count as a reflection of the spirit of late modernity because of their specific incorporation of urban space and failure.

A topography of this kind of designer store, founded or projected in the last 13 years, shows that out of the eight stores in this sample, only one is situated in the western part of Berlin, in the Kreuzberg neighbourhood.[15] All the others are in the central and semi-central eastern part of the city – Mitte (5), Prenzlauer Berg (1) and Friedrichshain (2). They are in »young«, scene-oriented neighbourhoods, although only three of them are in the

14 With 1,300 design enterprises and ca. €130 million turnover, this branch dominates the sector, labelled »artmarket« (*Kunstmarkt*) in the Cultural industries' report and figures in the top 12 percent of design enterprises in Germany. Between 1998 and 2002 this sector registered a 24 percent growth and a € 380 million turnover in 2002 (see Kulturwirtschaft in Berlin 2005: 65–67).

15 Nine department stores correspond, to my knowledge, to the characteristics mentioned above. In the case studies, I will only refer to three of them.

heart of these neighbourhoods, like a special street or place (one in Kreuzberg, one in Mitte, one in Prenzlauer Berg). Six are in post-war buildings (one in Kreuzberg, four in Mitte, one in Friedrichshain). The locations contain the word »department store« (3) or Berlin (5) in their name; one links the neighbourhood's name to »department store«. All stores are structured along the lines of the department store with its manifold articles from different labels – in these cases exclusively from Berlin cultural industries. Three are both atelier and store, adding to the authenticity of the products. The products range from on-location-handmade through to designer items, which are industrially produced. They include clothes, jewellery, furniture, games such as cards or memory, and all kinds of Berlin souvenirs.[16]

Between Old and New Cultural Economies: The Community-Based Department Store

The first case I wish to present is a department store project that was started by a group of three entrepreneurs who planned to open an alternative shopping centre in the heart of the symbolically highly-charged district of Kreuzberg. The images of this district range from »eldorado of squatters« in the 1980s to »small-Istanbul« and »immigrants' ghetto« in the late 1990s. In the new milennium it is catching up as the topos of the creative city makes Kreuzberg the place to nurture cultural production.[17] The entrepreneurs had already successfully run several music clubs in Kreuzberg, with sub-cultural and gay-lesbian public since the late 1980s. In 2002 this group of business associates and friends saw an opportunity to bring together like-minded individuals (from Kreuzberg) interested in setting up business. Based on the model of Affleck's Palace in Manchester, the store was meant to offer all kinds of »creative ideas«, presented in about 50 small shops within a department store.

16 For her masters thesis (Berlin, Humboldt University 2007) Anja Früh conducted systematic research on the design-souvenirs produced in Berlin since 1989.
17 See Barbara Lang (1998) for the symbolic gentrification of this district and Giacomo Bottà for the implementation of the music industry in this volume.

*Fig. 1: Neighbourhood management leaflet publicises department store project under the
headline »Colourful scene department store and lively meeting point at Kottbusser Tor«*

(Source: Quartiersmanagement Kottbusser Tor)

The economic practices conformed to the economic model that these
alternative entrepreneurs were trying to implement corresponded to two
different cultural logics. Firstly they referred to alternative models of self-
fulfilment and a sub-cultural notion of creativity that draws on authenticity
and resistance as in the »do-it-yourself« movement (Müller 1991). Secondly
the legal economic form for the enterprise was meant to rely on self-
employment (following a government-funded scheme) which resonated
perfectly with the post-industrial form of the entrepreneurial self (Bröckling 2007, McRobbie 2003). Paradoxically, the historical, cultural and social
patterns of Kreuzberg embedded the potential tension between alternative,
post-industrial and late-modern »lifestyles«.

The history of the department store project was comparatively short.
After six months, acquiring possible participants for the department store
and negotiating rent with the company who owned the space, the three
entrepreneurs were ready to quit the idea of opening the store in the famous social housing complex in the heart of Kreuzberg, Kottbusser Tor.
They realized that the company, running the complex, was deeply inscribed
in »old West-Berlin fraud« mentioned above (Rose 2003). It seemed more
important to raise public awareness of the living conditions in the social
housing complex where the store should have been located. Slowly a
neighbourhood initiative was born, still under the guidance of the three
would-be store managers. Thus the economic and cultural space turned
into a more explicit social and political space, a space of civic commitment
or engagement and also a symbolic space.

The entrepreneurs knew Kreuzberg as a business and cultural space.
This group of friends/colleagues had left their imprint to the neighbourhood with former economic/cultural engagement. Their new department

store project had been influenced by previous professional experiences and was therefore appropriate for this particular place. At the same time, because of their cultural and social commitment to the neighbourhood, they could not ignore their political engagement. The initiators abandoned the project as they thought it was best to protect their collaborators from further business risk and potential personal failure. They explained that they thought it would be irresponsible to keep these future entrepreneurs waiting to start their businesses until the whole procedure could begin i.e. searching for another space to rent, negotiating a contract etc. It was their cultural logic of alternative and sub-cultural engagement that was stronger than potential business success. Failure was rationalised by the fact they took responsibility for others.

Within the New Cultural Economy but without a Community

This second department store is not inscribed so deeply into the neighbourhood's history and lacks some of the community-based aspects that were so important for the project in Kreuzberg. Nevertheless it is structured along similar lines to the store described in the first case. It is located in the Friedrichshain district, in two stores of an old building that hosted first a department store for textiles and until the end of the 1990s the East German social organisation *Volkssolidarität*. Based on the participation of individual entrepreneurs, who manage their own shops (situated in different rooms throughout the building) it started in 2004 with seven collaborators from four different countries: Sweden, Russia, Lithuania and Germany. As stated in the press release, the department store »offers international designs – made in Berlin« while the »cosy atmosphere provides a relaxed shopping tour through a new, small, but nice highlight in Berlin's fashion scene«. While the Kreuzberg project was open to all kinds of »creative services and articles«, the Friedrichshain store specialised in handmade products, mainly from the fashion world, and in the beginning workshops. The individual space is shop and studio at the same time, which from the self-representation of the department store is meant to add handmade authenticity to the articles echoed in the slightly alternative styles of clothes (patchwork, knitwear or felt), jewlery and children's games.
The business structure of this initiative relies on the government-subsidized self-employment scheme (*Ich-AG*) that enabled individuals to

set up in business whilst the neighbourhood management supported the collective project. However, one designer holds the main contract for rent with subleases to the others. All contracts are renewed once a year until users with a more important capital asset are found.[18] In 2007, there were about six shops left on the first floor. For those who do not want to rent an entire shop, it is also possible to »rent a board« to display and sell products.

Fig.2: Minimising risk by sharing space and management of the building. Studio/shop in Friedrichshain department store.

(Source: Photography by the author)

Being part of this enterprise involves low (financial) risk: I was told from one designer that ten percent of each entrepreneur's income has to be invested in marketing the whole store and the renovation of the building etc. (also infobox. Stadtteilzeitung Boxhagener Platz, April 2006, 2). Also, each designer has to invest time in the communal space and take over the

---

18 For the officialised format of »temporary use«, where rents are below average or only running costs have to be paid, see Overmeyer et al. 2007.

opening hours one day a week selling articles from which s/he receives ten percent. In essence, the concept relies strongly on the minimisation of risk – gained by shared space and joint-responsibility for the store – which would not be possible if an individual ran a unit on their own. This is especially important since some of the individual entrepreneurs are selling or producing their articles for the first time.[19] Others are also selling their products on markets and in other Berlin shops. Therefore, their shop/studio in the department store is part of a range of business enterprises. These aspects point to the prevalence of the economic space of cultural economy before the participation within local community space. As such, this specific department store may be considered as an opportunity (»for beginners« or »re-starters«), which then opens up other possibilities without requiring a lot of financial resources and only some commitment such as time. As such it could be considered as a business enterprise almost exclusively based on the model of individual self-employment which leads to a partial local engagement and resonates only slightly with an enthusiastic entrepreneurial mood, ready to take *any* risk.

In the Heart of Cultural Industries: Berlin as Icon

Situated not far from the above-mentioned store but not so close to the young, alternative scene in this district, the third example may count as the most successful designer store business. It is a »retail platform«, founded in 2003 in a 300m² location on one of the main streets in the Friedrichshain district. With a big shopping mall at one end and the district's city hall at the other, this part of the street is characterised by the typical landscape of small shops and restaurants which regularly change hands or are often vacant in the very low price sector.[20]. Here, the designer department store appears quite detached from its local context where it is only one of two shops that offers high priced designer products (the other shop specialises in clothes). At the time of research, the store included a small café and was

---

19 One designer started a business only after he had heard about the concept of the store.

20 This situation has lead to the creation of a street association, financed by the CCI, the local adminsitration and EU. Created in 2004/2005 under the heading »Mittendrin Berlin: Die Zentren Initiative« (»Right in the middle of Berlin: initiative for (shopping) centres«) it aims to support entrepreneurs in this area and prevent the decline of this street as a shopping area. The design department store, however, does not take part in this association.

selling items from around 140 Berlin designers. Products on display included furniture, jewelry, clothes and Berlin souvenirs. The managers, selling the design products here, sought to set trends in their specific segment and cater for a young, fashionable clientele.

Besides the growing number of designers represented at the store and since its opening, the business has expanded spatially and conceptually in two ways. In 2005 it opened a second branch in the famous *Galerie Lafayette*, situated in the exclusive shopping area of Friedrichstraße, Mitte. In 2006 it added another 180m² to the first location in Friedrichshain, providing a special section for young Berlin designers from the numerous Berlin fashion institutes. This last initiative was launched in collaboration with a semi-public association, supporting Berlin designers (partly funded by the EU), and is supported by the local administration.

Fig. 3: Outsourcing failure: the department store as a design platform.

(Source: Photography by the author)

The managers of this designer store, who are not designers themselves, take part in another network – »create berlin«. Here they present their global vision as follows:

»PPG is a projects' and production company that aims to produce products for designers from Berlin and to acquire projects for the design scene in Berlin. [...] with its creative background of 140 designers from Berlin, it addresses the industry and offers innovative and individual solutions for merchandising, furnishings, shop concepts and product design« (http://www.create-berlin.de/berlinomat_de.html, January 15, 2007, translation I. Sch.).

Two aspects seem to be relevant to the character of this store:

1) the *products* offered by the store reach far beyond the role of selling designer articles to individual customers. It is rather about a whole set of *projects*, as the shop manager told me, that were initialised by the department store and which were still not enough known. The store addresses and articulates, in particular, the different economic actors in the Berlin cultural economy, which has become home »not only to newly self-employed individuals but also to established designers« (http://www.xerus-berlin.de/anbieterinfo/52, January 15, 2007) – including the public sector. The activities established with the help of the designer store might be considered as an attempt to become an unavoidable actor in the construction of a Berlin cultural industry.

2) If the aim is to offer services to other designers, this goal relies on the assumption that there would be a need for such »solutions« as the quote suggests. Here it is probably less the »established designers« who are addressed and more those who are in the process of setting up their businesses and in the situation of calculated risk and possible success. The topos »risk« and »possible failure« cannot be ruled out within the concept of this enterprise. Nevertheless its partial spatial practice, especially the section reserved for the so-called »young stars« with financial support from semi-public funds points towards anticipated failure or success, absorbed by the store and the owner's experience. However, with this support service, failure has successfully been extracted and transferred to the possible failure of »the others«.

Conclusion

The three perspectives presented in this paper helped to point out the relationship between cultural products, economic practices, the city and its imagery. In identifying cultural industries as a growing part within Berlin's economic wasteland a »high risk sector with extremely variable market chances« had been created at the same time (German Commission for UNESCO 2007, 25). The outlines of the three department stores, presented here, demonstrated their use of space, their management of risk and failure, and their self-representation, as different forms of inscription in the Berlin cultural economy and its cultural logic.

The first was deeply inscribed into a neighbourhood-based community logic. In the project envisaged for the department store, the risk imposed by the rental contracts was considered partly too great, and the possible failure of the individuals involved was seen as the failure of the whole project.

The second case reflected temporary community practices that involved sharing not only space but also income and time. But, the success of each economic enterprise was partly taken as a first attempt, supported by the subsidised format of self-employment (*Ich-AG*), and relied not only on the participation in the store but also on a range of other activities (markets, other stores etc.). Thus, risk and failure were individualised and the fluctuation within the store was relatively high.

For the third case, one could say that risk had been inverted. It had been turned into a resource for self-fashioning and self-centring of this quite successful designers' department store. This has been possible by turning failure into the possible failure of others that one is ready to prevent with the space and services offered by the store.

Thus, the designers' department stores have different links to cultural production not only because these are the products they offer. They are closely linked to the idea of being the product of a »creative idea« or being undertaken by culturepreneurs. Finally they are involved in the urban imagineering, making sense of the simultaneity of wasteland and that of growth.

The case of Berlin after the fall of the Wall suggests that to understand the impact of cultural production on urban economy and the impact of economy on urban culture, it is important to capture the cultural logic that binds these spheres together. The notion of urban imagineering may count as one sphere where this cultural logic is expressed in economic practices and self-representation. Contributing to the urban imagineering gives shape to participation in city space and urban society – even if, like in the case of Berlin, this requires inscribing ones own enterprise into an imagery of the city that is economically, successfully unsuccessful.

Bibliography

Boltanski, Luc and Eve Chiapello (2003). *Der neue Geist des Kapitalismus*. Konstanz.

Bröckling, Ulrich (2007). *Das unternehmerische Selbst. Soziologie einer Subjektivierungsform*. Frankfurt am Main.

Bunz, Mercedes (2006). »Meine Armut kotzt mich an«. *zitty*, 4, Berlin, 17–19.

DIW – Deutsches Institut für Wirtschaftsforschung (1992). *Kultur als Wirtschaftsfaktor in Berlin*. Berlin.

Färber, Alexa (2007). »Urbanes Imagineering in der postindustriellen Stadt: Zur Plausibilität Berlins als Ost-West-Drehscheibe«. In Thomas Biskup and Marc Schalenberg (eds.). *Selling Berlin: Imagebildung und Stadtmarketing von der preußischen Residenz bis zur Bundeshauptstadt*, 279–296. Stuttgart.

Fezer, Jesko and Axel John Wieder (2004). »Space of Limited Opportunities – Urban Development Berlin after 1989«. In *Komplex Berlin. Katalog der 3. Berlin Biennale*, 73–82. Köln.

Frank, Björn, Kurt Geppert and Dieter Vesper (2002). *Kultur als Wirtschaftsfaktor in Berlin. Eine Studie des DIW Berlin im Auftrag der IHK Berlin*. Berlin.

Friebe, Holm and Sascha Lobo (2006). *Wir nennen es Arbeit. Die digitale Bohème oder: Intelligentes Leben jenseits der Festanstellung*. München.

IHK Berlin and HWK Berlin (eds.) (2007). *Berliner Wirtschaft in Zahlen*. Berlin.

Kulturwirtschaft in Berlin (2005). *Entwicklung und Potenziale. Hrsg. Von Senatsverwaltung für Wirtschaft, Arbeit und Frauen in Berlin, Senatsverwaltung für Wissenschaft; Forschung und Kultur*. Berlin.

Klein, Christian (2005). »Vom Glück des Scheiterns. Lebens- und Gesellschaftskonzepte in Kästners ›Fabian‹ und Regeners ›Herr Lehmann‹«. In Stefan Zahlmann and Sylka Scholz (eds.). *Scheitern und Biographie. Die andere Seite moderner Lebensgeschichten*, 255–264. Gießen.

Lang, Barbara (1998). *Mythos Kreuzberg: Ethnographie eines Stadtteils (1961–1995)*. Frankfurt am Main.

— (2005). »Culturepreneurs in Berlin: Orts- und Raumproduzenten von Szenen«. In Alexa Färber (ed.). *Hotel Berlin – Formen urbaner Mobilität und Verortung. Berliner Blätter Vol. 37*, 53–64. Münster.

Litichevsky, Georgy (2003). »Berlin – Hauptstadt des dritten Jahrtausends«. In Pawel Choroschilow et al. (eds.). *Berlin Moskau/Moskau Berlin 1950–2000. Chronik*, 18–22. Berlin.

Lindner, Rolf (2003). »Talking about the imagery«. *monopolis. Globalisierung & Stadtforschung. sinn-haft*, 14/15, 10–13.

— and Lutz Musner (2005). »Kulturelle Ökonomien, urbane ›Geschmackslandschaften‹ und Metropolenkonkurrenz«. *Informationen zur modernen Stadtgeschichte*, 1, 26–37.

Lloyd, Frank (2006). *Neo-bohemia: art and commerce in the postindustrial city*. New York.

McRobbie, Angela (2003). »I was knitting away night and day. Die Bedeutung von Kunst und Handwerk im Modedesign«. In Marion von Osten (ed.). *Norm der Abweichung*, 99–117. Zürich.

Müller, Birgit (1991). *Towards an alternative culture of work: Political idealism and economic prectices in West Berlin collective enterprises.* Boulder/San Francisco/Oxford.

Niermann, Ingo (2003). *Minusvisionen. Unternehmer ohne Geld. Protokolle.* Frankfurt am Main.

Overmeyer, Klaus and Senatsverwaltung für Stadtentwicklung Berlin (eds.) (2007). *Urban pioneers. Berlin Stadtentwicklung durch Zwischennutzung.* Berlin.

Page, Max (1999). *The creative destruction of Manhatten, 1900–1940.* Chicago.

Projekt Zukunft Berlin (2006). *Berlin – City of Design.* Berlin.

Rose, Matthew D. (2003). *Eine ehrenwerte Gesellschaft. Die Bankgesellschaft Berlin.* Berlin.

Schlussbericht der Enquête-Kommission »Eine Zukunft für Berlin« (Abgeordnetenhaus Berlin, Drucksache 15/4000, 15. Wahlperiode), 9. Mai 2005.

Senatsverwaltung für Finanzen (2002). *Erklärung zur extremen Haushaltsnotlage Berlins.* Berlin.

Statistisches Landesamt Berlin (2005). *Berliner Statistik. Gewerbeanzeigen in Berlin.* Berlin.

Vogt, Sabine (2005). *Clubräume – Freiräume: musikalische Lebensentwürfe in den Jugendkulturen Berlins.* Kassel.

Zukin, Sharon (1995). *The culture of cities.* Oxford.

Authors

Peter Borsay is Professor of History at Aberystwyth University, a member of the international advisory board of *Urban History*, and a committee member of the British Pre-Modern Towns Group. His recent publications include *The English Urban Renaissance: Culture and Society in the Provincial Town, 1660–1770* (Oxford Univ. Press, 1989); *The Image of Georgian Bath, 1700–2000: Towns, Heritage and History* (Oxford Univ. Press, 2000); (edited with L. Proudfoot). *Provincial Towns in Early Modern England and Ireland: Change, Convergence and Divergence*, Proceedings of the British Academy 108 (Oxford Univ. Press, 2002); and *A History of Leisure: the British Experience since 1500* (Palgrave, 2006). Recent papers include, »Why are Houses Interesting?«. *Urban History*, 34, 2 (2007); »New Approaches to Social History. Myth, Memory and Place: Monmouth and Bath 1750–1900«. *Journal of Social History*, 39, 3 (2006); »From Bath to Poundbury: The Rise, Fall and Rise of Polite Urban Space 1700–2000«. In R. Leech and A. Green (eds.). *Cities in the World 1500–2000* (Leeds: Maney, 2006). He is currently engaged in research on various aspects of seventeenth- and eighteenth-century British towns, on the history of Welsh seaside resorts 1750–1914, on heritage and history, and is preparing a book on *The Discovery of England* (Continuum).

Giacomo Bottà is a postdoctoral research fellow in the Network for Urban Studies, Department of Social Policy, at the University of Helsinki. His doctorate, in comparative and cultural studies, was awarded from the Libera Università di Lingue e Comunicazione IULM (Milan, Italy) in 2003. His dissertation is entitled *Ich steh' auf Berlin! City, Individual, and Text in Berlin Prose of the 1990s*. His research interests include the representation of the city in arts and popular culture, the creative city debate, interculturalism and the cultural history of European cities. His recent publications include: »Pop Music, Cultural Sensibilities and Places: Manchester 1976–1997«. In J. Fornäs (ed.). *ESF-LiU Conference. Cities and Media: Cultural Perspectives on*

Urban Identities in a Mediatized World. Vadstena, Sweden, October 25–29, 2006. http://www.ep.liu.se/ecp/020/; »Interculturalism and New Russians in Berlin«. In *CLCWeb: Comparative Literature and Culture*, 2, 8 (2006). http://clcwebjournal.lib.purdue.edu/clcweb06-2/botta06.html

Christopher Breward is Deputy Head of Research at the Victoria & Albert Museum London and a Visiting Professor at the University of the Arts London (London College of Fashion) and Kingston University. His research interests include the cultural history of fashion and its relationship to concepts of place/space and gender (particularly London and masculinity). He sits on the Editorial Boards of the Journal of Design History and Fashion Theory. Recent publications include: Intoxicated on Images: The Visual Culture of Couture. In *The Golden Age of Couture*, London: V&A Publications, 2007, pp. 175 – 199; Fashion's Front and Back: Rag Trade Cultures and Cultures of Consumption in Post-War London. In *The London Journal* Vol. 31: 1 (2006), pp.15-40; *Fashion's World Cities* (co-editor), Oxford: Berg, 2006; Introduction and Post-script. In *Swinging Sixties: Fashion in London and Beyond 1955-1970* (co-editor), London: V&A Publications, 2006, pp.8-21, 120-123; *The London Look: Fashion from Street to Catwalk* (co-author), New Haven: Yale University Press, 2005.

Alexa Färber is postdoctoral researcher at the Department of European Ethnology at Christian-Albrechts-University, Kiel. Her research interests include the cultural economy of the city and new consumption spaces and practices, Islam in European urban space, and the anthropology of knowledge. Between 2003 and 2007 she has worked on a comparative research project on urban culture and ethnic representation in Berlin and Moscow at at the Department of European Ethnology, Humboldt University Berlin. She is member of the editorial board of the journals *Zeitschrift für Kulturwissenschaften* and *Berliner Blätter. Ethnographische und ethnologische Beiträge.* Recent publications include *Weltausstellung als Wissensmodus: Ethnographie einer Repräsentationsarbeit* (Münster, 2006); (edited with Riem Spielhaus). *Islamisches Gemeindeleben in Berlin* (Berlin, 2006); (ed.). *Hotel Berlin: Formen urbaner Mobilität und Verortung* (Münster, 2005).

David Gilbert is Professor of Urban and Historical Geography at Royal Holloway, University of London, where he is Director of the Social and Cultural Geography Research Group. From 2003-2006 he was Co-Director with Chritopher Breward of the ESRC/AHRC funded 'Shopping Routes' project that focused on the connections between fashion and urban change in post-war London. His current research interests include the relationships between fashion and world cities, planning and the West End of London, and the connections between fashion and tourism in post-war London. He has a broader interest in the history of Modern London and has published articles on the influence of imperialism on the city, on suburban cultures and on urban tourism. His earlier work focused on local cultures of collective action and political identity in inter-war Britain. Recent publications include (edited with Christopher Breward). Fashion's World Cities. Berg, Oxford, 2006; (edited with Christopher Breward and Jenny Lister). *Swinging Sixties: Fashion in London and beyond.* London, 2006, and Blues Interactions, inc. Tokyo, 2006 (Japanese version); (edited with David Matless and Brian Short). *Geographies of British Modernity: Space and Society in the Twentieth Century.* Oxford 2003; (edited with Felix Driver). *Imperial Cities: Landscape, Display and Identity.* Manchester 2003.

Simon Gunn is Professor of Urban History at the University of Leicester, UK. His main research interests are in the cultural history of the industrial cities of northern England in the nineteenth and twentieth centuries. He has also written on theory and historical practice. He is an organiser of the Urban History Group and joint editor of the journal *Urban History,* published by Cambridge University Press. Recent publications include »Elites, power and governance«. In S. Couperus et al. (eds.). *Changing Times: Elites and the Dynamics of Local Politics* (Leuven, 2007); *History and Cultural Theory* (London, 2006); with Alastair Owens. »Nature, technology and the modern city«. *Cultural Geographies,* 13 (2006); »From hegemony to governmentality; changing conceptions of power in social history«. *Journal of Social History,* 40, 2 (2006); »Translating Bourdieu: cultural capital and the English middle class in historical perspective«. *Journal of British Sociology,* 56, 1 (2005).

Martina Heßler is Professor of Cultural History and History of Technology at the Hochschule für Gestaltung, Offenbach am Main (Academy of Arts and Design). Her main research interests are urban history, history of technology, consumption history and history of visual cultures. Recent publication include: *Die kreative Stadt. Zur Neuerfindung eines Topos* (Bielefeld, 2007); (ed.), *Konstruierte Sichtbarkeiten. Bilder von Wissenschaft und Technik seit*

AUTHORS

der Frühen Neuzeit. (München, 2005); *Mrs. Modern Woman. Zur Sozial- und Kulturgeschichte der Haushaltstechnisierung* (Frankfurt am Main, 2001).

Marjatta Hietala, Ph.D. in history, MA in political sciences, is a professor of General History at the University of Tampere, Finland. She teaches at the Universities of Helsinki, Turku and Jyväskylä in Finland. In 1999 she was a Visiting Professor at the Department of History, University of Minnesota, in 1988–1989 Visiting Professor at the Graduate School and University Center of the City University of New York, in 2002 visiting Research Fellow at the University of Freie Universität Berlin, Institut für Vergleichende Geschichte Europas. Currently she is working with the project: *Universities, research centres and networks of scholars making cities attractive. A long term analysis,* financed by the Finnish Academy. Publications include: (edited with Tanja Vahtikari). *Landscape of Food. The Food Relationship of Town and Country in Modern Times,* (Tampere, 2003); (edited with Marjatta Bell). *Helsinki – The innovative City. Historical Perspectives,* (Jyväskylä, 2002); *Services and Urbanization at the Turn of the Century. The Diffusion of Innovations,* (Helsinki, 1987).

Thomas Höpel is Privatdozent of Comparative Cultural and Social History at Leipzig University. His research focuses on the history of cultural policy in Europe, on the history of cultural transfers between France and Germany, on urban history and on the history of the French Revolution of 1789. He is co-editor of the journal *Grenzgänge. Beiträge zu einer modernen Romanistik.* Recent publications include: (ed.), *Neue Forschungen zur Französischen Revolution von 1789. Grenzgänge. Beiträge zu einer modernen Romanistik,* 20, 2003; (ed. with Steffen Sammler), *Kulturpolitik und Stadtkultur in Leipzig und Lyon vom 18. zum 20. Jahrhundert* (Leipzig, 2004); »Geschichte der Kulturpolitik in Europa: vom nationalen zum europäischen Modell«. In Matthias Middell (ed.). *Dimensionen der Kultur- und Gesellschaftsgeschichte,* 184–205 (Leipzig, 2007); »Städtische Kulturpolitik in Deutschland und Frankreich 1918–1940«. *Historische Zeitschrift,* 284, 3 (2007), 623–658; *Von der Kunst- zur Kulturpolitik. Städtische Kulturpolitik in Deutschland und Frankreich 1918–1939* (Stuttgart, 2007).

Gert-Jan Hospers teaches economic-geography at the University of Twente in Enschede, the Netherlands. He has published on creative cities, regional innovation, place marketing and old industrial regions. Specialisation areas include the Ruhr Area, the North-East of England, the Oresund Region and Vorarlberg. Besides his research Hospers writes reports on German and English cities for the Dutch *Financial Times*. Publications include: »Borders, bridges and branding: the transformation of the Øresund Region into an imagined space«. In *European Planning Studies*, 14 (8) 2006, 1023-1041; with R. van Dalm. »How to create a creative city? The viewpoints of Richard Florida and Jane Jacobs«. In *Foresight: The Journal of Future Studies, Strategic Thinking and Policy*, 7 (4) 2005, 8-12; »Creative cities: breeding places in the knowledge economy«. In *Knowledge, Technology & Policy*, 16 (3) 2003, 143-162.

Habbo Knoch is Assistant Professor at the History Department, University of Göttingen. University studies at Göttingen, Bielefeld, Jerusalem and Oxford in Modern History, Philosophy, Political Sciences, and Sociology. Ph.D. in 1999, published in 2001 as *Die Tat als Bild. Fotografien des Holocaust in der deutschen Erinnerungskultur* (Images of the Holocaust. Photographs of Nazi Crimes and Germany Memory after 1945). Main research interests include Contemporary European history, Social and cultural history 1880–1930, History of mass media representations. His current research project is on »Grand hotels in Berlin, London and New York, 1860–1930«.

Jan Andreas May studied History and Art History at Berlin, Venice and Rome. He wrote his PhD on the history of the Venice Biennale which was defended in summer 2007 at Technical University Berlin. He received scholarships from the Centro Tedesco di Studi Veneziani, Venice; the German Historical Insitute, Rome; the Center for Metropolitan Studies, Berlin; and the Isabella Stewart Gardner Museum, Boston. His research interests are on the international exhibition and festival history in the first half of the twentieth century. Recent publications include: »Portus Artium – die venezianische Ausstellungspolitik des 20. Jahrhunderts«. *Zeithistorische Forschungen*, 4, 2007; »La Biennale di Venezia. Eine Ausstellungsinstitution im Wandel der Zeit«. In Ursula Zeller (ed.). *Die deutschen Beiträge zur Biennale Venedig 1895–2007*, 17–30 (Cologne/Stuttgart, 2007).

Birgit Metzger studied at the Saarland University in Saarbrücken (»Historisch orientierte Kulturwissenschaften«) and at the Laval University, Québec (Québec)/Canada; 2006. Her diploma thesis was on »Kreative Milieus in der Stadt. Geschichte und Gegenwart. – Chinatown an der Saar?«;. Since October 2006 she works as research associate in the DFG-funded project

Und ewig sterben die Wälder. Das deutsche Waldsterben im Spannungsfeld zwischen Wissenschaft und Politik (And yonder die the the woods. The German ›Waldsterben‹ between politics and science) at the Albert-Ludwig University in Freiburg im Breisgau. Her research is on the subject *›Waldsterben‹ as a political issue in West-Germany in the 1980s.*

Sandra Schürmann is currently doing research on cigarette advertising at the Museum of Work, Hamburg. Her research interests are the cultural history of modern urban space and the cultural history of advertising. Recent publications include: with Tino Jacobs, »Rauchsignale. Struktureller Wandel und visuelle Strategien auf dem deutschen Zigarettenmarkt im 20. Jahrhundert«. Werkstattgeschichte, 45 (2007); (edited with Jochen Guckes). *Stadtbilder und Stadtrepräsentationen. Informationen zur modernen Stadtgeschichte*, 1/2005; (edited with Jan Haack). S*tadt Natur. Unterwegs in Hamburger Landschaften*, (Hamburg: Museum der Arbeit, 2005); *Dornröschen und König Bergbau. Kulturelle Urbanisierung und bürgerliche Repräsentationen am Beispiel der Stadt Recklinghausen 1930–1960* (PhD thesis, Paderborn, 2005).

Jill Steward is Senior Lecturer in Cultural History at Northumbria University, Newcastle upon Tyne. Her research interests are the tourism in the nineteenth and early twentieth centuries, the development of spa culture and the role of visual culture and the media in the promotion of tourism and the formation of social and cultural identities. She is a member of the *European Urban Culture Group* (Northumbria and Newcastle Universities). Recent publications include: (edited with Alex Cowan). *The City and the Senses, Urban Culture since 1500* (Basingstoke, 2006); »Performing abroad: British tourists and travel to Italy: 1840–1914«. In D. Medina Lasansky and Brian McLaren (eds.). *Architecture, Performance and Space* (Oxford/New York, 2004); »How and where to go‹. Tourism and the Growth of the Travel Press, 1860–1914«. In John K. Walton (ed.). *Tourisms: Identities, Environments, Conflicts and Histories* (Clevedon, 2005); »Representations of spa culture in the nineteenth-century British media: publicity, the press and the *villes d'eaux*: 1800–1914«. In Annick Cossic and Partic Galliou (eds.). S*pas in Britain and France in the 18th and 19th Century* (Newcastle, 2006).

Jörn Weinhold is coordinator of the Bauhaus Research School and lecturer at the Institute for European Urban Studies at the Bauhaus-University Weimar. His main research project is *London's Middle Class Nature: Social and*

Spatial Practises of Environmentalists in Victorian England. He was engaged in exhibitions at the German Historical Museum in Berlin and the Ruhrland Museum in Essen. Research interests inculde the history of the industrialised and urbanised world, history of science and the environment as well as the theory of historical exhibitions. Recent publications include: (ed. with Alexander Geppert and Uffa Jensen. *Ortsgespräche. Raum und Kommunikation im 19. und 20. Jahrhundert* (Bielefeld, 2005);»Das Hochhaus«. In Alexandra Geisthövel and Habbo Knoch (eds.). *Orte der Moderne. Erfahrungswelten des 19. und 20. Jahrhunderts* (Frankfurt am Main, 2005);»Die Stadtrandsiedlung«. In Alexandra Geisthövel and Habbo Knoch (eds.). *Orte der Moderne Erfahrungswelten des 19. und 20. Jahrhunderts* (Frankfurt am Main, 2005).

Clemens Zimmermann is Professor of Cultural and Media History at Saarland University, Saarbrücken. His research interests are the social history of urban and rural areas, cultural and educational policy in Europe, the perception of new information and media technologies and the cultural economy of the city. He is chairman of the *Gesellschaft für Stadtgeschichte und Urbanisierungsforschung*; he is co-editor of the encyclopedia *Enzyklopädie der Neuzeit* and of the journals *Zeitschrift für Agrargeschichte und Agrarsoziologie* and *Informationen zur Modernen Stadtgeschichte*. Recent publications include: (ed. with Manfred Schmeling). *Die Zeitschrift – Medium der Moderne/La presse magazine – un média de l'epoque moderne. Deutschland und Frankreich im Vergleich/Etude comparative France-Allemagne* (Bielefeld, 2006); (ed.). *Politischer Journalismus, Öffentlichkeiten und Medien im 19./20. Jahrhundert* (Ostfildern, 2006); (with Werner Trossbach). *Geschichte des Dorfes* (Stuttgart, 2006); (ed.). *Zentralität und Raumgefüge der Großstädte im 20. Jahrhundert* (Stuttgart, 2006); *Medien im Nationalsozialismus. Deutschland, Italien und Spanien in den 1930er und 1940er Jahren* (Wien, 2007).

Social Science

Felix Kolb
Protest and Opportunities
The Political Outcomes of Social Movements
2007, 341 p., ISBN 978-3-593-38413-9

Karolina Karr
Democracy and Lobbying in the European Union
2007, 209 p., ISBN 978-3-593-38412-2

Stefani Scherer, Reinhard Pollak,
Gunnar Otte, Markus Gangl (Hg.)
From Origin to Destination
Trends and Mechanisms in Social Stratification
Research
2007, 323 p., ISBN 978-3-593-38411-5

Johannes Harnischfeger
Democratization and Islamic Law
The Sharia Conflict in Nigeria
2008, 283 p., ISBN 978-3-593-38256-2

Helmut Willke
Smart Governance
Governing the Global Knowledge Society
2007, 206 p., ISBN 978-3-593-38253-1

Michael Dauderstädt, Arne Schildberg (Hg.)
Dead Ends of Transition
Rentier Economies and Protectorates
2006, 249 p., ISBN 978-3-593-38154-1

Mehr Informationen unter
www.campus.de

campus
Frankfurt · New York